Economics of the
International Financial System

Economics of the International Financial System

Sukumar Nandi

LONDON NEW YORK NEW DELHI

First published 2014 in India
by Routledge
912 Tolstoy House, 15–17 Tolstoy Marg, Connaught Place, New Delhi 110 001

Simultaneously published in the UK
by Routledge
2 Park Square, Milton Park, Abingdon, OX14 4RN

Routledge is an imprint of the Taylor & Francis Group, an informa business

© 2014 Sukumar Nandi

Typeset by
Bukprint India
B-180A, Guru Nanak Pura, Laxmi Nagar
Delhi 110 092

All rights reserved. No part of this book may be reproduced or utilized in any form or by any electronic, mechanical or other means, now known or hereafter invented, including photocopying and recording, or in any information storage and retrieval system without permission in writing from the publishers.

British Library Cataloguing-in-Publication Data
A catalogue record of this book is available from the British Library

ISBN: 978-0-415-66023-5

To
My parents
Late Jatindra Nath and Durga Rani Nandi

Contents

List of Tables   *xiii*
List of Figures and Exhibits   *xv*
List of Abbreviations   *xvii*
Preface   *xix*
Acknowledgements   *xxi*

1. Introduction: The International Monetary System   1
2. Money in Economics of the Open Economy   6
   - 2.1 Introduction: What is Money?   6
   - 2.2 David Hume and the Quantity Theory of Money   8
   - 2.3 Purchasing Power Parity Theory   11
   - 2.4 The Monetarist Arithmetic   13
   - 2.5 Balance of Payments Adjustment   14
   - 2.6 The Absorption Model of the Balance of Trade   15
   - 2.7 The Monetary Approach   16
   - 2.8 Classical and Keynesian Models: A Comparison   17
   - 2.9 Money in New Open Economy Models   18
   - 2.10 Extension of OB-RO Model   19
   - 2.11 The Steady State Again   20
   - 2.12 Uncertainty and Stochastic Nature   20
   - 2.13 Equilibrium Exchange Rate and Pass-through   21
   - 2.14 More on Micro Structure of Exchange Rate   22
   - 2.15 Stabilization Programme in Crisis Economies: Monetarist Approach and Polak Model   23
   - 2.16 G-3 Exchange Rate Volatility   25
3. Money Growth, Inflation and Seigniorage   28
   - 3.1 Introduction   28
   - 3.2 Measurement of Seigniorage   31
   - 3.3 Broader Definition of Seigniorage   31
   - 3.4 Seigniorage and Exchange Rate   33
   - 3.5 Dynamic Effects   33
   - 3.6 Cost of Seigniorage   34
   - 3.7 Conclusion   35
4. Multinational Corporations and Emerging Economies   37
   - 4.1 Greenfield Investment and Merger and Acquisition: A Comparison   39
   - 4.2 Technology Issue   40
   - 4.3 Indian Case   41

	4.4	Market Structure and Competition	42
	4.5	Sequential Market Entry: A Case Study of Sony Corporation in the United States	43
5.	International Financial System: A Historical Evolution		
	5.1	The Gold Standard	45
	5.2	The Demise of Classical Gold Standard	46
	5.3	The Bretton Woods International Monetary System	47
	5.4	Multilateral Payments Mechanism	49
	5.5	Resources of IMF	49
	5.6	The Structure of Organization	50
	5.7	Historical Stages of the Bretton Woods Agreement: 1946–60	50
	5.8	The Period 1960–67	51
	5.9	The Liquidity Problem	52
	5.10	Special Drawing Rights (SDR)	53
	5.11	Market Price of Gold and Confidence Issues	54
	5.12	Demonetization of Gold	55
	5.13	Gresham's Law at International Level	55
	5.14	Decline of the System	56
	5.15	Post-Bretton Woods Era: Managed Floating Exchange Rate	57
	5.16	The Second Amendment of IMF Article	57
	5.17	Appreciation of USD	58
	5.18	The Plaza Accord	58
	5.19	International Capital Flows	59
	5.20	The Financial Architecture	59
	5.21	Exchange Rate Arrangements	60
	5.22	The Tobin Tax Proposal on Capital Movement	61
	5.23	The G-7 Study of World Monetary Reform	62
	5.24	Stronger Financial Regulation	62
	5.25	Strong Macroeconomic Policy	63
	5.26	Crisis Prevention and Crisis Management	63
	5.27	Formation of a New Group: G-20	64
	5.28	New Initiative of IMF and the Poor	64
	5.29	The New International Financial Architecture	64
	5.30	A New International Economic Order	65
	5.31	European Union and Euro	66
	5.32	European Union as Optimum Currency Area	67
	5.33	Euro and a Historical Introspection	68
6.	Recent Changes in the International Financial Structure		72
	6.1	Introduction	72
	6.2	The Role of International Monetary Fund	73
	6.3	Creation of New Arrangement to Borrow	74

6.4	Special Drawing Rights (SDR) Allocation	74
6.5	Role of the USD	77
6.6	Global Macroeconomic Imbalances	79
6.7	Financial Markets in Emerging Economies	80
6.8	Conclusion	80

7. National Government and Sovereign Currency — 82
- 7.1 Introduction — 82
- 7.2 The Gold Standard Implications — 84
- 7.3 Competing Currencies: Competition among Governments — 85
- 7.4 Some Barriers to International Competition in Money — 86
- 7.5 A Market Approach to Currency Provision — 87
- 7.6 Indian Rupee in a Controlled Regime: An Empirical Approach in Historical Perspective — 87
- 7.7 The Arrangement of Currencies — New Method of Reserve Bank of India — 88
- 7.8 Indian Rupee in Historical Perspective — 88
- 7.9 Emergence of Dual Rates — 90
- 7.10 International Transactions — 90
- 7.11 Price Level and Exchange Rate in India — 91
- 7.12 Real Exchange Rate — 93
- 7.13 Exact Exchange Rate — 93
- 7.14 Exchange Rate of Indian Rupee and Current Account — 96
- 7.15 Empirical Estimation — 97
- 7.16 Black-Market Premium and Price Ratio — 98
- 7.17 Currency Basket and Indian Rupee: The SDR Approach — 98
- 7.18 Choice between a Peg and a Currency Basket — 99
- 7.19 The System of Currency Basket — 99
- 7.20 Official and Black Market Exchange Rate of Rupee: A Time Series Study — 101
- 7.21 Black Market Exchange Rate of Indian Rupee: An Empirical Exercise — 102
- 7.22 Relative Price Movement and Black Market Exchange Rate — 103

8. International Banking System and Global Money Flows — 104
- 8.1 Introduction — 104
- 8.2 Role of Banks: Intermediation and Interest-Rate Expectations — 105
- 8.3 International Banking Operations — 105
- 8.4 Determinants of International Banking Activity — 106
- 8.5 Offshore Banking and Tax-Haven Centres — 107
- 8.6 Why Offshore Finance Centre a Preferred Destination — 108
- 8.7 Panama: An Offshore Centre — 109
- 8.8 The Isle of Man: Offshore Financial Centre — 109
- 8.9 The Fixed Coefficient Model of the Banking System — 110
- 8.10 The Eurodollar System — 111

Contents

	8.11 Capital Inflows and Financial Opening	112
	8.12 Asian and Latin American Experiences of 1990s	112
	8.13 Dollarization	113
	8.14 Currency Board and Dollarization: A Comparison	115
	8.15 Dollarization and Function of Money	116
	8.16 Dollar Deposits in Foreign Banks	116
	8.17 Seigniorage and Dollarization: Multiple Equilibrium Points	116
	8.18 Cost of Complete Dollarization	118
	8.19 Dollarization in Latin America	119
	8.20 Corruption and Open Economy Implications: The Developing Country Perspective	119
	8.21 International Gold Market Connections	121
9.	Exchange Rate and Foreign Exchange Market	130
	9.1 The Players	130
	9.2 Trading Location	132
	9.3 Favorite Currencies	133
	9.4 Quotations in Foreign Exchange Transactions	134
	9.5 Direct and Indirect Quote	134
	9.6 Direction in the Market	134
	9.7 Inter-Banking	135
	9.8 Foreign Exchange Account	135
	9.9 Reimbursement Claim Solution (RCS)	135
	9.10 Export and Import Transactions	136
	9.11 Marshall–Lerner Conditions	137
	9.12 The J-Curve	138
	9.13 Contractionary Devaluation	139
	9.14 Forward Speculation	139
	9.15 Market Efficiency	140
	9.16 Hedging and Interest Arbitrage	140
	9.17 Covered Interest Parity and Forward Premium	140
	9.18 Measuring Capital Mobility	142
	9.19 The Real Exchange Rate	143
	9.20 Monetary and Fiscal Policy in Open Economies	144
	9.21 Mundell–Fleming Model of Fixed Exchange Rates	145
10.	Modern Theory of Exchange Rate Determination and International Parity Relationship	149
	10.1 Introduction	149
	10.2 Determination of Exchange Rate	150
	10.3 Gold Standard: A Brief History	150
	10.4 Models of Exchange Rate Determination	152
	10.5 PPP and Real Interest Parity	154

10.6	Monetary Approach to Exchange Rate	154
10.7	Overshooting Exchange Rate	155
10.8	Dornbusch Model of Flexible Exchange Rates	156
10.9	The Portfolio-Balance Approach	158
10.10	News and Volatility in the Exchange Rate	159
10.11	The Foreign Exchange Market	161
10.12	Currency Substitution and Exchange Rate	161
10.13	Disequilibrium Models	162
10.14	Exchange Rate Systems and Policy	163
10.15	Rigidly Fixed Exchange Rate	163
10.16	Currency Boards	164
10.17	Currency Union	164
10.18	Pegged Exchange Rate	164
10.19	Managed Exchange Rates	165
10.20	Freely Floating Exchange Rate	166
10.21	Multiple Exchange Rates	166
10.22	The Relative Merits of Different Exchange Rate Regimes	166

11. International Transmission of Interest Rates and Monetary Independence — 169
    - 11.1 Introduction — 169
    - 11.2 Exchange Rate — 170
    - 11.3 Financial Integration and Capital Mobility — 171
    - 11.4 The Policy Trilemma — 172
    - 11.5 USD as International Currency — 172

12. Capital Mobility, Currency Crisis and Problems of Contagion — 176
    - 12.1 Introduction — 176
    - 12.2 The Crisis — 176
    - 12.3 Currency Crisis — 177
    - 12.4 First-Generation Models — 177
    - 12.5 Second-Generation Models — 178
    - 12.6 Third-Generation Models — 178
    - 12.7 Contagion: The Definition — 179
    - 12.8 Washington Consensus — 180
    - 12.9 Evolution of Washington Consensus — 181
    - 12.10 Globalization — 182

13. Foreign Direct Investment in India and Emerging Economies — 185
    - 13.1 Introduction — 185
    - 13.2 Objective — 186
    - 13.3 Approach towards FDI in India — 187
    - 13.4 Role of Infrastructure — 187
    - 13.5 Hypothesis of the Study as Pursued in this Chapter — 188
    - 13.6 Data and Methodology — 188

  13.7 FDI: A Model in the Making   188
  13.8 Empirical Exercise   189
  13.9 Technology Transfer, Capital Formation and International Trade   191
  13.10 Inter-Industry Variation in FDI   192
  13.11 Indian Economy and Foreign Capital   192
  13.12 Foreign Direct Investment and Emerging Economy Perspective   193
  13.13 Technology: Policy and Reality   193
  13.14 FDI: A Segmented Analysis   193
  13.15 Sector-Wise Inflow   194
  13.16 Nature of FDI Inflow   194
  13.17 Infrastructure and FDI Inflow   197
  13.18 A Quantitative Exercise to Ascertain the Role of Infrastructure   200
  13.19 Conclusion   202

14. International Reserve and Liquidity   215
  14.1 Introduction   215
  14.2 Review of Literature   217
  14.3 Adequacy of and Demand for Reserve   219
  14.4 Reasons for Holding Reserve   221
  14.5 Monetarist Controversies and Reserve: A Macro World View   222
  14.6 Theory, Model and Estimation   223
  14.7 Conclusion   230

15. Optimum Currency Area, European Union and the Euro   232
  15.1 Introduction   232
  15.2 The British Problem   233
  15.3 Maastricht Treaty, 1992   233
  15.4 The European Union   235
  15.5 Euro as the Single Currency of the European Union   236
  15.6 Euro vis-à-vis USD   238
  15.7 Conclusion   239

Select Bibliography   241

About the Author   257

Index   259

List of Tables

3.1 Seigniorage and its Components, 1997
3.2 Expropriation through Currency Debasement in Europe: Nineteenth Century

6.1 Calculation of Currency Amounts in SDR Basket

7.1 Real Exchange Rate and Estimated Exact Exchange Rate in India

8.1 Reported Ratios of Foreign Currency Deposits (FCD) to Broad Money with IMF Arrangement
8.2 Inflation and Dollarization Rates in Selected Countries
8.3 Deposits in Foreign Currency as Percentage of Money Supply

9.1 Top 10 Currency Traders in the World (Percentage of Overall Volume), May 2010
9.2 Geographic Distribution of Global Foreign Exchange Market Turnover: Some Principal Centres
9.3 Foreign Exchange Trading by Currencies, April 2010

11.1 Countries and their Exchange Rate Regimes

13.1 Indian Case of Regression Results
13.2 Malaysia: Regression
13.3 Sectoral Inflows of Foreign Direct Investment in India
13.4 Regression: Level Terms
13.5 Regression: Residual Plot
13.6 Regression: Log Transformation
13A Total FDI: (Approvals and Inflows)
13B Sector-Wise Approval of FDI
13C Sectoral Inflows
13D Sector-Wise Inflows as a Percentage of Approvals
13E Sector-Wise FDI Inflows as a Percentage of FDI Approved from 1991 to 98

14.1 Possible Effects of a Rise in Reserves on a Country's Policies
14.2 Regression Results of Countries
14.3 Regression Results of Some Countries

15.1 Alternative Measure of Debt Securities as Share of Currencies

List of Figures and Exhibits

Figures
- 7.1 Inflation in India and the World since 1980
- 8.1 Inflation Laffer Curve
- 9.1 J-Curve: After Depreciation
- 9.2 Production Possibility Frontier
- 9.3 Mundell–Fleming Model
- 10.1 Dornbusch Model: Monetary Expansion with Overshooting
- 10.2 Demand and Supply of Dollar Changes the Price: A Shift of the Demand Curve

Exhibits
- 13.1 FDI Inflows into India
- 13.2 Shares of Automatic Route and Government Route in the Total Inflow of FDI
- 13.3 FDI in India: Approved to Actual
- 13.4 FDI Inflow into India from Select Countries
- 13.5 Actual FDI as Percentage of Approved FDI (1991–99) (Country-wise)
- 13.6 FDI Inflows (1991–99) in Major Sectors
- 13.7 FDI (Approved and Inflow)
- 13.8 FDI in Different States
- 13.9 Relationship between State-level FDI and Infrastructure Index
- 13.10 Relationship between State-level FDI and Percentage of Man-days Lost
- 13.11 Relationship between State-level FDI and Urbanization Growth
- 13.12 Relation between State-level FDI and GDP Growth Rate

List of Abbreviations

ASEAN	Association of Southeast Asian Nations
BIS	Bank for International Settlement
BOP	Balance of Payment
BRIC	Brazil, Russia, India and China
CIS	Commonwealth of Independent States
CU	Currency Union
EC	European Community
ECB	European Central Bank
ECU	European Currency Unit
EEC	European Economic Community
EME	Emerging Market Economies
EMS	European Monetary System
ERM	Exchange Rate Mechanism
FDI	Foreign Direct Investment
FEM	Foreign Exchange Market
G-7	Group of Seven
G-20	Group of Twenty
GATS	General Agreement on Trade in Services
GATT	General Agreement on Tariff and Trade
GDP	Gross Domestic Product
IBRD	International Bank for Reconstruction and Development (World Bank)
IDA	International Development Association
IFC	International Finance Corporation
IMF	International Monetary Fund
IR	International reserve
LDC	Less Developed Country
LOOP	Law of One Price
LTCM	Long Term Capital Management
M&A	Merger and Acquisition
MFN	Most Favoured Nation
MNC	Multinational Corporation
NAB	New Agreement to Borrow
NAFTA	North American Free Trade Agreement
NIEO	New International Economic Order
OECD	Organization for Economic Cooperation and Development

OFC	Offshore Financial Centres
PBA	Portfolio Balance Approach
PCI	Per Capita Income
PPP	Purchasing Power Parity
PMLA	Prevention of Money Laundering (Amendment) Act, 2009
QTM	Quantity Theory of Money
R&D	Research and Development
SDR	Special Drawing Rights
UN	United Nations
UNCTAD	United Nations Conference on Trade and Development
US	The United States of America
USD	United States Dollar
WC	Washington Consensus
WTO	World Trade Organization

Preface

In this era of globalization, people think of keeping financial liquidity at the international level, and for that, understanding the nature of international money is necessary. The essence of money is that it is any marketable good used by a society as a store of value, a medium of exchange or a unit of account. Many objects can meet all of these needs. Since the needs arise in a natural process, society organically creates a money object when none exists. In other cases, a central authority creates a money object. In this way, money came into being in classical times in the early phase of civilization. And the process was transplanted in the international level when people felt the need for commodities not available within the national boundaries, and those were to be procured from other countries. Thus international money came into existence based on gold and this was the beginning of Gold Standard.

The present book presumes the knowledge of basic macroeconomics at the undergraduate level. The book deals with the structure of international money. Starting with the historical origin, it has elaborated the present international financial system. Money is sovereign within the state and the government uses this as a policy tool to meet the pressing needs of the society.

Important topic coverage includes the following:

- The nature of money in an open economy framework (Chapter 2)
- The role of money in economic growth and also inflation (Chapter 3)
- Implications of the operations of multinational corporations (Chapter 4)
- Evolution of the international financial system (Chapter 5)
- Recent changes in the international financial structure (Chapter 6)
- Nature of sovereign currency and its implications with the functioning of the government (Chapter 7)
- Operations of the international banking system (Chapter 8)
- Operations of the foreign exchange markets (Chapter 9)
- Theories of exchange rate determinations and international parity conditions (Chapter 10)
- International transmission of interest rate and interest rate convergence (Chapter 11)
- Role and complexities of international capital mobility (Chapter 12)
- Foreign direct investment in emerging economies (Chapter 13)
- Role of international reserve to maintain international liquidity of countries (Chapter 14)
- Structure and operations of the European Union as an optimum currency area (Chapter 15)

Economics of the International Financial System is primarily meant for three groups of people. First, the students at the postgraduate level can use this book in their course on international monetary economics and also international corporate finance. Second, advance students and researchers can selectively read this book for their studies and references. The third group consists of professionals who can have a quick look to get necessary knowledge about the way international financial system works nowadays. One can read and understand the contents of the chapters without the hassles of mathematical reasoning.

Acknowledgements

There are many well-known scholars in the field of international financial system whose contributions have enriched my ideas on the subjects and I have elaborated those ideas in the present book. I owe a deep intellectual gratitude to all of them including Jagadish Bhagawati and Joseph Stiglitz of Columbia University, Paul Krugman of Princeton University, Barry Eichengreen of University of California, Berkeley, and Sebastian Edwards of University of California, Los Angeles. Of course, I alone remain responsible for any error or inadequacy that may remain while presenting the theories in this book.

I also express my deep intellectual debt to my teachers both at Calcutta University and Utah State University, including Asim Dasgupta, Dhiresh Bhattacharya and Santosh Bhattacharya at Calcutta University, and Basudeb Biswas and Kenneth Lyon at Utah State University.

The treatment of the subject matter covered in this book has been honed by several years of classroom testing at Indian Institute of Management, Lucknow; Indian Institute of Foreign Trade, New Delhi; and Vidyasagar University of West Bengal. I owe many thanks to several generations of students who have helped sharpen my insights on many issues addressed in this book by their intelligent questions and sometimes ingenious interpretations.

I also thank my publisher Routledge Taylor and Francis Books India Private Limited and the editorial team for their strenuous efforts in editing and in other processes that have brought the book in its present form. I do appreciate their efforts.

Finally, I thank my wife, Karabi, for her moral support, and specially, for her understanding during the time I spent preparing the text. My daughters, Susmita and Nabanita, continuously urged me to finish the manuscript through phone and writings while remaining busy at their workplaces at distant locations. I thank them too.

1
Introduction: The International Monetary System

The notion of a 'global monetary system' usually means the gold exchange standard that was adopted after World War II in the Bretton Woods Agreement, in which each member state is to fix its currency with specified units of gold. In reality, it is a fixed exchange rate system in which each country is to maintain a fixed exchange rate vis-à-vis the USD while the USD is to maintain fixed parity with specified units of gold. The agreement adopted the USD as the international currency, and the United States made the commitment of giving one ounce of gold for every 35 USD surrendered. From 1960 onwards, the United States became involved in the war in Vietnam and that military expenditure drained their economy too much. The result was the quick depreciation of the USD and that had been reflected in the continuous higher prices of gold. From the official 35 USD per ounce that anchored the international monetary system, the USD declined to 40 USD/oz in 1968, 65 USD/oz in 1972 and 100 USD/oz in 1973.

The decline of the USD being the symptom of the decline of American economic system induced the French critique of the political implications of the USD-centric international monetary system, a gold exchange standard where the USD was designed to be used as the underlying reserve assets, in lieu of gold. Charles de Gaulle, the President of France in the 1960s, campaigned against USD as international currency and the huge economic power the United States enjoyed as a result. Also, the United States experienced a huge outflow of gold through the committed gold window mainly to the European countries. In the face of it, the United States came out of the commitment of gold window of giving one ounce of gold for every 35 USD in 1971, and with it the Bretton Woods system collapsed.

Post-1971, the world adjusted to a flexible exchange rate system whereby the member countries have adjusted the exchange rates of their domestic currencies vis-à-vis USD, which continued to depreciate, and it was reflected in the increasing price of gold in terms of USD. Economists call it as Bretton Woods II phase when USD continued to maintain its principal currency status. As the issuer of the currency, the United States enjoyed advantages from its role at the centre of the international monetary system. The principal benefits that accrue to a country as the issuer of reserve currency (USD) is the seigniorage, that is, the difference between the face value and the cost of issuing new money including interest payment and also the cost of monitoring the currency outside the country. Apart from the seigniorage, the country also enjoys advantages like balance of payments flexibility and competitive advantages for the domestic financial services.

What is the future of the USD as an international currency? The analysis of this question raises a prior question: why does any particular national currency come to be used extensively at the international level as a means of exchange, unit of account, and store of value? This question has attracted the attention of the economists, as they have highlighted various economic determinants of international currencies like confidence of the foreigners on the stability of the value of the currency, the existence of a well-developed and open financial market within the issuing country, and the extensive transaction network of the issuing country. Thus, economists have identified three factors — confidence, liquidity and transaction network — to be the key determinants of international currencies, though there is no consensus. Some economists predict that the dollar's international role is about to decline in the near future, while others foresee little change in its status in the coming years. The lack of consensus is also sometimes a product of the fact that economists are focusing on different functions that the USD performs as an international currency.

The emergence of the euro from 2000 onwards has shifted attention to its possibility of becoming a rival of the USD as the currency of the second largest economy Japan, the yen, could not muster the confidence of nations to be used as a reserve currency. Confidence in a currency is derived not just from the economic fundamentals, but from the size of the issuing state and also the broader international security power of the issuing country. According to Andrews Walter (2006), monetary power can be cultivated by a consistent conservative monetary policy at the domestic level that is credibly embedded within domestic politics and institutions, as he highlights the case of stable value of the pound sterling in the nineteenth-century United Kingdom that inspired such confidence. Walter also notes that the atmosphere of the United Kingdom was linked to its limited government, the narrow electoral franchise and the conservative financial control of the Bank of England.

If one wants to assess how the international and domestic political sources as mentioned above can influence the future of the USD as an international currency, one seems to pull in different directions. On one hand, the domestic military power of the United States boosts foreign confidence in the USD, particularly at the moments of international political instability when the USD has been regarded as a 'safe haven' currency. On the other hand, the atmospheres of inflation in the domestic level in the United States and the high levels of public debt have created doubts about the soundness of USD.

Foreign confidence in the currency of European Union, Euro is boosted by the fact that it has been embedded by the Union in a very conservative 'domestic' institutional context. Not only the European Central Bank has been mandated to pursue low-inflation policy, but its ability to fulfill this mandate has been strengthened by its legal independence from the government influences. On the other hand, confidence in Euro is undermined by the broader uncertainties about the strength of European political cooperation and the inability of Europe to project its power in a unified manner at the international level (McNamara, 2008).

Foreign confidence in a currency is also influenced by the openness of the financial market at the domestic level as well as the projected political power of the country at the global level. The inadequacy on both counts makes the Chinese yuan a non-starter at the present moment, in spite of the huge international reserves, China has accumulated and has achieved a very fast economic growth that makes the economy second in the world in size (Water, 2010).

The analysis projected above indicates that it requires many-dimensional considerations to understand the implications of an economic event at the global level. The chapters in this book try to explain these aspects in a theoretical as well as practical manner. For the latter, many cases are added to explain the geo-political situations. First, the concept of international money is taken in Chapter 2. The history of money shows that its origin is connected to a temple of Hera, that is located on the top of a hill called Capitoline. The latter is one of the famous seven hills in the city of Rome. Explaining the origin of money, the discussion continues to explain the relationship money has with gross domestic product and price level. The strength of money as a store of value is reflected in its purchasing power, and the purchasing power of monies of different countries can be compared through the theory of purchasing power parity. In the context of open economy, growth of money supply creates twin effects in the economy — its effect on interest rate and its effect on price level. If interest rate is treated as a price of capital, then the growth of money supply at the domestic level creates effects on the balance of payments of the economy through the price effects on commodities and capital.

One important power of the sovereign state is the authority to issue paper currency that can be treated as sovereign debt, and citizens accept that as money and use it as a medium of exchange. This paper currency may or may not be fully backed by reserves in gold and other foreign currency, and if it is not backed, then it is called fiat money or fiduciary issues. In today's world, all currencies are fiat money. This aspect of money sometimes creates potential problem as the sovereign state issues paper currency to claim resources from the market. This is the genesis of inflation in an economy. This interrelationship between money and inflation is explained in Chapter 3, which also analyses the concept of seigniorage, which the issuer of paper currency enjoys as the difference between the face value of the currency and the cost of production of the currency and the cost associated with the maintenance of the currency.

The multinational corporations (MNCs) are important players at present in the international financial system. The integration process in the world economy has been quickened by the activities of the multinational corporations through the expansion of business. The nature of their activities is explained in Chapter 4. The activities of the MNCs in the emerging market economies have been supplemented by capital flows often in the form of direct foreign investment. Different forms of this investment along with the role of technology in the market expansion in the emerging market economies have been explained.

The present form of the international financial architecture is the outcome of a long historical process of evolution in response to different financial events at various points of history and this has been taken up in Chapter 5. After World War I, many countries adopted an exchange standard that included both gold and foreign exchange, and this system paved the way for the use of USD exchange rate regime after World War II. The international monetary system set in place at Bretton Woods differed from the gold exchange standard, as USD had been given the all-important role of key currency. The United States committed to exchange USDs for gold at the fixed rate of 35 USD an ounce and other currencies were to keep their par values at a fixed exchange rate vis-à-vis the USD. The burden of intervention was to be borne by the non-reserve currency countries. The system broke down in 1971 when the United States came out unilaterally from the commitment of gold window and after that Bretton Woods Agreement collapsed. But a new system has been continuing since then with flexible exchange rate system, though the USD remains the international currency.

Since 1980, international economic system has undergone rapid changes most of which were to address the challenges of globalization of the world economy. One of the many facets of the challenges is the international liquidity problem that persisted in spite of the Robert Triffin's special drawing rights (SDR) experiment that started in late 1960. In this perspective, Stiglitz (2006) describes the global greenbacks system as one in which new reserves could be created every year and which would not be given to the wealthiest countries. He proposes the creation of a trust fund of conventional hard currencies so that countries in crisis can exchange their global greenbacks for currencies needed for payments. Chapter 6 analyzes all changes made post-1980 period including the responses from International Monetary Fund (IMF).

Chapter 7 explains the dynamics of sovereign currency and how governments in member states deal with it. One principal duty of the government is to take measures so that domestic economic system runs smoothly with stability and currency is an important instrument in that process. So each government issues currency in the domestic market that acts as money. But many governments use this power for the exploitation of domestic citizens by printing currency and commanding resources from the economy in lieu of it. The result will be runaway inflation as historic inflation in Germany before the World War II is recorded. Apart from dealing with all these aspects, this chapter also explains the economics of Indian rupee along with its historical roots.

Money is truly international in nature whether it is the Indian rupee or the Euro. The international flows of money as the reverse flow of commodities at some times are facilitated by the international banking system. The latter maintains wide networks in the world to transfer money from one corner of the globe to another. This complex process has been explained in Chapter 8 that also explains the activities of the offshore financial centres. In this connection, the activities of money laundering, that has become a chronic problem in the newly emerging markets, has been examined in detail.

The value of the domestic currency in terms of the foreign currency (say, USD) is determined in the foreign exchange market in case of a currency that is a fully floated one. The foreign exchange market is integrated with both money market and the capital market of the domestic economy, and the interest rate plays an important role in determining both the spot rate and forward rate of the foreign currency. All these dynamics are explained in Chapter 9. Again, Chapter 10 analyzes the dominant theories of exchange rate determination. The determination of exchange rate of the domestic currency is influenced both by monetary factors and real factors. While interest rate plays a crucial role, the situation in balance of trade of a country can influence the course of movement of the exchange rate. Economists also try to determine the equilibrium exchange rate in terms of the equilibrium of the balance of trade of the country, as the exchange rate of the domestic currency is an important factor for the competitive strength of the domestic economy in foreign trade transaction. Apart from this, there is the concept of purchasing power parity of the domestic currency that relates the purchasing power of the domestic currency with the exchange rate.

In open economy situation, a country faces the 'open economy trilemma', which means that of the three factors a country faces — a fixed exchange rate, perfect capital mobility and an independent monetary policy — the country is to choose any two of the three, as it cannot get all the three simultaneously[1]. Thus the country faces capital mobility along with the transmission of changes in the foreign interest rate in the domestic economy. This influences the movement of the exchange rate of the domestic currency. This is a complex process and the country has to adjust its monetary policies for maintaining stability of the exchange rate. This theoretical explanation is provided in Chapter 11.

Under globalization, capital flows in the reverse direction of water, i.e., capital flows upwards in terms of returns on it. Also, the country as the issuer of domestic currency should maintain the economic policies in such a way that the citizens have confidence in the currency they hold. When this is absent, people want to get rid of the currency like a hot potato. Thus, capital flight and also flight from currency have been common in history, and a recent example is the Asian currency crisis during 1997–99 when countries like Thailand, South Korea, Malaysia, Indonesia, and Philippines suffered in the form of a contagion. These aspects are explained in Chapter 12.

Foreign direct investment has played an important role in the industrialization of emerging countries mainly in two ways: it brought necessary capital in some capital-poor economies and the industries established by foreign direct investment led to diffusion of improved technology to the existing firms in the host country. The situation is not different in the case of India and all these are analyzed in Chapter 13.

From 1980 onwards, one common experience in the development history of the world is that many emerging economies have attempted to build up large international reserves as a cushion for the stability of the exchange rate and also for unforeseen fluctuations in the balance of trade situations. In this context, some Asian countries like China and Japan top the list. In 2010, about 40 per cent of the world's international reserves was held by the Asian region, and the size of China's international reserve was about USD 3 trillion. What is the optimum size of international reserves and what are the factors that determine the size of it are theoretical issues and these are explained in Chapter 14.

The formation of the European Union and the adoption of euro as the common currency by the member states of the European Union are unique experiments in recent history, and it has been the logical outcome of Robert Mundell's thesis of optimum currency areas. This aspect has been explained in detail in the last chapter, i.e., Chapter 15.

Conclusion

The broad objective of this book is to bring into focus the overall situation of the international financial system in its present dynamic context. Each chapter gives the up-to-date situation along with the theoretical background so that the reader can understand the inner dynamics of the situation. The references list of further reading help the potential researchers to move ahead in their further intellectual pursuits. All other annotations made in the text are placed in references at the end of the book.

---

[1] For explanation, see Obstfeld and Taylor, (2003).

2
Money in Economics of the Open Economy

2.1 Introduction: What is Money?

Economists define 'money' as a set of assets in the economy that people use to buy goods and services from other people. According to Friedman (1992), anything can be money like gold, silver, copper, etc., as what makes these commodities valuable is not what they are but what they are used for. The value of money is the value people attribute to what they want to exchange in exact quantity. As a medium of exchange, money establishes a *standard of value* and as money, in whatever form, is held in between exchanges, money becomes *a store of value.*

The definition of money, as explained above, has a reference to relationship and this aspect has attracted the attention of philosophers. According to Simmel (1978, 120),

> Since money expresses the value relationship between goods, measures them and facilitates their exchange, it enters the world of useful goods as a power of entirely different origin; either as an abstract system of measurement or as a means of exchange which moves between tangible objects as does ether between objects possessing weight.

Therefore, money stands as the measure and means of exchange between valuable objects, and these values are denoted with units of money, as the latter is treated as a numeraire.

History of Money

There is a general belief that the word 'money' originated from a temple of Hera, that is located on top of a hill named Capitoline, which is one of the famous seven hills in the city of Rome in Italy. In the ancient world the goddess Hera was often associated with money[1]. In the beginning, money was commodity money, representing any durable standard commodity that got the people's recognition, often through a dictat, to be used as a medium of exchange of other commodities. Slowly, metal coins were invented to be used as money.

Historically, a large number of coinage metals (including alloys), apart from gold and silver, have been used in the production of coins for circulation. Coins were also used for collection,

---

[1] Roman Gods began taking on the forms during the dynasty of the Etruscan kings that ruled the city of Rome in the sixth century BCE. These gods had been worshipped regularly at the temples on the Capitoline hills and as a result it became known as Capitoline Triad. The Triad were represented by Jupiter (Zeus), Juno (Hera) andMinerva (Athena) (North, 2000).

and metal investment as bullion coins, made from precious metals like gold and silver, kept as a store of value or as investment, and seldom used as medium of exchange. Bullion coins are generally made of gold or silver. The exceptions are *Krugerrand* of South Africa and *Vreneli* of Switzerland which are made of gold only. Also, the American Eagle series are made of gold, silver and platinum. Again, Canadian maple leaf series are made of gold, silver, platinum, and palladium.

Some archaeologists believe that Indians invented coinage sometime during the period 500–400 BCE. However, some historians think that first coins might have originated circa 600–550 BCE in Anatolia, which is in the modern-day Turkey. But, the debate continues. Along with Anatolia and also China, India played an important part in the development of coinage. *Puranas* or punch-marked coins were the earliest money made in India around 600 BCE. They were in circulation long before the beginning of the Christian era as Sanskrit writers such as Manu and Panini and also Buddhist Jataka stories have mentioned the aspects of such coins (Friedberg, 2003; Yeoman, 2010).

Representative Money

As trade and commerce had increased with the advance of human civilization, use of metallic coins became disadvantageous, and that was mainly for two reasons. First, more and more use of coins had meant carrying more weight over a long distance. Second, supply restrictions created problem as precious metals like gold, silver, platinum were really scarce. These twin problems were addressed by the invention of Representative Money. According to William Stanley Jevons (1875), representative money came into being because metal coins were variously clipped or depreciated during use, but using representations for value stored in banks ensured its worth. This evolved as gold and silver merchants or banks would issue receipts to their depositors which were redeemable for commodity money deposited. Later on these receipts were generally accepted as a means of payment and were used as money.

According to historians, banknotes or paper money was first used in China during the Song Dynasty. These notes known as 'jiaozi' had evolved from promissory notes that were used from seventh century CE. And these banknotes were used alongside metal coins. In Europe, banknotes were first issued by Stockholms Banco in 1661 CE and these were used along with metal coins. Starting from seventeenth century CE, Gold Standard became established in Europe. It was a system in which the medium of exchange were paper notes that were convertible into pre-determined and fixed quantity of gold and as a result paper notes replaced gold coins in the period seventeenth to nineteenth century in Europe. These gold standard notes were declared as legal tender and their redemption into gold coins were discouraged. With the dawn of the twentieth century, almost all countries started using paper notes under gold standard and those were backed by fixed amount of gold. Thus, modern money came into being. The rapid use of money had its effects on the dynamics of the economic operations of countries. The theoretical mechanism of this effect of money is very interesting. We now turn towards this aspect.

2.2 David Hume and the Quantity Theory of Money

The Quantity Theory of Money (QTM) is the first attempt of the classical economists to give a full theory of price level, and it establishes the relation between price level and money stock of a country. The origin of the theory can be traced back to the writings of David Hume (1828). Through his writings, Hume proved the position of the mercantilist[2] belief, that countries could become rich by generating balance of payments surpluses and accumulating gold, was wrong. Also Hume's book is dominated by several interrelated causal mechanisms in economics and Quantity theory is one of these. Here QTM places the stock of money in relation to the stock of available goods and this relation determines the equilibrium price level. Given the prices of commodities in foreign country, an increase in the domestic stock of money causes domestic prices to rise relative to foreign prices.

The second causal mechanism is the specie-flow mechanism, which shows that relative prices cause money (precious metals like gold) to vary inversely. The third relation is the loanable fund doctrine, which states that, the supply of and demand for loans together are the cause of the change in the interest rates. Hume also established the causal relation between the interest rates and profit rates. This is known as the arbitrage principle.

The issue of causality in macroeconomics has been debated extensively and part of that debate has attained philosophical undertones (Hoover, 2001). The causality aspect of the quantity theory of money has been debated and researched in two parallel schools — one later on led by the University of Chicago and the other by the famous group of economists known as Keynesians who were based mostly in two universities — Harvard University, Cambridge, Massachusetts and Cambridge University, Cambridge, the United Kingdom. Some even suggest that it is the nature of the initial construction of QTM that creates controversy always (Laidler, 1991). With this brief note we turn to the QTM proper.

The classical tradition of money begins with the following identity:

$$PQ = MV \qquad \text{Equation (2.1)}$$

where M is the quantity of money in the economy, V is the velocity of circulation of money, P is the price index, and Q is full employment output, a proxy for total economic activity.

This equation (2.1) as it stands is an identity. If the quantity of money is low, and there is a lot of activity in nominal terms, then money must be turning around fast, or velocity must be high. However, if the quantity of money is high, and velocity is high as well, but little real

---

[2] The doctrine of Mercantilism dominated both economic and political thinking for over a century from the publication of Machiavelli's *The Prince* in 1532 to Thomas Mun's *England's Treasure by Foreign Trade* published posthumously in 1664. The doctrine was associated with the concept of a strong State, with a positive balance of trade and the accumulation of foreign exchange (gold and other precious metals). The latter was seen as the means of acquiring political strength and national prosperity. Edward Misselden was perhaps the first writer to use the term 'balance of trade' in his book *The Centre of the Circle of Commerce* (1623). He argued that the policies of the State should be to secure a favourable balance of trade by promoting exports and discouraging imports, the country thereby receiving treasure and growing rich. The writers were not sure about the precise means by which the accumulation of treasure would make a country rich. Thomas Mun is taken as the typifying mercantilist thinking in the seventeenth century.

production is taking place, then prices will be high. The government is expanding money, and people are trying to get rid of it to get the purchasing power, so that prices will be high.

What the classical economists implied was that if people have more real money, they will buy more goods and services. If their wealth increases in the form of possession of more money, they will increase their consumption. So, a fall in prices keeping the level of money constant will increase the real money wealth and that will lead to more consumption. This was emphasized by A.C. Pigou (1943), and is known as real balance effects in the literature.

The first step in the evolution of the quantity theory from a mere tautology to a theory came from the Cambridge, UK 'cash-balance' interpretation of Equation (2.1), and this interpretation came from the writings of Alfred Marshall and A.C. Pigou. The above equation was reformulated as a demand-for-money function:

$$M = k\, PQ, \text{ where } k = 1/V \qquad \text{Equation (2.2)}$$

The Cambridge school simply took the real quantity of money (M/P) as the endogenous variable, set Q as the exogenous variable, and assumed that V, the velocity of circulation, was constant. Once the level of output is determined, the amount of real quantity of money M/P becomes a solution value of money market equilibrium. This development is a classical rebuttal to the Keynesian position that an increase in the quantity of money can ensure full employment. But Keynes at one place attributes unemployment to inadequate supply of money:

> Unemployment develops, that is to say, because people want the moon; — men cannot be employed when the objects of desire (i.e., money) is something which cannot be produced and the demand for which cannot be readily choked off. There is no remedy but to persuade the public that green cheese is practically the same thing and to have a green cheese factory (i.e., a central bank) under public control (Keynes, 1964, 235).

One may wonder how Keynes reconciled this 'green cheese' statement with the rest of his book *General Theory*, where he forcefully put the argument that economy might reach an equilibrium at less than full employment (ibid.)!

This approach is a well-defined hypothesis: it states that demand for money depends in a proportional way, or with unitary elasticity, on real output. It is thus a transactions-based demand for money. It also tells us that interest rates do not matter for the demand for money. It is a clear and simple theory, which can in principle be falsified by the evidence. In this sense, it is not trivial.

The second approach to understanding Equation (2.1) as a theory comes from Irving Fisher. His approach is not a theory of demand for money, but a theory of price adjustment. The relation becomes the following model of prices:

$$P = (V^*/Q^*)\, M$$
$$P = q \cdot M, \text{ with } q = V^*/Q^* \qquad \text{Equation (2.3)}$$

Fisher assumes that both output and velocity are constant in the long-run. Thus, prices are proportional to money stocks. Thus, the quantity theory money is a theory of price-level determination. Fisher affirms that this theory is a long-run theory and he is careful to point out that things may be different in the short-run. This led to the debate regarding the neutrality of money in later years.

Quantity Theory as Theory of Output

Fisher (1982) argues that the adjustment of prices and output may be sluggish and asymmetrical. Thus while money is doubled, prices may not double immediately, but it increases slowly, while output may initially decline, then increases from the present level and ultimately comes down to initial level. This is a long-run process and it ultimately leaves prices proportional to money supply. In this sense QTM is a long-run theory. Most economists today accept the Fisher interpretation of the quantity theory of price adjustment. It is a long-run theory of price adjustment, *ceteris paribus*. Prices will double if money doubles. In the short-run, other factors, such as oil shocks and supply shortfalls will affect the behavior of the overall price index.

Fisher's theory holds true only in the absence of nominal government bonds in the economy. Because if there are nominal bonds, an increase in the quantity of the money supply will put upward pressures on the price level. This reduces real value of the bonds, and thus lowers interest rates. The latter may affect saving, investment, and production, and this makes the relation between money supply and price level less than proportional. The Fisher approach assumes money as the only issue of the government.

Again, the Fisher approach is only valid when money is 'fiat money', the paper issued by the government. In a commodity money standard, when gold or silver serves as the media of exchange, or when these are used as 100 per cent backing for the paper currency, neutrality does not hold. An increase in the quantity of gold, for example, has direct effect on the price of gold, on employment and investment in the mining sector, and thus has relative price effects as well as "real effects". Thus, a monetary expansion in the form of an increase in gold is far from being neutral.

The debate between monetarists, Keynesians, and new classical economists (arising from rational expectations) 'centres' on the adjustment process of output. Is the output 'hump' following a monetary expansion a tidal wave or merely a ripple? Should monetary authorities attempt to fine tune the behavior of aggregate output through money stock changes? In this perspective, economists in the Keynesian tradition believe that there is scope for the monetary authority to help the economy move out of recession by appropriate expansionary policies. On the other hand, the monetarist tradition argued forcefully by Milton Friedman and Anna Schwartz in A *Monetary History of the United States, 1867–1960* (1963), establishes the position that money stock changes have long, variable and unpredictable lagged effects on output. Thus, the economists in the monetarist tradition believe that any attempt to fine tune output by monetary policy may backfire: expansion policies during a time of slackness may kick in just when the economy is in an expansion, and could stimulate inflation. The monetarist approach argues in favour of a policy of constant, smooth monetary growth, which, they believe, would lead to stable prices, and this is the famous *x-per cent rule* of constant money supply.

The rational expectation approach (REA) (that is also known as New Classical Approach) is a new twist on the monetarist tradition. This approach holds that the monetary authority can affect output temporarily, but only if the policy change is unexpected. When people expect monetary policy to become expansionary, they will forecast high prices, and thus will not feel richer, and spend more, when the money stock increases. If people are caught off-guard with a sudden increase in the money stock, then there may be temporary effects.

The rational expectations approach also raises the issue of time consistency in central bank behaviour. The central bank may find it optimal to say one thing (no expansion in the money stock) and do another (expand the money stock), in order to finesse an increase in output. One of the key contributions of this approach has been its focus on the credibility of government policy. While the central bank may find it optimal to dissemble once or twice, it cannot do so forever as people will understand the model behaviour of the central bank and neutralize it. Whatever the opinions about the short-run adjustment, and the 'real' effects of monetary policy on output, the message of the Fisher model is clear and straightforward: In the long-run, monetary expansion means higher prices, or continued higher rates of monetary growth mean higher rates of inflation. In this perspective, how the people form their expectation about the future price level under the premise of rational expectation hypothesis has been explained by Thomas Sargent in the following way:

> An alternative "rational expectations" view denies that there is any inherent momentum to the present process of inflation. This view maintains that firms and workers have now come to expect high rates of inflation in the future and that they strike inflationary bargain in the light of these expectations. However, it is held that people expect high rates of inflation in the future precisely because the government's current and prospective monetary and fiscal policies warrant those expectations ... An implication of this view is that inflation can be stopped much more quickly than advocates of the "momentum" view have indicated, and that their estimates of the length of time and the cost of stopping inflation in terms of foregone output are erroneous ... this is not to say that it would be easy to eradicate inflation. On the contrary, it would require more than a few temporary restrictive fiscal and monetary actions. It would require a change in the policy regime ... How costly such a move would be in terms of foregone output and how long it would be in taking effect would depend partly on how resolute and evident the government's commitment was (Sargent, 1983, 45–46).

2.3 Purchasing Power Parity Theory

The Purchasing Power Parity (PPP) theory states that prices of traded goods will be same everywhere in the world whether one buys these at New Delhi or New York if we neglect tariffs and transport costs. The PPP theory is a natural open-economy extension of the quantity theory of money. Like the quantity theory, it starts with the tautology:

$$P = E P_f \quad \text{Equation (2.4)}$$

where P is the price index for tradable goods in the domestic economy, expressed in domestic currency, P_f is the price index of tradable goods in the world market, expressed in foreign money, and E is the exchange rate, the price of one unit of foreign money in terms of domestic money.

Equation (2.4), as it stands, is trivial. Excluding tariffs and transportation costs, it states that the domestic cost of traded goods is simply equal to the foreign price, quoted in foreign money, multiplied by the exchange rate. For highly mobile traded goods, assuming no transport cost, simple goods arbitrage would see that Equation (2.4) is true.

Equation (2.4) becomes a causal monetary theory of exchange rate determination when we couple it with Fisher's monetary theory of prices, for the domestic and foreign economies. Rewriting Equation (2.4), and making use of the information in Equation (2.1), the following expression emerges:

$$E = P/P^f \qquad \text{Equation (2.5)}$$

And $P = q M^d$

$$P = q^f M^f \text{ we get from Equation (2.3)}$$

This gives the following

$$E = (q/q^f) M^d/M^f \qquad \text{Equation 2.5(a)}$$

Or, if the first term is taken as a constant, it implies that exchange rate between two countries becomes proportional to the ratio of the two countries' money stock, provided it is true that domestic and foreign price levels are proportional to the money supplies in two countries.

Purchasing power parity is one building block of monetary theory of exchange rate determination. Like Fisher's theory, it is a long-run theory: we are talking about long-run relations between money and prices in each country, and thus long-run relations between relative money supplies and the exchange rate. In the short run, events like oil shocks, supply shortages, or technological changes can and do affect the exchange rate as well as price level of the countries. We will discuss more about PPP doctrine in Chapter 10 when it is discussed as a theory of exchange rate determination.

It is important to see that the tautology of Equation (2.4) becomes a causal theory of exchange-rate determination in Equation (2.5). Money determines prices in different countries, and relative money supplies determine the exchange rate. Both price levels and the exchange rate are endogenously determined by the money supplies.

If one interprets Equation (2.4) as a causal theory of domestic-price determination, it may lead to misguided policy decision. If one believes that all goods in the economy are tradable, and that foreign prices are more or less stable, then one way to stop inflation, and keep domestic prices constant, is to simply freeze the exchange rate, or at least slow down its rate of change.

Purchasing Power Parity: An Elaboration

The purchasing power parity theory is about the long run, and leaves open the question of short-run adjustment, or dynamics like Fisher's quantity theory. Many papers are written on the deviations from PPP in academic journals, but still it is very popular. For a given monetary expansion in the home country, given a constant money supply in the foreign country, if the home country increases its money supply, prices adjust sluggishly, or 'crawl' to their long-run level, while the exchange rates jump more than double, and then come down, and may move to their long-run level either from above or below. The PPP theory gives broad hints about the exchange-rate movement. It is monetary policy that drives both prices and exchange rate in the long-run. Failure to come to terms with control of the money supply will only lead to upward movements in both the exchange rate and the price level.

2.4 The Monetarist Arithmetic

The classical tradition focuses on the quantity of money and its effects on the aggregate price level and the exchange rate. Why do governments bother to issue money? The question, of course, comes down to alternative means of financing government deficits. Governments have two options: (i) print money, or (ii) issue bonds. The following expression represents the government budget deficit:

$$\frac{G}{P} + \frac{iB}{P} - \frac{T}{P} = \frac{\Delta M}{P} + \frac{\Delta B}{P} \qquad \text{Equation (2.6)}$$

where G is nominal government spending, B is the stock of bonds, i is the interest rate, T is tax revenue, M is money supply, P is the price level, and Δ is the first-difference operator. Government spending and interest payments on existing debt in excess of tax revenue must be financed either by printing money or by issuing more bonds.

Regarding the financing of fiscal deficit, Sargent (1987) raises an interesting and provocative question. They point out that sooner or later, a government following a policy of bond-financed deficits will be forced to default on its debt. As the amount of outstanding bonds increases, so do the debt-service payments of the government increases with the amount of outstanding bonds. Sooner or later the, government will have to 'destroy' its outstanding debt, if its own deficit is to be brought under control. One way to destroy its debt is to print money, increase the price level, and wipe away the real value of outstanding government bonds. In this way, inflation becomes an instrument of government policy, rather than an objective of economic policy.

Sargent points out that without a fiscal correction (an increase in T or a decrease in G), increased bond expansion sooner or later becomes unsustainable. The government will have to run an inflation, to get the deficit under control. What the author points out is that the corrective inflation at the end after a period of bond financing of deficits, will result in a higher rate of inflation, than if the government had simply financed its deficits from the beginning by printing money (ibid.).

Why? If the government prints money to finance its deficits, from the start, inflation will show up. But the government does not have to pay interest on past issues of money that remain in circulation. Period-by-period, the government prints money to pay for the excess of G over T, but the government does not owe any interest on past issues. When following the bond-financing scheme, however, inflation does not show up, but the government has to issue new bonds at each period, not only to cover the excess of G over T, but also the interest payments on the outstanding bonds held by the public. As bond issues mount, so do the interest payments.

When the crisis point finally arrives, there is a large stock of bonds to destroy. To liquidate that higher inflation is necessary compared to printing of money for financing deficit period-wise.

The 'unpleasant' aspect of the Sargent's monetarist arithmetic is that bond-financing does not negate the quantity theory, but brings it back with a vengeance, in the absence of a fiscal reform. The use of bond instruments for financing deficits can defer inflation for some time, but sooner or later, bonds will lose their worth if the government does not put its fiscal house in order. This is an important lesson for many developing countries today.

2.5 Balance of Payments Adjustment

In 1931, gold standard was abandoned. Since the automatic adjustment mechanism of balance of payment (BOP) was no longer possible, different explanations were given to explain the BOP disequilibrium and these are:
 (1) it is a problem of distorted relative prices in international trade,
 (2) it is a problem of excessive expenditure of the country relative to output, and
 (3) it is a problem emanating from the domestic monetary disequilibrium.

The above three ways of viewing the BOP difficulties correspond to the so-called elasticity approach, absorption approach and monetarist approach in the literature.

The Elasticity Approach

The elasticity approach to balance of payments adjustment focuses on the current account of the balance of payments. On the assumption that there may be distortion in relative prices in the international market, it explores the question: what conditions must prevail in the foreign exchange market for a devaluation or depreciation of the currency to improve the balance of payments starting from equilibrium, with the balance of payments measured either in foreign or domestic currency? It is basically a partial equilibrium analysis — holding constant everything else that may affect the supply of and demand for foreign or domestic currency, except the change in the relative price of foreign and domestic goods arising from the change in the exchange rate itself. It also assumes that the supply elasticity of all goods are infinite. It implies that the domestic price of exports, the foreign price of imports, and the prices of import and export substitutes are constant. Also autonomous expenditure in money terms is held constant.

Under these assumptions, the condition for a devaluation to improve the balance of payments is known as the Marshall–Lerner condition, which states that devaluation will improve the balance of payments on current account, if the sum of the price elasticity of demand for exports (η) and imports (ψ) exceeds unity in absolute value i.e., if:

$$|\eta + \psi| > 1 \qquad \text{Equation (2.7)}$$

The intuitive explanation of the condition is as follows. Consider a small x per cent devaluation which leads to a x per cent fall in the foreign price of domestic exports. If the demand for exports rises by less than x per cent, foreign exchange earnings will fall; if demand rises by more than x per cent foreign exchange earnings will rise, and if demand rises by exactly x per cent, foreign exchange earnings will remain the same. In this last case of unitary elasticity of demand, it would then only require a minute cutback in import demand (an elasticity of demand for imports slightly above zero; $\psi > 0$) for foreign exchange earnings to improve in total. Any combination of price elasticity of demand for exports and imports will improve foreign exchange earnings provided they sum-up to greater than unity.

A seemingly contrary result was derived by Harberger (1950), and is repeated by Stern (1973). They suggest that the income effects of devaluation alter the Marshall–Lerner condition, making it more stringent. The explanation is that these models hold *real* expenditure constant implying a rise in autonomous expenditure in *money* terms, so that in a two-country model, money expenditure rises in the devaluing country and falls in the appreciating country. This raises imports and reduces exports for the devaluing country, and the condition for balance of payments improvement becomes:

$$|\eta + \psi| > 1 + m_1 + m_2 \qquad \text{Equation (2.8)}$$

where m_1 is the marginal propensity to import of the devaluing country and m_2 is the marginal propensity to import of the other countries. Of the two specifications, which one should be preferred depends on whether a successful devaluation is interpreted to mean one which improves the balance of payments *with* real income falling or *without* real income falling.

2.6 The Absorption Model of the Balance of Trade

The Keynesian tradition, like the classical tradition, starts with the following identity in an open economy situation:

$$Y = C + I + G - T + EX - IM \qquad \text{Equation (2.9)}$$

where Y is national product, C consumption, I investment, T tax payments, EX exports, and IM imports. As it appears, equation (2.7) is trivial: it must be true. However, the absorption approach, assumes that the trade balance (EX-IM), is the dependent variable:

$$(EX - IM) = Y - (C + I) + (T - G) = (Y - A) + (T - G),$$
where $\qquad A = C + I \qquad \text{Equation (2.10)}$

Equation (2.10) tells us that the trade balance depends on how much an economy produces in excess of its domestic absorption (consumption and investment), and how much its government saves. Thus, this relation would predict chronic trade deficits for countries which have (1) chronic fiscal deficits, with $T < G$, and for countries which have (2) low private saving or high investment relative to domestic production, with $Y < A$.

Equation (2.10) offers a simple and striking explanation of chronic trade deficits. It tells us that chronic fiscal deficits are mirrored in trade deficits. It also predicts that countries that keep their fiscal house in order and that have high saving rates (low C relative to Y) will have chronic trade surpluses.

This equation shows the trade balance of a country with the fiscal policy. The correct policy for correcting a trade deficit, then, is fiscal stabilization, and in the longer term, a policy of increasing domestic production relative to domestic absorption, through increasing productivity and personal saving.

In a functional macroeconomic sense, the absorption approach to the balance of payments may be regarded as superior to the partial equilibrium elasticity approach. But it unfortunately gives the impression that it is *plans* to spend in excess of *plans* to produce that is causal in the explanation of balance of payments deficits. In practice, this may not be the case. Equations (2.9) and (2.10) which portray the balance of payments as the difference between income and expenditure, or savings and investment, are derived from the national income *identities*, and causation must never be inferred from identities. A deficit in the first instance may be caused by an autonomous fall in exports, by an autonomous rise in imports, or by an autonomous deterioration in the real terms of trade. This may be quite independent of decisions to spend more than output, because real income has been depressed. For the simultaneous achievement of macroeconomic goals, the diagnosis of the true *initial* source of the deficit is important if the correct policy response is to be adopted.

Suppose the deficit is not caused by excess demand at full employment, but it is due to an exogenous fall in real income. In this case, dampening demand to cure the deficit will simply lead to an even lower level of real income. This confusion is similar to the IMF adjustment programmes in developing countries that is taken as stemming from *ex ante* excess demand whereas the real root of the problem may be poor export performance, import penetration, or a cyclical worsening of the terms of trade.

In an important paper, Johnson (1958) establishes the impression that balance of payments deficits are not simply associated with excess monetary demand for goods. The latter may cause the former. He distinguishes between what he calls a stock deficit and a flow deficit. The former is self-correcting through a rise in interest rates caused by a once-for-all switch out of domestic assets. The latter is not self-correcting and the monetary authorities accommodate the deficit by expanding the money supply. In either case, the deficit is *caused* by an excess supply of money, with equilibrium in the money market being restored by a loss of international (foreign exchange) reserves. This interpretation of the absorption approach led to the emergence of the monetarist approach to BOP.

2.7 The Monetary Approach

The essence of the monetary approach to the balance of payments is that it takes the balance of payments as a whole, that is, the current and capital account together. It assumes that changes in international reserves are a function of disequilibrium between the supply of, and demand for, money. An excess supply of money leads to a loss of international reserves and an excess demand for money leads to a gain in international reserves. Again, the changes in the level of reserves is the mechanism by which the balance between the supply and demand for money is restored. A currency depreciation can only be successful if it increases the nominal demand for money relative to the supply, as the price level rises. This is achieved by reducing the real supply of money in relation to the real demand. Johnson (1977) once asserted that 'all balance of payments disequilibria are monetary in essence'.

Further Implications

The trade balance is simply exports less imports, evaluated in domestic currency: thus we can write balance of trade (BOT) as,

$$BOT = EX - e \cdot p^* IM \qquad \text{Equation (2.11)}$$

where e is the exchange rate, p* the foreign price level, EX exports and IM imports.

The current account is simply the balance of trade, BOT, plus the net interest receipts of the home country — interest income on foreign capital owned by domestic residents, Kf,d, less interest payments on domestic capital owned by foreign residents, Kd,f:

$$\text{Current Account} = BOT + e \cdot i^* \, Kf,d - i \, Kd,f \qquad \text{Equation (2.12)}$$

where i* is the foreign interest rate and i is the domestic rate.

The capital account is simply net capital inflows, or changes in domestic capital owned by foreigners, less the changes in foreign capital owned by domestic residents, and this can be written as,

$$\text{Capital Account} = \Delta K_{d,f} - e \, \Delta K_{f,d} \qquad \text{Equation (2.13)}$$

Finally, the net foreign asset position of a country is simply the amount of foreign capital owned by domestic residents less the amount of domestic capital owned by foreign residents. The net foreign asset position of a country tells us if a country is a net creditor or a net debtor, and this can be written as,

$$NFA = e \cdot Kf,d - Kd,f \qquad \text{Equation (2.14)}$$

With these definitions, one can readily understand that the persistent trade deficit, financed by capital inflows, sooner or later, will change the net foreign asset position of a country from the status of a net creditor to that of a net debtor. The result shows in the changes of the international reserve of the country. Sometimes international reserve may increase even though balance of trade is adverse. This happens through the capital inflow in capital account, Fiscal and External Balances, US.

2.8 Classical and Keynesian Models: A Comparison

On the surface, there does not seem to be any consistency and similarity between the classical models of the quantity theory of price adjustment and purchasing power parity with the Keynesian absorption model of trade. The classical models take stocks as the exogenous policy variables, while the absorption model concentrates on flow variables (fiscal balance, income, consumption, and investment). The classical models concentrate on the adjustment of price indices, either the aggregate price level or the exchange rate, while the Keynesian model looks at the adjustment of a flow, the trade balance. Finally, the classical models speak of the long-run effects of policy changes, while the absorption models are interested in the short-run adjustment of flow variables.

The key difference is that economists in the classical tradition believe that the economy is inherently stable and will adjust to long-run equilibrium without the need of government intervention. The classical economists believe that government intervention is usually part of the problem, not the solution. Keynesians, however, believe that the economy can get stuck in the short-run disequilibrium of a persistent trade deficit, with high unemployment, and that corrective government intervention may be called for in order to help the economy move smoothly from short-run adjustment of trade-flows to balance, and to long-run adjustment of prices and exchange rates.

The discussion of market failure of course admits the need for government intervention like the standard case of public goods with externality. Whether this case can be extended to the macro economy is still a debate that goes on in a different plane.

2.9 Money in New Open Economy Models

A series of papers published since the late 1980s had changed the main theoretical contours of traditional international economic theories. The latter had largely been built on the solid foundations of Heckscher–Ohlin model, though some extensions had been achieved in some papers published in the 1980s. These were mainly concerned with the inclusion of the assumptions of imperfect competitions, counter trade and to some extent, price rigidity. But the basic premise of the H–O model remained intact. While the pure theory of international trade remains tied to H–O framework, the monetary theory, i.e., balance of payments and exchange rate determination had been built upon either the Keynesian framework or the monetarist framework.

In 1995, Maurice Obstfeld and Kenneth Rogoff (henceforth OB–RO) jointly published a paper (Obstfeld and Rogoff, 2000) that started a series of research changing many assumptions of traditional theory of international economics. The basic model of OB–RO is a two-country dynamic general equilibrium model with the provisions of nominal price rigidities, imperfect competition, and a continuum of agents who both produce and consume. Each agent produces a single differentiated good and all of them have identical preferences. The latter are characterized by an intertemporal utility function that depend positively on consumption and real money balances but negatively on work efforts. The work efforts are positively related to output. While two countries are home and foreign, exchange rate is the price of foreign currency in terms of home currency. The exchange rate works as the bridge between the domestic price and the foreign price.

The OB–RO model assumes that there are no restrictions on international movements of commodities. This implies that law of one price (LOOP) holds for individual commodity and internationally identical commodity basket is governed by PPP, i.e., each traded commodity attracts the same price when converted to a single international currency. Strict version of PPP implies a fixed real exchange rate, as the latter is defined as the nominal exchange rate adjusted for relative national price levels, or,

$$RER = NER \times (CPI / CPI^*)$$

where CPI and CPI* are price levels of home and foreign respectively. Thus twin assumptions of LOOP and continuous PPP imply a fixed RER for the home country. When PPP holds only in the long run and not on continuous basis, RER may have fluctuations over time.

OB–OR model assumes that two countries can borrow and lend in the integrated capital market of the world. The only asset traded internationally is the risk-free real bond denominated in consumption goods. Agents maximize their lifetime utility subject to budget constraint.

Each agent decides his optimal choice of consumption, money holding, labour supply and also determines the price of his output. Nominal rigidity is introduced into the model by fixing prices one period in advance. The system is first solved for the steady state of the model. A log-linear approximation is made of the steady state to study the effects of a monetary shock. Since prices are sticky for one period, the solution distinguishes between the impact effects of a shock and the long-run, steady-state effects. The welfare effects of a shock are the sum of the short-run change of utility and the long-run change in steady-state utility.

The model also considers the experiment of an unanticipated permanent increase in domestic money supply (a la Dornbusch). The effects of a monetary shock is an increase in output and consumption. The real interest rate of the world declines and a nominal depreciation of domestic currency boils down to a decline in domestic terms of trade. Both these factors lead to an increase in foreign consumption. Since the increase in aggregate consumption and the shift in relative prices work in opposite dimensions, the effects on foreign output are ambiguous. The current account of the home country moves to a surplus. This implies a permanent improvement in net foreign assets. When the latter is translated to positive net investment income inflow, this increases consumption permanently above domestic output and that leads to a domestic trade deficit. Again, the wealth effects of an increase in net foreign assets reduces domestic labour supply as leisure consumption increases, domestic output declines and this leads to a permanent improvement in the home country's terms of trade. Thus money is not neutral in this model.

In the model, the monetary shock's impact on home and foreign welfare can be calculated. The different effects of the money shocks on consumption both in the short-run and in the long run, real balances and leisure can be aggregated adjusting to the respective weights implicit in the utility function. It follows from the model that home and foreign welfare increase in the same proportion, though the output effects of the shock are asymmetric. This is because the first order effects of the monetary shocks are the initial increase in world demand. But the distortions will be there because of imperfect competition, and the initial levels of output will be too low compared to the world total; a demand-driven increase in the world output increases welfare to the equal benefits of both countries.

2.10 Extension of OB–RO Model

The OB–RO model has been extended by later research works. Nominal rigidity is one particular assumption. Harald Hau has generalized the model in three ways with the objective of investigating the role of factor price rigidities and non-tradable for the international transmission mechanism (Hau, 2000). First, the model allows for factor markets and also for nominal rigidity originating from sticky factor prices. Second, Hau's paper also allows for non-traded goods.

Third, it is assumed that there is no international goods arbitrage and there is flexible price setting in local currency. Because of optimal monopolistic price fixation, law of one price still holds, though non-tradable in the consumer price index will create deviations from the purchasing power parity.

The main result of the Hau's paper is that factor price rigidities have similar implications to rigid domestic producer prices. In the context of a market structure with factor price rigidities, the conclusion of OB–RO model is confirmed here also. However, a large share of non-tradable goods in consumer's budget implies that exchange rate movements are magnified, because money market equilibrium depends on a short-run price adjustment that are associated with fewer tradable commodities. This is important as this effect may explain the high volatility of the nominal exchange rate relative to price fluctuations as observed in the market.

2.11 The Steady State Again

In OB–RO framework, current account plays an important role in the transmission of shocks across the countries. But the steady state is indeterminate, and both the consumption differential between countries and the net foreign assets of a country are non-stationary in character. After a monetary shock, the economy will move to a new steady state, and continue there till another shock arrives. Later formulations of OB–RO have not emphasized the role of net foreign assets accumulations as a channel of macroeconomic transmissions between countries. This is achieved with two assumptions:

(1) the elasticity of substitution between domestic and foreign goods is unity, and,
(2) financial markets are complete in the sense that international capital market is complete with perfect capital mobility.

Under complete financial markets and law of one price, full risk-sharing means that there will be no shift in wealth between countries arising out of monetary shocks. This makes the persistence channel non-functional, and there is no longer a shift in relative wealth having a permanent effect on relative labour supplies, that causes permanent effects on relative prices and outputs. As a result of these, the assumption of complete markets help to simplify the analysis by denying both the current account and net foreign assets the role of dynamic propagation mechanism.

The two assumptions (1) and (2), by denying the current account to generate dynamic persistent effects have helped for the achievement of the determinacy of the steady state. The assumption may be strong, but the role of current account dynamics in the generation of persistent effects of transitory shocks have also been found to be quantitatively not important in the literature (Kollman, 1996).

2.12 Uncertainty and Stochastic Nature

OB–RO has introduced the effects of an unanticipated monetary shock in a sticky price general equilibrium model with a stochastic setting. Thus monetary uncertainty is introduced by assuming home and foreign money stocks follow log-normal stochastic process. Since uncertainty affects equilibrium prices, it has effects on expected consumption levels, the terms of trade and also relative output levels. For example, if the home country faces monetary uncertainty, the corporate of this country will add a risk premium in the prices of commodities. This will reduce production, but will improve terms of trade. Thus uncertainty has first-order effects on equilibrium welfare levels. These effects are symmetric on welfare levels of both countries, home and foreign, despite ex-ante differences in price setting and ex-post differences in relative output levels. This induces both the countries to design an optimum global exchange rate system, and this will hold irrespective of the relative size of home and foreign countries.

The model as developed in OB–RO (1998) has another interesting implication. Regarding its predictions for asset pricing, the risk premium on a volatile currency may be negative if exchange rate movement hedges consumption volatility. This again explains a puzzle related to forward premium: a high inflation country may have a relative volatile and unstable currency that hedges consumption risk, and thus it simultaneously generates a positive expected depreciation and a negative forward premium. Also monetary uncertainty has magnified effects on the level of exchange rate relative to the forward premium. When the latter is volatile, the analysis then provides an explanation for the high volatility of the level of exchange rate. This also explains that not only does a high interest rate lead to potential depreciation of the currency, but also the expectation of a depreciation of the home currency due to monetary shock may increase the interest rate.

The results obtained above in the extended OB–RO model are based on the assumptions specific to the model along with the micro foundations. This aspect has been questioned in subsequent literature and some papers have attempted to relax some strong assumptions (Sarno, 2001).

2.13 Equilibrium Exchange Rate and Pass-through

Empirical evidence in the literature indicates that changes in the nominal exchange rates are not fully passed through to the prices of commodities. It seems that consumer prices are not very responsive to nominal exchange rate changes. One implication of this is that the *expenditure switching* effects of exchange rate changes might be very small, which means that a change in the nominal exchange rate might not lead to much substitution between domestically produced commodities and internationally produced commodities, as the relative prices of the commodities do not change much for the consumers.

When the exchange rate changes have small effects on the behaviour of final users of commodities, it will require a large change in the exchange rates to achieve equilibrium after some initial shock to the fundamentals. Suppose there is a shock that reduces the supply of imported commodities, then that implies that a very large home depreciation might be required in order to increase the relative prices of imported commodities enough to reduce demand for that sufficiently. This shows that low pass-through of exchange rates may imply high exchange-rate volatility in equilibrium.

The central issue is market segmentation and practice of local-currency pricing of traded commodities. This practice of local-currency pricing impedes the linkages of commodity prices across the countries that again cause the deviations from purchasing power parity (PPP) doctrine and also high exchange-rate volatility. But there are some caveats to this conclusion and these are as follows.

First, international finance markets often allow for complete risk-sharing across countries. This means that the exchange rate will be determined by risk-sharing conditions, in spite of the fact that local currency prices are independent of exchange rate movements.

Second, even in situations of limited risk-sharing in the sense as above, the linkage of asset prices through bond markets will impose a very narrow limit of exchange rate movements, and that rules out high volatility.

Apart from local-currency pricing, two other factors are added in the literature to explain high volatility of exchange rates — heterogeneity in the distribution of internationally traded commodities and the existence of 'noise traders' in the foreign exchange markets. The first comes through the way commodities are sold and prices are set in the international markets. Some firms market their products directly, while others have foreign distributors. In the latter case the exporters set the price in home currency, and the distributors translate that in the currency of the importing country. The second one, i.e., traders adjust changes in the exchange rate changes by the information of interest rate differentials. The expectations of these traders regarding the interest rate changes are said to be conditionally biased as reported in empirical literature (Devereux, 2002). All these cause high volatility in the exchange rate while the economy reaches equilibrium.

2.14 More on Microstructure of Exchange Rate

There has been further research to explain the short-run volatility of the exchange rate. It is argued that dispersed information is rapidly summarized in the public quote of macro variables. This contention is challenged in recent literature (Lyons, 2002). The argument is as follows. The market information of important macro variables like exchange rate gives a set of information in *abstract* form, and the argument in favour of this abstraction is not tenable as it lacks empirical support, while dispersed information approach Evans and Lyons, 2002; Payne, 1999) has better credibility so far as empirical support is concerned. Again research has revealed that real exchange rate volatility can have significant impact on the long-term productivity growth of the economy, though the magnitude of the impact depends on the level of financial development of the country (Philippe Aghion et al., 2006). It is seen empirically that volatility of real exchange rate reduces the rate of economic growth in the countries with a low level of development in the financial sector, but for financially advanced countries there is no significant impact.

The difference between the public information approach and the dispersed information approach is the importance of the variable *order flow* in the latter. Order flow is a concept borrowed from microstructure finance. The latter has two main strands — market design and information processing. The latter is important for dispersed information approach as it borrows heavily from it. Order flow concept also belongs to it, i.e., information processing.

Order flow is the transaction volume that is signed according to whether the transaction is initiated from the buy side (+) or the sell side (−). Over time, order flow is measured as the sum of signed buyer-initiated and seller-initiated orders. Of the two types of cash flows, if the buyer-initiated order exceeds the seller-initiated order, then it yields a positive sun. Order flow as a concept has some similarity with *excess demand,* but with a difference. Excess demand will be zero in equilibrium, but this is not the case with order flow. In foreign exchange market, orders are initiated against a market maker, who stands ready to absorb imbalances between buyers and sellers. These *uninitiated trades* of the market maker make the difference between the two concepts — excess demand and order flow.

Order flows convey information about dispersed fundamentals because these contain the trades of those who analyze those fundamentals. It is a transmission mechanism. The dispersed information approach (DPA) may speak to longer horizon exchange rates in the same way that microscopes speak to pathologies with micro impact. This helps solve the puzzles in exchange rate movements like why the latter are virtually unrelated to macroeconomic fundamentals or, why exchange rates are excessively volatile. The DPA links these puzzles with another important phenomenon — how market participants form their expectations of future fundamentals — and this DPA does through expectation formation. The focus is on information types and how information maps into expectations. The issue of information type and mapping to expectations are the important tools of analysis of the microstructure finance to resolve the puzzles as said earlier.

2.15 Stabilization Programme in Crisis Economies: Monetarist Approach and Polak Model

Money supply is recognized as one of the determinants of the aggregate demand of the economy. When we treat money supply as a policy variable, we implicitly assume that the monetary consequences of payments imbalances are sterilized. It is recognized that when devaluation of exchange rate increases price level, it reduces the real money balances and so it reduces real demand. Therefore, money is important, and the monetarist approach starts with placing money at the core of the argument.

The monetary approach to balance of payments was developed by two schools. The first was based at the University of Chicago under the leadership of Robert Mundell and Harry Johnson. The second was initiated by J.J. Polak at International Monetary Fund (IMF) and the justification for the new approach as stated was that it would try to develop models that would be usable to monitor macroeconomic management when only rudimentary statistical information is available. We develop the Polak model briefly in the following paragraphs.

The objective of the model was to study the effects on both income formation and the balance of payments of the two important exogenous variables — autonomous changes in exports and the creation of domestic credit. A model that requires to reveal the effects of these two variables needs a demand for money function.

In a simplified banking system of a country, the consolidated balance sheet will reveal the identity:

$$\text{Money supply} = \text{Reserve} + \text{Domestic Credit, or,}$$
$$H = R + D \qquad \text{Equation (2.15)}$$

When there is a deficit in the balance of payments, it implies a loss of international reserve. It follows then from Equation (2.15) that there must be a counterpart to a deficit in balance of payments in the form of either credit creation (sterilization) or dehoarding (which implies a fall in H). Since dehoarding is a disequilibrium phenomenon (and a temporary thing), a payments deficit can persist *only if it is accompanied by credit creation.* In other words, any additional credit creation will ultimately leak out abroad. This is the central theorem of monetary approach to balance of payments. In this category, the Polak model is a model of payments adjustments under a fixed exchange rate regime.

The Polak Model is based on a number of assumptions. First, the country is having a fixed exchange rate regime and capital mobility is not allowed. Second, exports are treated as exogenous and so is the domestic credit creation. So the latter can be treated as a policy variable. Third, velocity of circulation of money is constant. This enables one to normalize velocity as unity, and then one can write to generality:

$$Y(t) = H(t) \qquad \text{Equation (2.16)}$$

Fourth, imports are always a fixed proportion (m) of the value of nominal income with one period lag, or,

$$M(t) = m \cdot Y(t-1) \qquad \text{Equation (2.17)}$$

This is rather a simplifying assumption, as it means that the propensity of import is independent of whether a given nominal income is the result of high price level and low output, or high real output and low price level.

The model is completed by the money supply and balance of payments identities:

$$\Delta H(t) = \Delta R(t) + \Delta D(t) \qquad \text{Equation (2.18)}$$
$$\Delta R(t) = X(t) - M(t) \qquad \text{Equation (2.19)}$$

And the symbols are:

H = Money supply
R = Monetary reserve
D = Domestic credit
X = exports
M = Imports
Δ = a change operator

A substitution of equations (2.16) and (2.17) into equation (2.19) gives,

$$\begin{aligned} Y(t) &= H(t) \\ &= H(t-1) + \Delta H(t) \\ &= Y(t-1) + \Delta R(t) + \Delta D(t) \end{aligned} \qquad \text{Equation (2.20)}$$

Equation (2.20) gives the basic monetary theorem. Since in equilibrium,

$$Y(t) = Y(t-1),$$

A payments deficit (that is $\Delta R < 0$) can persist only when domestic credit creation is positive or, $\Delta D > 0$.

The dynamic nature of the model derives from the fact that it contains both income and the change in income. The solution of the model gives the endogenously determined values of income, changes in the reserve and change in the domestic credit of the banking sector.

The model is simple but robust. The message is clear that any expansion of domestic credit will create disequilibrium in the domestic money market and the spill over in the external sector will make the balance of payments worse. Based on this conclusion, IMF has traditionally given to limiting domestic credit expansion as an important element of programme of the adjustment in balance of payments. The implicit assumption is that the fall in nominal income (a result of limiting domestic credit) will come through fall in price level and *not through a fall in real output*. But the critics argue that the contraction of domestic credit may lead to a fall in output.

Critics of the IMF stabilization programme argue that IMF uses the same programme for all countries without realizing that conditions may differ. Recent experience of the stabilization programme in countries like Russia, Argentina, and even in some countries in South Asia has not been good. Some countries have suffered severe contraction in Gross Domestic Product (GDP) that have caused huge unemployment.

As if in response to the critics' arguments, Polak (1997) in a recent paper has argued that the model addressed the persistent problems of the late 1960s and early 1970s of the twentieth century. But the world financial system has undergone some fundamental changes during the last two decades. For this, IMF should consider some modifications in its policies while applying the model. Polak suggests three changes and these are:

First, the flexibility of international capital movements imply that that variable can no longer be treated as exogenous as in the original model. Capital movements depend on domestic interest rates and exchange rate expectations. The required modification is a challenge to IMF.

Second, in the present scenario, domestic interest rate depends strongly on the size of the government deficit irrespective of the mode of financing of it, that is, whether that deficit is financed from the banking system or in a domestic capital market. The interest rate is not in the model, but that should be accommodated.

Third, the exchange rate is to be incorporated in the model, as it is important in its effects on the trade flows and also on inflation expectations.

Though Polak argues for the extension of his original model on lines suggested by him, he has not done the necessary extension. In the absence of that, he rather suggests that IMF should take into account some other macroeconomic conditions of the country before setting forth the conditionality[3].

2.16 G-3 Exchange Rate Volatility

In recent times, the exchange rates of USD, yen and euro are going through large fluctuations and this volatility has caused huge problems in the stabilization programme of developing countries. This is because the latter have tied their currency to USD and the volatility in dollar/yen and dollar/euro rates are creating stability problems in their exchange rates.

---

[3] In the absence of a theoretically sound model, the IMF has recently tended to adopt an 'all risk' policy regarding its approach to CIS countries with a triple set of conditions: a ceiling on domestic credit, a floor under net international assets, and an indicative target for base money.

In an important paper, Reinhart and Reinhart (2002) have tried to address this issue with the hypothesis whether there is a trade-off between the exchange rate and interest rate volatility. The paper reviews the traditional North–South links through trade, commodity markets and capital flows. It also adds transmission channels in the form of interest rate and exchange rate volatility. The empirical part of the paper finds no clear support for the hypothesis that limiting G-3 exchange rate volatility is desirable from the perspective of the emerging market economies.

Ricardian Equivalence:

Regarding the nature of funding the social works Ricardo wrote;

> In point of economy, there is no real difference in either of the three modes: for twenty million in one payment, one million per annum for ever, or 1200,000 for 45 years, are precisely the same value; but who pay taxes never so estimate them, and therefore do not manage their private affairs accordingly. We are too apt to think that war is burdensome only in proportion to what we are at the moment called to pay for it in taxes, reflecting on the probable duration of such taxes.
>
> (1817, 186–87)

In an influential paper, Barro (1974) posed the question as to whether government bonds are net wealth or not, and many economists explored this topic on both theoretical and empirical grounds. If the answer to Barro's question is 'no', then changes in the composition of government expenditure finance have no real effect on consumption.

The above stance of Barro, which is the main issue of what has been known as Ricardian Equivalence in subsequent literature depends on the following assumptions:

(1) Families act as infinitely lived dynasties because of intergenerational altruism.
(2) Capital markets are perfect, i.e., any one can borrow and/or lend at the *single* rate.
(3) The path of government expenditure is fixed.

In the context of the above assumptions, when governments finance deficit by issuing bonds, the bequests that families give to the next generation will be just sufficient enough to offset the higher taxes that will be required to pay off those bonds. In this perspective Barro (ibid.) wrote:

> In the case where marginal net-wealth effects of government bonds is close to zero ... fiscal effects involving changes in the relative amounts of tax and debt finance for a given amount of public expenditure would have no effect on aggregate demand, interest rates, and capital formation.
>
> (1974, 1116)

Later Barro (1979, 941) defined the Ricardian Equivalence as 'shifts between debt and tax finance for a given amount of public expenditure would have no first-order effect on the real interest rate, volume of private investment, etc.'.

Barro has refined the concept of Ricardian Equivalence subsequently, perhaps in response to several criticism in the literature (Barro, 1979, 1989) and subsequent literature has come out with both theoretical and empirical arguments. In effects, Ricardian Equivalence (RE) implies that government budget imbalance is irrelevant to resource allocation. If in a particular year the government goes for higher expenditure based on huge deficit the citizens understand that the resulting debt accumulation would require future tax increase for servicing the debt. Thus the effects on the consumption will be minimum[4]. But history contains few Ricardian experiments in which taxes are changed independently of other events which may simultaneously influence consumption and savings[5]. Further, many of the empirical tests one might conduct require strong assumptions about the nature of consumption function, interest rate and income expectations, and other features of economic parameters.

But literature reveals that both time-series and cross-section data indicate a generally positive correlation between consumption and measures of government deficits. The government deficits capture the intergenerational impact of tax policy imperfectly. Nonetheless, some research studies suggest that current accounts might be negatively related to government deficits that is similar to the results of overlapping generation model, and these two are not completely unrelated as claimed in Ricardian equivalence.

Topic for Further Discussion

In the context of globalization, what type of problems does a small open economy face while pursuing independent monetary policy? Discuss.

Further Reading

Sriram, Subramanian S., 'A Survey of Recent Empirical Money Demand Studies', *IMF Staff Papers*, 47(3), International Monetary Fund, 2001, 334–65.

Takats, E., 'Was it Credit Supply? Cross Border Bank Lending to Emerging Market Economies During the Financial Crisis', *BIS Quarterly Review*, June 2010, 49–56 .

---

[4] Although David Ricardo explained the theoretical arguments for equivalence in his book *Principles of Political Economy and Taxation* (1817), he did not believe that the results would be applied in practice. He warned against the dangers of high public debt levels as he feared that labour and capital might migrate abroad to avoid the taxe needed for servicing the national debt (Ricardo, 1951, 247–49).

3
Money Growth, Inflation and Seigniorage

3.1 Introduction

Gold standard was the first modern international monetary system operating during the late nineteenth and early twentieth centuries. An international gold standard required that more than one country ought to be on gold and also have freedom from both of international gold flows and of foreign exchange transactions. In a country which is on gold standard, the currency is either made of gold, or it is convertible into gold at a fixed rate. Then the fixed mint parity of any two countries on the gold standard imply a fixed exchange rate between the countries' currencies. The mint par is an expression of the ratio of weights of gold used for the coinage of the currencies. For example, before World War II, British and American currencies were on gold standard. The mint par between these two currencies was 4.86 USD per one British pound.

In principle, a country could make a choice among four types of international gold standards — the pure coin standard, the mixed gold standard, a gold bullion standard and a gold exchange standard. The first two categories are explained above. Under gold bullion standard, gold coin neither circulates as money nor it is used as bank reserves, and the government does not mint gold coins. But the monetary authority stands ready to transact with private parties buying or selling gold bars at pre-determined prices for its paper currency.

'World War II had brought large-scale destruction in Europe and with the decline of the economic system, the gold standard also had become dysfunctional. Meanwhile the United States emerged as the leading economic and military power in the world. The result had been the new world order under the Bretton Woods System.

The Bretton Woods System adopted in July 1944 replaced the earlier gold standard by USD standard, in the perspective of the commitment of Federal Reserve of America to maintain a gold window, which was to replace USD at the rate of 35 dollars per one ounce of gold. USD was adopted as international currency and all members of the United Nations were asked to maintain fixed exchange rate system against the USD. In this way, gold parity of countries' currency had been tried to maintain through USD. The situation continued smoothly till 1971, but in that year US authorities unilaterally withdrew the gold window facility with the declaration that US was no longer committed to replace USD by gold at the rate of 35 USD per ounce of gold. This declaration had several important effects on the world financial metal system. First, price of the yellow metal started rising both in American domestic market and in other countries. Second, the member countries started adjusting the exchange rates of their currencies vis-à-vis USD and that paved the way for flexible exchange rate regime. Third, the disconnect between gold and money supply created the background of the emergence of fiat money where money supply of a country had not been fully backed by gold.

The flexible exchange rate regime had created problems for the small, less-developed countries. The financial systems of these countries were not developed enough, and maintaining a stable flexible exchange rate regime of the domestic currency had become a difficult proposition for such countries. Though some could have come out with stability of their currency regime, many suffered for a long time. This instability in the financial sector has had a profound effect on the growth and stability of the real sector of the economy. This chapter will explore all these aspects in greater detail.

Money in the modern world is a fiat paper currency as its intrinsic value depends on the legal guarantee of the sovereign government. By issuing paper currency the government earns income that is known as seigniorage in the monetary theory. Seigniorage (SNG) is defined in the literature as ' a duty levied on the coinage of money for the purpose of covering the expenses of minting, and as a source of revenue to the crown, claimed by the sovereign by virtue of his prerogative.' (McKinnon, 1979, 283)

According to Black (1989), seigniorage is the excess of the face value over the cost of production of the fiat money. Seigniorage is generally associated with the revenue income of the government from its monetary monopoly. But in practice, the issue of high–powered money is delegated to the central bank in most countries. Although the government owns the central bank, this does not mean that all revenue from money creation accrues to the government. In the United States of America, during the period 1946–1981, total revenue from money obtained was — 131.7 USD billion, if measured by money issuance, whereas 102 billion USD was transferred by the Federal Reserve to the US Treasury, and it was only 77.9 per cent of the former (Barro, 1982). Also the evidence of Barro reveals that, on a year to year basis, there is no connection between seigniorage and the revenue of Federal Reserve. Recent empirical evidence shows that for the Federal Republic of Germany, only 38.3 per cent of total seigniorage has been transferred to the government during the period 1960–87 (Klein and Neumann, 1990). All these evidences cast doubt on the rationale of measuring the contribution of seigniorage (SNG) to the finance of the government by the amount of money creation (Drazen, 1989).

One interesting aspect of SNG is that it remained more or less absent during the era when money meant metallic coins, either silver or gold. The reason was obvious as the difference between the face value of the coin and the cost of production including the cost of the metal was not significant. This prevented the rulers to issue reserve money for the sake of reaping the SNG. The invention of paper money facilitated the process as such type of money could be released in the economy with a minimum cost.

During the period of metallic currency, principal gain from SNG was the premium or the commission charged when the coins were first released to the economy. Once the money was released, coins were to be maintained at a cost for its storage and transport. Even coins used to lose its weight through wear and tear leading to the situation that the face value of the coin became less than the metal value.

During the regime of metallic coins, excess supply of money leading to inflation should had been a rare phenomenon as that would necessitate a large supply of the metal at a relatively less cost[1]. Inflation in a commodity money situation may happen only when the commodity used in the minting of coins becomes excess in supply or the cost of minting of coins becomes less. Both are unlikely events and so we see a long period of price stability during this phase of history. But once paper money came into circulation, these commodities, like gold and silver, were released for other social use. In a sense, the introduction of paper money brought a huge amount of social savings in the society.

The introduction of paper brought huge advantage to the governments as they found in it larger scope for marshalling resources from the economy by giving paper money, which is very cheap to produce. This is the disadvantage of fiat money as a system. The intrinsic value of paper money depends on a strict control on its supply and the legal backing of the government. But its cheapness leads to its abuse by the issuer and then it loses its credibility. In this perspective, J.M. Keynes observed, there is no subtler, no surer means of overturning the existing basis of society than to debauch the currency. The process engages all the hidden forces of economic law on the side of destruction ... (Keynes, 1923, 80)

We have observed that paper money, also called fiat money, has no intrinsic value. Fiat money can retain its market-perceived value if asset-holders remain confident that its rate of supply to the economy will remain strictly controlled. This remains true because the demand for paper money is derived from how readily it is accepted rather than how fully it is backed. This has been proved many a time through historical events and more recently it is revealed in the events of Thailand, Indonesia, South Korea, Russia, Brazil and Argentina. The governments of these countries fully backed their currencies. In spite of that, the individuals and institutions that were holding monetary instruments denominated in these currencies, lost confidence in the credibility of the governments and substituted these financial instruments with other forms of money. The public perception was found true when it was revealed that the central banks of these countries were unable to purchase the domestic currencies at prices fixed by them. That led to large scale devaluation of these currencies as were seen in cases of Thai baht, Indonesian rupiah, Russian rouble, and Brazilian real, etc. In fact we see a sequence of financial crisis in history starting from England's fourteenth century default to the very recent financial crisis in the United States (Reinhart and Rogoff, 2008).

One important element common in all the cases stated here is that the governments of these countries tried to finance their budget deficits by the seigniorage reaped through the increase in the supply of money. This makes SNG inter, related to budget deficit and inflation, which shall be discussed further.

---

[1] Even the history of metal coins is full of situations when debasement of currency happened by reducing the silver content of coin. This was the devise through which the dictators expropriated their subjects' money by supplying debased metal currency. Table 3.2 in the appendix to this chapter reveals what happed in Europe in the nineteenth century.

3.2 Measurement of Seigniorage

The common measure of SNG is the real rent from issuing reserve money, and it is defined as the currency in circulation plus the reserve of the bank held by the central bank. The real rent is computed as the change in the reserve money divided by the price level. This we can write:

$$SNG = dM/P \qquad \text{Equation (3.1)}$$

Here d denotes change in the sense of differential calculus, M the reserve money as defined and P the price level. Since the differential d (M/P) can be expanded as;

$$d(M/P) = [P \cdot dM - M \cdot dP]/P^2 = dM/P - (M/P) \cdot dP/P,$$

therefore,

$$dM/P = d(M/P) + (M/P) \cdot \Pi \qquad \text{Equation (3.2)}$$

where

$$\Pi = dP/P \text{ i.e., rate of inflation.}$$

Combining Equations (3.1) and (3.2), we can write,

$$SNG = d(M/P) + \Pi \cdot (M/P) \qquad \text{Equation (3.3)}$$

The SNG has two components. The first term on the right is the change in the real reserve money. It measures the increasing command over the commodities available to the government through its release of additional reserve money. The second term is the inflation tax that the authority collects from the holders of fiat money as the extent to which inflation erodes the intrinsic value (purchasing power) of the fiat money held by the public. It measures the capital loss suffered by the holders of paper money as price level changes. One interesting aspect of fiat money is that once the asset holders start thinking that the supply of fiat money is far in excess than what is warranted, the newly issued money debases the existing money in circulation. This is equivalent to the capital loss of the holders of the fiat money, and the first term is a measure of that as it indicates the change in the real reserve money.

3.3 Broader Definition of Seigniorage

A rapid expansion of reserve money — and hence money supply — can lead to a gain to the government in the form of inflation tax and seigniorage, and it may lead to a cost as the holders of existing money stock think it as a form of capital loss. These capital gains or losses induced by a rapid expansion of money supply can be measured by making the concept of seigniorage a bit broader. This can be pursued by using the stylized set of accounts for the monetary authority that McKinnon used. According to McKinnon (1979), total assets consist of money reserves and investment denoted by I and total liabilities consist of deposits, say D. From this SNG is computed as

$$SNG = r \cdot I - r^* D - C \qquad \text{Equation (3.4)}$$

where   r = open market rate of interest on investment
   r^* = deposit rate of interest on the holding of international currency
   C = cost of servicing the existing stock of money

One implication of this McKinnon identity is that if the government has a large external liability (that makes a negative I, or I < 0), it will lose seigniorage. This is an interesting result as extended money creation by the government leads to loss of revenue on account of SNG. We will see more on this later.

Neumann (1992) has deduced a formula of 'extended seigniorage' (ESN) by using a similar format. His identity is:

$$ESN = SNG + (iD + i^* F + GR)/P \qquad \text{Equation (3.5)}$$

where ESN = extended seigniorage
SNG = seigniorage as defined above
i = interest rate on the stock of private debt (D) held by the monetary authority
i^* = interest rate on official foreign loan made by the monetary authority
F = amount of foreign loan of the authority
P = consumer price level
GR = unrealized capital gains on assets

These equations put together a system that links inflation, seigniorage, exchange rate movements, interest rate, fiscal deficit and some other macro variables. We can show the link between seigniorage and exchange rate movements through a simplified version of monetary authority's accounts. Whenever there is changes in the balance sheet of the monetary authority, reserve money changes. Put in symbols, change in the reserve money (dM) is the sum of the changes in the net foreign assets (dF), changes in the net domestic credit (dD) and change in other items (dZ). We can write,

$$dM = dF + dD + dZ \qquad \text{Equation (3.6)}$$

where Z = proxy for other items, or parameters that influence macro variables in the economy.

Dividing through by the price level P, we write

$$dM/P = dF/P + dD/P + dZ/P \qquad \text{Equation (3.7)}$$

Similar to Equation (3.2), we can manipulate

$$d(F/P) = dF/P - (F/P).dP/P, \text{ or,}$$

$$dF/P = d(F/P) + \Pi.(F/P) \qquad \text{Equation (3.8)}$$

Similarly,

$$dD/P = d(D/P) + \Pi.(D/P) \qquad \text{Equation (3.9)}$$

and,

$$dZ/P = d(Z/P) + \Pi.(Z/P) \qquad \text{Equation (3.10)}$$

Combining Equations (3.7) to (3.10) we can write,

$$dM/P = d(F/P) + \Pi.(F/P) + d(D/P) + \Pi.(D/P) + d(Z/P) + \Pi.(Z/P)$$

$$\text{Equation (3.11)}$$

We can now interpret equation (3.11). We see that the generation of SNG depends on factors that change net foreign assets, net domestic assets and net change of other items (Z) being a proxy of some macro variables, along with rate of inflation and the extent the latter affects the parameters as mentioned.

3.4 Seigniorage and Exchange Rate

Net foreign asset F can be written as

$$F = e.F^*, \qquad \text{Equation (3.12)}$$

when $F^* = $ dollar value of foreign assets, and
$e = $ exchange rate of domestic currency.

Expanding the expression we can write,

$$dF = de.F^* + e.dF^*,$$

or after a little manipulation, we get

$$dF/P = [de/e + dF^*/F^*]. F/P \qquad \text{Equation (3.13)}$$

When money supply is increasing rapidly, both the exchange rate (e) and the dollar value of foreign liabilities will increase. This means both de and dF^* will be positive. For a highly indebted country, net foreign asset (F/P) will be negative and that makes the value of the right hand side of (3.13) negative.

When net foreign assets of the monetary authority are large and negative, the effects of exchange-rate changes (as measured by dF/P in equation 3.13) subtract in a major way from the generation of SNG as in Equation (3.11). So, a country with a huge foreign liability and high inflation is caught in a bind, as further money creation leads to a negative seigniorage and more money creation is needed to compensate the latter. This aspect will be clear if we analyze the cases of two highly indebted countries, Russia and Zambia.

Table 3.1 *Seigniorage and its Components, 1997*

Country	dM/P	dF/P	dD/P	F*	a**	b**
1	2	3	4	5	6	7
Russia	1.76	0.49	1.27	1.85	0.10	0.36
Zambia	1.22	−0.15	1.36	−28.6	−2.27	1.92

Note: $a^{**} = (de/e). F/P$, $\qquad b^{**} = (df/f). F/P$

Source International Financial Statistics, IMF, March 1999.

Column 4 shows direct gains from seigniorage to GDP. Its value becomes low when the growth of reserve money becomes fast. In the case of Zambia, growth of money supply became very high, that reduced the value of the gains from seigniorage to GDP.

In column 3, the value shows the effects of exchange-rate changes. When net foreign assets of monetary authority are large and negative (liability), the effects of exchange-rate changes subtract in a major way from the generation of seigniorage. Here the data of Zambia are striking as the figure is negative.

3.5 Dynamic Effects

Some economists prefer the study of the dynamic effects of reserve money changes. In the developed countries, the growth of reserve money is stable and budget deficit does not lead to money creation. That leads to the discussion of seigniorage in terms of a 'steady state' equilibrium. But critics point out that in the developing countries, the growth of the reserve money is volatile and rapid. Even the economists have emphasized the existence of a Laffer Curve (named after Professor Laffer showing retrograde relation between rate of tax and tax revenue) relating seigniorage to the rate of inflation and the growth of reserve money in the perspective of hyper-inflation. The idea boils down to the existence of an optimum seigniorage point and whether a country makes a transition back to optimum point once it crosses the limit. Economists argue that this transition is very important for the highly indebted countries that have moved beyond their optimum international credit limits. They find themselves in a dilemma. They are caught in a spiral of accelerating inflation as they try to gain access to the increasing amount of foreign exchange needed to meet the debt service obligations. As the rate of reserve money creation increases, the task of meeting foreign obligations becomes increasingly difficult.

From the theoretical exercise above we can write briefly the policy implications faced by the highly indebted countries today. The countries that face twin problems of a large amount of foreign debt and its servicing obligations and a potential high inflation may have the temptation of servicing the foreign debt obligation by the creation of reserve money and appropriating the seigniorage. But this boils down to a large scale debasement of the domestic currency and hyper-inflation. In such a situation, the country better seek a rescheduling of debt obligation even if that means a default and adverse international repercussions.

3.6 Cost of Seigniorage

Some developing countries are prone to maximizing revenue from seigniorage, and in the process, these countries face trouble in unstable currency. There is also a cost of seigniorage and that can be placed as follows.

The important cost of SNG is the resource cost of printing, issuing, storing and maintaining the stock of fiat money. Sometimes countries facing very high inflation have to import large stock of printed currency at a substantial cost.

Another cost of SNG is the *inflation tax* imposed on the economy as hyper-inflation sets in. The authority may collect resources through inflation tax, may even facilitate a desirable redistribution of income, but this also leads to currency substitution and a capital loss on fixed-income liabilities.

The literature has noted that through currency substitution and asset substitution the public can reduce their holdings of financial instruments denominated in domestic currency. The asset holders in unstable economies with a track record of high inflation have become efficient in using this method, and this way they insulate their assets from the negative effects of monetary disruptions. This situation is common in countries like Russia, Argentina, Peru, Bolivia, Serbia and some others.

A country with a large external debt faces capital loss when hyper-inflation becomes chronic. A commitment to repay foreign liability is associated with several risks. International interest rates may increase, and that will increase the cost of debt. The country faces the same effects when the domestic currency depreciates. While the first increases the cost in foreign exchange, the second increases the cost in domestic currency.

3.7 Conclusion

The monetary authority enjoys seigniorage and inflation tax through the release of reserve money. So long the latter maintains an equilibrium relation with the country's GDP and other macro parameters, the economy faces no problem. Instead, the society as a whole is benefited by the positive externality of the existence of money as an institution. Apart from that the control of reserve money gives several benefits to the authority and these are: (*i*) accrual of monopoly rents due to the difference of yields on official liabilities, and (*ii*) real gains to the issuers of financial instruments.

The authority gets the monopoly rents as the official financial instruments held by the private sector at rates below the market rates. One example is the reserve requirements of banks.

The authority issues fixed coupon bonds and when inflation continues due to rapid increase of reserve money, the real value of these bonds are deflated. The difference between the face value of the bond and the real value is the gain to the issuer.

Does sovereign money matter? Or, is it a desirable thing in the global scene that some 200-plus independent nations should have their own sovereign currencies? These are somewhat complex questions. In the above, we get the theoretical backdrop about the cost and benefit of the issuance of reserve money, and now we are in a position to pursue this issue in detail in Chapter 7.

Topic for Discussion

In the context of serious debasement of the home currency by the government, what type of problems does the economy face? Discuss.

Further Reading

Aarle, B. van and Budina, N., 'Financial Repression, Inflation and Seigniorage: The Polish Experience', *Weltwirtschaftliches Archiv*, 133 (4), 1997, pp. 683–707.

Mankiw, N. Gregory, 'The Optimal Collection of Seigniorage', *Journal of Monetary Economics*, 20, 1987, 327–41.

Sahay, R. and C. Vegh, 'Inflation and Stabilization in Transition Economies: A Comparison with Market Economies', *IMF Working Paper* 95/8, 2995.

Winiecki, J., 'The Regional Survey', in J. Winiecki and A. Kondratowicz (eds), *The Macroeconomics in Transition: Developments in East Central Europe*, London, Routledge, 1993.

Appendix

Table 3.2 *Expropriation through Currency Debasement in Europe: Nineteenth Century*

Country	Period Covered	Cumulative decline Silver Content of (per cent)	Largest Debasement (per cent) and Year	
Austria	1800 – 1860	– 58.3	– 55.00	1812
Germany	1800 – 1830	– 2.2	– 2.2	1816
Portugal	1800 – 1855	– 12.8	– 18.4	1800
Russia	1800 – 1899	– 56.6	– 41.3	1810
Turkey	1800 – 1899	– 83.1	– 51.2	1829
United Kingdom	1800 – 1899	– 6.1	– 6.1	1816

Source: Robert C. Allen–Richard W. Unger Database: European Commodity Prices 1260–1914

4
Multinational Corporations and Emerging Economies

Multinational corporation is a business concern with operations in more than one country outside the company's home country. These inter-country operations may be linked with parent concern by merger, operated as subsidiaries, or the subsidiaries may enjoy considerable autonomy. Multinational corporations (MNC) are often perceived as large enterprises with little regard for the social and economic conditions of the countries in which they run their operations (Nuruzzaman, 2005).

At present there are well over 40,000 MNCs operating in the world economy with more than 2,50,000 overseas affiliates doing businesses across the world. In 1995, the top 200 MNCs had combined sales of approximately USD 7.1 trillion, and that was about 28.3 per cent of the world gross domestic product of the same year[1]. The top MNCs have head quarters in the United States, Western Europe and Japan. These corporations have the capacity to shape global trade, production and also financial transactions (Meyer, 2004).

MNCs through their cross-continent operations have capital investment in the countries of their operations. These are treated as foreign direct investment and this has the effect of integration of world capital markets. Thus, MNCs have an important role in the integration of world economy. With the advancement of technology, there has been tremendous development in communications and this has helped the functioning of the MNCs so far as coordination and monitoring their worldwide operations are concerned. This has been the favourable perspective of the integration of the world capital markets.

The degree of integration of the capital markets of different countries has increased in recent times with the tremendous surge of capital mobility across political boundaries. This phenomenon has also increased the role of MNCs in the economic development of the developing countries. Conceptually, there are five ways in which an MNC can serve a foreign market:

(1) invest directly by a Greenfield venture,
(2) invest directly by acquiring a local firm,
(3) invest directly by starting a joint venture with a local firm,
(4) enter into a strategic alliance with a local firm.

---

[1] Encyclopedia of Business, 2nd Edition, 5 November 2010, posted by Remington.

The fifth alternative is no direct investment in the host country, but the MNC can serve the host country market by exports or giving license to the local firm. The first four alternatives involve foreign direct investment (FDI) on the part of MNC. Whether the latter will go for FDI or the fifth alternative depends on both the economic conditions of the host country and the business strategy of MNC. In the case of developed countries like Organisation for Economic Co-operation and Development (OECD) economies, the MNC has a free choice among the first four alternatives. But in the case of developing countries and transition economies[2] there are restrictions and the choices are limited. This is because capital markets in most of the developing countries are not open and their currencies are not fully convertible. This places restraints on the behavior of the MNCs who aspire to enter such countries.

In developing countries, with a developed capital market and a large industrial sector, the acquisition of private firms is a realistic alternative to Greenfield entry[3]. Except in countries like South Korea with an advanced technology base, merger with local firms is troublesome because of the huge gap in the level of technology, size and management philosophy. The same problem remains with strategic alliance with local firms of the host country.

In the early phases of liberalization of the transition economies, the state-owned firms are often put on sale and MNCs see it easy to acquire the state-owned firms and thus they enter the market of the host country. After that Greenfield entry becomes more feasible with merger and acquisition remaining for the future. The behaviour of the MNC regarding their entry and operations in the developing countries has attracted the attention in the literature. It has identified three aspects regarding the MNC behaviours:

(1) target country characteristics
(2) investment characteristics, and
(3) industry characteristics

The most common framework is the transaction-cost analysis, that is, the MNC chooses the mode of entry that involves minimum cost (Meyer, 2004; Prahalad and Lieberthal, 1998). The findings in the literature can be put in the following form:

First, larger MNCs are more prone to acquire firms in other countries than small ones. However, in recent times, smaller firms also have become more prone to acquire as the transaction cost of merger and acquisition (M&A) has reduced.

Second, MNCs with lower R&D intensity are more likely to buy technological capabilities abroad by acquisition, and firms with strong technological advantages are likely to set up Greenfield ventures.

Third, the greater the cultural and economic differences between the home and the host countries, the less is the probability that the MNC will go for acquisition. Generally, M&A concentrate in countries with similar cultural and business practices.

---

[2] These are former command economies like Russia, Ukraine, Poland, and other east European countries, CIS countries like Uzbekistan and others, China and Vietnam. The significant change of economic policies of these economies has changed the perception of foreign capital and FDI is welcome now.

[3] Where the MNC starts a new enterprise with the import of both capital and technology. This is done to take advantage of cheap labour and/or source of raw materials.

Fourth, acquisitions by MNC are encouraged by capital market imperfections that lead to the undervaluation of the assets of firms. The same thing may happen in times of economic crisis like the Asian Currency Crisis of 1997.

Fifth, horizontal acquisitions are driven by the search for new markets, products, and brand, and seldom for cost rationalization. But such acquisitions may lead to 'asset rationalization' of the acquired firm and this often damages the capabilities of the latter.

Sixth, Greenfield investments offer the MNC greater control and more ability to mould affiliate structure, system and culture than acquisition. Everything can be replicated from the investing country.

In sum, the entry of the MNC in the developing countries induces certain important changes including technology transfer to the host country. But, over time, there is more reciprocal process of technology transfer and sharing of intangibles like tacit knowledge (Bressman et al., 1999). From the investor's perspective, M&A offers certain advantages over Greenfield investment of rapid entry and access to existing proprietary assets. In the case of developing countries, M&A creates advantage of rapid entry, access to local market knowledge and distribution system. It also creates contacts with the governments, suppliers and the consumers, and also it may be the only form of FDI where other opportunities are absent.

Sometimes, established cultural and organizational inertia may create problem for the MNC after acquisition of firms in the host country and the MNC may find it costly for the necessary assimilation process. Even valuation of assets of the firms in the host country for acquisition may be difficult as the capital market is often imperfect and not developed. Such problems generally emerge in large developing countries that are opening to international competition for the first time. In such situations, Greenfield investment will be more suitable for the MNCs.

4.1 Greenfield Investment and Merger and Acquisition: A Comparison

Both the developing countries and the transition economies are rapidly integrating their economies with the world economic order. In the process, the firms in such countries face intensifying competition, accelerating technological change and increasingly integrated world production. They seriously lack two things: capital and new technology. Here lies the importance of the entry of the MNC. Now a comparison of two principal modes of entry — FDI in Greenfield investment and M&A route — can be made from the perspective of the host country.

It is recognized that FDI inflow in the developing country helps in upgrading competitiveness. It is a powerful tool in the case of countries where domestic technological capabilities and skills are weak, and that cannot be raised at international level within a short period. Even when the country is strong in the availability of skill, the pace of technical change at global level is so strong that without the MNC participation it becomes difficult for the developing country to compete effectively (UNCTAD, 1999). In this case, M&A as a mode of FDI inflow is an important way to restructure and upgrade competitive capability of the host country firm.

FDI investment in both the modes — M&A and Greenfield way — adds to the financial resources of the host country as neither is financed by raising resources domestically. While Greenfield investment adds new productive facility which is an addition to the existing production capacity of the economy, M&A transfer the ownership of the existing asset into foreign hands. But money flows in both cases, and the M&A transfer resources to the existing owners that can be invested in the economy. So, the net financial effects are the same in normal times except in one situation, when the acquired company is broken up and different components are sold separately at a much higher price. This is known as *asset stripping* in the literature. This is a sign of imperfect capital market as the latter fails to assess the true value of the assets.

But in a crisis situation (as in south Asia in 1997–98), many firms are sold at depressed prices and foreign capital acquires firms in the host country through M&A cheaply. This involves a cost to the host country. The cost increases and becomes a net loss to the host country if the firm acquires through M&A is sold later when markets become normal and asset value increases. This can be prevented if the host country can manage extra liquidity in crisis times when FDI through Greenfield investment becomes rare.

4.2 Technology Issue

The inflow of FDI is associated with the inflow of new and frontier technology to the host country. The effects of technology transfer to the host country will be the same in normal situation in either type of entry — Greenfield investment and M&A mode. A Greenfield investment involves the setting up of a new facility that brings new technology with new capital. The running of this new plant requires new and improved skill formation. This may not happen in the case of M&A, at least in the short run. For this reason, Greenfield investment is preferred in the developing country.

In the case of M&A, the acquired firm may need considerable technological upgrading to bring it to the world level. As a result, it may experience rapid change compared to the new facility under Greenfield mode that is already using frontier technology. The evidence for Asia and Latin America shows that M&A can lead to considerable technological upgrading, and the MNC can boost expenditure on research and development (R&D), if the acquired firm already possesses research capabilities (WIR, 1998). Moreover, M&A may lead to the preservation and increase of technological capabilities in the firms, under competitive pressure, in an open economy.

Sometimes, FDI through M&A mode may lead to the downgrading of R&D activity and status of the acquired firm, if the latter does not possess technological assets regarded as valuable by the foreign company. In such a case, M&A brings negative effects to technology of the host country. This is evidenced in East Europe and Latin America, where the affiliates of the MNC engage themselves in simpler activity and put less emphasis on R&D.

In normal circumstances, an MNC will tend to preserve the R&D base of a newly acquired firm and maintain links with local technological resources. Sometimes, it goes further and tries to strengthen local technological efforts and linkages for the absorption of technology in the host country. This is known as *asset seeking FDI,* and this type of FDI in the United States has been used by Mexico, South Korea and Taiwan to improve their domestic technological base. The result, in terms of defusing new and improved technology and knowledge locally, depends on the strength and economic efficiency of the linkages established by the acquired firms. When these are positive, MNCs will retain and strengthen these, in which case FDI through M&A mode will lead to better diffusion than the mode of Greenfield investment in the short run. But when the linkages are weak and inefficient, FDI through M&A will lead to less diffusion, and that makes little difference compared to the Greenfield mode.

The interaction between the existing domestic firms and the new foreign firms either through M&A mode or through Greenfield investment is complex and dynamic over time. Wang and Blomstrom (1992) isolate two channels for this interaction process. The interaction leads to the spill-over of superior technology across the firms having strong linkages. The more disembodied aspects of superior technologies used by foreign firms can spread to domestic firms through the mobility of trained workers and managers, and through technical guidance provided to vertically linked domestic suppliers. Thus, the mere presence of foreign firms exposes domestic firms to superior technologies: this is the demonstration effect. Two, competitive pressure exerted by foreign firms (in the form of lower prices or higher product quality) forces domestic firms to improve their technologies. Productivity gains materialize only if competition is effective — that is, it encourages domestic firms to catch up — and if domestic firms have the ability to innovate or imitate successfully. The latter requires that the technological gap should be small enough relative to the learning capabilities of the domestic firms. If it is not, isolated instances of foreign entry can degenerate into foreign monopoly. At the same time, the extent of spillovers may be limited by the tendency of multinational firms to concentrate their R&D activity in their developed country headquarters — the so-called 'headquarters effect'. The relative importance of these effects may explain why spillover effects have been stronger in some countries and for some sectors.

4.3 Indian Case

Did the foreign-controlled firms in India differ from the domestic firms in terms of their conduct and performance? The literature reveals discriminating characteristics of domestic and foreign-controlled firms and it is found that as a proportion of sales, foreign-controlled firms spent less on R&D (presumably because they rely on technology imports) than domestic firms, but expenditure on advertising was broadly similar for the two groups of firms (Kumar, 1994). However, foreign-controlled firms were significantly more profitable in their operations, a result corroborated by other studies; Kumar concluded that the profitability of foreign-controlled firms was protected by entry-barriers: in knowledge-and-skill-intensive industries, their technological strength, access to global marketing networks and brand names gave them a clear edge over domestic firms. He found that the degree of seller concentration did not seem to affect profitability but there was market segmentation: foreign-controlled firms competed on the high-value end of the market while domestic firms concentrated on the low-value end.

How did the multinationals defend these profit margins? Advertising intensity, measured as the ratio of advertising expenditure to net sales, was greater for foreign-controlled firms, but domestic firms relied more heavily on selling commissions. Of course, different industrial sectors differ in the advertising intensity: the overall difference in marketing strategies might reflect the difference in industrial concentration of foreign-controlled and domestic firms. Also, it is seen that domestic firms have increased their expenditure on technology imports, especially in recent years, and have overtaken foreign firms in this respect. Unfortunately, we do not have comparable data for R&D expenditure, but these were typically quite small for all manufacturing firms in India. On the whole, the observable differences in conduct were not that large.

4.4 Market Structure and Competition

During the last two decades, FDI has been a powerful instrument for the developing countries to exploit their existing comparative advantage and also create new competitive power in their effort to enhance their participation in world trade. This has been possible as long as the countries are able to create new skills and capabilities and attract the MNCs into higher value activities (WIR, 1998). In the process, the entry of MNCs has certain effects on the domestic market structure of the host country, though the effects are not clear. Usual measures like concentration ratios are misleading indicators, particularly when the country is open to import competition, and MNCs concentrate in industries that are scale-and technology-intensive. Again, the entry of large MNCs poses serious challenge to competition policy. Here the host country should be cautious with rules and regulation to maintain competitive conditions for the domestic firms.

Generally speaking, the relationship between openness to foreign investment and market structure is complex. Caves (1996) notes the positive relationship between the extent of foreign investment and the degree of market concentration found in empirical studies. In theory, this could be due to rent-seeking foreign investment being especially attracted to sectors or countries with high concentration, and ensures high profitability too. Even so, the short-run effect of foreign entry, especially when it is Greenfield investment, is to increase the number of firms and reduce concentration. The long-run effects depend on the nature of competition between the entrants and the incumbents. If incumbent firms are moderately competent, there may well be virtuous cycles of technological competition. On the other hand, inefficient domestic firms with poor learning capabilities would lose market share to foreign firms. Further, small and inefficient domestic firms may face insurmountable technological barriers and further, economies of scale may drive such firms to the fringe of the market. Foreign entry might thus increase market concentration through mergers and acquisitions, and occasionally, through predatory-pricing.

4.5 Sequential Market Entry: A Case Study of Sony Corporation in the United States

A sequential market entry by a multinational corporation happens when the MNC seeks to penetrate a new market often through foreign direct investment. It involves acquisition or establishment of a firm operating in the niche market related to the parent company's product line. Sony Corporation of Japan utilized the method of sequential entry into the United States with the establishment of a small television assembly plant in San Diego, California, in 1972. For some years, Sony's US operations remained confined to the manufacture of television. But Sony branched out with the establishment of a magnetic tape plant in Dothan, Alabama, in 1974. Again, Sony's operation expanded further in 1977 with the creation of an audio equipment plant in Delano, Pennsylvania.

The unfavorable exchange rate movement between Japanese Yen and USD forced Sony to wait for consolidation. But Sony later continued to diversify its US operations by creating facilities for the production of computer displays and data storage system during the 1980s. In 1990s, Sony further diversified its operations with the start of the production of semiconductors and personal telecommunications products. This case also shows how the operations of MNC help the integration of not only the capital markets of the world but the product lines of major commodities.

Topic for Discussion

Explain how globalization is helping MNCs leverage emerging markets for growth.

Further Reading

Friedman, Thomas L., *The World is Flat*, Farrar, Straus and Giroux, New York, 2006.
Roach, Brian, 'A Primer on Multinational Corporation', in Alfred D. Chandler, Jr. and Bruce Mazlish (eds), *Leviathans: Multinational Corporations and the New Global History*, Cambridge, Cambridge University Press, 2005, 19–44.
Stiglitz, Joseph E., *Making Globalization Work*, W.W. Norton and Co., 2006.
Strange, Susan, *The Retreat of the State: The Diffusion of Power in the World Economy*, Cambridge, Cambridge University Press, 1996.

5
International Financial System: A Historical Evolution

The period between 1919 and 1944 had been very volatile and uncertain in the world financial system as it — before getting the respite from the disruption of World War I — got embroiled again with the start of World War II. By that time, US had come to the world scene as the first world power both militarily and financially. The US financial planners developed a perspective of liberal international economic system that would enhance the possibilities of secure world peace through the free movement of capital and traded commodities across countries. This understanding came from the belief that the fundamental causes of two World Wars lay in economic discrimination practiced by Nazi Germany on the one hand and members of the British Empire on the other, regarding trade preferences to countries. The US position was articulated by Cordell Hull, the US Secretary of State, 1933–44 in the following words:

> unhampered trade dovetailed with peace; high tariff, trade barriers, and unfair economic competition, with war … If we could get a freer flow of trade … Freer in the sense of fewer discriminations and obstructions … so that one country would not be deadly jealous of another and the living standards of all countries might rise, thereby eliminating the economic dissatisfaction that breeds war, we might have a reasonable chance of lasting peace (Hull, 1948, 81).

The urgency of the situation was felt by the financial planners of the United States so much so that in 1944, 730 delegates from all 44 Allied nations gathered at Mount Washington Hotel in Bretton Woods, New Hampshire, US, for the United Nations Monetary and Financial Conference. Upon long deliberation on the need for a world financial order, the delegates signed the Bretton Woods Agreement during the first three weeks of July 1944. Thus the international financial system was born in its new avatar.

History

The evolution of the world financial system to come to its present form was a long journey: it passed through five principal types of financial systems that the world had experienced: the gold bullion standard, paper gold standard, Bretton Woods standard, flexible exchange rates and very recent cooperative joint intervention. Each system evolved depending on the need of the time and the will of the leading nations of the world who were able to carry the 'burden' of the world currency. But the major characteristics of the financial system determine the dynamics of the money supply of the countries who are partners in trade and the common world system. We need to know about the different financial systems that prevailed in the world to understand the evolution of world money. A better understanding of the world monetary system would help us understand how the domestic money supply in member countries was affected by the change in the world financial system. Though we are aware today that the domestic financial system cannot be fully insulated from the global phenomenon, the situation in the immediate post-war period was not much different in the Group-of-Ten countries[1]. The level of economic integration among these countries made them inter-dependent.

5.1 The Gold Standard

The classical gold standard emerged as a true international standard by 1880 when a majority of independent countries agreed to switch from bimetallism, silver monometallism and paper to gold as the basis of their currencies. The key rule was maintenance of gold convertibility at the established par. When the countries adhered to the fixed price of gold vis-à-vis their currencies and maintained it, it amounted to a fixed exchange rate. According to recent evidence, the exchange rates throughout the period 1880–1914 were characterized by a high degree of fixity of the main countries, and violations of gold-parity points and devaluation was rare. The stability in the price of gold and the ease in the supply of gold compared to the world demand did facilitate this situation. The period was an ideal example of classical full-employment equilibrium situation in the industrial world with real income changing very little, and so the increase in the demand for monetary gold was small enough to be met by the available production and supply.

According to established literature, a time-consistent credible commitment mechanism is necessary for an international monetary arrangement to be effective among the countries. The adherence to the gold convertibility rule provided such a mechanism. Also, apart from the reputation of the domestic gold standard and the constitutional provisions regarding the same, some other mechanisms like improved access to international capital market, the operation of the rules of the game, and the hegemonic power of England might have enforced the countries to adhere to the international gold standard rules.

The main countries at the time realized that gold standard did provide improved access to the international capital markets and hence the support for the regime increased. Also, countries believed that gold convertibility would be a signal to creditors of sound government finance. Again, this had been the case for both developing and developed countries seeking access to long-term capital, such as Austria, Hungary and Latin America. Japan also used short-term loans to finance the Russo-Japanese war during 1905–06. The example of England being on the gold standard was an added attraction for other countries to be on the same standard. In fact, England had been the centre of the world monetary system because of its economic might and political influence. The fixed relation of the British pound with gold assured the countries to stick to the gold standard.

---

[1] The group of ten were Belgium, Canada, France, West Germany, Italy, Japan, Netherlands, Sweden, United Kingdom, and the US.

The success of the gold standard had been largely due to the commitment mechanism the participating countries followed regarding the internal adjustments of policies faced with external shocks. Since rules were followed sincerely and adjustments facilitated, the commitment to the convertibility of gold was strengthened and there was less chance of leaving the gold standard. Further, the hegemonic power of England acted as an anchor. The literature mentions that the classical gold standard of 1880–1914 was a British-managed standard. There were several reasons for this. At that time London was the centre for the world's gold, commodities and capital markets. Second, many countries substituted sterling for gold as an international reserve currency. Third, there had been extensive outstanding sterling-denominated assets outside Britain. Fourth, the Bank of England could attract whatever gold it needed by the manipulation of its bank rate, and other central banks would adjust their discount rates accordingly. In this way, the Bank of England did exert a strong influence on the money supply and price level of the member countries. The central banks of other countries accepted the leadership of the Bank of England because they benefited from using sterling as a reserve asset, even though they might have been constrained from following independent discretionary policies that might have hurt the cause of gold standard.

Gold standard was an asymmetric system (Giovannini, 1989). England was the centre country and the Bank of England used the bank rate to maintain gold convertibility. While Britain could follow an independent monetary policy, other countries like France, Germany, etc., accepted the dictates of fixed parities and allowed their money supply to adjust passively. England, as the leader, had been benefited in multiple ways. It enjoyed the seigniorage earned on foreign-held sterling balances. Also financial institutions in London got handsome returns for the central location and easy access to international capital markets.

In an influential study, Professor Nurkse (1944) has argued that in crucial times, the principal member countries did not behave properly in the sense that they partially sterilized their gold inflows, and the result had been that domestic and foreign assets of these countries moved in opposite directions during this period of gold standard. The rules of the game dictated that they should not interfere with the influence of gold flows on the money supply. Perhaps they became concerned about the potential inflation and thus became proactive in the control of money supply.

5.2 The Demise of Classical Gold Standard

World War I created a massive shock that the financial system could not endure and the classical gold standard ended. The war reduced the economic strength of the main European countries in general, and England in particular. The anchor role England used to provide for the stability of the system ended as the US pushed England back from the leadership role. A reformed system — gold exchange standard — prevailed for a short period 1920–29; it was an attempt to restore the salient positive features of the classical gold standard while allowing a significant role of domestic stabilization policy, in response to specific needs. But frictions emerged as the conflict between adherence to gold standard rule and discretion of policy for domestic compulsion could not always be resolved. Also, there was an attempt to economize the use of gold as reserve by restricting its use to central banks and by encouraging the use of foreign exchange as a substitute for gold.

The gold exchange standard was destined to be a failure as it suffered from a number of defects. First, the use of two reserve currencies — sterling and USD — was creating problems as there was an absence of leadership as a hegemonic power unlike the earlier period when Britain shouldered the role. Second, there was little cooperation among the key members — Britain, France and the US. Two strong members, i.e., France and the US, were reluctant to follow the rules of the game. They created deflationary pressures in the world by persistent sterilization of their balance of payment surpluses. The system could not bear it and ultimately it collapsed with the Great Depression. But by that time it had transmitted deflation and depression across the world (Eichengreen, 1989; Friedman and Schwartz, 1963; Temin, 1989).

5.3 The Bretton Woods International Monetary System

With the end of World War II, the victors assembled at Bretton Woods, New Hampshire, US, to build up the World Monetary System, which came to be known as Bretton Woods International Monetary System (BWIMS). The principal objectives were to remove the ills from the financial system and to create a stable world monetary order. For this several measures were adopted. First, the floating exchange rate system was stopped. Second, the gold exchange standard was scrapped as it was thought to be responsible for the international transmission of deflation in the early 1930s due to its vulnerability to the problems of adjustment, liquidity and confidence. Third, the new system sought to stop the beggar-thy-neighbour devaluation, trade restrictions, exchange controls and bilateralism prevalent after 1933.

A group of economists led by J.M. Keynes, E.N. White and Ragnar Nurkse argued for an adjustable peg system, which was expected to combine the good features of stability of the exchange rate under the fixed-exchange-rate gold standard, on the one hand, and the monetary and fiscal independence under the flexible-exchange-rate standard, on the other. The coordination role of an international monetary agency was also planned. The latter was supposed to have considerable control over domestic financial policy of the members. But the two sides had differences over minor details. The Keynes plan contained more domestic policy autonomy than the White plan, and the latter put more emphasis on exchange rate stability. While both the teams — the British and the American — were not in favour of a rule-based system, the British team was primarily interested in preventing the deflation of the 1930s, and it attributed that partly to the deflationary monetary policies of the US and partly to the constraints of the gold standard rules. Thus the British team was in favour of an expansionary system.

But the American team led by the US Assistant Secretary of the Treasury, Harry Dexter White, presented a system which was closer to the gold standard as it put emphasis on the fixity of the exchange rates. The nature of the proposed system was as follows. Though the importance of rules as a credible commitment mechanism was not formally mentioned, they proposed strict regulations on the linkages between *unitas* (the proposed international measure account) and gold. In case any member country did face fundamental disequilibrium in the external sector, it could change the exchange rate parity with approval from three-quarter majority of all the members of the new institution.

Ultimately, the prescription of both the teams prevailed as the Articles of Agreements of the International Monetary Fund incorporated the elements of both the Keynes plan and the White plan, with an emphasis on the latter. The acceptance of the Plan came to be in conformity with the ground reality that it was the United States which was going to shape the international financial system.

Two institutions emerged out of the Bretton Woods Agreement — the International Monetary Fund (IMF) and the International Bank for Reconstruction and Development (IBRD). The latter was planned to take care of the long-run growth of the war-ravaged economies of the world, and the IMF was assigned the role of maintaining the world monetary order and stability of the exchange rate system. With these objectives in mind, the articles of the IMF were written. The main points of the articles were :

(1) The creation of par value system
(2) Multilateral payments
(3) The use of Fund's resources
(4) The powers of IMF
(5) The nature of the organization

The Par Value System

Article IV of IMF defines the numeraire of the international monetary system as either USD or gold of the weight and fineness on 1 July 1944. All the members of the Fund were asked to declare a par value of their currencies and maintain it within 1 per cent margin on both sides. If any country faces fundamental disequilibrium, it can exchange the parity after consultation with other members. If the change of parity is within 10 per cent, the decision of the members will not be rejected. However, if the change is more than 10 per cent, the concerned country needs to have the approval of the IMF. In case a decision is made for a uniform change in par value of all currencies in terms of gold, it is to be done after the approval by a majority of all voting members of the Fund, and by each member separately with voting quota of more than 10 per cent.

The Article IV, Section I (a) of the Agreement reads as

> Expression of par values. The par value of the currency of each member country shall be expressed in term of gold as a common denominator or in terms of the United States dollar of the weight and fineness in effect on July 1, 1944.

The importance of gold as the numeraire was obscured mostly when most of the countries excluding the US had chosen to define their par values in terms of USD. John Williamson suggested that the neutral gold numeraire had been chosen to give the United States the symmetrical option to change its exchange rate of dollar along with other countries. Gold was chosen as a conveniently neutral numeraire for defining par values of the exchange rates of the currencies, but gold was not perceived as the fundamental asset which would act as a brake on the issue of currencies and help in the determination of the common price level of the commodities in the member countries the way it had been in the nineteenth century (Williamson, 1977). No single currency, not even the USD had been recognized as the 'key' currency linking the principal currencies in the world in 1945.

5.4 Multilateral Payments Mechanism

Article VIII of the IMF states that members are supposed to make their currencies current account convertible though they can keep capital control as stated in Article VI(3). The members are to avoid discriminatory currency and multiple currency arrangements. Again, Article XIV allows the countries to keep their currencies not convertible for a period of three years and, during this period, exchange control can be maintained. In fact, it had taken a long time for the developing countries to make their currencies convertible in current account transactions.

Countries would adjust their exchange rates depending on the domestic equilibrium for which the current account balance is one important parameter. Here Mundell raised one interesting issue when he stated the following:

> Only (N-1) independent balance of payments instruments are needed in an N-country world because equilibrium in the balance of (N-1) countries implies equilibrium in the balance of Nth country. The redundancy problem is the problem of deciding how to utilize the extra degree of freedom (1967, 195.

Because of the demonetization of gold in all private transactions, as well as its virtual demonetization in official transactions too, the redundancy problem as stated by Mundell had arisen in a very strong form after 1945. All currencies operating in the system were potentially independent national fiat monies. The amounts of these fiat monies were neither related to their base of monetary gold, nor were the exchange rates of these monies tied to the traditional gold parity. As gold failed to act as the Nth currency, USD slowly took its place. This created the conditions for the Fixed-Rate Dollar Standard.

5.5 Resources of IMF

The size of the total fund of IMF, contributed by the members' quota in the form of 25 per cent in gold and 75 per cent in national currencies, was initially USD 8.8 billion, and the amount could be increased every five years if the majority of the members wanted. Under the scheme of the White Plan, members could obtain resources from IMF to help finance short and medium term payments, disequilibrium in external transactions. IMF established a number of conditions for the use of its resources by the countries suffering from balance of payment deficits. It set the requirements and conditions for the repurchase, i.e., the repayment of loan. All these were to facilitate the management of currencies which are of greater demand for the payments of international obligations. The conditions imposed on the member country seeking loans from IMF are derived from a monetarist model of Professor Polok, and in many cases this has been resisted by the countries.

5.6 The Structure of Organization

The IMF is governed by a Board of Governors who are appointed on the voting strength of the members. The Board makes the policy decision regarding the actions of the members. Also a number of Executive Directors and one Managing Director are selected by the members. The power of the members is reflected in the voting rights, which are proportional to the members' quota (of contribution).

Under the agreement, the United States had to maintain a fixed price of gold at USD 35 per ounce, and when the members were maintaining fixed parity, the gold price used to be an anchor of the system, which converted the gold standard into a dollar standard.

The architects of the Bretton Woods Agreement were not very much specific about the functioning of the system. The evolution of the system was partly based on subsequent interpretations of the economists who were engaged in research. Several important features were mentioned (Tew 1988; Williamson, 1985). One such feature is that all currencies were treated as equal in the articles of agreement, which implies that each country was required to maintain its par value by intervening in the currency of other countries. This position dictated by theory would not have been meaningful, as other countries could fix their parities in terms of USD, as the United States was the only country that pegged its currency in terms of gold.

5.7 Historical Stages of the Bretton Woods Agreement: 1946–60

The period of transition from war to peace in the post-World War II was very long and painful, and the functioning of the Bretton Woods system had not been on the desired lines. The system started functioning normally by 1955, and till 1958, full convertibility of the currencies of the major industrial countries could not be achieved. Under the Article XIV of the Bretton Woods Agreement, the countries could continue to use exchange controls for an indefinite period of transition after the establishment of the IMF in March 1947. The countries used exchange control to preserve their foreign exchange and in addition, every country negotiated a series of bilateral payment agreements with each of its trading partners. The countries in war-ravaged Europe were in desperate need for imports of raw materials and capital goods, and thus the allocation of scarce foreign exchange had come under the control of the government.

Even before the start of World War II, political uncertainty in Europe induced massive capital flight from Europe to the US. In 1934, American administration resorted to the devaluation of dollar and the price of gold was raised from 20.67 USD per ounce to 35.00 USD per ounce. These phenomena induced the flow of gold to the US from the rest of the world and when the War came to an end, the US had become the holder of two-thirds of the world's monetary gold stock. Simultaneously, Europe experienced a depletion of the dollar and gold stock, and the economy had been running well below capacity. The Organization for European Economic Cooperation (OEEC) experienced a huge trade deficit with its trade with the US. OEEC was established in 1948 to coordinate the funding of the Marshall Plan, and the latter facilitated huge inflow of capital to the economies of Europe for reconstruction and development. In fact, a huge amount of foreign capital, mainly from the US, was invested in the European countries to lead the economies towards reconstruction and development.

The period 1946–60 saw some dynamic events which had a significant effect on the international financial system.

In 1949, Great Britain devalued pound sterling by 30.5 per cent and after this 23 countries reduced their parities with USD by more or less similar magnitude. This spate of devaluation helped the European countries to adjust their external sector efficiently and, as a result, they could eliminate their large trade deficit. But large-scale changes in the parity conditions by a number of countries created the impression that monetary authorities could perpetuate their disequilibrium situation for some time and that would create a condition for speculation. In any case, there was perceptible resistance from the monetary authorities to change their parity and slowly, the Bretton Woods system had been reduced to a fixed exchange rate regime even though it was an adjustable peg system in the initial thinking stage. It is interesting from an academic standpoint that the authorities preferred the spill-over of domestic disequilibrium into the external sector in their adverse balance of payments rather than correcting their exchange rates.

Even before the British devaluation of pound, France devalued French franc in January 1948, and this created a multiple exchange rate system, which created problems in the form of broken cross rates between pound and dollar. The system was rectified with the devaluation of pound. In 1950, Canada also floated its dollar and this situation continued till 1961.

There was another problem towards the end of 1950s; it was the inadequacy of the IMF's resources to meet the liquidity problem of the world, which the growth of the world's monetary gold stock could not meet. The gap was bridged by the holding of USD. The supply of the latter was due to the balance of payment deficits of the US. During this period, the latter used to have surplus in the current account, but owing to huge investments abroad and the outflow of capital in the capital account, the balance of payment became negative. The important thing was that the dollar substituted gold in a significant way and the problem of the shortage of gold was taken care of.

5.8 The Period 1960–67

From the year 1960, the Bretton Woods system started functioning normally as the principal members started intervention in the foreign exchange market to buy or sell USD for the maintenance of parity of their currencies. The US Treasury started buying or selling gold with the central banks of other countries at the pegged price of 35 USD per ounce. The member countries on their part pegged their currencies with USD at fixed rate within a band of 2 per cent on either side of the parity. Thus, each currency being anchored to USD had been indirectly pegged to gold.

The evolution of the system in the 1960s turned out to be a bit different compared to the ideal situation the architects had visualized. Instead of the original system of equal currencies, the mechanism evolved into a variant of the gold exchange standard in a sort of gold-dollar system. The British pound lost its importance in the international field and the USD became the single important international currency. The decline of pound happened because of a multiplicity of reasons, the principal reason being the relative decline of the British economy in the world. As it had been fully convertible, by the end of 1960s, dollar was used as a currency of international reserve.

Further, while the intention of the Bretton Woods Agreement had been the adjustable peg system in the exchange-rate mechanism, the system that evolved over time could be called a fixed rate system. The reason that monetary authorities became too conservative regarding the adjustment of the parities was perhaps because they were unwilling to take the risk of changing the parities as that might lead to the possibility of speculative capital flows and follow-up behaviour by others. Thus the resulting system took the shape of a fixed exchange-rate dollar gold standard. This evolution created some problems in the international financial systems which were not uncommon in the inter-war period also and these can be placed into two categories: liquidity and confidence.

5.9 The Liquidity Problem

Towards the end of 1960s, US started experiencing deficit in its balance of payments and this was mainly due to a huge capital outflow in the capital account transactions. Since the US is a reserve currency country, it did not have to adjust its domestic policies to the changes in the balance of payments. The dollar outflows had been sterilized by the federal reserve as a matter of routine. The outflows of dollar meant that other countries, particularly European countries, had been holding dollar reserve. This created different perceptions in some main European countries and there was resentment against the do-nothing attitude of the US Federal Reserve on the deficit balance of payment situation. In 1965, France began to convert outstanding dollar liabilities into gold through the gold window. That created some pressure on the price of gold.

Meanwhile, US monetary authorities responded to the emerging world situation by initiating measures to improve the balance of trade, changing the fiscal-monetary policies, imposing curb on the export of capital, and taking measures to prevent the conversion of outstanding dollars into gold. But these policies could not change the situation much and the liquidity problem continued.

The liquidity problem in the international scene was due to the maladjustment of the demand and supply of gold, as the shortfall of the latter began to be felt in the early 1960s. All through the 1940s, the price of gold had been declining, and this reduced the production and supply of gold. The stagnant price of gold also reduced its production in the mid-1960s and it was apparent that the supply of gold from the Soviet Union would not bridge the excess demand gap. Meanwhile, the demand for gold had been increasing. Apart from a significant increase of private demand, the demand was increasing also due to increased volume of trade and commerce among the countries. The prospect of the world monetary gold stock growing fast enough to finance the growing world real output and the value of international trade seemed to be impossible. Even during 1957–58, the gap between the two in the Group of Seven countries had been significant.

Triffin (1978) pointed out that the supply of dollars arising out of the negative balance of payments of the US could not substitute monetary gold on a permanent basis as the US monetary gold reserve would decline significantly relative to the dollar liability held in foreign countries. The level of the world monetary gold stock held in Group-of-Ten countries did not grow in proportion to the growth of real gross domestic product and volumes of trade. The gap between the demand for monetary gold (to support the increasing money supply) and the available supply had been bridged by the dollar reserve. So long the dollar-gold convertibility at fixed rate had been there, dollar was considered as a substitute for gold. But everything has a limit and this was no exception, and some countries became apprehensive of the possibility of the United States not adhering to the gold-dollar convertibility.

5.10 Special Drawing Rights (SDR)

The discussion on the liquidity problem as stated in the previous paragraph implies that there had been a feeling that the growth of international reserves had not been adequate to supply reasonable liquidity to the growing international trade and commerce. Though apparently no real strain was visible, there was a fear that the lack of liquidity might act as a constraint on the economic growth of the world. Moreover, the mechanism of increasing the international reserve was too much dependent on the running of deficit balance of payments on the part of the United States. This was unstable by design, as Professor Triffin had shown. So the members of the IMF felt the need to create a supplementary reserve which would bolster international trade and commerce. The results had been the First Amendment of the IMF Articles of Agreement in 1967 and this empowered the IMF to create a Special Drawing Account to supplement its quota system that operates under its General Account. Under the new scheme a reserve asset was to be created by the IMF and that would be called Special Drawing Rights (SDR), and this would not be backed by the deposits of the members, but the value of SDR as a reserve asset would rest on it being regarded as an acceptable means of exchange between the IMF and the central banks of the member countries.

The value of SDR was initially set equivalent to one dollar or set at 1/35th of an ounce of gold. Under the scheme, each member was allocated a specified annual amount of SDR in proportion to their quota with the IMF, and the country could draw upon its SDR allocation if it experienced a balance of payments difficulties. The member was required to consult the IMF in the case of drawing the quota, but in drawing the SDR allocation, the member did not need to consult with the IMF. Further there was no conditionality attached with SDR drawing and it was not subject to repayment. The last thing implied that SDR had increased the amount of international reserve.

The cumulative total holdings of SDR allocated to a country was known as the 'net cumulative allocation' of the country and over a five-year period the member had to maintain its SDR balance at an average of 30 per cent of its net cumulative allocation. This percentage was reduced to 15 in 1979. The first allocation of SDR during the period 1970–72 was to the amount of USD 9.5 billion. In July 1976, the value of SDR was changed from one dollar to a weighted basket of 16 currencies. Later in January 1981, the value of SDR was redefined and pegged to a basket of five currencies, and these currencies were pound sterling, French franc, Japanese yen, USD and German mark.

A country upon drawing the SDR could exchange the same with other foreign currencies and increase its reserve. All members of the IMF were bound to accept the SDR in exchange for their currencies up to three times their net cumulative allocation. The country that drew its SDR allocation was to pay the rate of interest to the Fund and the country that exchanged the allocated SDR with its currency got the rate of interest. Thus the SDR was an indirect loan mechanism through the international liquidity increases.

5.11 Market Price of Gold and Confidence Issues

Gold had been the anchor of the system and it was supposed to give stability to it. But the pegging of the official price of gold at 35 USD per ounce by the US Treasury attracted the attention of the speculators, who pushed the free market price of gold in London market to 40 USD per ounce from the US Treasury buying price of 35.20 USD. But gold served as backing to the USD with a 25 per cent gold reserve requirement against Federal Reserve notes. So, the US monetary authority apprehended that the speculation in the gold market might spill over to the official demand for the conversion of dollar into gold. As a remedial measure, US Treasury supplied gold to the Bank of England to restore stability, and requested the monetary authorities of Group of Ten countries not to buy gold at prices higher than 35.20 USD per ounce. In November 1961, the London Gold Pool was formed by the US and seven other countries, and it could stabilize the price of gold. The central banks of the seven countries supplied 40 per cent of the gold stock in this pool.

The 1960s witnessed two phenomena not conducive to the stability of the financial system. First, there had been a growing scarcity of the gold as the production of the yellow metal leveled off by 1965–66. Also the demand for gold increased mainly from the private sector. Second, there had been a perceptible increase in the US, inflation rate as the money supply increased partly due to the Vietnam war. Some economists think that the US followed an inflationary policy at home at that time because of domestic compulsion.

The two phenomena cited above created a crisis of confidence regarding USD and during 1967–68, the London Gold Pool became a net seller of gold, losing gold of about three billion dollar equivalent at the pegged price. There was apprehension about the devaluation of dollar, though the scarcity of gold in the world was one reason (Gilbert, 1968; Johnson, 1968). The resulting situation had its consequences. In March 1968, the London Gold Pool was abolished and it was replaced by a *two-tier arrangement*. The monetary authorities of gold pool stopped buying and selling gold in the market, but instead they started transaction of gold only among themselves at a fixed price of 35 USD per ounce. This was the official tier in which central banks only could transact among them. But a private market was allowed in which gold as a commodity could be traded at free market prices. Along with that the US removed the 25 per cent gold reserve requirement against the Federal Reserve currency. Thus, the link between gold production and other market resources of gold and official reserves was severed. The result of these new arrangements was that gold had been demonetized at the margin. The system evolved into a de facto dollar standard, though gold convertibility remained.

By 1968, the system also reduced to a de facto fixed exchange rate system. The major industrial countries agreed not to convert their huge dollar reserve into gold. Meanwhile European countries and Japan became economic power houses and they became increasingly reluctant to absorb more dollar liabilities. These countries also were not ready to readjust their exchange rate upwards as they expected the US to make the readjustment. Faced with these contradictory pulls and pressures, the International Monetary Fund found itself helpless as its resources were not enough to prevent devaluation by major industrial countries by providing them adequate assistance for adjustment (Dominguez, 1993).

5.12 Demonetization of Gold

The establishment of the two-tier system after the closure of the London Gold Pool could not maintain the stability of the gold-dollar parity for long, and the US was forced to close the gold window in August 1971. The closing of the gold window to foreign official-holders signaled the end of the gold exchange standard. The last functional link between the dollar and monetary gold was severed. With this the Bretton Woods System collapsed, but the institutions created as a result of the agreement — IMF and IBRD — survived. IMF still had an important role as a clearing house for different views on monetary policies, as a centre of information, as the primary source of adjustment of the countries outside the Group of Ten, and as a monitor of the world financial system. Particularly, the developing countries needed the guidance and help of the IMF to standardize their financial system.

It took several years for the monetary authorities to formalize the demonetization of gold as an international reserve asset. 1 January 1975, the official price of gold was abolished as the unit of account for the international monetary system. Monetary authorities could enter into gold transactions at market-determined prices, and IMF terminated the use of gold. The US ended the 41-year ban on gold ownership for its residents. Within a short time, US Treasury started auctioning a portion of its gold stock. Thus gold became like any other commodity.

5.13 Gresham's Law at International Level

In the 1960s, the adverse price movements in the international level brought asymmetry in the intrinsic values of two principal assets — gold and USD. Under the Bretton Woods System, gold and USD parity was fixed at $35 per ounce of gold and at this rate, US authority was committed to buy and sell gold with foreign central banks. As the US economy experienced inflation by approximately 40 per cent during the 1960s, it was presumed that the price of gold too had risen. There was persistent upward pressure in the gold market. The market perception of gold being officially under-valued, US authority secured an agreement from the foreign central banks not to convert their USD reserve into gold. But that could not save the situation, and US president Nixon announced the suspension of dollar-gold convertibility in 1971. Thus USD had driven out gold from the market which was stated in a Law by Thomas Gresham in the sixteenth century. The Law states that whenever there exists a discrepancy in the prices of two assets by market perception, and if the nominal values are the same, the asset which is undervalued will disappear from the market and the asset which is overvalued will remain. This is an explanation of the decline of the Bretton woods System given by Niehans (1984) and De Grauwe (1989).

5.14 Decline of the System

The Bretton Woods Agreement had the design of making the United States the center country so that it could perform the anchor role for the stability of the system. Unfortunately, the United States could not perform that role because of a set of reasons. The United States was to fix the price of gold at 35 USD per ounce and also to maintain domestic price stability to safeguard the intrinsic value of the dollar. Of course, the price of gold could be adjusted with the consent of the majority of the members having quotas in IMF at 10 per cent or more. But there was no enforcement mechanism for the US, and only the credibility of the country and a commitment to gold convertibility had assured the sustainability of the system. The rest of the world, the (n-1) countries, had to accept the price level set by the US through their commitment to fixed parities of their currencies vis-à-vis USD. This had the implication that the (n-1) countries had to follow a definite set of fiscal and monetary policies which were consistent with the fixed parities. But the countries could change their parities because of the adjustable peg. In the process disequilibrium in the domestic economy might happen, but this contingency was not spelled out in the sense that there had been no constraints placed on the member countries regarding the extent to which the domestic monetary and fiscal policy could deviate from the pattern set by the US (Giovannini, 1993; Mundell, 1968).

The crisis of liquidity in the world financial system had not been properly addressed. The countries were to keep reserves against their currencies either in the form of gold, or in some principal currencies such as the dollar. But in reality, USD had been the main currency which was used as the reserve currency because of the gold convertibility. There had been the gold convertibility clause and a crisis of confidence too, and these prevented the US from supplying the monetary reserve demanded by the (n-1) countries. In addition, the US followed an inflationary policy in the late 1960s, but was unwilling to devalue the dollar. This reinforced the confidence problem regarding the USD. So, when some countries tried to liquidate their dollar liabilities and transform them into gold, the US got panicky and closed the gold window in 1971, signaling the collapse of the system. Thus the American decision to suspend gold convertibility ended the important aspect of the Bretton Woods system. The second part of the system — adjustable peg — disappeared 19 months later.

The system collapsed for several reasons. First, there were two major flaws that undermined the system. One flaw was the gold exchange standard. This placed the US under threat of a convertibility crisis, and the country addressed this problem by the pursuit of policies that made adjustment more difficult.

The second flaw was the adjustable peg. Since the cost of discrete changes in parities with the dollar was high, the system evolved into a disinclined fixed rate system without an effective adjustment mechanism. This they had to do in the face of growing capital mobility.

Finally, America followed an expansionary monetary policy that was not appropriate for a key currency. The creeping inflation, though low in magnitude, was sufficient to initiate a speculative attack on the world's monetary gold stock in 1968. That led to the collapse of the Gold Pool. By that time the system had evolved into a *de facto* USD standard. So the United States had the obligation to maintain price stability. The country failed in it and that ultimately destroyed the system.

5.15 Post-Bretton Woods Era: Managed Floating Exchange Rate

The period between 1971 and 1973 had been one of shock and adjustment for the major countries of the world, and in March 1973, the world turned to a generalized floating exchange rate. In the new system, the monetary authorities started extensive intervention to influence both the levels of volatility and the exchange rates of their currencies. By 1980, the dynamism of the system stabilized and members started intervening only to control the volatility of the system. The Group-of-Seven countries started a coordinated attempt of exchange market intervention to bring stability. The decade following 1980 witnessed enormous capital flows across political boundaries and a relative dis-intermediation of the international banking system. This had an impact on the world financial system, particularly on the viability of the international banking system. Some banks in Japan could mobilize enough capital and became very large in terms of the asset size. The countervailing power emerged and the Basle Committee introduced capital adequacy norms for all banks operating in the international market. The capital adequacy ratio (CAR) initially proposed as 8 per cent of the risk-weighted assets acted as a constraint on the expansion of the credit portfolio of the banks. The latter had an important impact on the money supply of the member countries.

5.16 The Second Amendment of IMF Article

The Second Amendment of the IMF Articles came into effect in April 1978 and it formally gave the IMF members a large degree of discretion in the selection of their exchange rate arrangements. IMF had been urged to adopt a policy of 'firm surveillance' over the exchange rate policies of the members.

The Second Amendment Article IV defined the responsibility of the members. Each member was obliged to notify the IMF of its exchange rate arrangement. The members were free to select the exchange rate arrangement they would think right for their interest, but they were to supply information to the Fund. Also a member was to avoid manipulating exchange rates in order to prevent effective balance of payments adjustments or to gain an unfair competitive advantage over the other members which might hurt the interest of the latter. In a way the Second Amendment reduced the power of the IMF drastically.

5.17 Appreciation of USD

During the period 1980–85, USD experienced substantial appreciation against major currencies. The nominal effective exchange rate appreciated by 50 per cent and the same thing happened with the real rate. This was the result of the divergent macroeconomic policies pursued by the US, Japan and European countries. The US authorities followed a relaxed fiscal policy but a tight monetary policy, with the budget deficit skyrocketing from USD 16 billion in 1979 to USD 204 billion in 1986. As the US real interest rate increased relative to other countries, capital from other countries flowed into the United States to finance the growing current account deficits, and the dollar appreciated. The US government argued that the dollar appreciation was the reflection of the growing strength of the domestic US economy.

The appreciation of dollar hurt the export and import competing industries of the US and this increased the balance of payment problems. The public sentiments went in favour of protection, and the trade partners of the US were convinced that the negative balance of payments of the US was a reflection of its growing budget deficits. But a parallel thinking also developed that USD should be allowed to have its true level.

5.18 The Plaza Accord

Finance ministers of G-5 countries — France, West Germany, Japan, US, and United Kingdom — met at Plaza Hotel in September 1985 and after deliberations of their respective view points, they issued a Communiqué which is known as Plaza Accord. According to it, the exchange rate of USD did not accurately reflect the changes in the economic fundamentals like the measures Japan was to take to stimulate domestic demand, or the US commitment to reduce budget deficits. There was also agreement about the depreciation of dollar, and the countries agreed to cooperate on this issue. The dollar started to decline and the extent of the decline of dollar caused concern among the members.

In February 1987, the G-7 countries (Canada and Australia together with G-5 group) met in Paris to consider the situation of the declining USD and reached an agreement known as Louvre Accord. Consequently, the G-7 countries agreed that further decline of dollar was not desirable and the then-exchange-rates were a true reflection of the economic fundamentals. Implicit had been the agreement that the USD should be kept within a 5 per cent target band against the deutschmark and the yen. But the accord could not completely prevent the decline of dollar.

In October 1987, there had been a collapse in the stock markets around the world and as a consequence, the dollar came under pressure as the crash in the stock market induced the fear of a world recession. The governments of some industrialized countries started loosening their monetary policies and reducing the interest rates. In January 1988, the trade deficits of the United States showed signs of improvement, and USD started the recovery phase.

5.19 International Capital Flows

The flexible exchange rate system in the world had been associated with an increasing strength of the international money managers, who were able to make large-scale capital movement from one country to another within a very short time. The trans-border capital flows had been effected to make profit either from the possible fluctuations of the exchange rates due to the potential changes in the short-term interest rates, or the potential changes in the prices of the stocks in well-integrated stock exchanges of different countries. The first reason had been man-made, on some occasions leading to a pre-planned attack on a currency, and this led to a destabilization of the currency, when the concerned central bank failed to take care of its total liability denominated in the form of total currency in circulation with the banks and the public. This type of situation had been very common in the 1990s when several countries became victims of the international currency predators. However, we will discuss this aspect in detail in Chapter 12.

5.20 The Financial Architecture

The period 1990s had been marked by a series of currency crises, and the intervention of different governments in response to these crises came first in the European Monetary System (EMS) countries and then in Mexico. The crisis then spread to South East Asia and it soon spread to other countries like Brazil and Russia. Though each country had its own unique feature in the currency crisis, there were certain stylized facts in this phenomenon. The EMS crisis of 1992 was initiated by German reunification and the reluctance of other member states to pursue policies, which could have checked inflation. The Mexican crisis had resulted as a combination of several factors after Mexico experienced huge capital inflow till 1994 when the crisis occurred. The forces were as follows. First, interest rates increased in the US making investment in Mexico less attractive. Second, a rebellion in the state of Chiapas increased doubts among the investors about the political stability. Besides, when one presidential candidate of a political party was assassinated, capital inflow to Mexico reduced drastically and Mexico had to use its depleted reserve to save the currency.

The Russian crisis in the aftermath of 1998 was a culmination of external shock like a decline in the prices of raw materials to an asymmetric expectation of the creditors. The decline of tax receipts of the government due to the fall in the price of oil led to an imbalance in the budget of the Russian government. The parliament blocked the reform proposal of the government and the currency became weak due to capital flight. In this situation Russia sought help from the IMF and after some controversy got a loan of 11.4 billion USD. This created an upward expectation in the financial market and investors started buying short-term rouble debt to earn very high interest rates. Interestingly, no one understood that rouble might depreciate further because of high interest rates, and this precisely did happen. In August 1998, Russia allowed the rouble to float and suspended the redemption of rouble-denominated debt. The depreciation of rouble initiated a 'run' on the bank, as depositors wanted to withdraw roubles to buy dollars. The banks were holders of large debts which were 'frozen' and so they could not pay their depositors. The country had to suffer for the irrational decision of the investors first to put money with wrong expectations and then withdraw capital leading to the collapse.

Looking at the evolution of the international monetary system, one finds several important conclusions. First, the maintenance of the fixed exchange rate system in the beginning and the flexible exchange rate system since the early 1970s always had to face the n-country problems, as the number of independent exchange rates would be always smaller than the number of currencies. Thus, it is impossible in theory for all the governments to pursue independent exchange rate policies. The history of the evolution of the system since 1950 has shown how the governments had to solve the n-country problem at different times. IMF had not been successful in controlling exchange rate policies, though it had been the source of balance-of-payments credit. The willingness of the US to allow other countries to adjust their exchange rates vis-à-vis USD solved the n-country problem in the initial years till 1960. Later on, the United States experienced deficit in the balance of payments, and other countries accumulated dollar reserves and they substituted gold reserves by dollars. The US tried to solve this problem by a realignment of the exchange rates by Smithsonian Agreement in 1971. But this arrangement fell apart in 1973 when the US devalued the dollar unilaterally. This induced other governments to float their currencies.

The second lesson of the evolution of the international financial system is the market behaviour in the pegged exchange rate system. When the latter is firmly in order, investors are tempted to take advantage of the interest rate differences without covering their foreign exchange exposure. But the moment market suspects the durability of the pegged rate system, the investors rush for cover. The resulting conversion of currencies and the large amount of capital flows can produce the anticipated exchange rate change, which the investors apprehended. This has happened time and again; this happened in Europe in 1992–93, Mexico in 1995, Asia in 1997–98 and in Russia in 1998 (Adams et al., 1998; Goldstein, 1998). The repeated crises has reopened the debate about whether restrictions should be imposed on the international capital flows, what should be the appropriate exchange rate arrangement for the new market economies, and whether IMF needs restructuring. Some economists are in favour of introducing some sort of a tax on the international capital flows as suggested by Tobin. This will make the transfer somewhat costly but opinion differs on this issue. However, we will have a close look at this issue later in this chapter. Again the enormity of the crisis as seen in Asia in 1997–98 has induced thinking along the line whether the IMF in its present form can take care of this sort of problem in the future.

5.21 Exchange Rate Arrangements

In recent times different countries have made different types of exchange rate arrangements and broadly these can be put in the following categories:
   (1) Currency pegged to another strong currency or SDR
   (2) Currency pegged to a currency composite
   (3) Flexible exchange rates of a single currency
   (4) Flexible exchange rate under cooperative arrangement

(5) More flexible or managed floating exchange rate
(6) Independent floating exchange rate

Countries like Angola, Liberia, Iraq, Oman, Panama, Syria, and Beliz have pegging arrangements with USD. Again countries like Benin, Cameroon, Congo, Mali, and Senegal have a fixed peg system with French franc. Countries like Libya and Myanmar have pegged their currency with SDR, while some countries have pegging arrangement with specific currency like Bhutan with Indian rupee, Brunei with Singapore dollar, Estonia with German mark, and San Marino with Italian lira.

The countries who have a pegging arrangement with a currency composite are: Bangladesh, Burundi, Cyprus, Fiji, Iceland, Jordan, Malta, Slovak Republic, Tonga, and Vanuatu.

Countries like Bahrain, Qatar, Saudi Arabia, and UAE have currencies which are quite flexible though not of the elite group. On the other hand, countries like Austria, Belgium, Denmark, Finland, France, Germany, Ireland, Italy, Luxembourg, Netherlands, Portugal, and Spain have flexible and elite currencies which are also stable through cooperative arrangements. These countries belong to the elite OECD group.

Some countries have currencies whose exchange rates are described as managed floating. Their list is quite long and the principal countries in this group are Algeria, Brazil, Chile, China, Costa Rica, Egypt, Georgia, Hungary, Indonesia, Israel, Iran, Malaysia, Pakistan, Russia, Singapore, Sri Lanka, Thailand, Venezuela, and Vietnam. This position was as on June 1997.

Some countries have opted for an independent floating exchange rate regime and this list is very long. Some of these countries are: India, Albania, Australia, Canada, Ghana, Jamaica, Kenya, Lebanon, Mexico, Peru, Sweden, Switzerland, United States, and Zambia.

This shows that exchange rate arrangements of different members of the IMF are of various nature and this has made the system much more complex. Each country follows a course regarding its currency's exchange rate according to the strength of the economic fundamentals. In fact, the Second Amendment of IMF Articles in 1978 has empowered the members to choose their own exchange rate regime and supply information to the Fund accordingly.

5.22 The Tobin Tax Proposal on Capital Movement

James Tobin argues that in a world of flexible exchange rates the dynamics of the short-term capital flows has a destabilizing effect on the stability of the exchange rates, and in fact, it can disrupt the whole process (Tobin, 1978, 154):

> National economies and national governments are not capable of adjusting to massive movements of funds across the foreign exchanges, without the real hardship and without significant sacrifice of the objectives of national economic policy with respect to employment, output, and inflation.

Tobin argues that in the highly integrated world of today, it is difficult for the national economies to pursue independent monetary policies. If domestic interest rate rises, this can induce a sharp appreciation of the currency in real sense. Again, a fall in the interest rate will lead to a real depreciation. This sort of effect will have adverse impact on the economic parameters of the economy, and Tobin suggests that a tax can be imposed on all foreign exchange transactions so that the destabilizing effects are reduced. The proposed tax will reduce the incentive for the speculators to instigate huge capital flow-in and flow-out of the economy in response to a small interest rate change. Tobin suggests that this type of tax should be imposed on all types of foreign exchange transactions without exception and then only it will be effective. Though it may have a negative effect on the international trade, Tobin thinks that the trade-off is worthwhile as it will have a stabilizing effect on the exchange rate, and through that, on employment and income.

Many economists believe that Tobin's tax is a harsh measure as a flat tax on all foreign exchange movements can reduce the depth and breadth of the markets, and the consequent reduction in liquidity can increase the volatility of the market, and it is an opposite and unwelcome situation from what is desired. Also, with today's innovative financial markets, it is highly probable that the tax will be circumvented as financial innovation will induce a replication of instruments that would remain unaffected by the tax.

5.23 The G-7 Study of World Monetary Reform

The Asian crisis in 1997 induced the G-7 countries (the seven countries are: the United States, Canada, United Kingdom, France, Germany, Italy and Japan) to a fresh study for revamping the world monetary system and the finance ministers of the seven countries brought out a Report entitled 'Strengthening the International Financial Architecture' which was accepted in a summit in Cologne in June 1999. The Report identifies five main areas which are to be looked into for strengthening the world monetary system (G-7, 1999). The areas are:

(1) transparency and best practices
(2) strong financial regulation in industrial countries
(3) strong macroeconomic policies and financial system in emerging countries
(4) improving crisis and management with private sector involvement
(5) promoting social policies to protect the poor

Regarding *transparency* the Report emphasizes that transparency is needed to ensure that information about existing conditions, decisions and actions of the authority should be made accessible, and easily understood by the economic agents. When the latter gets sufficient market information, they can efficiently allocate the resources to minimize the risks. Transparency also promotes healthy market expectations of the agents that help maintain stability in the system.

Monetary authorities should publish information about their reserve position, the leverage position and external indebtedness. The countries are to be encouraged to apply uniform standards and sound practices to foster the development of a sound financial system. International institutions should disclose their evaluations of the respective countries' financial system.

5.24 Stronger Financial Regulation

The Report emphasizes that inadequate and inefficient evaluation of the credit proposals are also responsible for the creation of bad asset. Excessive risk-taking along with a high degree

of leverage can make the financial system fragile and spread negative expectations. The Report identifies three areas which are to be addressed by the industrial countries and these are:
(1) improving risk measurement and its management
(2) assessing the implications of the activity of the *highly leveraged institutions,* and
(3) evaluation of the implications of the activities of the Offshore Financial Centres

The three areas are interconnected as it is the offshore regions where the probability is very high that highly leveraged financial institutions are engaged in high–risk business. The resultant loss, when it happens, erodes the bottom line of the parent institutions.

5.25 Strong Macroeconomic Policy

The Report devotes considerable space to discuss the spectrum of macroeconomic and financial policies the emerging countries should adopt in the current global scenario. One important area is the exchange rate regime which should be supported by consistent macroeconomic and fiscal policies by the respective governments. The financial system should also work in an efficient manner by maintaining a proper leverage position.

The Report also asks the G-7 group for its firm commitment to work together with the important financial institutions of the world to improve the standard of supervision of banking and financial system. It also requests the governments of the emerging countries to narrow down the zone of the government guarantee for the private sector loan so that the problem of *moral hazards* can be minimized.

The G-7 countries also caution the emerging countries (there are 11 in the group and they are Argentina, Australia, Brazil, China, India, Mexico, Russia, Saudi Arabia, Korea, South Africa, and Turkey) to go for capital account liberalization with proper sequencing of policies and creation of necessary infrastructure. The International Monetary Fund and other similar institutions are asked to monitor closely the trans-border capital flows to minimize the potential destabilizing effects of the latter. It is recognized that the international capital market has an important role for the improvement of productivity in the emerging countries. The Report also asks the emerging market countries to adopt best practices regarding debt management with greater reliance on long-term debt, as it helps adopt stable taxation policy on the part of the government. Short-term debt induces frequent changes to taxation policies that create distortion in the economy.

5.26 Crisis Prevention and Crisis Management

Regarding crisis prevention, the G-7 report envisages a framework for preventing crisis without introducing moral hazards. The main element in this framework is the involvement of private creditors in all the aspects of debt management strategies. The Report recognizes that the official financial assistance in certain situations can play an important role in the prevention of crisis, and even when crisis occurs, in limiting the risk of contagion. It urges the emerging countries to develop a mechanism for a more consistent and systematic dialogue with the main creditors for the restructuring of loan, and thus spreading the liability over a larger time horizon so that the risk of contagion remains limited.

The Report advises the debtor countries to establish sound and efficient bankruptcy procedures, and a strong judiciary to promote transparency and equity in the insolvency regime. It puts emphasis on both the commitment of countries to meet their obligations and market discipline.

5.27 Formation of a New Group: G-20

On the initiative of G-7, a new group has been created in the world scene and it is called G-20, which comprises seven members of G-7, a representative each of European Union and jointly of the International Monetary Fund and the World Bank, and 11 major emerging countries. The G-7 is of the view that they propose to establish a new mechanism for informal dialogue in a framework of Bretton Woods institutional system, and broaden the dialogue on key economic and financial issues among major emerging economies for the promotion of world growth and stability. Some sort of a *collective management of the world financial system* has been the motivating force behind the formation of G-20, as this group constitutes the largest mass of the world economy on the basis of the market size. Whether countries outside this grouping will cooperate with this idea is a question which only the future will answer.

5.28 New Initiative of IMF and the Poor

The financial crisis of 1997 had proved that it was the poor in the affected countries who were hit the hardest, and a realization dawned among the academics that there should remain some safeguards for the protection of the people in the lower rung of the economic ladder in case any financial crisis erupts. The World Bank has taken the initiative in this field, and it has developed a set of *Principles and Good Practices in Social Policy* in April 1999 with the objective of identifying and managing the social dimension of financial crisis. Also, the IMF programme 'Enhanced Structural Adjustment Facility' has been renamed as *Poverty Reduction and Growth Facility*. This exercise signals an important shift of emphasis towards the achievement of social objective in the programmes supported by the IMF.

Both the World Bank and the IMF are committed to achieve significant result, and these twin institutions supported other measures which are consistent with the objective of poverty reduction. They also supported the G-7 initiative of debt reduction of heavily indebted poor countries. But the approach relies on the positive aspects of the market mechanism and they advise the poor countries to do the necessary reforms so that the fruits of the progress reach the real poor.

5.29 The New International Financial Architecture

In the last two decades, the world financial system has undergone significant changes and there is a growing concern among the academic community about the stability of this system (Blinder, 1999; Eichengreen, 1999; Goldstein, 1997). There has been a broad consensus about what the emerging countries should do regarding external financial transactions and these are: adoption of a floating exchange rate regime, less reliance on foreign currency borrowing, and extreme cautious approach regarding capital account liberalization. Along with these elements, there has been an emphasis on the role of market in the new scheme of things.

There are still certain gray areas which are to be looked into. The stability of the world system depends on the interdependence between the macroeconomic policies of the global financial powers, particularly the US, European Union and Japan. But the present arrangement may not be considered as sufficient. As for example, the low interest rate policy as well as weak yen policy pursued by the Bank of Japan since the middle of 1995 had been necessary to fight the domestic recession. But this policy led to a huge Japanese investment in the US at a cheap cost, and a huge Japanese loan to South Asia. In early 1999, there had been a sharp reversal of the yen decline vis-à-vis USD and the G-7 passively accepted that it was not good for the recovery of Japan. The market took the signal that the yen was going to appreciate further which was consistent with the American attempt to reduce the deficit in current account in its trade with Japan.

There is perhaps another issue which should be addressed properly and it is the liquidity of IMF, which obtains its resources through quota subscriptions from members. In return, IMF creates international liquidity. This is supplemented with the creation of the Special Drawing Rights (SDR). But in the present scenario of market-led world financial system, what is feared is that IMF may create too much liquidity in the system which may not endure. Being the international lender of last resort, IMF should not create any moral hazard problem so far as the management of the current account of an individual member is concerned. But the market perception should be clear that IMF has the means to prevent a crisis situation of a particular member from degenerating into a systemic instability.

5.30 A New International Economic Order

Since the breakdown of the Bretton Woods system in 1971, and despite increased trade and financial liberalization, the world economy has not performed particularly well. There have been two major oil shocks in 1973 and 1979; there was a major debt crisis in the developing countries throughout the 1980s. There have been over one hundred episodes of systemic banking crises including the dramatic financial crisis in East Asia in 1997, and continued growing divisions in the world economy between the rich and the poor. According to the *World Development Report 2002* published by the World Bank, the average level of per capita income (PCY) in the rich developed countries, which constitute only 17 per cent of the world's population, is nearly 28,000 USD per annum compared to a figure of about 500 USD in the poorest developing countries, that contains about 40 per cent of the world's population. The gap is big enough, but even this understates the degree of income inequality because it compares only the average income for rich and poor countries. The gap becomes much wider if we also consider the distribution of income within countries. For example, the ratio of the average income of the richest 5 per cent of the world's population to the average income of the poorest 5 per cent is over 100:1. There are nearly three billion people in the world living in primary poverty, and nearly one billion suffer various states of malnutrition because they live on the equivalent of less than one dollar per day.

The situation has not improved. Meanwhile, population has increased and the absolute numbers in primary poverty has increased too. The world distribution of income shows little sign of equalizing. If we consider international inequality between countries measured by the Gini ratio, the Norwegian Institute of International Affairs (2000) calculates a figure of 0.59 (excluding China from the sample) compared with 0.6 in 1950. For the average developing country growing at 3 per cent per annum, it would take 80 years to catch up with the current living standards in developed countries, let alone narrow the absolute gap. Apart from the colossal income differences, there are huge discrepancies in other indices of welfare such as literacy, life expectancy, housing provision and other basic needs between the two groups of countries.

Against this background, it is no wonder that there have been frequent periodic calls from international development agencies, international statesmen, professional economists and the developing countries themselves for a New International Economic Order (NIEO) to address the issue of global inequality, or what is sometimes called the 'North–South' divide. When this is a reality, the issues that require urgent attention are:

(1) the nature of commodities produced by the developing countries
(2) the term of trade
(3) the volatility of primary product prices
(4) the deflationary bias in the world economy.

The last issue is related to the restructuring programme of the IMF when it is to bail out a member from a chronic balance of payments crisis. The IMF is to recognize the structural characteristics of the particular developing country before suggesting measures. Perhaps this type of restructuring of the institutions will lead to a revival of the new international financial system (Dooley et al., 2003).

This chapter explains in detail the evolution of the world's financial system, and the description of the new financial architecture will not be complete without a discussion of the new experiment of the twentieth century, i.e., the formation of European Union and the new currency euro. We discuss this in the next section.

5.31 European Union and Euro

The single currency of the European Union, euro was launched on 1 January 1999, when it replaced European Currency Unit (ECU) that was an artificial 'basket' currency, which was used by the European Union as their internal accounting unit. ECU is a composite currency consisting of 12 currencies whose weights are proportionate to the importance of the economy[2]. Theoretical value of one ECU was equal to USD 1.17 and that remained the value of one euro at the time of adoption.

As on 2011 European Union consists of twenty-seven members and they are — Austria, Belgium, Bulgaria, Croatia, Cyprus, Czech Republic, Denmark, Estonia, Finland, France,

---

[2] The weights of the twelve currencies are like Belgian Francs (8.183), German Marks (31.915), Danish Krones (2.653), Spanish Peseta (4.138), French Francs (20.306), British Pounds (12.452), Greek Drachmas (0.437), Irish Punts (1.086), Italian Lira (7.840), Luxembourg Euro (0.322), Dutch Guilders (.87) and Portugese Escudos (0.695).

Germany, Greece, Hungary, Ireland, Italy, Latvia, Lithuania, Luxembourg, Malta, Netherlands, Poland, Portugal, Slovakia, Slovenia, Spain, Sweden, and United Kingdom.

Of these 27 countries, 10 countries have not adopted euro as their sovereign currency and they are maintaining their own currencies and they are — Bulgaria, Czech Republic, Denmark, Hungary, Latvia, Lithuania, Poland, Romania, Sweden, and United Kingdom. Other 17 member countries have adopted euro as their sovereign currency which created the Euro Area in Europe. Euro was introduced physically on 1 January 2002 in both paper currency and coins forms and members were advised to keep the legacy currencies in circulations legal tender for two months starting from 1 January 2002, that is, till 28 February 2002.

5.32 European Union as Optimum Currency Area

The success of the euro becoming the single currency of the European Union (EU) depends on the EU becoming an optimum currency area. To fulfil the latter criterion, EU should satisfy some conditions. First, the members of EU should possess similar economies in the sense that they should have compatible economic structures with the same level of economic diversification. In that case, the countries would get the same type of external shocks and they can follow the same type of exchange rate. In the absence of similarity, same type of external shocks would create different type of effects and the countries would require different exchange rate policies.

Second, the economies of the countries under EU should be properly integrated so that they face the same phase of business cycles at the same time. This will facilitate adopting same interest rate policy and one monetary policy. This condition is tough but very important, because if interest rates deviate from one another, diverse capital movements will create problems for the single monetary policy. The latter is crucial for the credibility of Euro being the single currency in EU. It will be a difficult proposition for the European Central Bank (ECB) to fight inflation in one country with high interest rate and tackle recession in another country with lower rate of interest.

Third, the member states should have a common economy in the sense that the movement of capital, labour as well as commodities should face no restrictions across the political borders. This implies a single market condition and the industries in the concerned countries should be ready to face this competition.

The three conditions as outlined above are necessary for the establishment of the optimum currency areas. The fact is that EU member states are yet to achieve this stage. But the Maastricht Treaty tried to ensure that the eleven countries were similar by imposing four *convergence criteria* related to the exchange rate, inflation rate, interest rates, and the public deficit (budget deficit) in relation to the gross domestic product. First, the exchange rate of the country must remain within the *normal fluctuation margin* of the Exchange Rate Mechanism [ERM] for two years. Second, the rate of inflation should be no more than 1.5 per cent above the average rate of the three best performing member states. Third, the long-term interest rate should be in line with the best countries in terms of performances. Fourth, the budget deficit should be no more than 3 per cent of the gross domestic product of the country.

On the surface, the success of the convergence criteria in the case of 11 countries shows the success of the common currency. But ground reality may remain different. When all capital market instruments are converted to the common currency, the interest rates will converge, but that will not ensure the similarity of the objective situations of the capital markets of the member states. Failure of this implies that capital will not move to the capital-poor regions as expected initially. All these show the difficulties in the way of the member states under EU forming the optimum currency areas.

The literature explains the optimum currency areas as an ideal state, and it defines whether a group of countries can enter into a monetary union without much negative externality. In a sense, every country with its own currency is a monetary union, but that does not guarantee that the country presents an optimum currency area. Big countries like the US, Russia, China, and India are not optimum currency areas, as different states either in the US or in India do not exhibit the similarity of the economic structures as described under the optimum currency areas.

But the monetary unions do function and this they do with relative success because of the functioning of some adjustment mechanism like flexibility of factor prices, and mobility of labour and capital across the regions. Flexible wages and interest rates will clear the markets and that takes care of unemployment and under-employment of the factors of production. Free and unrestricted mobility of capital and labour is very important in this adjustment mechanism without which sectoral unemployment will prevail.

What is the real situation in European Union? Different studies suggest that the cultural and linguistic differences among the countries in Europe form a significant barrier to labour mobility. It has to try hard to achieve the type of labour mobility as seen in the US. But sociologists raise a more fundamental issue and that is whether the social friction that may result due to labour mobility in the face of cultural differences are desirable from the stability aspect of the society. This is an apprehension and for this economics has no answer.

The success of the euro will depend largely on the role of the European Central Bank (ECB), which is located in Frankfurt and which is controlled by a set of independent central bankers who are not vulnerable to political opinion. The ECB will see rough days ahead as it tries to impose strict monetary and fiscal discipline on the weaker countries for the stability of euro and its success will depend on to what extent it can withstand the potential political pressure. The hegemony[3] of euro over Europe will depend on the success of the core members of the Union to carry out the system with stability. The formation of European Union and its impact is discussed in this chapter from the perspective of the theory of optimum currency areas.

5.33 Euro and a Historical Introspection

Euro is a unique experience in recent times and many minds are inquisitive about the stability of the new currency. The stability of a currency depends on three factors — the credibility of the

---

[3] Regarding hegemony of a single currency, the term 'dollar hegemony' was coined first by Henry C.K. Liu (2002) to explain the hegemonic role of the US dollar in the globalized economy.

government that backs it, the breadth of its market, and the constancy of its purchasing power. Since the currency is, in general, a fiat currency, the acceptability depends on the credibility of the issuer, and here the role of the government is important. The breadth of the market in space depends on the transaction domain of the currency, and it is proportionate to the gross domestic product of the country. The constancy of the purchasing power of the currency depends on the monetary policy which, again, depends on the political stability. This is linked to the first one, and stable currencies are protected by a strong state power.

The British pound and the USD have been the most important international currencies of the last two hundred years. The pound was the dominant international currency of the nineteenth century because of the following reasons: Britain's monetary policy tied to the Gold standard had a history of stability. Again, British empire had become the greatest empire of its time and it was run from the financial centre of London. The pound faded with the end of World War I as British economy became weak and after World War II, Britain's empire crumbled and USD took over as the world's principal currency (Mundell, 1998).

The famous international currencies in history had been produced by strong political powers in their golden times. The story remains the same for the Persian daric, the Macedonian stater, the Byzantine bezant, the Arabian dinar, the Greek drachma, the Roman denarius, the Venetian ducat, the Spanish maravedi, the French livre, and of course, more recently, the British pound and the American dollar.

The great currencies of history had always been made of precious metals and the viability of the currency was not dependent entirely on the existence and security of the state. In the Middle Ages when Genoa, Florence or Venice suffered military defeat, their currencies — sequins, florins, and ducats — still enjoyed a fall-back value of about 3.5 grams of gold. But this is not applicable to paper currencies, and Confederate paper currencies lost their value at the end of the Civil war in the US in 1864 (ibid.).

After the end of World War II, USD replaced pound sterling as the world currency and it was waiting in the wings since the end of World War I. In the 1920s, the gross domestic product of the US was more than three times of its economic rival Great Britain. During this period, dollar was anchored to gold standard and the economy had been enjoying a high and stable rate of growth, unemployment, and price stability. So it was no accident that dollar replaced British pound as the world currency after the end of World War II.

The 1944 Bretton Woods meetings missed a great opportunity for the creation of a genuine multilateral world currency and that was a theoretically interesting option. But history reveals that international monetary reforms in the direction of a world currency had been blocked by a strong and presiding superpower. Great Britain did it in the nineteenth century and the US also blocked the international monetary reforms that would reduce the role of its currency in international financial system. In the Bretton Woods meetings, both Keynes plan of Britain and the White plan of the US put forward provisions for a world currency — *bancor* for the Keynes plan and *unitas* for the White plan. But the US rejected the idea of a world currency. The Bretton Woods system finalized the agreement with a world financial system based on gold and USD, and there was no provision for a separate world currency. Thus the USD became the international currency through the commitment of gold window on the part of Federal Reserve of the United States.

Stability of Euro

Viewed from the perspective as described in the above paragraph, Euro is a unique experiment in recent times. It is now the currency of European Union with the exception of the United Kingdom. Several more countries are to join EU soon. The once-famous currencies like French franc, German mark are all now history. Generally, the question that comes in the discussion is: how stable will euro be? We have seen above that stability of a currency depends on the strength of the state, the size of the transaction domain, and the backing for the currency. In this case, euro has some weaknesses. The European Union cannot be considered a strong central state. Again euro will have no formal gold or foreign exchange backing. But these weaknesses are offset by two important considerations.

First, the European System of Central Banks (ESCB) will have a huge amount of gold and foreign exchange reserve. Second, though the EU is not a central state, it has the binding force of NATO backed by the United States, and it survives and becomes stronger with the inclusion of members who were former communist states. With countries already having euro as the currency of medium of exchange, the stage has been set for the core of a single currency area and it has all the potential to become a worthy alternative to the USD. Even if that time is not near, the euro–dollar exchange rate will be very important for the stability of the world financial system.

Role of the World Stock of Gold

It has been estimated that total amount of gold mined in the world by the end of the year 2009 totaled 165,000 tons, and at the 2011 price of USD 1900/oz the value of this stock will be approximately USD 9.2 trillion. As of June 2009, the International Monetary Fund held 3217 tonnes of gold, which had been constant for some years. Of the top gold holding countries in the world, the United States held 8133.5 tonnes in December 2010, and the position of some major countries at the same time are — Federal Republic of Germany 3396.3 tons, Italy 2451.8 tons, France 2435.4 tons, China(PRC) 1040.1 tons and Switzerland 1040.1 tons[4].

Topic for Discussion

The way the international economic system has evolved over the last four decades is strongly influenced by unprecedented wave of globalization and movement of inter-country capital. Discuss.

---

[4] World Gold Council Statistics, 2010.

Further Reading

Bergsten, F., 'The Dollar and Deficits: How Washington can Prevent the Next Crisis', *Foreign Affairs*, 88(6), December, 2009.

Berry, R. Albert, and Gustava Indart, *Critical Issues in International Financial System,* New Brunswick, Transaction Publishers, 2003.

Stiglitz, J.E. and Jose A. Ocampo (eds), *Capital Market Liberalization and Development*, 2008, Oxford University Press, Oxford, New York, 2008.

Tirole, Jean, *Financial Crises, Liquidity and the International Monetary System*, Princeton University Press, Princeton, 2002.

6

Recent Changes in the International Financial Structure

6.1 Introduction

The global financial crisis that had shaken the US economy and the member states of the European Union in 2008–09 began with the downturn of America's subprime housing market in 2007. It happened in the backdrop of a peculiar inter-bank liquidity system among US banks. In early August 2007, US banks held approximately USD 12 billion of reserves deposited in accounts with the United States Federal Reserve System[1]. During an average day, these USD 12 billion reserves were used to make daily inter-bank transfer amounting to approximately USD 4 trillion. This implies that, on an average, a dollar in reserves changes hands 300 times per day[2]. A change in this large multiplier driven by banks' desire to hoard reserves can lead to a sudden enormous drop in liquidity. While this system continued, the subprime crisis had been brewing.

In the perspective of a recession like atmosphere in 2001–02, the Federal Reserve reduced the interest rate to a historical low level so much so that in 2004 the real interest rate became negative. Thus the extended period of low interest rates from June 2003 to June 2004 became a key contributor to the housing boom and also a marked increase in household debt relative to after-tax income. In the context of very low interest rates, demand for housing started increasing and prices of houses started increasing also. This propelled many households to buy houses in the expectation of capital gains as banks were ready to provide loans based on mortgages. The eagerness of the banks to lend money induced them to over-estimate the credit-worthiness of prospective borrowers. This had been the genesis of subprime mortgage.

The mortgage brokers used to lend money to subprime borrowers[3] at very high rates of interest without proper assessment of the credit-worthiness of the borrowers. These mortgage loans were then sold to wholesale mortgage buyers; the latter then sold these to investment banks who repackaged and restructured them into mortgage-backed bonds and collateralized

---

[1] UNCTAD, Trade and Development Board, Notes, September, 2007.
[2] Stephen G. Cecchetti, Federal Reserve Policy Actions in August 2007, http://www.voxeu.org/index.php?q=node/460 (accessed 27 August 2013)
[3] This adjective became popular after the financial crisis in 2008 in the US, and it indicates those households that became ready to borrow funds from the banks to buy houses at high interest rates though their income could hardly meet the monthly installments for the payment of the mortgage loans.

debt obligations (CDO). This cascade of derivative products would become fragile if any point in the structure went wrong and that precisely happened with the defaults of the borrowers. The crisis had been a combination of subprime borrowers defaulting on loans that then have to repossess their houses, dragging down the overall housing market as well as many of these structured securitized products suffering due to the many defaults in mortgages. Many hedge funds such as Goldman Sachs and two subsidiaries of JP Morgan had large exposure to these structured products and they suffered due to that.

The collapse of the housing prices in the US had its negative effects on consumption and hence demands. The situation became complex as banks became risk-averse, the supply of credit became squeezed, and overall American economy faced recession. This, along with the problems in the financial system, cast its shadow on some countries in the European Union through transmission channels and the problem became global in 2008–09.

6.2 The Role of International Monetary Fund

Recent operations and responsibilities of the International Monetary Fund (IMF) can be divided into three distinct areas: surveillance, lending and technical assistance. Surveillance involves monitoring economic and financial developments of the member states and providing policy advice to the member states when needed. Lending necessitates the provisions of financial resources under specified conditions to help a country experiencing balance of payment difficulties. Technical assistance includes help in designing or improving the quality and effectiveness of domestic policy-making.

The IMF had to face a major challenge in 2008 when, as an institution, it was in no position to lend to the US or other European countries affected by the financial crisis. The IMF's total financial resources as of August 2008 were USD 352 billion, of which USD 257 billion were usable resources[4]. The IMF was unequipped to provide by itself the necessary liquidity to the US and other affected Western countries. Further, the US and other Western countries, along with some oil states in the Middle East, are the primary contributors to IMF resources, and it was unlikely that these very countries would seek IMF assistance.

Since the financial crisis of the US, many emerging market economies have built up huge foreign reserve positions in order to avoid having to turn to the IMF, should a financial crisis happen to them. From a level of around USD 1.2 trillion in 1995, global foreign exchange reserve exceeded USD 8.3 trillion in the first quarter of 2010[5]. According to the IMF tabulation, by the second quarter of 2008, developing countries' foreign exchange reserves were USD 5.47 trillion compared to USD 1.43 trillion in the industrialized countries.

Emerging market economies' (EME) foreign reserve accumulation had been fuelled by rising commodity prices and large current account surpluses, along with the flows of foreign direct investment. But this meant less demand for loans from the IMF on the part of developing

---

[4] IMF resources that are considered non-usable to finance its operations are (*i*) its gold holdings, (*ii*) the currencies of member states that are using IMF resources, (*iii*) the currencies of other members with relatively weak external positions and (*iv*) other non-liquid IMF assets.
[5] Bank of America, Global Finance, December 2010.

countries. In the year 2003, IMF credit outstanding was USD 110.29 billion and this figure stood at USD 92.6 billion in September 2008. Since the IMF earns income on interest paid on IMF loans, this means lower income for the IMF. This has induced the IMF to seek authorization from national legislatures to sell a portion of gold that it holds in reserve to create an investment fund so that its profits can be used to finance the operations of the IMF.

6.3 Creation of New Arrangement to Borrow

The New Arrangement to Borrow (NAB) was proposed by some member states in 1994 and it was created in 1998 after the Mexican debt crisis raised concerns about the adequacy of IMF resources in the face of a major worldwide crisis. An earlier facility, the General Arrangement to Borrow (GAB), was created in 1962 to increase the IMF resources in case it were needed to give last-minute support to major European currencies after they had become freely convertible after the Second World War.

The NAB is a set of credit arrangements between the IMF and 26 developed country members and institutions. These arrangements are renewed periodically and the last time it had been done in November 2007 for a further period of five years from November 2008. The NAB are a supplemental and emergency mechanism, and they provide temporary financing for the IMF only when it is necessary. They are a non-quota based source of financing for the IMF. And NAB is not intended to substitute for a quota or capital increase.

At the G-20 meeting in April 2009, the major countries agreed that the resources of the NAB should be increased by USD 500 billion. This would not expand the IMF's core resources, but it would triple the funds available to the IMF for use in fighting future financial crises like what happened in the US in 2008. The G-20 countries agreed that USD 250 billion should be made available through bilateral arrangements between the IMF and individual countries. In that context, countries like Japan, European Union members, South Korea, Canada, Norway, Switzerland, and the US have pledged funds of different denominations to bolster the financial position of NAB.

6.4 Special Drawing Rights (SDR) Allocation

The G-20 countries proposed in their meeting of 1994 that the IMF should create additional USD 250 billion worth of Special Drawing Rights (SDR) and allocate them to member states. Further, with a general SDR allocation that took effect on August 2009 and a special allocation in September 2009, the amount of SDR increased to SDR 204 billion (which was equivalent to USD 318 billion of the 2009 exchange rate). The First Amendment to the IMF Articles had become effective in 1969, and it authorized the IMF to create a new international reserve asset that could be used to supplement the member countries' foreign exchange reserves. The SDR is distributed to member states in proportion to their IMF quotas. They are held in the SDR department of the IMF and are separate from quota resources. The SDR serves as the unit of account of the IMF and some other international organizations. Its value is based on a basket of key international currencies.

Under the Articles of Agreement (Article XV, Section 1, and Article XVIII), the IMF may allocate SDRs to member countries in proportion to their IMF quotas. Such an allocation provides each member with a costless and unconditional international reserve asset on which interest is neither earned nor paid. However, if a member's SDR holdings rise above its allocation, it earns interest on the balance.

The SDR is neither a currency nor a claim on the IMF. It is a potential claim on the freely usable currencies of the IMF member states. Holders of SDR can obtain these currencies in exchange for their SDR in two ways. First, through the arrangement of voluntary exchanges between member states, in which one member state can get the desired currency from the other member in lieu of SDR. Second, IMF can designate member states with a strong external position to purchase SDR from members with weak external positions.

The value of SDR was initially defined as equivalent to 0.888671 grams of fine gold in 1969, and that was also equivalent to one USD. After the collapse of the Bretton Woods System in 1973, the SDR was redefined and it was pegged to a basket of five currencies — US dollar, pound sterling, Japanese yen, German mark, and French franc. At present the basket consists of four currencies — the US dollar, euro, pound sterling, and Japanese yen. The value of SDR is calculated now as the sum of specific amount of the four currencies valued in USDs on the basis of daily exchange rates quotation in London market[6].

The basket of four currencies to which SDR is pegged, is reviewed every five years by the Executive Board to ensure that it reflects the relative importance of currencies in the world financial system. In the recent review in November 2010, the weights of the currencies in the SDR basket were revised (Table 6.1).

Table 6.1 *Calculation of Currency Amounts in SDR Basket (as on 30 December 2010)*

Currency	Initial new Weight (%)	Illustrative currency Amount	Exchange rate on 30/12/2010	US dollar equivalent
Euro	37.4	0.4230	1.32500	0.560475
Japanese Yen	9.4	12.100	81.6300	0.148230
Pound Sterling	11.3	0.1110	1.54350	0.171329
USD	41.9	0.6600	1.00000	0.6600
SDR 1 = USD				1.54003

Source IMF, Special Drawing Rights — A Fact sheet, 30 December 2010.
Note: The exchange rate for yen is expressed in terms of currency units per USD; other rates are expressed as USDs per currency unit.
Currency amounts (Col 3) are based on average exchange rate during 1 October to 30 December 2010.

Role of SDR in the Present Scenario

It is expected that in the context of desirable stability in International Monetary System (IMS), the SDR can play a crucial role in the following ways.

---

[6] The details of the SDR valuation is in Appendix A.

First, if the stock of SDR can be expanded through regular allocations among the member states, that can meet some of the need for precautionary reserves, and this will contribute to alleviate the shortage of global safe asset which, in turn, will reduce the global imbalances.

Second, if the use of the SDR is encouraged as a unit of account to price global trade and denominate financial assets, that could mitigate the impact of exchange rate volatility and create natural demand for official SDR as an alternative store of value.

Sovereign States and International Finance Institutions can start the development of a market for SDR-denominated assets, by issuing and investing in those assets to increase their liquidity and create the impetus for a private market to develop. The IMF can also issue such assets strictly to meet the need to supplement its resources.

IMF Bond Sales

Several developing countries with large foreign exchange reserves have been approached for contributing to the G-20 pledge to increase IMF resources. Many have disagreed on this proposal and demand broader governance reform at the IMF type of functioning. At the IMF's Spring 2009 annual meetings, Brazil, India, China and Russia expressed their interest in purchasing bonds issued by the IMF in SDRs. For countries with large reserves, these bonds could prove an attractive way in diversifying the currency composition of their foreign exchange reserves, apart from receiving some secured interest returns.

Article 7 of the IMF's Articles of Agreements provides the IMF the authority to borrow from the capital markets. While the IMF has never issued bonds in its long history, the framework for issuing bonds in the official sector was developed in the 1980s. So far as the available framework goes, it is expected that the bonds would be traded only amongst official agencies, and countries would not be allowed to sell the bonds to private firms or individuals on the secondary markets.

Gold Sales by IMF

The IMF Executive Board approved gold sales in September 2009, and the sales were to be strictly limited to 403.3 metric ton, which was one eighth of the IMF's total holding at that time. The gold sales programme was completed in December 2010.

According to the modalities for the gold sales adopted by the Executive Board, the IMF initially stood ready to sell gold off-market directly to central banks and other governments at market price. During October and November 2009, the IMF sold a total of 212 tons of gold to the Reserve Bank of India, the Bank of Mauritius and the Central Bank of Sri Lanka. The Fund also sold 10 metric tons of gold to Bangladesh Bank in September 2010[7]. The gold sales programme of the IMF generated total proceeds of SDR 9.5 billion, which is about USD 15 billion[8].

---

[7] IMF, Questions and Answers, IMF Gold Sales, April 2011.
[8] Ibid.

The Executive Board decided that the proceeds from the gold sales by the IMF would help the financing of the IMF on a sound footing, and boost the IMF's capacity to provide concessional loans to low-income countries. The Executive board also proposed a new income model in its meeting in April 2008. The new income model would provide more diverse sources, apart from the resource pool from gold sales, that are better aligned with the variety of functions performed by the IMF.

6.5 Role of the USD

The USD is a major form of cash currency used by the citizens of the world. According to one estimate, about 75 per cent of 100-dollar notes, 55 per cent of 50-dollar notes, and 60 per cent of 20-dollar notes are held outside the United States, and about 65 per cent of all US bank notes are in circulation outside the US (US Treasury Department, 2006). Foreign holdings of the US banknotes offer some advantage to the US as it creates a larger base over which the country now collects seigniorage. The estimate of the seigniorage that the US derives from its currency held outside by foreign citizens is done by computing a rate of return based on the interest earned on the Treasury portfolio held by the Federal Reserve. This calculation suggests an annual savings of about USD 30 billion. (Federal Reserve Bank of New York, 2010). But this savings is offset to some extent by the cost borne by the US for maintaining a currency outside the national borders for controlling counterfeiting, and providing depository vaults for new currencies to be exchanged in lieu of old ones.

The USD is also important in the exchange rate arrangement of many countries. According to one study, seven countries are now dollarized or have currency boards using the dollar, and 89 have pegged exchange rate against dollar (Ilzetzki et al., 2008, cited in Federal Reserve Bank of New York, 2010).

The use of USD is very predominant in the overall foreign exchange reserves of sovereign governments that has grown sharply during the first decade of current century and crossed USD 7 trillion in 2008 (TMF, 2010). In 2010, while USD accounted for 61.4 per cent of total foreign exchange reserves of all countries, euro accounted for 26.3 per cent, pound sterling 4.0 per cent, Japanese yen 3.8 per cent and others 4.5 per cent (IMF, 1995–99, 2006–10).

The predominant position of the USD in the reserve assets of sovereign states has created debate in international forum about the potential role of other currencies in place of USD. For obvious reasons, there is diversity in opinion and the currency composition of official reserves is purely the decision of the individual sovereign governments. The major reasons cited for a possible change in the dollar's role are the following: the relatively higher growth rates in some other parts of the world, the large size of the Euro area, the chronic imbalance in the balance of payments of the US and the potential changes in the pattern of economic and military strength (Pisani-Ferry and Posen, 2009).

The dollar is a leading transaction currency in the foreign exchange market with 86 per cent share in the forex transaction in 2007, the share of euro being 37 per cent, that of yen 16.5 per cent and other industrialized countries' currencies 40.5 per cent[9].

Dollar as International Currency

At the risk of some loss in generalization, economists have identified three economic determinants of international currencies. First, a currency is more likely to achieve an international standing as a store of value and unit of account if foreigners have confidence it its stable value. This kind of confidence is inspired if a currency has a proven stable value over time, and this feature is possible for a currency if the issuing country has the track record of a sound macroeconomic fundamentals in the domestic economy.

The second determinant of international currency identified is the existence of well-developed and open financial markets within the issuing country. These types of markets make the currency an attractive one in which to hold assets. Since 1960, the unparalleled depth and openness of American financial markets have become the main pillar for the international role of dollar.

The third economic determinant of international currency relates to the extensiveness of the issuing country's transactional networks in the world economy. The extensive networks induce the foreigners to use the country's currency in their international trade and investment activities.

Thus, the three economic factors — confidence, liquidity and transactional networks — have made the USD as the international currency, and its continuation will depend on how long the system remains the same at international level. This does not deny the political compulsion though as some political scientists argue (McNamara, 2008, 439-59).

Since 1971, when dollar was delinked from the commitment attached to gold window, the dollar has seen its ups and downs: a substantial fall at the end of 1970s, a significant appreciation vis-à-vis major currencies of the world, an engineered decline after 1986, and a period of steady strength during 1994 and 2002. In the 1990s, the dominant role of dollar in international economy remained unchallenged. Measures of that dominance had been reflected in the rising level of dollar-denominated debt owed both to foreign and domestic creditors by borrowers in countries other than the US, the share of dollar assets in the international reserves holdings, and the amount of dollar held and exchanged outside the United States by residents of other countries.

While the international currency status of the dollar has given significant advantages to the US, questions about its sustainability are often raised in some quarters. Any country issuing international currency will experience capital inflows, and the resulting investment in its credit instruments will increase the availability of credit and allow its citizens the luxury of spending more while saving less. But the steady stream of capital inflows can continue if the international-currency-issuing country is able and willing to run the trade deficits, which will enable other countries to earn the currency they hold as part of international reserves.

---

[9] The currency per centages are of 200 per cent, as each transaction involves two currencies (Bank for International Settlements, 2009)

The concerns about the continued payments imbalances have failed to provoke thinking about the reform of the global monetary system. After the crisis period in the US starting from 2008 passed, there has been a growing opinion among the economists that the currency of the European Union, euro, will increase its share in the international monetary system and the current strong-currency regime will continue. But the European Union is unlikely to assume the American role of importer of last resort, and if no country or region within the European Union is willing to run the trade deficits that creates opportunities for other trading partners to accumulate euro as reserve currency, a global system based on national currencies cannot continue. This is the genesis of global imbalances prevailing in the beginning of the twenty-first century. Some innovative and bold steps are needed to bring near equilibrium in the world financial system.

6.6 Global Macroeconomic Imbalances

The financial crisis in the US in 2008 and afterwards has induced thinking among the economists regarding the possible causes of the crisis of that proportion and the culprit being identified in the increasing global imbalances. Considering the fact that global imbalances and financial crisis are intertwined in character, we can infer three patterns in the world financial system that have been conducive to persistent global imbalances and unsustainable financial fragilities.

First, real domestic imbalances have increased over the last decade. A large increase in productive capacity occurred in the emerging world during 2000–07. A shift in the primary share of income took place worldwide. The share of wages in gross domestic product (GDP) in China declined from 55 per cent in 1992 to 48 per cent in 2008. In the US, the median real wage has been stagnant since 1995 despite the fact that the real GDP has grown annually by about 3 per cent every year during the same period[10]. In contrast, consumption trend has been divergent. In China, the share of consumption has reduced by 10 per cent of the GDP in relative terms during 2000–08, but consumption continued to grow in relative terms as a per centage of GDP in the US.

Second, financial development across countries has been asymmetric and also haphazard. Whether we look at capital account regime or the breadth and depth of domestic financial markets, countries actively participating in the world system are in very different situations. Even countries within the European Union differ regarding the respective domestic financial system.

Third, the international financial system faced a shortage of safe assets. This shortage, in turn, provided incentives in the private financial sector to generate apparently safe assets through innovation. Some economists consider this as the fundamental reason why bubbles have emerged in many countries with increasing frequency either in financial markets or in real estates. Only the US economy has the financial depth and skill to produce liquid and safe assets in industrial quantities. No wonder US capital markets act as a magnet for world savings, especially for official foreign-exchange reserves.

---

[10] Banque de France, *Financial Stability Review*, No. 15, February 2011.

6.7 Financial Markets in Emerging Economies

Since 2000, developing countries have recorded rapid growth, averaging about 6 per cent per year. A recession in the US and a sudden increase in risk-aversion may have a large negative impact on emerging markets. The main transmission mechanism would be a decline in demand for the developing countries' exports to the developed industrial countries and also a significant change in international investors' appetite for the assets of the emerging economies. What will happen to the emerging markets would depend on the way both the US and the European Union manage to come out of the economic recession. The effect on the individual emerging economies would depend on the level of economic integration with the developed world.

6.8 Conclusion

There has been a significant geographical shift of the world growth centre from the developed world to the emerging market economies in Asia. The share of G-7 countries[11] in the aggregate world GDP fluctuated around 65 per cent from 1971 to 2002, and after that it started falling and reduced to 51 per cent in 2010[12]. As the large emerging economies like China and India develop as the core of the international monetary system, there is likely to be a large shift in world saving and investment behavior. This sort of adjustment will respond over time to factors as diverse as the possible decline in precautionary household savings as social safety nets are extended, rising productivity, and needs of the development of the infrastructures, and also increasing depth of the financial system. There are ageing phenomenon in the advanced economies and it would have an impact in the form of a large shift in asset allocations and their relative prices.

As the global GDP and financial assets become more and more diversified, the possibility arises that the preeminence of USD will erode over time and, it will lead to a multi-polar system with several currencies playing a key role in the global financial system. The speed at which this transition takes place will have a critical bearing on the stability of the global financial system. With that in view, there should be necessary reforms in the functioning of the International Monetary Fund.

Topic for Discussion

Explain the rationale of soft lending by the International Monetary Fund to countries in need.

Further Reading

Caballero, R.J. and A. Krishnamurthy, 'Global Imbalances and Financial Fragility', *NBER Working Paper No. 14688*, January 2009.

Carney, M., 'Global Imbalances: The International Monetary System and Financial Stability',

---

[11] It was formed in 1975 as the Group of Six: France, Germany, Italy, Japan, United Kingdom, and US. The following year, Canada was invited to join.

[12] IMF, World Economic Outlook, 2010.

Financial Stability Review, No. 15, Banque de France, February 2011.

Helleiner, Eric, 'Political Determinants of International Currencies: What Future for the US Dollar ?', *Review of International Political Economy*, 15(3), 2008, 354–78 .

Kirshner, Jonathan, 'Dollar Primacy and American Power: What's at Stake?', *Review of International Political Economy*, 15(3), August 2008.

Palais-Royal, 'Reform of the International Monetary System: A Cooperative Approach for the Twenty First Century', February 2011.

7

National Government and Sovereign Currency

7.1 Introduction

Researchers in history have established that use of money predated minting of coins by about 3000 years. And in this respect the Chartalists[1] advanced two explanations for the origin of money. First, Goodhart (1998) and Wray (2001) are of the opinion that money originated in the ancient penal system which established compensation schedules of fines as a means of settling one's debt for inflicted wrongdoing to the affected party. These debts were settled through an elaborate system of disbursement, and the latter were centralized into payments to the state. These payments were by money, in whatever form it had been in the relevant time.

The second explanation is offered by Henry (2004) and Hudson (2004) and this traces the origin of money to the Mesopotamian temples and palaces that developed an elaborate system of internal accounting of debts. These public institutions played an important role in establishing a general unit of account and store of value. In this process of history, money evolved as standardized weight independent of the practice of injury payments either to the affected party or to the state. According to Goodhart:

> money first arose as an acceptable way of resolving inter-communal debt obligations, and only subsequently (when money's functions had thus become accepted and ratified as a unit of account and means of payment), became widely accepted in market transactions (2003, 186).

On similar lines J.M. Keynes argues that:

> ... the age of Chartalist or State Money was reached when the State claimed the right to declare what thing should answer as money to the current money-of-account — when it claims the right not only to enforce the dictionary but also to write the dictionary (1930, 5).

These paragraphs explain in brief how sovereign money had evolved through the process of history. Thus modern money is state money and its intrinsic value, either as unit of account or as

---

[1] The word chartal has its origin in the Latin word 'Charta', and it means a token or a ticket. From this the means of payments to the power that be (say tax payments) have this token *or Chartal form.* Thus, Knapp (1973) provides the definition of money as:

'Money always signifies a Chartal means of payment. Every Chartal means of payment we call money. The definition of money is therefore a "Chartal means of payment' (Knapp, 1973, 38).

store of value, is largely dependent on the actions of the state. The nature of money as explained implies that it is an important invention in modern civilization for the smooth functioning of the present-day exchange economy. Considering the fact that money has a positive externality in the economy, every government finds its duty to provide a stable currency to its citizens.

One of the best documented histories of sovereign currency is the dollar of the United States. The history records that Abraham Lincoln, in his 1839 speech before the Illinois legislature, spoke about the government's ability and obligation to provide a stable currency so that the exchange economy can function smoothly (Lincoln, 1839). The record of the successive governments in this field is not very encouraging though. One can establish convincing evidence in the somewhat dubious experience of the Greenback period, initiated in 1861 and lasting until 1879, when paper money issued by the government during the Civil War was made convertible into gold.

Even after more than 150 years of Lincoln's remark, economists find themselves still wrestling with this same issue: *Is government the solution or the problem when it comes to protecting the purchasing power of money?* History is filled with examples of what governments may do when their power of mintage is unlimited and the cost of it is not prohibitive. The hyperinflations of Germany in the 1920s, and of Russia, Argentina, Bolivia, and Brazil in the 1990s are sobering reminders of the effects of excessive money creation.

The important question today is: What can be done to ensure that governments and their central banks deliver on their responsibility of protecting money's value?

In modern times, money means fiat money or currency released by the monetary authorities that are not backed by gold and/or other foreign currency assets fully. This fiat money is a monetary standard that is not supported by convertibility into intrinsically valued commodities like gold or silver. The combination of historical experience and the near-universal evolution to fiat money systems has created a widespread recognition that national monetary authorities will not deliver price stability unless careful attention is given to the incentive structures under which they operate.

Nobel Prize winning economist Friedrich von Hayek (1976, 27) put it this way: 'History is largely a history of inflation, and usually of inflations engineered by governments and for the gain of governments.'

What Hayek refers to in the above quote is the debasement of national currency done by the government to pursue shortsighted ends[2]. This action had destabilized many nations by ruining the financial system. Germany during the period 1920–39 is a classic example in this regard.

What is crucial is that the international financial system is to evolve a mechanism that will prevent such history from repeating itself. The challenge remains to devise sustainable institutional monetary arrangements that can protect the public from debasement of the value of its money.

---

[2] The following quote of J.M. Keynes on the subject of currency debasement is particularly noteworthy: 'Lenin was right. There is no subtler, no surer means of overturning the existing basis of society than to debauch the currency. The process engages all the hidden forces of economic law on the side of destruction, and does it in a manner which not one man in a million is able to diagnose.' (Keynes, 1920, 226–51)

In recent times, several nations have taken up this challenge by legislating price stability as the sole, or dominant, objective of their central banks. Such legislation with price stability as the principal objective of the central bank has already been passed in New Zealand, Canada, the United Kingdom, and Sweden. While these new initiatives are laudable, it is too soon to tell whether they will be sufficient to ensure that governments and their central banks consistently deliver price stability. The stability of a currency and its credibility to the citizens depend on a set of macroeconomic and social factors. Such legislation is but one of many environmental factors that may contribute to the protection of a nation's currency.

The history of money over the past two centuries shows nations groping for lasting institutional structures, that provide incentives to limit their own governments' temptation to debase their currency, in order to satisfy short-sighted political objectives. The approaches used in the past have stemmed directly from both the nature of money prevailing at the time and societies' views about the proper role of government.

In the perspective of the widespread temptation of the governments of the developing countries, to debase their currencies to maximize the seignorage and inflation tax, some economists have proposed a novel idea and this can be put as follows: Perhaps the most innovative and lasting way countries can achieve stable purchasing power for their monetary assets is by competing against each other in the provision of money. Nations that excel at providing a superior standard of value may find citizens in other countries who prefer to import their currency. Facing such competition, the providers of domestic currencies will have to improve their own products.

7.2 The Gold Standard Implications

Since historical times, governments have taken some role in providing money to the economy. In the beginning, the role was limited to 'authentication', verifying that coins contained the standard weight of metals as indicated. Even in this limited role, however, the authorities occasionally violated the public trust concerning the soundness of money. In the era of pure fiat monies, methods are devised to maintain the credibility of the money. The primary approach to keeping governments 'honest' and credible has been to remove the power to inflate from those with the most incentive to do so. This objective has been achieved by building in a high level of independence between the central bank, which has the power to inflate and the Treasury, which has the incentive to inflate.

The central bank has been given independent responsibility for monetary policy, and this is meant to serve as a way for a government to commit to lower rates of inflation that would be realized without the existence of a separate monetary authority. Though this institutional structure is not a panacea, this has proven especially useful: studies have shown that countries with more independent central banks have lower rates of inflation. This is one important finding suggesting the importance of central banks in the developing countries.

Despite central bank independence, the experiences of 1980s show that the central banks in some countries failed to maintain the stability of the currency. This has induced many countries to move toward more explicit central bank accountability for protecting the purchasing power of money.

Hayek was of the opinion that private agents (banks) may be given the responsibility of supplying money, subject to certain constraints imposed by the monetary authority. He contended that as long as private monies were allowed to circulate freely, competition would keep the value of these currencies constant over time. In case any issuer attempted to collect too much seigniorage by inflating away the value of its money, consumers would substitute into competing money. In the process, currency issuers would have an incentive to remain honest. Hayek's proposal has historical precedent. So-called 'free banking' in some countries like Canada and Scotland tested the idea that money need not be provided by the central government. Under free banking arrangements, private banks competed against each other to provide the public with currency.

Critics of traditional private money systems have often used Gresham's law to argue that money must be provided by governments. This famous dictum states that bad money will always drive good money out of circulation. In other words, it argues that only monies with the worst inflation rate would circulate. This led many to believe that a government monopoly on printing money is necessary.

Though there is a possibility that private companies and banks could compete in the provision of money, it is not clear that such private arrangements are sustainable as a practical matter, given the seigniorage opportunities inherent in government-controlled money or in any currency provided by a monopoly. Thus, governments have powerful incentives to tax private money out of existence, in order to become the sole provider of legal tender.

7.3 Competing Currencies: Competition among Governments

One aspect remains open in Hayek's proposal, and that is, what might make governments less inclined to intervene now than in the past. Furthermore, convertibility of private note issues into specie was taken as a given in all historical free-banking regimes. What incentives do governments have to forgo the seigniorage opportunities inherent in their provision of fiat money and return to the world of privately issued monies that are ultimately redeemable in specie?

Some economists argue that with the advent of flexible exchange rates, Hayek's vision of competition among currencies that can effectively regulate the quantity of notes may become a reality. Privately issued monies may not be allowed to compete as that may lead to a chaotic condition, but competition among different national currencies may serve the same purpose.

In today's world of close cooperation and integration, international currencies are increasingly competing to become the currency of choice. The dollarization in Eastern Europe, Russia and Latin America shows how a foreign currency can become a legitimate substitute for a domestic currency that has failed to maintain its value. Even in countries like Argentina that have a currency board system, individuals' ability to hold dollar accounts encourages the government to maintain the integrity of its monetary system.

7.4 Some Barriers to International Competition in Money

Once the US and the rest of the world broke away from the anchor provided by the gold standard, inflation rates almost universally trended upward and, in some cases, spun rapidly out of control. Effective demonetization of gold happened with the delinking of gold price to USD that came with the unilateral declaration of the US in 1971, and with that, Bretton Woods Agreement collapsed.

Though a price stability mandate would help to shift the focus of monetary policy away from short-term fine-tuning to long-term price stability, such legislation cannot be viewed as a panacea in the absence of clear incentive structures that remove the government's temptation to violate the mandate. However, in the light of increasing integration of world markets, one suggestion can be made that the same competitive forces that have served market economies so well may ultimately constrain the excessive money creation that has been problematic for fiat money regimes in the past.

Why might competition among sovereign nations in the provision of money prove to be sustainable where private competition did not? The answer lies in the very same seigniorage possibilities that induce governments to undermine private competition in the first place. Unlike the case for domestic economy, individual countries have no power to legislate their own monetary monopoly in the global economy. The USD will circulate as a medium of exchange in foreign countries only if it is considered superior in value to other national currencies. This means the US, or any country, will enjoy the benefits of seigniorage outside its borders only if it wins the competitive battle in the monetary marketplace.

But the interesting question is: Why would a sovereign nation willingly give up its seigniorage to a 'competing' country? The answer comes from considering the mutual advantage of trade, wherein nations benefit from comparative advantage. A nation should be willing to import a competing currency when it needs a stable payments medium to strengthen a developing market economy with necessary liquidity. If a nation's monetary credibility is weak, importing a standard of value may enhance wealth within the country, and thus tax receipts, by more than the revenue gained from seigniorage.

This competitive mechanism for protecting the value of money can be enhanced by changing existing protectionist laws to foster more effective competition among currencies. We should heed Hayek's argument that countries around the world should abolish 'any kind of exchange control or regulation of the movement of money between countries' and provide 'the full freedom to use any of the currencies for contracts and accounting.' (Von Hayek, 1976, 29).

Legislation requiring that the courts enforce 'specific performance' would also increase the opportunity for currency competition. Currently, in most countries of the world, when there is a dispute involving a contract that is stated in terms of a currency or unit other than the national currency (such as gold), courts do not require performance in the stated unit, but only require an 'equivalent payment' in the national currency, weakening the power of competition among national currencies.

7.5 A Market Approach to Currency Provision

Clearly, important goals are within reach. Inflation is low, and price stability is beginning to be recognized as the predominant long-term monetary policy objective of the central banks around the world. Flexible exchange rates, coupled with more-open capital markets, are enabling international currencies to compete with one another. Central banks cannot be complacent, however, because new challenges will surely arise. Just as fiat money replaced specie-backed paper currencies, electronically initiated debits and credits are likely to become the dominant payment modes in the future. The concept that money is like any other good and that competition among issuers can best guarantee its value should not be forgotten.

We will now see one of the best managed and controlled currencies in the world that is Indian rupee.

7.6 Indian Rupee in a Controlled Regime: An Empirical Approach in Historical Perspective

Indian rupee, the sovereign currency of India, has undergone a long process of evolution since 1950, before becoming a fully convertible currency in current account in March 1993. The formal administrative systems of the rupee is as follows. The Reserve Bank of India, in accordance with the policy formulated by the Government of India, administers the foreign exchange control system through its exchange control department. In this area, a number of commercial banks assist the Reserve Bank in the implementation of its policies. The Controller of Imports and Exports issues the foreign trade license. India joined the International Monetary Fund in Washington on 18 December 1946. It became a member of the International Finance Corporation on 18 April 1956.

During the period 1973–1993, the exchange rates were computed from the value of rupee, which was determined on the basis of the relationship of rupee to a basket of currencies of India's major trading partners within a margin of 5 per cent value adopted. The number of currencies and the value of weights attached remained a secret. Exchange rate of the rupee in terms of the pound sterling was accordingly fixed by the Reserve Bank of India. Exchange rates for spot and forward purchases of deutsche mark, Japanese yen and USDs were based on the latest available rates, and Reserve Bank used to announce such rates every day. Exchange rates of other currencies were derived from the cross rates of the pound sterling with the rupee. Reserve Bank stood ready to purchase currencies of some member countries of Asian Clearing Union (ACU), deutsche mark, Japanese yen, pound sterling and US dollars, spot and forward, and to sell spot ACU currencies and pound sterling. The Reserve Bank started selling USD spot since February 1987. The Reserve bank permitted authorized dealers to fix the floor and ceiling rates for purchases and sale of USD and pound sterling on the basis of a formula furnished by it.

Authorized dealers were permitted to maintain balances and positions in 'permitted currencies', which are divided into two groups, Group A and Group B. Group A consisted of 20 listed currencies (currencies like Australian dollars, Austrian shillings, Bahrain dinars, Belgian francs, Canadian dollar, Danish kroner, deutsche mark, French francs, Hong Kong dollar, Italian lira, Japanese yen, Kuwait dinars, Malaysian ringgit, Netherlands guilders, Norwegian kroner, pound sterling, Singapore dollars, Swedish kronor, Swiss francs, and US dollar). Authorized dealers are also permitted to buy and sell spot any permitted currency from and to banks in any currency outside the Bilateral Group (consisting of former East Germany, Czechoslovakia, Poland, Rumania, and former USSR).

7.7 The Arrangement of Currencies — New Method of Reserve Bank of India

All countries were divided into two groups for the prescription of the currency: the Bilateral group of countries and the External group of countries. Payments to and from the Bilateral group must be settled in Indian rupees through the appropriate clearing account. Payments to the External group of countries (countries outside the Bilateral group) may be made in rupees to the account of a resident of any country in the group of any permitted currency. Regarding Asian Clearing Union (consisting of Bangladesh, Burma, Islamic Republic of Iran, Pakistan, Sri Lanka, and also Nepal) countries, all payments on account of current international transactions between India and other members, except Nepal, are required to be settled through the ACU arrangement. The residents of Nepal obtain their foreign exchange requirements from the Nepal Rastra Bank.

7.8 Indian Rupee in Historical Perspective

Before 1947, Indian economy could maintain a set of separate policies for the stability of the external value of its currency, the Indian rupee, though the relation with the pound sterling was of primary concern. After independence, the rupee was pegged to the pound sterling at a fixed parity of ₹ 1 = 1 s. 6 d. Since USD had a fixed parity with gold at 35 USD per ounce of fine gold, the rupee, through its relation with pound sterling, established a fixed parity with gold at ₹ 1 = 0.2686 gm of fine gold. The exchange rate of rupee for other currencies was determined on the basis of the cross-rates of these currencies against the sterling and the rupee–sterling rate. In 1949, the rupee was devalued against USD along with the devaluation of pound sterling, and the gold content of the rupee was reduced to ₹ 1 = 0.1866 gm fine gold. This system continued until the mid-1960s. Meanwhile, the expansion of the money supply to finance the budget deficit created pressure on the price level. This disequilibrium in the domestic money market had a spillover effect on the balance of payments and on the black market exchange rate of the rupee. A spurt in the activity of the black market occurred in the early 1960s as the unofficial parallel economy began to flourish, thanks to the complexities of official control and licensing policy.

In the 1960s, the disequilibrium in the domestic money market had its effects on two fronts. First, sizeable black market activities flourished along with significant deviations of the black market exchange rate for the rupee from the official rate (Pick, 1960). Second, a mounting deficit in the balance of trade revealed that the rupee had become significantly over-valued leading to a loss of a competitive edge of Indian exports in the international market. This induced the devaluation of rupee in June, 1966 by 57.5 per cent against pound sterling. The corresponding devaluation of the rupee against the dollar brought the rate to 1 USD = ₹ 7.50. The gold parity of the rupee was reduced to ₹ 1 = 0.11888 gm.

In August 1971, the Bretton Woods system broke down and an interim floating arrangement emerged for major currencies. The rupee was pegged to the USD at 1 USD = ₹ 7.50, but the pound sterling was continued as the intervention currency. The rupee-dollar parity was used for determining the rupee–sterling rate based on the market rate of pound sterling against the dollar. In December 1971, the Smithsonian realignment of currencies was made, and the rupee was delinked from the dollar and relinked to the pound sterling at £ 1 = ₹18.968. This led to an effective devaluation of the rupee against the pound by 5.38 per cent. Under the Smithsonian Agreement, the dollar was devalued against gold, and the external value of the rupee against the dollar was adjusted accordingly at 1 USD = ₹ 7.279.

In September 1975, the rupee was delinked from the pound sterling and linked to a currency basket. The sterling continued to be the intervention currency and also the currency against which the components in the currency basket were valued regularly. But the identification of the currencies and their respective weights remained a secret. The system continued till the end of February 1993.

Since the middle of the 1970s, there have been considerable uncertainties in the international money market. As a developing country, India had to peg its currency with any one major currency of the world. And when all the major currencies were floating, it meant unintended depreciation of the rupee. Thus the objective of the basket link was to prevent further depreciation of the rupee against other currencies which it had been undergoing since 1972 along with the floating pound. In the background of supply constraint of exportable goods, the government felt that the depreciation of the rupee, a result of a pegged currency in a floating world, would not help much in increased export earnings. On the contrary, it might lead to an increasing inflationary pressure via rising expenditure on imports. When the rupee was linked to the currency basket, the Reserve Bank of India announced that the currencies contained in the basket were for those countries who were important trade partners.

The discrepancy between the Indian stance on its currency (a basket-linked currency) and that of the International Monetary Fund (a managed-floating currency) was significant. The IMF used to exercise surveillance over the exchange rate policies of member countries in order to discourage the manipulation of exchange rates. Again, member countries were required to intimate to the IMF the particular exchange rate arrangement adopted by them and also any change. In these situations, the discrepancy in the respective position of India and the IMF led to the conclusion that India had opted for an arrangement permitting discretionary management of the external value of its currency. The multi-currency basket was expected to provide a ready technique for managing the daily rate of the rupee against the intervention currency, in order to stabilize the average level of the rupee, while at the same time achieving a desirable market-related level for the USD.

7.9 Emergence of Dual Rates

Throughout the period from 1950 onwards, the free market value of rupee vis-à-vis USD had always been lower compared to the official rate. The free-market rate (the so-called black market rate) deviated from the official rate time to time depending on the foreign exchange reserve position, the crisis in balance of payments, the level of exports over and above the unaccounted factors like illegal inflow of gold into the country. The deviations of the black market rate from the official rate is important in the sense that it is the black market premium which determined to a large extent the inflow of remittances through unofficial channels. The Reserve Bank of India adjusted the exchange rate of rupee consistently downward in the 1980s leading to 8–9 per cent depreciation of the rupee every year on an average. A look at the data of official exchange rate and black market exchange rate of rupee indicates that rupee has been much more flexible downwards in the 1980s, but the gap between the official rate and the black market rate had been wider compared to the earlier decade. The reasons for the fluctuation of the black market (read free market) exchange rate should be sought more outside the legal and organized sectors of economic activities.

In July 1991, the Reserve Bank of India announced the partial convertibility scheme of Indian rupee in the 60:40 ratio. Thus exporters could convert 60 per cent of their export earnings of foreign currency by free market rate, while they had to convert the remaining 40 per cent through official rate. Considering the fact that the prevailing free market rate had been approximately 15 per cent higher than the official rate (read the rupee value of USD), the exporters were getting some 12 per cent less value of their earnings in terms of rupees. That in the new system they were getting higher value of their export earnings compared to what they used to get during the fixed exchange rate regime was completely lost on them, and their comparison with the potential free convertibility of USD by market rate convinced them that their export earnings were subjected to taxation. Ultimately, in March 1993, the rupee was freely floated, thus abolishing the official rate.

Is Indian rupee a free currency now in the sense that Japanese yen is one? The answer is no. Indian rupee is not freely convertible and trade in Indian rupee is practically banned. But the external value of rupee is now determined by the market forces and their rate is used now to convert export earnings of foreign currencies in terms of rupee. Thus Indian rupee has entered a new era, and the researcher requires some more time to understand the full implications.

7.10 International Transactions

The Indian rupee is a restricted currency in the sense that the foreign exchange regime in India is a controlled one. Thus banks involved in international transactions are to function within well-defined parameters, which change too often by new circulars.

The accounts of banks are of two categories: resident accounts and non-resident accounts. The accounts of Indians, and of Nepalese and Bhutanese nationals resident in these countries, and the accounts of offices of Indian, Bhutanese and Nepalese firms and companies in Nepal and Bhutan are treated as resident accounts. All other accounts in the banks related to foreign countries are non-resident accounts. Again, corresponding to the division of countries for prescription of currency purposes, the accounts of banks are directed into two groups: the accounts of banks in the Bilateral group of countries and the accounts for the External group of countries. Accounts of banks for the latter may be credited with payments for imports, interest, dividends, etc., with authorized transfers from the non-resident accounts of persons and firms provided that both parties belong to the same country or countries in the External group. They may be debited for payments for exports and for other payments to residents of India. The balances in the accounts of banks in the countries in the External group may be converted into any permitted currency. The prior approval of the Reserve Bank of India is required for all other entries on bank accounts. All these show the nature of the complex foreign exchange regime which maintains a large number of regulations for non-resident account holders. Since such economies are prone to capital flight, rules are made to prevent that, though one of the accepted facts is that in spite of all these regulations capital flight takes place on a regular basis.

From 1991, some relaxations have been made to attract foreign capital in non-resident accounts. Some concessions in the form of higher interest rates have also been provided. The result has been encouraging though inflow and outflow has become a common feature in these accounts. As a part of ongoing economic reforms, exchange control rules are being made much more liberal and its impact on the inflow of foreign capital have become positive. There has been perceptible change in the interest structure of the country and the interest rate is expected to come down further. It is expected that domestic interest rate will converge with the world rate in the long run.

7.11 Price Level and Exchange Rate in India

Exchange rate of a currency is a price of the currency in terms of foreign currency. This leads to the implication that it determines the price of the exportable in foreign countries in terms of foreign currency. The price of tradable commodities in the foreign market is linked with the domestic price level through the exchange rate when the latter is fixed. In Indian case, the movement of the price level in India is not compatible with the movement of world price level and this is shown in Figure 7.1. We find that relative inflation is much higher in India since the middle of 1984. Thus, following the large-scale deviations of the domestic price level compared to world price level in case of a continuous inflation, if the exchange rate is not adjusted downward to compensate the price rise (to maintain the purchasing power parity), the foreign currency price of the exportable will be higher in foreign market, and the operation of the law of demand will reduce the export of the country. This analysis leads to one additional responsibility of the monetary authority of the country following a fixed exchange rate regime, and that is, it is to adjust the exchange rate in face of inflation in the country so that the foreign currency prices of the exportable are not adversely affected. Technically speaking, two concepts are involved here and these are the purchasing power parity doctrine (PPP) and the real exchange rate (RER).

Figure 7.1 Inflation in India and the World since 1980

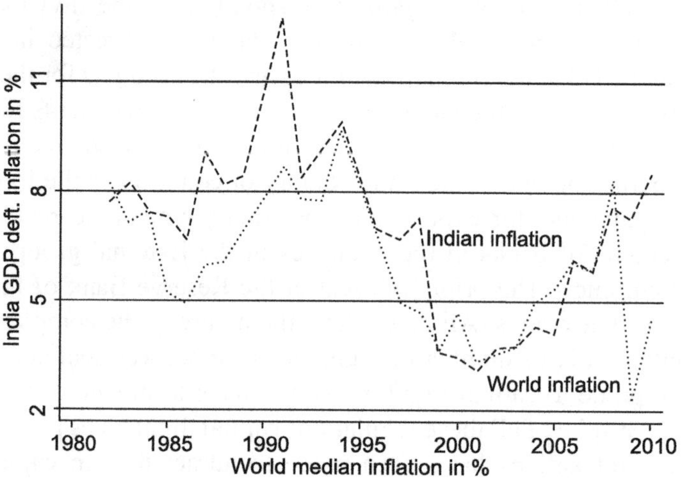

Source: Developing Trends, March 2011, Vol. 1, Issue 1.

The purchasing power parity (PPP) doctrine relates the price of a commodity in the home country, p, with its own-country price in another country e P* or

$$P = e P* \qquad \text{Equation (7.1)}$$

where e is the nominal exchange rate, and it represents the home-currency value of a unit of the foreign currency. The relationship (7.1) is a 'strong form' of PPP, and it implies that, neglecting the transport cost, the price of an internationally traded good, say gold, should be same everywhere when expressed in some common currency. Thus an Indian, while buying his HMT watch, should pay same amount of money either in Bombay or in London.

Though appealing, the empirical support of PPP has always been mixed in the literature. While Edison and Klovland (1987) find some support for PPP in their studies based on long-run time series data, Dornbusch (1985) and Giovannetti (1992) have failed to find any evidence of support for PPP. In the later portion of this section, we will see the empirical position of PPP in India.

The limited success of the PPP is sought to be explained in the literature in several ways. First, it is said that there are flaws in the actual price level compared, because price indices in different countries include different goods, including non-traded goods, with different weights and thus PPP may fail when relative price changes. Thus the failure of the PPP is more apparent than real.

The second approach places a renewed emphasis on theories that postulate that there is no long-run and stable relationship between prices in different countries. These theories seek to explain the movement of the exchange rates by other factors including the price level.

The logarithmic transformation of (7.1) will be

$$\log e = \log P - \log P* \qquad \text{Equation (7.2)}$$

and the estimable form of (7.2) is

$$\log e = a_0 + a_1 (\log P - \log P^*) \quad \text{Equation (7.3)}$$

Thus equation (7.3) has been estimated using quarterly data of India for the period 1973 to 1991. The Cochrane-Orcutt method of estimation has been used to take care of auto-correlation.
. For official exchange rate, the estimation is as under:

$$\log e = 1.554 + 0.056 (\log P - \log P^*) + u$$
t-statistic   (0.912) (0.673)
Adjusted R^2 = 0.987   SEE = 0.089
D.W. Statistic = 1.726   n = 73

Thus a look at the result shows that PPP does not hold in the case of India during the period 1973–91 as the coefficient of the relative price level ($\log P - \log P^*$) is not significant.

7.12 Real Exchange Rate

A related concept of Purchasing Power Parity (PPP) condition is the Real Exchange Rate (RER), which can be derived by rewriting the strong form of PPP (equation 7.1). Thus, we can write

$$RER = e \frac{P^*}{P} \quad \text{Equation (7.1a)}$$

RER represents domestic currency price of foreign goods relative to home goods. The strong form of PPP indicates that real exchange rate should be a constant. Thus RER may deviate from the equilibrium value (some constant) in the short run, but in the long run it cannot go too far from the equilibrium value (some constant) as suggested by PPP.

When both the domestic and foreign price levels equilibrate in the long run, RER becomes one and then the test of the PPP in strong form becomes equivalent to the test of RER, i.e., whether RER hovers around unity or not.

Using the price levels of India and the US (as a proxy of foreign price level), we have calculated the RER for India during the period 1973–91. A look at the nominal and real exchange rates shows that the RER also depreciated overtime. Thus the adjustment of the nominal exchange rate following the currency-basket regime has over-compensated the price rise in India.

7.13 Exact Exchange Rate

We see that real exchange rate depends on the domestic price level. In India many prices are government-administered and thus the government has power to influence the real exchange rate through the price level. In view of this, another exchange rate is estimated. It is called Exact Exchange Rate (EER). Corresponding to a particular price level, EER is that exchange rate for which the real exchange rate will remain constant. If we take the 1973 price level, then we calculate EER as

$$EER = (RER \text{ of } 1973.1) \times \frac{CPI}{CPI^*}$$

The calculated values of both RER and EER are given in the following table. The discrepancy between the two rates shows actual deviations of the RER from the 1973 level.

One can interpret EER as the equilibrium exchange rate provided the anchor period (the rate that is taken for calculation) is assumed to have the equilibrium rate. The subsequent changes in the nominal rate are to compensate the relative inflation only. Since the concept of equilibrium exchange rate is hazardous and full of controversy, the information about the EER can be used as a good proxy for the equilibrium rate.

The calculation of both RER and EER is done in the Table below for a limited period, 1973.1 (First quarter of 1973) to 1991.1. The reader can easily calculate these two rates by following the same formulas.

Table 7.1 *Real Exchange Rate and Estimated Exact Exchange Rate in India (1973.1–1991.1)*

Time/Year	Real Exchange Rate (RER)	Exact Exchange Rate (EER)
1973.1	7.24	8.33
2	6.58	8.79
3	6.81	9.08
4	6.92	9.34
1974.1	6.51	9.48
2	6.17	10.05
3	6.00	10.67
4	6.02	10.67
1975.1	6.05	10.25
2	6.54	10.15
3	7.26	9.82
4	7.57	9.39
1976.1	7.96	9.82
2	8.11	8.81
3	7.81	8.95
4	7.82	9.03
1977.1	7.75	9.02
2	7.75	9.03
3	7.49	9.21
4	7.12	9.16
1978.1	7.63	8.79
2	7.66	8.57
3	7.33	8.63
4	7.55	8.62

(Contd.)

(Contd.)

Time/Year	Real Exchange Rate (RER)	Exact Exchange Rate (EER)
1979.1	7.87	8.23
2	7.76	8.17
3	7.65	8.35
4	7.53	8.35
1980.1	8.07	8.07
2	7.75	8.00
3	7.51	8.21
4	7.69	8.20
1981.1	7.87	8.27
2	8.19	8.43
3	8.37	8.65
4	8.35	8.66
1982.1	8.99	8.26
2	9.20	8.25
3	9.08	8.47
4	8.90	8.61
1983.1	9.12	8.69
2	8.94	8.96
3	8.70	9.32
4	8.85	9.43
1984.1	9.10	9.35
2	12.67	7.02
3	9.88	9.56
4	10.33	9.58
1985.1	10.10	9.78
2	10.36	9.54
3	9.78	9.75
4	9.84	9.83
1986.1	9.88	9.89
2	9.79	10.18
3	9.67	10.43
4	9.81	10.63

(Contd.)

(Contd.)

Time/Year	Real Exchange Rate (RER)	Exact Exchange Rate (EER)
1987.1	9.80	10.49
2	9.70	10.60
3	9.50	10.96
4	9.20	11.12
1988.1	9.53	10.81
2	10.22	10.97
3	10.32	11.22
4	10.40	10.43
1989.1	11.21	11.09
2	11.80	11.14
3	11.65	11.38
4	11.89	11.39
1990.1	12.26	11.17
2	12.07	11.50
3	12.19	11.78
4	11.93	12.04
1991.1	12.78	12.21
2	13.65	12.34
3	15.78	12.98
4	15.45	13.29

Source: Based on Nandi (1996)

Note: RER = NER (CPI*/CPI), where CPI* is US price level
Exact Exchange Rate (EER) = 7.24 (CPI/CPI*)
i.e., estimated exchange rate to keep the RER fixed at 1973.1 level.

7.14 Exchange Rate of Indian Rupee and Current Account

The monetarists argue that the equilibrium in the domestic money market influences the changes in the exchange rate of the currency. Money is one important asset in the portfolio of individuals, and some economists developed the asset-theory approach to the exchange rate determination. Along with this development, another approach emerged in which the current account position of the country is considered as an important determinant for the changes in the exchange rate. By emphasizing the relationship between the current account and the exchange rate, this approach developed a model of exchange rate determination that integrated the role of relative prices, expectations of the economic agents, and the asset markets (Dornbusch and Fischer, 1980). This approach strikes a middle course, or some sort of a synthesis, between the two earlier approaches — the monetarist one suggesting the importance of monetary equilibrium and price level, and the alternative one suggesting the importance of current account. But since trade flows out of changes in the current account are linked with the changes in the portfolio of international assets of the country at the macro level, and since money is an important asset, the two approaches can be linked together. The intuitive explanation follows:

When deficits in the current account of a country are financed from the international reserve and the surplus in the current account augments the volume of the same international reserve, the changes in the current account position changes the holding of foreign currency position of the country. This also affects the supply of money at the domestic level. Seen from a different angle, a continuous surplus in current account will increase the supply of foreign currency leading to a relative decline in the price of that currency. Thus the exchange rate of the foreign currency valued in terms of the domestic currency declines or the exchange rate of the domestic currency appreciates. Thus the present exchange rate (spot rate) is influenced by the realized trade flows. This argument also implies that the future spot rate will be influenced by the expected changes in the trade flows. If there is a sudden change in the perception of the traders engaged in the international trade that Indian economy is to import more petroleum in the near future due to a surge in demand and a near stagnation in the domestic production, the expected demand for foreign currency, say USD, will go up and the future spot rate of rupee will decline. The expected depreciation of the domestic currency will induce the individuals to shift from domestic currency to foreign currency, where it is possible, and thus further depreciation of the domestic currency becomes a possibility. Currency substitution is not possible in India, but traders can hedge the possible change in the expected trade flows due to exogenous shocks by withholding the stock of foreign currency. This may influence the free market exchange rate of Indian rupee in the recent situation.

The above analysis suggests that current spot exchange rate of rupee is influenced by changes in the expectations about the future position of current account, as well as the current position. Again, the short-run effect of an exogenous shock affecting the current account can be different from its long-run effect. If the country remains initially at equilibrium and an exogenous shock like Gulf war induces an expectation of a large trade deficit, exchange rate will fluctuate, though in the long-run, all prices and quantities adjust to the situation and equilibrium is restored to the current account. The new long-run exchange rate will be a depreciated one, which will equilibrate the trade flows and the current account. The short-run spot rate approaches the long-run rate over time. All these point to the fact that the position of current account may influence the exchange rate with time lags and this consideration should be taken care of in formulating the model.

7.15 Empirical Estimation

Here figures of current account position in India since 1973 onwards are taken as the difference between exports and imports of the country. The equation for estimation is of the form:

$$E_t = b_0 + b_1 CA_t + u_t \qquad \text{Equation (7.4)}$$

The presumptive sign of the coefficient b_1 should be negative.

The estimation for the period 1971–1991 with quarterly data is as follows (using Cochrane-Orcutt method of estimation):

$$E_t = 8.296 - 0.018 \, CA_t + e$$
t-statistics (9.41) (3.38)
D.W. statistic = 1.87   SEE = 18.595
Adjusted R^2 = 0.985   n = 73
(ρ hat) = 0.015

The result of estimation shows that the coefficient of CA_t is of expected sign (negative) and significant. The result shows the importance of current account in the exchange rate behavior.

7.16 Black-Market Premium and Price Ratio

The parallel movement of the official exchange rate and the black market rate all through the period 1973–91 is an important characteristic of Indian economy. People used to sell foreign currency in unofficial market as that gave them a premium. The premium is calculated by using the formula.

$$\text{Premium} = \frac{\text{Black market rate}}{\text{Official rate}}$$

It is argued that the black market premium depends on the relative price level of the domestic economy. It means that if domestic inflation rate deviates too much from the world inflation rate (i.e., becomes much higher), the black market rate (read free market rate) will move away from the official rate. Thus the black market premium is related with the relative price ratio, or the ratio of domestic price level to world price level.

In search of an empirical relationship, we have regressed the black market premium (PRM) or current account, the ratio of prices (that is CPI/CPI*), where CPI* is the US price level and the rate of change of official exchange rate (DER), and the result of the estimation is placed below:

$$PRM = 1.08 - 0.0003 \, CA_t + 0.223 \, (CPI/CPI^*) - 0.208 \, DER + e$$
t-statistic (4.20) (−0.253)   (+1.162)   (−0.75)
Adjusted R^2 = 0.736   SEE = 0.602
D.W. statistic = 2.22   n = 73

We find that the value of adjusted R^2 is significant. This suggests that the operation of black market premium can be explained by the normal explanatory variables like current account, the price ratio and the rate of change of official exchange rate. The sign of the coefficient of current account is satisfactory (negative), though it is not significant. The same is true for the coefficient of price ratio which is significant at 25 per cent level. The coefficient of the exchange rate depreciation (DER) is of expected sign though not significant. The information on black market premium is available in Nandi (1996).

7.17 Currency Basket and Indian Rupee The SDR Approach

Since 1975, Indian rupee is linked with a basket of currencies of the countries who have been India's important trade partners. The number of currencies in the basket and the specific weights attached to these currencies have been kept a secret by the Reserve Bank of India, to safeguard the exchange rate of rupee from speculation. In this context, any discussion on India's currency-basket system can proceed on two lines. First, the system can be placed against the alternative systems of exchange rate management available for a country like India. This type of discussion can explain the pros and cons of the currency-basket system. Second, since rupee is supposed to be linked with the major currencies of the world, and these currencies are more or less floating, the SDR exchange rate of rupee can be compared with the same of some currencies, which are important for India's international trade.

With the collapse of the system of fixed exchange rate regime along with the Bretton Wood System in 1971, the weaker economies of the world faced the problem of instability of the exchange rate of their currencies. Strictly speaking, they could choose in between the two extremes: the exchange rate flexibility at the one end and the fixed exchange rate regime on the other. Which way the country should go depends optimally on the structural characteristics of the economy. If the economy is considerably open, a fixed exchange rate regime would ensure minimum external shocks. When the nominal exchange rate is fixed, the external shocks are absorbed through adjustment in domestic price structure and through a mobility of factors of production. Otherwise, some shocks can be absorbed by flexibility of nominal exchange rate.

When nominal exchange rate is made flexible, three courses are open to any country — full float of the currency, pegging to a single currency, and linking the currency to a basket of currencies. These are broad categories and many countries use a combination to maintain stability of the exchange rate.

7.18 Choice between a Peg and a Currency Basket

A single currency peg creates a small zone of stability with the fortune of the pegging currency tied with the dominant one. It is easy to administer and in this context, an adherence to the peg becomes also strong.

But the trade weight attached to the dominant currency may change over time and the fluctuation in the exchange rate of the dominant currency may create problems for the stability of the pegged currency. To provide a cushion to such an eventuality, the currency is pegged to a basket of currencies, and the negative effect of the wide fluctuation of a single currency remains limited to the value of the weight.

If the international trade is highly diversified both region-wise and commodity-wise, and if a single trade partner does not have a good record of macroeconomic stability, pegging to a currency basket is always preferable. Further, a single currency peg generally creates larger imbalances in the external sector, but again, in some situation, it facilitates capital movement within the region.

7.19 The System of Currency Basket

A particular country, say country i, links up its currency (say rupee) to a basket of (n–1) other currencies in such a way that it selects a positive base exchange rate vector

e^*_i (where $e^*_i = e^*_{i1}, \ldots, e^*_{i,n-1}$)
and it attaches non-negative nominal weights w_{ij} to the currency of country j (sum of the weights or $\Sigma_j w_{ij} = 1$). The optimum number of the currencies and the value of the weights w_{ij} can be determined by an optimizing procedure, say, the minimization of its variance. The ith country adjusts the supply of its currency so that the observed current exchange rate vector e_i (that is $e_i = e_{i1}, \ldots, e_{in}$) satisfies the condition

$$\Sigma_j w_{ij} e_{ij} / e^*_{ij} = 1$$

Such a currency basket can be made consistent provided it satisfies some conditions specified in the literature (Williamson, 1982). Since we intend neither to measure the optimum value of the weights nor the number of currencies by any programming exercise, we are not pursuing this case here.

Assuming that the basket should contain the currencies of some important countries, and these currencies are floating, an attempt is made here to explore the quantitative relation between the SDR value of Indian rupee with the same of five currencies, which are USD, Japanese yen, German deutsche mark, French franc and Italian lira. The data used in this exercise are the monthly SDR exchange rate of six currencies (including Indian rupee) during the period 1984–89.

The model can be written as:

Re/SDR = F (Dollar/SDR, Yen/SDR, Mark/SDR, Franc/SDR, Lira/SDR)

The estimation of the model is as follows:

Re/SDR = 7.3444 + 0.332 (Dollar/SDR) – 0.017 (Yen/SDR)
T-stat.   (0.278)   (2.30)   (–2.67)
– 0.036 (Mark/SDR) + 0.274 (Franc/SDR) – 0.005 (Lira/SDR)
(–0.024)   (0.68)   (–2.53)
   Adjusted R^2 = 0.996   SEE = 2.693
   D.W. Statistic = 2.003   n = 71

While the overall fit of the regression is good (evident in the value of R^2 and D.W. statistic), the coefficients of Yen/SDR and Mark/SDR are not significant. The sign of the co-efficient of Lira is negative and it is significant. The sign is puzzling and so is the sign of the co-efficient of Mark/SDR. Of course, this reflects the complex situation in the international currency world with near chaotic movement of some leading currencies.

One observation about the period of this quantitative exercise is important. The choice of the period 1984–89, though inadvertent, coincides with the period of liberalization initiated by the late Rajeev Gandhi, and it is characterized by at least two phenomena: more flexibility in the exchange rate at the official level and an increase in the foreign debt of the country. While the former helped the expansion of exports, liberalization increased imports too. The increasing gap between the imports and the exports had been filled up by increasing resort to international borrowing. The result has been an increasing volume of international debt though domestic industry registered phenomenal growth.

7.20 Official and Black Market Exchange Rate of Rupee: A Time Series Study

Black market or illegal market for a commodity emerges when legal barriers exist for the sale of the commodity or sale of the same for a maximum price for which adequate supply is not available. Thus it is the existence of excess demand for the commodity which acts as the origin of the black market. The nomenclature 'black' has been synonymous with lack of sanction of the law. Since 1950, most of the developing countries have been practicing rigid control in the foreign exchange transactions to safeguard their limited foreign exchange reserve. But excess demand for foreign currency has led to a parallel market for foreign exchange where the latter becomes available at a premium. Thus black market for foreign exchange, particularly USD, has been operating in India since independence and the quotations for the black market price of USD are available in Pick's Currency yearbook (Pick, 1968). In fact, the latter has been publishing the black market quotations for all the currencies of the developing countries since 1950.

The theory of black market of currency is well established in the literature (Bhagwati, 1978; Black, 1976). The theoretical underpinning of the operation of the black market and the movement of the black market exchange rate can be summarized as follows.

The exchange rate of a currency is determined in the long run by the purchasing power of it, and the latter is determined by the movement of the price levels of the two countries. The domestic price level depends on the excess money supply and the movement of the gross domestic product. If disequilibrium exists in the domestic money market and that creates a pressure on the price level, the spill-over of this phenomenon in the international front of the country will be on two aspects — the balance of payments of the country will worsen and the equilibrium value of the exchange rate will change. In the context of the fixed exchange rate regime, which had been the principal system under the Bretton Woods agreement, the official exchange rate cannot depreciate automatically. Thus, the free market exchange rate will depreciate and it will move away from the official rate.

In the demand-supply framework, the above analysis implies that the demand for foreign exchange cannot be met by the inadequate supply of it. The latter is conditioned by inelastic exports of the country as the higher price structure of the domestic commodities makes these non-competitive in the international markets.

The common theoretical explanations hold for all countries, but the mode of operation varies from one country to another. Thus the excess demand for gold in India and Pakistan, the demand for luxury consumer goods in Bangladesh, the demand for Western goods in former East European countries, the debasement of currencies in Latin American countries and present-day Russia — all these have created the black market for foreign currency, and particularly the USD.

7.21 Black Market Exchange Rate of Indian Rupee: An Empirical Exercise

All through the period 1950–91, the parallel exchange rate of rupee has been deviating from the official exchange rate depending on factors which are partly economic in nature. There has been an attempt in the literature to explain the movement of the black market exchange rate. One such attempt in the monetarist tradition tries to explain the movement of the black market exchange rate by the disequilibrium analysis of the domestic money market. It is the failure of the official exchange rate to adjust properly in response to the changes in the relative price level, which causes changes in the black market rate. Thus a model as given below is formulated in the literature to explain the movement of the black exchange rate (Blejer, 1978):

$$\log BMR = a_0 + a_1 (\log P - \log P^* - \log E) + a_2 (GP - GP^*) + u$$

With sign $a_1 > 0$, $a_2 > 0$

Where BMR = black market exchange rate
P = domestic price level
P^* = foreign price level
GP = domestic inflation rate
GP^* = foreign inflation rate
E = nominal official exchange rate

The above model is based on the Purchasing Power Parity theory. Using the quarterly data of India during the period 1973–91, the estimation of the model is as follows:

$$\log BMR = 2.795 - 0.446 (\log P - \log P^* - \log E) + 0.325 (GP - GP^*) + e$$

t-statistics = (1.33) (–2.04)   (2.13)

Adjusted R^2 = 0.962   SEE = 0.39

D.W. Statistic = 2.13   n = 73

The estimated value of the co-efficient a_1 is negative contrary to expectation, though it is significant only at 5 per cent level. The elasticity of the relative inflation rate $(GP - GP^*)$ is positive, and it is significant. Thus, this model fails to explain the role of Purchasing Power Parity vis-à-vis official exchange rate in the movement of the black market exchange rate in India, though the black market rate is explained by the relative inflation variable properly.

A slight different version of the model of black market exchange rate is as follows:

$$\log BMR = b_0 + b_1 \log P + b_2 \log P^* + b_3 \log E + b_4 (GP - GP^*) + u$$

With the presumptive sign as

$$b_1 > 0, b_2 < 0, b_3 < 0, b_4 > 0$$

The estimation of the model on the same data base (Nandi, 1996) is as follows:

$$\log BMR = -1.770 + 0.103 \log P + 0.407 \log P^* + 0.699 \log E + 0.048 (GP - GP^*) + e$$

(–2.33)   (0.34)   (1.30)   (3.117)   (0.26)

Adjusted R^2 = 0.96   SEE = 0.31

D.W. Statistic = 2.05   n = 70

(Figures in parentheses are t-statistics)

The sign of the estimated co-efficient of log P is positive as expected but not significant. The co-efficient of log P^* is positive but significant only at 20 per cent level. The sign of the coefficients of log E is positive and significant contrary to expectation, and estimated value of b_4 is positive but not significant. This shows that the variations of the official exchange rate have significant influence on the changes in black market rate and the elasticity is 0.699. This has important policy implications.

One common element we derive from the estimation of both the models and that is, the elasticity of the relative inflation (GP–GP*) is positive in both the situations. While it is significant in the first case, it is not so in the second. Strictly speaking, this theory gives a poor explanation about the behaviour of the black market exchange rate in India.

7.22 Relative Price Movement and Black Market Exchange Rate

One theoretical implication of the monetarist explanation of the movement of black market exchange rate (read free market rate as usual) is that the latter should reflect truly the movement of the relative price level. The idea is that if the domestic economy suffers from inflation and if the rate of inflation is higher compared to the world standard, the black market rate will be subjected to a high degree of depreciation when official exchange rate is fixed or depreciating slowly than what it should be. We have seen earlier that the depreciation of the official exchange rate more than compensated the relative movement of the price level.

The position regarding the black market exchange rate is as follows. During the period 1954–72, when India followed a fixed exchange rate regime, the movement of the black-market rate more than compensated the movement of relative prices (Nandi, 1996).

The nature of the movement of the black market rate convinces the researcher that it is not always related to the movement of relative inflation. In fact, it has its own dynamic nature and a study of that requires the analysis of the structure of the economy along with its organizational aspects.

Topic for Discussion

Explain the inadequacy of the macroeconomic fundamentals of an economy that leads to the emergence of the black market exchange rate of the domestic currency.

Further Reading

Davidson, P., *Financial Markets, Money and the Real World*, Northampton MA, Egward Elgar, 2002.
Reinhart, C. and K. Rogoff, *This Time is Different: Eight Centuries of Financial Folly*, Princeton, NJ Princeton University Press, 2009.
Wray, L.R., *Understanding Modern Money*, Northampton MA, Edward Elgar, 1998.

8

International Banking System and Global Money Flows

It may be helpful to think of the financial networks that converge on London as a recharged version of the British Empire, held together by modems rather than gunboats and overseen by the mother of all anachronisms, the British political system. As with the original empire, there is a good chance that the colonials will now be left to clean up the mass.
Daniel K. Finn, University of Richmond, *London Review of Books*, July 2009

8.1 Introduction

In any economy, the financial system plays the vital role of providing the requisite liquidity in the system, along with maintaining the balance between the surplus of financial assets in one section with the excess demand for the same in another section. The latter is done through the operation of the money market which provides a channel for the sale and purchase of financial assets for money. It establishes a continuous mechanism through which the holders of short-term cash surpluses meet the holders of short-term cash deficits. This market provides opportunities to meet the temporary cash requirements of firms, financial institutions and governments through the mechanism of granting loans as short as overnight and as long as one-year maturity. The market consists of a vast network of banks, security dealers and brokers. Like other economic agents, banks are both dealers and producers. They are dealers in the sense that they bring together lenders and borrowers, and they are producers as they transform raw base money or cash issued by the government into more convenient cheques or demand deposits, which have greater security than cash, and also they transform short-term deposits into longer-term loans. In the process they do the financial intermediation and maintain liquidity in the system.

In their role as dealers, bankers help to reduce risk in the economy. There are two types of risk: the more familiar default risk and the less familiar withdrawal risk. In reducing these risks, banks make their profits. Let us consider default risk for instance. A would-be supplier of credit, or lender-creditor, wishes to make a loan, in order to earn interest on excess cash-balances. The creditor may search out prospective borrowers from among the public. But the creditor must evaluate the individual risks of default. Further, to the normal costs of acquiring information, there is the higher risk of concentrating the loan with one or a few individuals. Because of this, the creditor would charge a high interest rate on this loan, in order to compensate for the risk. By going to a bank, with a long-standing reputation and a diversified portfolio of assets, the creditor markedly reduces the risk of any default on the loan. The rate of interest should be lower in this case.

8.2 Role of Banks: Intermediation and Interest-Rate Expectations

Banks do financial intermediation as they transform short-term deposits into longer-term assets or loans. Typically, short-term deposits are less risky for depositors, and so they require a lower rate of interest. Longer-term loans, on the other hand, offer borrowers a lower risk of withdrawal, so borrowers will be willing to pay a higher interest rate to the bank. For this reason, banks usually transform short-term liabilities (deposits) into longer-term assets (loans).

The banks generally borrow short to finance long-term assets and use this leverage to earn the spreads which accrue to them as income. They borrow short through a sequence of, say, two one-period deposits, offering rates r1 now and expected rate r2 next period. Again, the banks can borrow long. On the lending side, the bank can offer a two-period loan at an interest rate I, or it can extend a sequence of two one-period loans at interest rates i1 now, and expected interest rate i2 next period.

The time management of both deposits and credit portfolio will depend on the difference between the short-term interest and long-term ones. The business of the banks is the quantum of spreads that is defined as the difference between the average returns from the created assets and average costs of deposits.

8.3 International Banking Operations

International banking operations are essentially to facilitate the movement of goods across the political boundary of countries. Banking system came along with the development of money as an institution. As civilization narrowed down the social distances, and mankind learned about the benefits of exchanging commodities across political boundaries, the present-day international trade developed. The transaction of commodities across countries required financial intermediation at the international level and thus international banking business was born. What started with movement of gold and silver across country-borders became, ultimately, an efficient institution of international transfer of not only yellow metal but the currencies of sovereign countries. In this way, the emergence and growth of international banking is closely interwoven with the development of international trade and international capital movement.

The above gives the general perspective of the growth of international banking. But there are many aspects to this development. From a historical standpoint, the recent growth of international banking can be regarded as a reversion to the situation before World War I when European banks dominated the world capital market. During the period 1940–60, regulatory control on capital flow and convertibility of the currencies reduced the importance of international banking. From 1960 onwards, globalization of capital market started and the emergence of surplus in petro-dollars in the 1970s gave the much needed liquidity to the international banking business. The latter has been characterized by an increasing turnover in international trade, a phenomenal increase in the international flow of capital, and also an increasing flow of funds from the banks to non-bank sectors. To understand the causative factors properly, the literature has attempted to identify the factors supporting the internationalization of banking business. Thus, factors like non-financial multinational corporations, the proximity to customers abroad, the competitive advantage with better information technology, and the benefits due to international diversification have been mentioned in the literature in the contexts when these become relevant (Nandi, 1996). These factors, along with other forces of globalization, have established the huge international financial architecture which rule the international financial market today. The theoretical studies mentioning the factors helping the expansion of international banking are important, but in today's scenario, the major business of international banks is based on international trade, international transfer of capital and money and derivatives.

The literature abounds in the exploration of the causative link in the development of international banking, but not many studies are found testing the theory empirically. There have been several studies which attempt to measure empirically the role of the different factors behind the growth of the US banks in the international fields (Nandi, 1996).

8.4 Determinants of International Banking Activity

In today's world, no country can afford to be autarkic either in the field of international trade or in international banking. But the latter is subject to much more restrictions in almost all the countries compared to the former. What determines the growth of international banks in the domestic banking sector of a particular country? Analytically we can proceed as follows.

Since international trade is closely related to international banking, volume of international trade (imports and exports together) is a determinant of the growth of international banking, and the relationship is direct. Assuming that no specific restrictions are imposed on the operation of foreign banks, so far as their operations are concerned in international banking vis-à-vis the practice of international banking done by home country's banks, it can be said that an increase in the turnover of international trade should have positive impact on the growth of international banking. Alternatively, the ratio of export to gross domestic product can be taken as the explanatory variable. This alternative formulation can be tested.

Foreign direct investment has been cited as an important determinant for the expansion of international banking. In fact, the presence of international banks facilitates the inflow of foreign capital and it is expected that the increase in foreign direct investment should have a positive impact on the growth of international banking.

Banking service as a commodity is supposed to have positive income elasticity. As national income is growing, demand for banking service should increase. To what extent the increase in income will help the growth of foreign banking activity in domestic soil depends on the preference of the consumers and also the participation of the foreign banks in the trade, both domestic and international, of the host country. If we take per capita income as the explanatory variable for the growth of international banking activity, then the growth of per capita income may facilitate the growth of international banking in the host country on the assumption that foreign banks have complementary role in the domestic banking structure.

The growth of domestic deposit should have an influence on the activity of foreign banks. But in many countries, foreign banks are not allowed to create a domestic deposit base, though this facility is crucial for the increase in business. Foreign banks often face difficulties in the creation of domestic deposit base even when it is allowed as the cost of the maintenance of deposits may be too high compared to business. Many foreign branches of Indian banks operating abroad have not created the domestic deposit base for this reason.

An increase in domestic deposit is supposed to have a positive influence on the deposit mobilization of all banks including the foreign banks. That helps the building up of the asset portfolio. To what extent deposit mobilization will affect the activities of foreign banks depends on the competition between domestic banks and the foreign banks in the host country. Foreign banks prefer the creation of a domestic deposit base in the domestic currency as this helps in the expansion of business. Many countries do not allow the foreign banks to create a domestic base, as the latter is perceived to help the foreign bank to mount an attack on the domestic currency.

Again, the exchange rate changes affect the activities of the foreign banks. An increased volatility of the exchange rate increases the risk factor in international banking, and unless this aspect is properly taken care of, this acts negatively so far as the growth of international banking is concerned. We are to understand that the balance sheet of the foreign banks in the head office is in their mother currency. If Indian rupee appreciates vis-à-vis their mother currency, that would show good results in their foreign operations.

An index of activity of foreign banks may be their aggregate asset structure, though the number of branches may be another indicator. Some studies take both. We find that the expansion of international banking in a country depends on several factors like the importance of trade in GDP, the dynamism of the exchange rates, the deposit base and some others as explained in earlier paragraphs. The literature also examines the quantitative strength of different variables using an econometric model (Nandi, 1996). We will pursue here another type of international banking activity which is conducted in offshore areas and specially, tax-haven locations.

8.5 Offshore Banking and Tax-Haven Centres

Offshore banking initially started in offshore regions but in its current avatar, it has nothing to do with its geographical indications. It is more as a type of banking sharply different from the traditional type, and it is operational even from some important centres like New York and London, though jurisdiction varies in offshore operations. Also, it is a fact that major businesses in offshore type of banking are done from offshore areas like Hong Kong, Singapore, Bahamas, etc. Offshore banking comes under the category of external and Eurocurrency banking when we find currency $\neq$ location of the bank $\neq$ residence of the borrower/depositor.

This situation characterizes the international banking practice when an Indian citizen deals with a Korean one in a bank at Hong Kong. Offshore banking is conducted out of primary financial centres such as London, New York, Chicago, Tokyo, and also secondary ones such as those in the Caribbean and the Asia-Pacific region. The primary financial centres benefit from a strong industrial base on which the money requirements of the customers depends, while the secondary sectors derive their importance from the proximity of the economies, which are either the source of large financial resources or have substantial independent requirements for financial services.

8.6 Why Offshore Financial Centres are a Preferred Destination

In some situations, very small nations with good infrastructures and strategic locations create offshore financial centres (OFC), as a matter of policy, to attract foreign capital so as to invest the same for the growth of domestic economy. These countries, hardly known outside the region, have escaped the agony of poverty through this process of foreign capital investment.

During the last two decades, many OFCs have been created as part of the developing countries' efforts, to initiate economic growth in their small domestic markets through the provisions of international financial services. These OFCs are classified along a spectrum of 'notional' OFC to 'functional' OFCs. While the former provide minimal financial services, hardly more than simply being a jurisdiction in which *nameplate operation* of the companies can be established, the latter provide a wide range of value-added services. Notional OFCs are costless to establish, and for that competition among tiny states is tough, and it contributes little to the economic development of the region.

The functional OFCs require elaborate infrastructure like communication, airport, labour force, and all these call for large investment. As a result, the region experiences over-all economic growth and the 'real' economies surrounding the region are benefited through backward and forward linkages.

The OFCs, with support from the local government, offer a large number of services to the potential investors in their banking system and these are:
(1) excellent communication links with the outside world
(2) absence of any tax burden (or even when tax exists, it is bare minimum)
(3) non-existence of any treaty to exchange tax information with other countries
(4) predominant use of major world currencies
(5) no exchange control
(6) the facility to disguise the ownership of corporate vehicles through the use of nominee directors and bearer shares
(7) no reporting requirements for companies like annual reports
(8) no system of supervision of companies such as Annual General Meetings.
(9) maintenance of secrecy and confidentiality

The list is long and the main idea is to give all facilities to the foreign investors so that the OFC can earn money by selling confidentiality.

A small sub-category of offshore banks exists in the tax-haven areas like Cayman Island, Nassau, Bahamas, Bahrain, Monaco, Andorra, etc. All offshore centres have the common denominators of customer confidentiality, very low taxes on offshore business and an absence of foreign exchange control. However, the activities in the centres vary depending on location, convenience to other financial markets, legal and accounting matters, and communications. Some of the specialized services are the following: company formation and management, administrative services for 'paper' branch and subsidiary banks, portfolio management for trusts, Euro-bond underwriting and placement, incorporation and management of captive insurance companies, ship registration, storage and trans-shipment of merchandise, etc. Thus, in today's world of globalization, the offshore centres have assumed great significance.

One should be clear about the difference between a tax haven and offshore centres. A tax haven is a jurisdiction with a high level of banking and commercial secrecy through which businesses or individuals can hold assets and earnings, and move the same to other places and different jurisdictions with little or no tax impact. While many offshore financial centres are tax havens, many are not. These two are different and these should not be confused. Perhaps the governments in the countries creating the offshore financial centres would like to state that these centres operate in tax-efficient zones and these are created to derive benefits of large-scale movement of finance capital.

Capital flight and so-called money laundering are two phenomena from which the developing countries suffer most. The offshore financial centres in tax-haven regions are often the conduit for large-scale transfer of funds. The mechanism of transfer and volumes have been studied in the literature (Nandi, 1999).

8.7 Panama: An Offshore Centre

Panama is an independent republic with no exchange control and very liberal tax laws. It is bilingual, as both English and Spanish languages are used here. It has a very good infrastructure both in air transport and telecommunications. There are a large number of local and foreign financial institutions, and also a large spectrum of legal and accounting expertise. The banking secrecy is protected by various laws. There is no tax on offshore business and its legal system is well established. Panama has a long tradition in commercial banking and offshore business. The legal system is liberal in the incorporation of companies, Eurocurrency business, banking secrecy, and private banking. The huge amount of capital deposited in the banks here are often used in the domestic investment. Also the fees generated in the business and the small level of taxes facilitate the generation of income and employment. Of course, a large amount of cash of doubtful origin pass through the OFCs like Panama, and this is part of international money-laundering nexus.

8.8 The Isle of Man: Offshore Financial Centre

The Isle of Man (IM) is outside the sovereign jurisdiction of United Kingdom. It is in the centre of Irish Sea and 80 miles away from Manchester. This tiny territory has its own government for the last 1,200 years, and it has obtained the status of an offshore centre. This island takes pride in its numerous attractions along with its ability of providing a safe, tax-free environment for the investors. The well-established company laws of the island allow a variety of corporate vehicles including companies limited by guarantee and hybrid companies, and also companies limited by share capital.

Companies that are not owned by the residents of the IM and those that conduct their business completely outside the IM, even if they may have an office there, are granted exemption from all IM income taxes. Non-resident companies from other jurisdictions like Panama or Irish non-resident can maintain their base at IM and can apply for IM residency under Part F of Isle of Man Companies Act, and they are eligible for income tax exemption. The ownership of the companies need not be a matter of public record, and this way complete secrecy can be maintained. The companies can carry on lawful business in any country and in any currency that they desire according to their convenience.

The island has an excellent financial infrastructure, and most banks, accountants, and insurance companies are represented there. For example, Ulster Bank (Isle of Man) Limited is a wholly-owned subsidiary of Ulster Bank Limited, and the latter is a member of Nat West Group, which is one of the world's largest banking organizations. Under the rule of the Financial Supervision Commission responsible for the Depositors' Compensation Scheme, deposits are protected up to 75 per cent of the first GBP 20,000 per depositor. The investors are offered several options regarding the opening of account, the variations in minimum amount, minimum withdrawal and interest rate structure. For example, an investor can keep money in fixed deposits, the time may vary from one week to five years at an interest rate which is known in the beginning.

The list is not exhaustive, and some centres within well-established countries are providing the same level of services. Some OFCs are now targets of Russia's organized crime like Nauru, and the Russian syndicate has evolved an ingenious way of using front organizations to cover Russian connections. The crime branches of many countries in OECD group are trying to identify the Russian connections because of their potential of wrong-doing. The role of these OFCs in the illegal transfer of money across the globe has been explained in detail in Chapter 14 where money laundering has been explained.

8.9 The Fixed Coefficient Model of the Banking System

The economic position of the banks in the society and their roles in shaping the monetary policy can better be understood with the help of a model. An early model of the banking system, based on a fixed coefficient approach, explains how banks engage in monetary expansion. The model rests on three equations:

$$R = r D \qquad \text{Equation (8.1a)}$$
$$C = k D \qquad \text{Equation (8.1b)}$$
$$MB = R + C \qquad \text{Equation (8.1c)}$$

where 'R' represents the reserves of the banking system, 'C' the currency in circulation, 'D' demand deposits, and MB, monetary base, equal to the sum of reserves and currency in circulation. The coefficient 'r' represents the required reserve ratio of bank, with respect to deposits, while 'k' is the ratio of cash to deposits, a ratio determined more by the state of communications and financial technology, as well as custom. For example, the less financially developed an economy is, the greater the need for cash for ordinary payments rather than cheques. Substituting the reserve and cash equations in the monetary base definition, one can obtain the following deposit multiplier:

$$MB = rD + kD$$

And from this we get

$$\Delta D/\Delta MB = 1/(r + k) \qquad \text{Equation (8.2)}$$

With a required reserve ratio of 0.15 and a cash/deposit ratio of .05, for example, the deposit multiplier is 1/.20, or 5. For every one dollar of monetary base that the government injects into the economy, deposits expand by a factor of five. This model shows the role that the banking system plays in the money supply process. The government can reduce the money supply either by reducing monetary base, or by changing reserve requirement, since a higher required reserve ratio r will lower the multiplier, and reduce the amount of deposits offered by the banking system.

There is no role of interest rate in the model. Particularly deposit and lending rates can be accommodated in the model as these are important in the functioning of the banking system.

In an expanded model, let us assume that the reserve ratio would depend on the lending rates i, and the discount rate idisc, the rate at which banks can borrow to supplement reserves. Thus the interest rate r would become a function like the following:

$$R = r(i, idisc), \text{ with } r1 < 0, \quad r2 > 0 \qquad \text{Equation (8.3)}$$

The first negativity implies that higher lending rates would lead banks to keep less reserves. Again, the second positive sign implies that higher discount rates would force banks to hold more reserves so they would not have to borrow from the central bank.

Similarly, the cash–deposit ratio k would depend on the deposit rate r, or we can write,

$$k = k(r), \text{ with } k' < 0, \qquad \text{Equation (8.4)}$$

since higher deposit rates would provide incentives to put more cash in the banking system.

8.10 The Eurodollar System

The Eurodollar system evolved through a complex process of history. Some countries in East Europe preferred to deposit dollars in non-American banks in Europe. Also some American banks were eager to do banking outside the legal arms of the Federal Reserve of the United States. Again, there is a surplus of dollar depositors relative to dollar borrowers in the United States, and the opposite has been the case in Europe with a surplus of dollar borrowers, relative to dollar depositors.

Eurodollar system developed as an inter-bank market. Given the assumptions of regional imbalances in dollar deposits, differences in legislative requirements, differences in transactions costs, it made sense for US banks to shuffle funds from surplus US banks to London branch banks, for later distribution to European banks. In the process the Eurodollar system grew, in its early development, from the mid-1960s up through the early 1970s, as an inter-bank market for dollars. The interest rate in the Eurodollar markets is known as the LIBOR rate or London Inter-bank Offered Rate.

Since ruble was not fully convertible, the Russians wanted to store the proceeds of this gold sale in a hard currency. However, Russia could hardly deposit the money in Chase Manhattan for fear of siege. The London banks accommodated the Russians, and started taking deposits, and making loans in dollars. It is important to see the Eurodollar bank facilitating the development of the dollar as the vehicle currency or key currency, in world business. Bilateral payment imbalances were settled in dollars, or in gold, under the Bretton Woods fixed exchange rate system. Again, multinational firms kept their consolidated accounts, across several countries, in dollars. There were obvious savings, in terms of information and accounting costs, in doing business in dollars.

The American banks doing the Eurodollar business outside of the jurisdiction of the Federal Reserve System, could offer deposit rates that were not regulated at zero (the famous Regulation Q), and could charge borrowers rates without ceilings set by state usury laws in the United States. The result was that borrowing and lending in dollars in the Eurodollar markets was much more a 'market-oriented phenomena', or a much less distorted market, compared to the internal US market.

The market grew and stabilized through the mid-1970s. Many thought that the Eurodollar market had peaked. Then came the Organization of Petroleum Exporting Countries (OPEC) crisis and that paved the way for rapid expansion of the Eurodollar markets.

8.11 Capital Inflows and Financial Opening

In Dornbusch model, under a flexible exchange rate system, a capital inflow will lead to a nominal appreciation of the exchange rate, and in the short run, a real appreciation. We see from the Mundell–Fleming model that a capital inflow will lead to an increase in reserves and an increase in the money stock. This will lead to a drop in interest rates, and lead either to inflationary pressures, or to an ensuing capital outflow. However, the inflationary pressures are hard to avoid in a fixed exchange rate system if the capital inflows are sustained and exogenous. Then some other measures become necessary.

If there is a sudden wave of massive capital inflows, it creates danger in the form of either a strong exchange rate appreciation, or a strong inflationary pressure in a fixed exchange rate system. The latter creates real exchange rate problems, and the ensuing speculation against the currency for a probable devaluation. Capital inflows may pose acute challenges for countries beginning, or in the midst of a stabilization effort.

8.12 Asian and Latin American Experiences of 1990s

There had been a marked pattern in the capital inflows to Asia and Latin America in the 1990s with some regular features: a marked increase in international reserves in the recipient countries and a surge in stock prices. However, there is one important difference between Asia and Latin America: in Latin America, the inflows have been accompanied by a real exchange rate appreciation, while in Asia, an appreciation has been less common.

In Asia, before July 1997, the capital inflows have gone hand-in-hand with large increases in investment as a percentage of GDP, usually an increase of 3 percentage points or more.

In Latin America, by contrast, the inflows have been associated with a decline in private saving. Another key difference is sterilization. Singapore was probably the most successful in limiting the expansion of credit and monetary aggregates. The literature shows that Asian countries could use foreign capital more efficiently compared to Latin America. Also, the latter experienced a decline in the savings–GDP ratio.

Capital inflow into the newly emerging market economies has another implication when the latter go for financial opening. Recent research has revealed that financial sector reforms and opening that sector to international competition has increased the risk of financial crisis in such countries. But, again, the financial sector opening has the potential of higher long-term growth of GDP. Clearly there is a trade-off between short-term crisis and higher long-term growth. In this perspective, the countries should undertake financial sector reforms with caution. The monetary policy has an important role in making the inflow of capital smooth and building up a hedge at macro level, in the face of potential fragility of the financial system.

8.13 Dollarization

Dollarization is a process in which a country adopts the currency of the US — the USD — as its official currency, which is used as the medium of exchange[1]. In a fully dollarized economy, the country's national currency ceases to exist, and the USD is made the only medium of exchange, store of value and the unit of account. Today Panama (since 2002), Ecuador (since 2001), and El Salvador (since 2001) are full dollarized economies in the world. A country with full dollarization has eliminated the monetary policy-making role of its central bank. Without a national currency to manage, the country's monetary policy is placed in the hands of the Federal Reserve in the US.

Partial dollarization occurs when USD circulates alongside a country's national currency. In this arrangement, the domestic currency continues to serve, to a great extent, as the medium of exchange, store of value, and unit of account. Partial dollarization exists in many countries in the world, notably in Latin America and former communist countries (the so-called CIS countries).

What Goes Wrong with Domestic Currency

A country's domestic currency is issued by its central bank, and domestic currency in circulation is considered as the liability of the central bank so much so that it should remain ready to replace the domestic currency by asset to its citizens on demand. In fact, several policies in monetary field followed by the central bank are inter-related and these are:

(1) quantum of domestic currency in circulation,
(2) policy regarding the rate of inflation in domestic economy,
(3) the exchange rate of the domestic currency vis-à-vis foreign currency.

---

[1] The term 'dollarization' is not only used as using the USD as the official currency, but using any foreign currency, e.g., euro, British pound etc, as the official currency of the country.

Since domestic currency issued by the central bank is the liability of the latter, every central bank maintains some reserve in the form of gold and foreign exchange (generally USD) as the backing of the domestic currency in circulation. In today's world, hardly any country maintains 100 per cent reserve, but the quantum of reserve determines the perception of the citizens regarding the intrinsic value of the domestic currency. A currency with partial domestic reserve is called fiat money. Here is the problem that arises for many countries who print money without any reserve, that leads to runaway inflation in the economy. This situation is ideal for citizens losing faith in the credibility of the domestic currency and consequently, they switch to a stable foreign currency (generally USD, or, Euro). This is the genesis of dollarization in many countries.

The list of countries with partial dollarization (residents holding a significant share of their assets in the form of foreign currency denominated assets) is rather long. This is reflected in the ratio of foreign currency deposits to broad money of the country. The names are in Table 8.1.

Table 8.1 *Reported Ratios of Foreign Currency Deposits (FCD) to Broad Money with IMF Arrangement*

Country	1991	1995
Argentina	35.1	43.9
Bolivia	76.8	82.3
Costa Rica	37.7	31.0
Guinea-Bissau	34.7	31.2
Lao People's Democratic Republic	39.4	35.6
Mozambique	11.8	32.6
Nicaragua	28.7	54.5
Peru	59.9	64.0
Turkey	29.7	46.1
Uruguay	78.5	76.1
Bulgaria	33.4	28.4
Egypt	50.7	25.1
Hungary	16.5	26.6
Jordan	13.0	15.2
Pakistan	8.9	13.6
Poland	24.7	20.4
Greece	13.2	21.6
United Kingdom	7.7	15.4

Source: IMF, Monetary Policy in Dollarized Economies, Occasional Paper # 171, 1999.

Table 8.1 shows that a large number of countries have significant percentages of dollarization and that shows the demand for the USD in these countries, as people substitute a percentage of their cash holding in USD.

One reason for the large currency substitution in countries is a very high rate of inflation in these countries that erodes the confidence of citizens in domestic currency. Thus inflation rates in Argentina were 88.75 per cent during 1986 and 1990. For the same period, the situation of some other countries was like this: Bolivia (58.45), Mexico (17.45), Peru (110.29), Uruguay (16.16). In fact, the decline of inflation followed with dollarization as seen in the following Table 8.2.

Table 8.2 *Inflation and Dollarization Rates in Selected Countries*

Country	Period	Inflation Rate	Dollarization Ratio
Argentina	1986–90	88.75	78.37
	1991–95	5.20	71.65
Bolivia	1985–1989	58.45	88.02
	1990–95	2.94	90.81
Mexico	1983–87	17.45	44.62
	1988–95	5.95	33.30
Peru	1986–90	110.29	84.79
	1991–95	11.24	80.48
Uruguay	1986–90	16.16	90.99
	1991–95	11.58	86.33
Hungary	1988–92	5.67	23.96
	1993–95	5.44	39.95

Source: Ize and Yeyati, 2003.

8.14 Currency Board and Dollarization: A Comparison

Currency Board (CB) is the nearest competitor of the full dollarization system. Under Currency Board system (CBS), the monetary authority commits to trade foreign exchange for domestic currency at a fixed rate on demand. Through this mechanism, the central bank can increase the base money supply and this is the only mechanism. There is no extension of domestic credit to the government or banks. So, the domestic currency is fully backed by a corresponding stock of foreign exchange, and the domestic currency remains fully convertible.

Under CBS, the monetary authority loses much of the independence of monetary policy, but it can capture the seigniorage of issuing the domestic currency. At this stage, a comparison with the dollarization is important. Dollarization means the country loses the seigniorage, and a more important fact is that it would be permanent.

The loss of seigniorage is sometimes significant. One estimate puts the domestic currency in circulation in Argentina as equivalent to USD 15 billion and the annual increase in demand for currency is USD 1 billion (at a rate of 0.3 per cent of GDP). The foregone interest earning on the stock of money is estimated to be USD 0.7 billion, and that is about 0.2 per cent of GDP of Argentina.

What are the benefits of dollarization? It is an extreme step for a country suffering from chronic instability in currency, and this saves the economy from currency instability. It is argued also that it helps integration to the economies of the USD area and Europe. We will see more of it at the end of this section.

8.15 Dollarization and the Function of Money

Non-US residents having dollars in their portfolio is not really dollarization. These dollars simply serve as a store of value, much like gold. Neither does it mean that a country's prices are quoted in dollars, especially in times of high inflation. It occurs when US currency becomes a medium of exchange. This is the decisive function of money. Dollars can serve as a parallel medium of exchange, or they can serve as the only medium of exchange.

It is easy to understand why dollars may become a parallel currency in times of high and unstable inflation rates. Domestic residents avoid the inflation tax on their domestic money holdings, and at the same time, have the convenience of using dollars as a medium of exchange.

Of course, it is a flight from the domestic money. But it also reduces the inflation tax base of the domestic monetary authority. If the need for inflation tax revenue does not abate, then a higher inflation rate will be needed to wring out the same inflation tax revenue, from the diminished tax base.

This problem, of forcing a higher inflation tax on those who are unable to acquire dollars, has regressive distributional effects. While the upper and upper-middle classes acquire dollars, and protect themselves from the inflation tax, the middle and poorer classes get stuck with an increasing share of the inflation tax burden. Inflation becomes decidedly regressive once dollarization takes place, and ultimately can lead to increased social and political instability.

8.16 Dollar Deposits in Foreign Banks

In several countries in Latin America, dollar deposits were permitted in domestic banks. The use of dollar deposits in foreign banks is similar to the Eurodollar phenomenon. The governments recognize that their citizens keep dollars as a store of value, and often use dollars as a medium of exchange. So instead of trying to de-dollarize, and forcing these citizens to put the deposits in Miami banks, why not simply permit dollar deposits in domestic banks? The country would avoid capital flight (legal or illegal), the banks would get the additional business, and finally, the government would gain additional reserves, which could be invested in US Treasury bills, and thus produce much needed revenue for the government.

8.17 Seigniorage and Dollarization: Multiple Equilibrium Points

Mode of financing the annual budget is the prime areas of fiscal policies and the government of any country is reluctant to sacrifice that power. In many developing countries, the government tries to part-finance the budget deficit by printing money. This is done by rationalization taking recourse to economic theories one way or the other. The government budget deficit, financed by money creation, is written as follows:

$$g - t = \Delta M/P = (\Delta M/M)(M/P) \quad \text{Equation (8.5)}$$
$$g - t = \Pi (M/P), \text{ when } \Pi = \Delta M/M \quad \text{Equation (8.5a)}$$

where 'g' represents real government spending, 't' real non-inflation tax revenue, 'M' the money supply, 'P' the price level, 'Δ' the first difference operator, 'π' the long-run inflation rate, equal to the rate of monetary growth, $\Delta M/M$. This second relation expresses the deficit as a tax on real balances held by the public, with $(g - t)$ equal to $\pi (M/P)$. The term 'π' (M/P) thus expresses the inflation tax needs of the government, for financing its deficit. The demand for money, especially during times of high and unstable inflation rates, is simply a function of the long-run inflation rates.

Phillip Cagan introduced the following non-linear exponential form, linear in logarithms, in his influential study of hyperinflation:

$$M/P = A \exp(-\eta)$$
$$\log M - \log P = \log A - \eta$$

Or, $\quad\quad\quad\quad m - p = a - \eta \quad\quad\quad\quad$ Equation (8.6)

The deficit or inflation tax need of the government is a straight line, whatever the inflation rate; the government needs fixed revenue from inflation, $\pi (M/P)$. The vertical line is thus a demand for seigniorage or tax revenue from inflation. The non-linear curve captures the demand for money effect on the private-sector supply of inflation tax revenue to the government. At low rates of inflation, inflation tax revenue increases, but at a certain point, when the parabola bends, higher inflation actually decreases the demand for money to such an extent, that the inflation tax revenue falls. As Phillip Cagan notes: 'The desire to subdue inflation is obviously not enough and must be confirmed by performance. The conclusion appears inescapable, therefore, that the reduction of inflation requires the maintenance of slack demand' (Cagan, 1979, 249).

The implication of this analysis is that for a given deficit of the government, and a given deficit-financing need for inflation tax revenue, there can be two equilibrium inflation rates, which equate the supply and demand for inflation-tax revenue. As seen in the diagram, at B, the low-inflation equilibrium, a given deficit can be financed with a relatively high demand for domestic money and a relatively low inflation rate. However, at A, the high inflation trap, the same deficit is financed under conditions of a low demand for domestic money and a relatively high inflation rate.

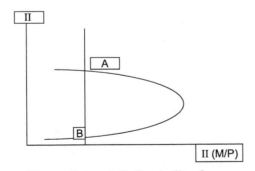

Figure 8.1: *Inflation Laffer Curve*

The lesson from this analysis is that dollarization, by decreasing the demand for domestic money, can lead to a jump in the equilibrium inflation rate from B to A. Fiscal deficits do not have to change — they can actually fall somewhat — but inflation rates can explode, when dollarization triggers a flight from domestic money.

Such inflationary explosions have been rather common in Argentina and Brazil, before their last stabilization plans. This analysis shows quite clearly that a continuing fiscal deficit, however moderate, can lead to both inflation and inflationary instability, once dollarization takes hold.

Of course, once a country is at the high-inflation equilibrium, there is no reason why it cannot fall back to the low-inflation equilibrium, if there is a positive shift in demand for domestic money. This is what happened in Ecuador in the early 1980s, with its securitizations plan.

Ecuador prospered during the oil boom years. As tax and oil revenues increased, so did social expenditures. Many dollar-denominated debts were contracted by the private sector during this time. After the drop in oil prices, as one can imagine, tax revenues fell, but social expenditures remained high. As expected, the deficit increased. Dollarization set in, and inflation jumped to over 80 per cent annually.

8.18 Cost of Complete Dollarization

In many Latin American countries, USD is used as medium of exchange alongside the domestic currency. For example, it is legal in Mexico to have and use USD as medium of exchange along with peso. This is also a form of dollarization, but it is incomplete dollarization. Complete dollarization happens when the country abandons the use of its own currency issue, except perhaps for small coins, and uses dollars as the media of exchange. This is what Panama has done, and what Liberia did for several decades.

The issue of complete dollarization is akin to the issue of the euro as the medium of exchange for members of the European Monetary System. The argument for a country giving up its own currency, in favour of a currency beyond its direct control, is that it imposes a harder budget constraint on the fiscal authority. The result is that the fiscal authority no longer has the option of printing money to finance its deficits. It must either tax or borrow in the bond market. Long-awaited tax and expenditure reform may finally come when a country has no other option other than facing the discipline of international bond markets.

The problems of dollarization are many. How can a country get the dollars to serve as the currency and monetary base? The only way, of course, is to run a surplus with the US. This once-over cost, a trade surplus equivalent of about 5 per cent of GDP, is a high price to pay for a currency system.

The second cost is a continuing cost. What if the US runs an inflation of 5 per cent, or 10 per cent? By adopting the currency of the US as legal tender, and rejecting any sort of domestic inflation tax, the citizens of this country, in effect, agree to pay an inflation tax to the United States government. Thus, complete dollarization appears to be a very drastic policy move for a country in need of fiscal discipline.

8.19 Dollarization in Latin America

In Latin America, several countries have been dollarized officially. Ecuador was dollarized in September 2000, and El Salvador in January 2001. Unofficial or partial dollarization is widespread in Latin America; it refers to a process when individuals substitute domestic money with USD in order to conduct transactions, and also to protect the intrinsic value of their savings by keeping money in dollar deposits. The degree of dollarization in these countries is calculated by taking bank deposits in foreign currency as a percentage of total liquidity. Table 8.3 shows this.

Table 8.3 *Deposits in Foreign Currency as a Percentage of Money Supply*

Country	1990	1995	2001
Argentina	33.7	45.1	62.8
Bolivia	66.2	67.3	84.8
Honduras	1.4	17.0	27.6
Mexico	10.0	17.5	5.5
Nicaragua	27.3	57.6	70.4
Peru	38.6	57.1	55.0
Uruguay	80.1	73.7	82.2

Source: *Federal Reserve Bank of Atlanta Economic Review*, and IMF reports

We have discussed different aspects of dollarization in the previous paragraphs. A dollarized economy will become dependent on a continuous flow of international reserve to maintain liquidity and thus the condition of international markets become important. Such an economy should be competitive internationally so that it can attract capital flows either as foreign investment or net borrowing. All these depend on how successfully the government can implement the fiscal discipline and maintain it.

8.20 Corruption and Open Economy Implications: The Developing Country Perspective

Money Laundering

In today's world of integrated financial system, money laundering (ML) has emerged as a menace to the policy makers. When it is linked to the unofficial black economy of many developing countries, the problem becomes very complicated.

ML, in general, is the disguising or concealing of illicit income in order to make it appear legitimate. The criminal anti-money laundering law of countries generally encompasses the money generated from numerous different crimes — e.g., drug trafficking, murder for hire, racketeering, prostitution, and embezzlement. There are many ways ML is perpetuated in different countries and we can describe some of these.

Method 1: How it works in a typical Latin American environment:
(1) Sell cocaine and get a million dollars.
(2) Take the million in cash to the Cayman Islands.
(3) Buy a legitimate corporation from a bank, complete with a board of directors.
(4) Open a bank account in the corporation's name and deposit the rest of the money. Enjoy the islands, get some sun, and then go home.
(5) When you get home, borrow $200,000 from the Cayman corporation's account and have it delivered via wire transfer.
(6) Open a restaurant.
(7) Deposit proceeds from the ongoing drug business along with proceeds from the restaurant every month into a legitimate bank account. Don't add too much illegal money, just enough to make it look as though your restaurant is doing a good, healthy business.
(8) Pay all of your taxes on the restaurant deposits, so the tax authorities do not start an investigation.

As stated above, the ML method is diverse and it exploits the legal system of the particular country and region. Another example of ML is the following.

Method 2: A second mode of operation:
(1) Open a Swiss bank account and routinely deposit receipts from illegal gambling operation by regular conversion of Indian rupees into USDs through hawala operations.
(2) Buy a string of carwashes in India worth ₹ 50 million.
(3) Put ₹ 10,00,000 in legitimate cash as a down payment and get a ₹ 25 million mortgage from a legitimate financial institution in India.
(4) 'Borrow' the other ₹ 24 million from the Swiss account in equivalent USDs. When you pay interest on this 'loan' you are really paying it to yourself. Much of this interest, since it is mortgage interest, is tax-deductible. Your tax refund comes from IT authorities.
(5) Once you have paid yourself back in the Swiss account, you can borrow from that account again and again and again[2].

Macroeconomic Effects of Money Laundering

The effects of ML on the health of the macroeconomy are negative. Such activities damage the financial sector institutions that are critical to economic growth. That also diverts resources and encourages crime and corruption. It further distorts the external sector of the economy, international trade, and capital flows, to the detriment of the long-term economic development.

Recent literature shows that strong financial institutions like banks, non-bank financial institutions, and capital markets are critical to economic growth. These institutions allow for the concentration of capital resources from domestic savings, and efficient allocation of such resources to investment projects facilitate the generation of sustained economic development. ML impairs the development of these institutions in two ways.

First, ML erodes the credibility of the financial institutions, as within these institutions, there is always a correlation between ML and fraudulent activities undertaken by employees. At a higher level of ML activities, entire financial institutions of the developing countries are

---
[2] Partly based on http://home.earthlink.net/~astrology/launder.htm

vulnerable to corruption by criminal elements as they try to gain further influence over their ML channels.

Second, customer trust is fundamental to the growth of financial institutions in a developing country. But the perceived risk to depositors and investors from institutional fraud and corruption is an obstacle to the growth of such trust (Fiorentini and Peltman, 1997; Quirk, 1997).

Sustained ML can also damage the economy through trade and international capital flows. The problem of illicit capital flight from the developing countries is generally facilitated by domestic financial institutions as well as their foreign counterparts ranging from offshore financial centres to major banks with branches in major financial centres of the world like London and New York. The illicit flight of capital from the capital-poor developing countries impairs the growth process of such economies. This also causes significant distortions in the country's exports and imports.

8.21 International Gold Market Connections

Many experts who regularly monitor international funds flow are of the opinion that gold transactions from the established markets of the world are an integral aspect of an ML scheme. The scheme operates in the following manner. Gold is purchased with the help of funds which are of illicit origin. It is then exported to another location where it is converted into cash by sale, and the proceeds are legitimized. If reporting requirements are there for the purchase of gold, it is circumvented by structuring the purchases to amounts which are below the reporting threshold.

Certain centres in the world are famous for gold markets and these are: Cordoba in Spain, Vicenza in Italy, Dubai in UAE, Paris region and Marseilles in France, and some offshore centres. In these areas, gold is often purchased by cash and mostly in non-indigenous currencies or USD. The yellow metal serves as both a commodity and a medium of exchange in the process of ML conducted between Latin America, the US, Europe, and South Asia. One such cycle is like this: Gold bullion enters into Italy via the Swiss brokers. This is converted into jewellery which is shipped to Latin America. This jewellery is then sold in the black market using the *black market exchange rate* of peso. This cycle is replicated elsewhere where restrictions prevail on the purchase of gold, and the exchange rate of the domestic currency is pegged making it off the equilibrium rate.

Hawala Transaction and Gold

Money laundering through the use of gold as a medium of exchange has another connection and it is the hawala or hundi, which is an alternative remittance system. The word 'hundi' means bill of exchange, and 'hawala' means trust. This is an alternative remittance system that facilitates the transfer of funds without the physical movement of it. People who use hawala as a means of fund transfer believe that it is cost-effective and less bureaucratic compared to the transfer of funds through the banking system. Hawala originated in South Asia (India is a prominent destination) and it is built on trust and close business contacts, but now this system is used in other parts of the globe as an alternative system of remittance.

A hawala broker based in one country facilitates the transfer of funds by receiving money in local currency. He then makes contact with another hawala broker (often his own men in the network) in another country and instructs him to make the necessary payments to the beneficiary in that local currency. The account is settled by sending postal money order or some other financial instrument to a gold house in the Persian Gulf region by the first broker. The gold house then effects payments to the second country hawala broker by sending gold, which is converted to cash in the South Asian country for making the payments. Gold may enter as a legal import item or in an illegal way.

In the ML associated with the hawala system, gold often plays the role of primary medium of exchange in some transactions, and it is for two reasons. First, gold enjoys a special place in the religion and culture of the region. Gold is not only a precious metal, it is a symbol of aesthetics and purity in religious and social rituals in the Indian sub-continent and South Asia. The second reason is purely economic, and it is that the citizens in many countries in this region have little trust in their local currencies, and gold is used as a hedge against inflation. In such a scenario, gold is the primary means of protecting the intrinsic value of wealth.

Money Laundering: Other Forms

Apart from the traditional form of laundering money, some other kinds of international crime are also seen among the activities like counterfeiting of currencies and other monetary instruments, the buying of banks by suspected criminal groups, cyber hacking, and direct access and pass-through banking. There is continuing concern as financial crimes and ML are taking place with varying degrees of intensity in more than 120 jurisdictions according to one international survey (USA-based), and many governments have not declared all forms of money laundering as criminal activities.

International Accords

There have been concerted efforts by many governments to fight the ML menace for the last two decades. The main international agreements addressing ML are the United Nations Vienna Convention against Illicit Traffic in Narcotic Drugs and Psychotropic Substances (the Vienna Convention), and the 1990 Council of Europe Convention on Laundering, Search, Seizure, and Confiscation of the Proceeds of Crime.

The Basel Committee on Banking Supervision, the European Union, and the International Organization of Securities Commissions (IOSCO) are busy to frame guidelines towards the role of financial institutions regarding the detection and prevention of ML.

The Vienna Convention adopted in December 1988, prepared the groundwork for the efforts to combat money laundering, by creating the rules obligatory for the member states (signatory) to make ML from drug trafficking a criminal offence. The convention promotes international cooperation in investigations and makes the extradition of the accused in money laundering case easy. It also establishes the principle that domestic bank secrecy provisions should not interfere with international criminal investigations. Thus, the banks in the countries that are signatory to the Convention cannot withhold important information regarding their client, if so desired by the investigating authority.

The 1990 Council of Europe Convention (CEC) was adopted in November 1990, and it establishes a common definition of ML and a common policy and measure to fight it. The convention lays down the principle for international cooperation among the signatory states, and some of them are outside the Council of Europe. However, the scope of the treaty may go well beyond just the money that comes from drug trafficking.

The G-10's Basel Committee on Banking Supervision issued a 'statement of principles' in December 1988, and with this principle the international banks of member states are expected to comply. The principles deal with the identification of the customers, avoiding suspicious transactions, and the cooperation with the investigation agencies. The committee related the transparency in operations of the member banks to their credibility to the depositors, which broadly guarantees the stability of the financial system.

The Council of the European Communities adopted a directive in June 1991 on the 'Prevention of the Use of the Financial System for the Purpose of Money Laundering'. There has been measures for the liberalization of capital movements and cross-border financial movements which created opportunities for ML and the Directive is aimed at curbing this type of crime. The member states are also obligated to enact laws for the financial institutions so that the latter conform to the rules for the prevention of ML.

The International Organization of Securities Commissions adopted a Report in October 1992, which encourages its members to take necessary steps in the form of making legislation to combat ML in securities and futures markets. A Working Group of IOSCO Consultative Committee is set up to collect information on ML, and exchanges that among the members to combat the crime.

The Egmont Group

In the year 1995, a group of Financial Intelligence Units (FIUs) met at the Egmont Arenberg Palace in Brussels in Belgium and decided to establish an informal group whose goal would be to facilitate international cooperation. Now known as Egmont Group, these FIUs meet regularly to find ways to cooperate, especially in the area of the exchange of information on international financial transfers as well as training and sharing of expertise. Any FIU that considers complying with the criteria of the Egmont Group of being a central and national agency responsible for receiving, analyzing, and disseminating to the competent authorities, disclosure of financial information, is eligible to apply to become a member of the Egmont Group.

The Secretariat was established in July 2007 and it is based in Toronto, Canada. It provides administrative and other support to the overall activities of the Heads of FIUs, the Egmont Committee, and the Working Groups. The Secretariat is headed by the Executive Secretary of the Egmont Group. The Egmont Committee serves as the consultation and coordination mechanism for the Heads of FIUs and the Working Groups. Its primary function includes assisting the Egmont Group in a range of activities, from internal coordination and administration, to representation at other international forums.

The Asia-Pacific Group

The Asia-Pacific Group (APG) on money laundering was officially established as an autonomous regional anti-money laundering body in February 1997, at the Fourth Asia-Pacific Money Laundering Symposium in Bangkok, Thailand. The purpose of APG is to facilitate the adoption, implementation, and enforcement of internationally accepted anti-money laundering and anti-terrorist financing standards set out in the recommendations of the Financial Action Task Force (FATF). The APG undertakes studies of methods and trends of money laundering and the financing of terrorism in Asia-Pacific region.

The Financial Action Task Force

The Financial Action Task Force is the main international body which is engaged in comprehensive efforts to promote the adoption of countermeasures to combat ML worldwide. FATF was set up by governments of the G-7 countries in 1989, and at present its membership comprises a large group of countries like Australia, Austria, Belgium, Canada, Denmark, European Commission, Finland, France, Germany, Ireland, Italy, Luxembourg, the Netherlands, Norway, Portugal, Spain, Sweden, Switzerland, Turkey, the United Kingdom, the US, and Japan.

The FATF has pursued three main functions: (*i*) monitoring countermeasures of the members to combat ML, (*ii*) reviewing the ML techniques periodically and planning countermeasures, and (*iii*) promoting countermeasures of ML in non-member countries.

The FATF made a detailed definition of countermeasures to combat ML and that is known as 'Forty Recommendations' which was adopted in 1990. These recommendations are placed in four categories according to themes and these are:

(1) The Overall Context giving the Perspective
(2) The Legal Framework
(3) The Role of Financial System
(4) The Strengthening of International Cooperation

In the overall context category, the recommendations urge member countries to ratify the Vienna Convention, and to ensure that the secrecy laws of the financial system do not facilitate ML.

The set of recommendations in the legal framework category prepare the ground rules so that the ML activities can be put in the category of criminal activities. It should make it possible for the government to monitor the movement of the funds that are related to crimes of ML type and if necessary, seize the cash and other assets.

The elements within the role of financial system category define the role of banks, life insurance companies, other non-bank institutions, and the regulatory authorities. In the recommendations, it is expected that the financial institutions will be able to identify their customers, maintain the records sufficient to allow the reconstruction of transactions, and be able to hand over the records to the investigating authorities for criminal cases and prosecution.

The recommendations in the last category encourage authorities to exchange information on currency flows and ML techniques and on doubtful transactions. International cooperation should be supported by bilateral and multilateral treaties based on generally shared common legal concepts. Also, there should be mutual assistance and cooperation regarding the identification, freezing, seizure, and confiscation of criminal proceeds, and further legal actions as needed.

The FATF members continue to re-examine their anti-ML measures and refine them when necessary. Several countries are working to extend preventive measures beyond the traditional banking sector. The Netherlands and some other European countries have introduced the legislation that requires money transfer businesses to report any doubtful transaction. Thus the upgrading of countermeasures to fight ML is a continuous process (FATF, 1999).

There are also other means available to fight ML at the international level and some of these are:
(1) The Uunited Nations Model Bill on Money Laundering and Proceeds of Crime, and Terrorist Financing, 2003.
(2) The United Nations Model Mutual Assistance in Criminal Matters Bill, 1998.
(3) The United Nations Model Foreign Exchange Bill, 1998.
(4) The United Nations Model Law on Money Laundering, Confiscation, and International Cooperation in Relation to Drugs, 1995.

The provisions of these laws are stringent enough to prevent ML, but the real issue is the enforcement of the provisions as often the political will is lacking.

Genesis

The United Nations General Assembly, in its Special Session (1999), came up with the political declaration that required the member states to adopt ML legislations and programmes. In case of India, with the changed economic scenario and the dynamic process of liberalization laws, like Foreign Exchange Management Act (FEMA) in place of earlier Foreign Exchange Regulation Act (FERA), it was felt to be much static and harsh. It was felt that a new law was required to curb the power of the launderers of money.

India: The Prevention of Money-Laundering Bill, 1999

The Prevention of Money-Laundering Bill, 1999 has been passed in the Indian parliament recently and it is now a law in the statute book. The provisions in the law are rigorous enough and these are comparable to the rules as in vogue in the FATF countries.

The definition of ML as stipulated in the Law is as follows:

Whoever (1) acquires, owns, possesses or transfers any proceeds of crime, or
(2) knowingly enters into any transaction which is related to proceeds of crime either directly or indirectly, or,
(3) conceals or aids in the concealment of proceeds of crime, commits the offence of money laundering.

The person who commits the crime of ML shall be punishable with rigorous imprisonment and the property connected to ML shall be attached. The provisions in the ML bill are sufficiently stiff and there are provisions in the bill for the cooperation with other countries to combat the crime of ML.

The Prevention of Money Laundering Act, 2002

The Prevention of Money Laundering Act, 2002 (PMLA) was enacted and the detailed rules were framed there under, and it came into force from 1 July 2005. Under the provisions of the Act, Financial Intelligence Units was set up as an apex body for coordinating India's efforts to curb money laundering. The PMLA and rules notified thereunder impose obligations on banking companies, financial institutions and intermediaries to verify the identity of clients, maintain records of transactions and furnish information to FIUs. PMLA defines ML offences and provides for the freezing, seizure, and confiscation of the proceeds of the crime involved.

The Schedule to the PMLA, 2002, lists some of the offences under the following legislations:
(1) Offences under the Narcotic Drugs and Psychotropic Substances Act, 1985 — e.g., contravention in relation to opium poppy and opium.
(2) Offences under Indian Penal Code (part B) — e.g., murder, kidnapping for ransom, counterfeiting currency notes.
(3) Offences under the Arms Act, 1959 — e.g., knowingly purchasing arms from unlicensed persons not entitled to purchase the same.

The activities enumerated in the above Acts generate huge amount of money, and the money launderers convert these sums into shares or deposit these in banks and in the process, they convert the essential character of the money.

The PMLA was a very peculiar legislation. The Civil Procedure Code, 1908 and the Criminal Procedure Code, 1973, were clubbed together and thus the Act could hit the sources of illegal money. As per the provisions of the Act, banks and financial institutions and financial intermediaries will have to report to the Government all suspicious transactions and those amounting to over ten lakh rupees. Moreover, every financial institution has to maintain a record of all transactions, the nature and value of which is being prescribed in the rules. All these institutions are to be registered with Securities and Exchange Board of India (SEBI).

Under the provisions of the PMLA, 2002, Financial Intelligence Unit, India, (FIU-IND) was set up as an apex body for the coordination of India's anti-money laundering efforts.

The Prevention of Money Laundering (Amendment) Act, 2009

The Prevention of Money Laundering (Amendment) Act, 2009 (PMLA, 2009) had come into force with effect from 1 June 2009. In terms of sub-section 2(a) of Section 12 of PMLA (2009), the records referred to in clause (a) of sub-section (1) of section 12, shall be maintained for a period of ten years from the date of transaction between the client and the banking company.

Maintaining time for furnishing information and verification and maintenance of records of the identity of the clients of the banking companies and financial institutions, both domestic and international, will permit reconstruction of individual transactions so as to provide evidence for prosecution of persons involved in criminal activity.

With a view to preventing the system of purchase and/or sale of foreign currency notes/travellers' cheques by authorized persons[3] from being used, intentionally or unintentionally, by criminal elements for money laundering or terrorist financing, the authorized persons should carry out full-scale Customer Due Diligence (CDD) before undertaking any money changing transaction[4].

The PMLA (2009) has certain sections that are aimed at regulating money transactions by politically exposed persons (PEP). Thus when a customer is recognized as PEP after business relation is established, elaborate CDD is to be performed on such customers and the decision to continue business relation with such persons should be taken at a senior level.

A Policy Problem

Money laundering has become a global problem, and its impact is most in the developing countries where the size of informal sector is relatively large, the legal system is not sufficiently effective, corruption has attained some degree of tolerance, the public in general are not conscious either for lack of proper education or wrong propaganda, and the nexus between politics and social life is strong. The offshore centres provide the necessary conduit to siphon money from the country first and then bring the money back in another form. The illicit trade in drugs and narcotics is a flourishing business in such economies. A prudent monetary policy is a first casualty in such a situation, and the link between money supply and price level, or the link between credit and gross domestic product are not significant. Economic development in such a society becomes highly distorted and a small minority controls the levers of both economic and political power (Lilley, 2000).

> We must reconsider what constitutes corruption. It is right to be concerned by bribery and embezzlement of public assets, but tax evasion is generally overlooked even though it represents theft of public assets and, in terms of orders of magnitude, has far greater impact on public revenues than bribery and embezzlement. Tax evasion involves abusive behaviour at the intersection between private activity and the public interest. It involves minorities bypassing accepted social norms, and provides one set of rules for the rich and well connected, and another set of rules for the poor and weak. More insidiously, it involves privileged elites, who use secrecy jurisdictions to undermine the will of elected parliaments. It is time that secrecy jurisdictions are recognised for what they really are: a full-on assault on the sovereignty of nation states, a direct attack on democracy, and a cancer running through the veins of contemporary capitalism.
>
> John Christensen, Director, Tax Justice Network, September 2008

The following gives some idea of the strength of ML that goes on in the world and that derives strength from the grey economy of different countries.

---

[3] 'Authorized persons' means an authorized person as defined in clause© of section 2 of the Foreign Exchange Management Act (FEMA), 1999.

[4] Prevention of Money Laundering (Amendment) Act, 2009. A.P. (DIR Series) Circular No. 18.

Country Estimates

- The following paragraph explains the strength of money laundering (ML) that goes on in the world and that derives strength from the grey economy of different countries.
- According to *Hospodarske Noviny* (2 April 1998), the model estimate of grey economy in Czech Republic was 10 per cent of the gross domestic product (GDP). In Mexico the amount of money laundering was estimated to be USD 26 billion States every year (*Chicago Tribune, 25 March 1998*)
- In Poland the amount of money laundering (ML) is about USD 2 billion every year (National Bank of Poland, Aprail 15, 1998).
- In Russia, the share of shadow business in the overall economy may range between 25 per cent to 50 per cent, and the model estimate of the ML is about 15 per cent of the GDP (TASS, 17 March 1998). Again, according to one estimate about USD 50 – 250 billion is illegally moved from Russia to the blanks in Western Countries (Russian Interior and Economics Ministries, April 1999).
- Accoring to Swiss Finance Ministry, Switzerland is implicated in USD 500 billion each year (as reported on 26 March 1998).
- The size of black economy in United Kingdom is between 7 – 13 per cent of GDP and the model estimate of total money laundering is 7.4 per cent of GDP of the country (*Sunday Telegraph, 29 March 1998*).
- Money laundering in Belarus in about 30 per cent of GDP (European Humanities University, 20 November 1998) and the model estimate shows 22.2 per cent of Belarus' GDP is laundered money.

Topic for Discussion

Explain how money laundering activities can be the reason for instability in the domestic financial system.

Further Reading

Alami, Tarik, 'An Econometric Investigation of Dollarization in Egypt', Journal of Development and Economic Policies, 2(2), June 2000, 7–24.

———, 'Currency Substitution Versus Dollarization: A Portfolio Balance Model', Journal of Policy Modeling, 23(4), May 2001, 473–79.

Algahthani, Ibrahim M., 'Currency Substitution, Gold Price and the Demand for Money in a Developing Economy: The Case of Kuwait', Middle East Business and Economic Review, 4(2), July 1992, 1–5.

Arifovic, Jasmina, 'Evolutionary Dynamics of Currency Substitution', Journal of Economic Dynamics and Control, 25(3–4), March 2001, 395–417.

Arize, Augustine C., 'Currency Substitution in Korea', American Economist, 35(2), 1991, 67–72.

Alsowaidi, Saif S., 'Factors Influencing Currency Substitution in Lebanon', Middle East Business and Economic Review, 12(2), December 2000, 10–20.

Bartlett, Brent, 'The Negative Effects of Money Laundering on Economic Development', in Asian Development Bank, Countering Money Laundering in the Asian and Pacific Region, Regional Technical Assistance Project No. 5967, , May 2002.

Dolar, Burak and William F. Shughart II, 'The Wealth Effects of the USA Patriot Act: Evidence from the Banking and Thrift Industries', Journal of Money Laundering Control, 10(3), 2006, 300–17.

Financial Action Task Force (FATF), 'Trade Based Money Laundering', Financial Action Task Force–Groupe d'action financière, Paris, 23 June 2006.

Hetzer, Wolfgang, 'Money Laundering and Financial Markets', European Journal of Crime, Criminal Law and Criminal Justice, 11(3), 2003, 264–77.

Naylor, R.T., Wages of Crime: Black Markets, Illegal Finance, and the Underworld Economy, Ithaca NY, Cornell University, 2002.

Qorchi, Mohammed El, Samuel Munzele Maimbo and John F. Wilson, Informal Funds Transfer Systems: An Analysis of the Informal Hawala System, Washington DC, International Monetary Fund, 2003.

Ridley, Nicholas, 'Financial Enmeshment — Banking Systems in Western, and Central and South-Eastern Europe: The Interacting Factors of Anti-Money Laundering, the Rigours of Transitional Economy, and the Underground Illicit Economy', Journal of Money Laundering Control, 9(1), 89–98, 2006.

Rosdol, Alexa, 'Are OFCs Leading the Fight against Money Laundering?' Journal of Money Laundering Control, 10(3), 2007, 337–51.

Web Sources

http://www.bis.org (accessed 24 May 2013)

http://www.euribor-ebf.eu (accessed 13 July 2013)

http://www.riskmetrics.com (accessed 24 May 2013)

For Money laundering information and literature the relevant web links are::

http://www.fincen.gov (accessed 13 July 2013)

http://www.imolin.org/imolin/en/bibliogr.html#GENERAL (accessed 13 July 2013)

http://www.oecd.org.corruption (accessed 13 July 2013)

9

Exchange Rate and Foreign Exchange Market

Like any other market in economic theory, the foreign exchange market is also a commodity relationship, and is defined as the relation between buyers and sellers for the purchase and disposal of the currencies of different denomination. A student desiring to send some amount of USDs to New York as an application fee has to approach a local bank for the purchase of the required dollars. He is asked to submit a specified amount of Indian rupees to the bank and he obtains a demand draft for USDs drawn on a New York bank. The relationship between the amount of Indian rupees and USDs is determined by the price of one unit of USD in terms of Indian rupee, and this price is the exchange rate of the Indian currency. *Exchange rate is the price of one unit of foreign currency in terms of the domestic currency.*

There is a *two-ness* in the transactions in the foreign exchange. Any transaction is between two currencies. Each person involved in the transaction is simultaneously a buyer and a seller of currencies. The bank in the above example is buying Indian rupee and selling USDs. The student is also doing just the opposite, selling Indian rupee and buying USDs. Each transaction again involves two banks as the Indian bank is using its dollar balances when it issues the draft to the student. Lastly, the Indian bank by selling USDs is making itself short of it, and it has to purchase equal amount of dollars to square its position. This aspect is unique in foreign exchange transaction, and it makes it a very complicated process.

9.1 The Players

By nature, the foreign exchange market (FEM) is a global market. The principal players are governments, central banks, commercial banks, other financial institutions, brokers, businesses, corporates, and individuals. The major transactions are between the commercial banks, which are authorized dealers.

The central bank is an important player as it has the primary responsibility of maintaining the stability of exchange rate of the domestic currency. The stock of the latter is issued by the central bank and it is in circulation in the domestic economy. Part of this may be floating in the international market. It is the responsibility of the central bank to preserve the intrinsic value of its liability. This gives credibility to the domestic currency in the international market. It is no accident that people are reluctant to hold Australian dollar or Indonesian rupiah.

Commercial banks are the providers of liquidity to the economic system, and this they do by facilitating the cash flow of currencies of multiple denominations. They hold foreign currency for this, and the portfolio of commercial bank has the important element in the form of foreign currency either as cash or as short-term monetary instruments. Trading in foreign exchange is an important source of revenue to the banks.

Corporate houses enter FEM to convert their asset or liability in foreign currency into the domestic currency. The latter being the currency of the balance sheet, the corporates insulate the balance sheet position from the fluctuation of the exchange rate. Firms doing international business should pay the suppliers in the local currency in each country in which they operate. They also receive payments in different currencies from their customers. These foreign currency cash flows are converted into domestic currency.

The brokers and individuals, though small players, have their important functions in FEM. The brokers give some crucial services to the banks when the latter are confused or, when the market behaves in an erratic manner.

Two more players are active in the area of international finance nowadays — investors and speculators.

Many corporate businesses own property and acquire business abroad. The capital flows both ways and the repatriation of earnings are in foreign currency. This they surrender to the central bank of the country and get the domestic currency. In the case of portfolio investment in bonds and shares abroad, larger sums are involved and the investors enter the FEM for regular conversion of domestic currency into a foreign one and vice versa.

Table 9.1 *Top 10 Currency Traders in the World (Percentage of Overall Volume), May 2010*

Rank	Name	Market Share (per cent)
1.	Deutsche Bank	18.06
2.	UBS AG	11.30
3.	Barclays Capital	11.08
4.	Citi	7.69
5.	Royal Bank of Scotland	6.50
6.	JP Morgan	6.35
7.	HSBC	4.55
8.	Credit Suisse	4.44
9.	Goldman Sachs	4.28
10.	Morgan Stanley	2.91

Source: Bank for International Settlements.

The large-scale presence of speculators in FEM has been a dominant phenomenon since the middle of the 1980s. They play in the FEM to buy and sell foreign currencies for a margin. The transactions are not backed by any genuine demand for trading in merchandise. It is trading in currencies only.

The dynamism and depth of FEM depends on the behaviour pattern of the players. Modern technology has provided full information to players, and it is how they decipher the market information and use it for their response that determines the course of market movement. The banks have realized the potential of trading in foreign currencies and many banks improve their bottom line though the operation of their currency trade. Table 9.1 depicts the top 10 currency traders in the world.

9.2 Trading Location

The currency market is truly global and it has no single physical location. Most trading in currency occurs in the inter-bank markets, among financial institutions located in different countries. Trading in FEM typically occurs through telephonic conversations and also through computer network around the globe. International markets remain always open during the weekdays. It opens first in Sydney, then Tokyo, Singapore, Hong Kong, Mumbai, Bahrain, Frankfurt, London, New York, and Chicago. Thus, when Europe is opening, Sydney is closed and markets remain open as the globe gets the sunshine during the day.

Most banks do their spot-market currency trading in the same centres though they have the technological capability to do trading with any distant corner of the globe. Still some centres have gained importance in the volume of trading. London is one such centre and New York follows it. The importance of principal centres of the world is shown in the following Table 9.2.

Table 9.2 *Geographic Distribution of Global Foreign Exchange Market Turnover: Some Principal Centres (as on 2010)*

Country/Location	Average daily turnover (USD bn.)	Percentage share
London (UK)	1853.59	36.66
New York & Chicago (USA)	904.36	17.89
Tokyo (Japan)	312.33	6.18
Singapore	265.98	5.26
Germany	108.60	2.15
Switzerland	262.58	5.19
Hong Kong SAR	237.57	4.70
France	152.62	3.00
Denmark	120.46	2.38
Canada	61.89	1.22
Other Centres (Countries)	776.46	15.36
Total	5056.44	100.00

Source: Bank for International Settlements.

In 2000, the amount of daily turnover in FEM all over the world was approximately 1500 bn USD and only 1 per cent of the sum accounted for the merchandise trade. Rest is pure speculation. The markets also deal with some financial products known as derivatives. These are hedge tools customers and/or financial institutions buy to safeguard against future potential risk due to adverse fluctuations in the exchange rate of the domestic currency. Typical products are currency futures, currency forwards, currency swaps, and options.

The nature of trading in currency futures is different and it started first in Chicago Mercantile Exchange. Even today, it is the predominant exchange for currency futures in the world. The exchange at Sao Paolo, Brazil comes next in terms of volume of trading. Trading in currency futures at other exchanges is minimum, as the customers prefer other forms of derivatives.

9.3 Favourite Currencies

The demand for a currency depends on the demand for the commodities to be imported from that country. If India wants to import machinery from Italy, India needs reserves in Italian lira, and India can buy that currency from FEM in exchange for some other currency or USD. The latter is international currency by the Bretton Woods agreement. But in global markets, several currencies are traded and that can be seen from the following Table 9.3.

Table 9.3 *Foreign Exchange Trading by Currencies, April 2010*

Currency	Percentage of turnover
USD	42.45
Euro	19.55
Japanese yen	9.50
British pound	6.45
Swiss franc	3.20
Canadian dollar	2.65
Australian dollar	3.80
Hong Kong dollar	1.20
Swedish krona	1.10
Other currencies	10.10

Source: Bank for International Settlements.

The USD is more dominant in spot markets trading compared to derivative trading. Also it has the predominant position in the foreign currency reserves of the member countries of the International Monetary Fund (IMF). Again, in 1990s, many transition economies had adopted USD as their *de facto* medium of exchange and that had increased the demand for dollar in a big way[1].

German D-mark and Japanese yen are two strong currencies, and many countries keep these two currencies as a part of their international reserves. Japan encourages trade in yen in the case of countries in the South and Southeast Asia. Other currencies including British pound are not much favoured, though euro is coming up fast. With the introduction of the euro in 11 countries of European Union, a significant realignment in the international currency holding is expected[2]. First, currencies like French franc, deutschmark, lira, escudo, etc. have been replaced by euro in the respective countries.

---

[1] In the transition economies like the so-called CIS countries, e.g., Tajikistan, Ulbekistan and East European countries like Hungary, Poland, etc. people started using USD as the medium of exchange. This happened mainly for two reasons: the countries were in the process of introducing their own currencies, and/or the people were waiting for stability of the home currency. In the intervening period, they were using the USD. In fact, in many countries dual currency systems are in operation, USD being the second currency.

[2] The new currency euro came into existence on 1 January and 11 countries that adopted euro as the sovereign currency replacing their own existing currencies are — Austria, Belgium, Finland, France, Germany, Ireland, Italy, Luxembourg, Netherlands, Portugal, and Spain. By 2011 another six countries joined the Euro area making the number 17, and these countries are — Estonia, Greece, Cyprus, Malta, Slovenia, and Slovakia.

9.4 Quotations in Foreign Exchange Transactions

In FEM the price quotations of any currency becomes a two-way quote, like for INR/USD, the quotation is like

$$1 \text{ USD} = ₹ 48.90/97$$

The above is an inter-bank rate, and bank is willing to buy at the rate of 1 USD = ₹ 48.90 and sell @ 48.97. This is said as bid/ ask rate and the difference between the two is known as spread.

Again, a dollar/D-mark quotation will read like 1.5000/10. The bank which quotes this rate reveals that it will buy mark (sell dollars) at 1.5010 and sell mark (buy dollar) at 1.5000. It means that it buys cheaper and sells dearer a particular currency in exchange for the other one. The opposite is true for the person who has asked for a quote. The difference between the purchase and sell rates is called 'spread'. Spreads change according to market volatility[3].

A foreign exchange rate consists of an integer part and 4 decimal points (sometimes 2 decimal points). Thus the decimals are expressed either at 10th thousands or hundreds. Each such 0.0001 is called *basis points* or *pips*. For example, a 40 pips change in the dollar/rupee exchange rate 1 USD = 48.0000/10 means 1 USD = 48.0040, or, 1 USD = 47.9960.

9.5 Direct and Indirect Quote

These prices showing a unit dollar in terms of rupees as 48.0000 is known as direct quote. This is the prevailing system and Reuter screen shows rates in this fashion except in the case of some currencies like the British pound. In this case the dollar/pound rate is shown as pound/ dollar rate.

If we take the reciprocal of the direct quote, we get the indirect quote and in case of the above dollar/rupee rate this will be Re 1 = 0.02128 USD, that is reciprocal of 48.0000. The indirect quote has one advantage. In this format, an increase in value means the currency is moving up. But in direct quote, an increase in value means the currency is moving down. In 1992, dollar/rupee rate was 31.3700 and compared to that, the rate in 2001 is 48.0000. It implies that Indian rupee has gone down about 50 per cent during the last nine years.

9.6 Direction in the Market

In FEM, the exchange rate is a relative price. So when one currency goes up, it implies that other currency is going down. In case dollar/rupee rate changes from 48.0000 to 48.0005, market signals that rupee is going down, and it also means that dollar is going up. Thus, unlike in the

---

[3] Spread is an important variable in FEM. This denotes the fraction $p(\text{ask}) - p(\text{bid})$. Sometimes spread is expressed in logarithm form

$$S = \log p \, (\text{ask}) - \log p \, (\text{bid}).$$

In the direct quote, spread is positive. Economists have used the change in spreads to predict the future behaviour of some macro variables like inflation and interest rates.

markets for stocks, *there is no direction for the market.* But there is direction of movement for the currencies. In the case of stock markets, the index of the market gives an average direction and that reveals the aggregate movement of the stock prices.

9.7 Inter-Banking

In the domestic or international transaction mechanism, inter-banking occurs when a customer doing banking with Bank AA wants to pay a customer doing banking with Bank MM. Thus, the system of inter-banking is important and the process of setting up of inter-banking involves the following steps:
(1) Each bank is to create a vostro account
(2) Each bank is to ask the other bank in a foreign country to open nostro account for itself
(3) Each bank is to send the list of nostro and vostro accounts to the clearing centre (like EuroPEN in Europe)

The EuroPEN system is a bilateral clearing system. It uses nostro and vostro accounts to settle inter-bank transactions. It does not act as a clearing house but as a distribution hub. This makes the system easier as the transactions of all banks come to a single point for settlement among the participating banks.

9.8 Foreign Exchange Account

When an Indian company approaches a bank for payments of Euro to a French Company in France for the imports, the Indian company pays Indian rupee to the bank at a rate offered by the bank. The bank gives a demand draft drawn on a bank in France. That French bank may be a branch of the Indian bank, or representative bank. In either case, the Indian bank maintains a Euro account with the French counterpart. This is known as a nostro account. This is an important instrument in the international payment process.

A nostro account is opened and maintained in foreign countries to settle foreign currency transactions like exports, imports, remittances and other similar things. Nostro accounts are currency-specific, that is, an Indian bank can open USD account in the US only, though a bank can maintain more than one nostro account in dollars in different cities of the US. All dollar deposits in the bank will be added to the nostro account that gives the liquidity to the bank so that it can meet the demand for dollars of the potential importers.

Parallel to the nostro account, when the foreign bank opens a rupee account in India with an Indian bank, it is known as vostro account. Thus, the Citi Bank in New York can open a vostro account with the State Bank in Delhi, and make all rupee payments in India on behalf of the American importers of Indian commodities.

9.9 Reimbursement Claim Solution (RCS)

For a large bank with a vast network and connection with a large number of correspondent banks, it becomes difficult to monitor all the transactions in multiple currencies. To address this problem some software are developed. Reimbursement Claim Solution (RCS) is a commercially available, fully integrated solution, designed for large network banks that offer a collection service to downstream correspondent banks for all export collection items, reimbursement, authorizations, and check collections. RCS is a fully scalable solution. It offers comprehensive functionality for the collection item transaction flow from the network of the downstream correspondents to the clearing centre of the correspondent service provider. This integrated approach provides an operating advantage to a network bank competing for correspondent banking services.

For a correspondent branch operation, RCS improves the operation by tracking and tracing payments on behalf of the customers of the branches. At the head office level of the correspondent, RCS automatically consolidates all claims by its branches and it provides a bank a wide view of all outstanding claim items. Thus, at a point of time the bank can have an overall picture regarding the claims in a consolidated form.

In sum, there are many types of transactions in the foreign exchange market. What has been most apparent in the last 15 years is that the majority of transactions in this market are not the ordinary exporters and importers settling their international accounts. The market is driven by the speculators and interest arbitrageurs, trying to take advantage of expectations about future exchange rates and international interest-rate differentials. In short, one's domestic currency can appreciate not because foreigners are trying to buy the products of the country, but because they are taking advantage of higher interest rates or expectations of an appreciation. Ordinary exporters, facing competitive international markets, may suddenly find their products 'price out' of competition, unless they pass-through the exchange rate effect, by cutting the prices of their exports in domestic currency, so that the international prices remain the same after the appreciation. This was the Japanese trick. However, the pass-through means lower profit margins in domestic currency, and exporters can do this just for so long. So large capital inflows can cause problems for exporters and export production, and thus for employment. In the next section, we will examine the different functions of the exchange rate, from the perspectives of the different transactors.

9.10 Export and Import Transactions

The first use of foreign exchange is for the settling of international export and import transactions, accounts receivable and accounts payable. An importer in India ultimately pays a foreign supplier in the foreign currency. An Indian taking a trip abroad will need foreign currency for day-to-day expenses.

The foreign exchange market determines the spot rate for demand and supply of foreign currency. This exchange rate is not the same as the rate for bank notes one finds at train stations and airports. This tourist rate may be slightly above the quoted spot rate, since tourist exchanges have the added risks of keeping currency on hand and currency dealers at work. The quoted spot rate is the inter-bank rate for switching currency from an account in a domestic bank to foreign currency in an account in a foreign bank.

The combination policy of devaluation and a fiscal austerity programme is the traditional IMF recipe for countries in a chronic balance of payments deficit. This is what the international money doctors prescribe, after their missions and diagnoses. It should be remembered that devaluation involves a cut in the standard of living. A devaluation means higher costs for imported goods, which could include food and medicine, as well as intermediate goods for production of manufactured goods. Fiscal austerity also means hardship. There is no question that the cure for a chronic balance of payments deficit is often harsh.

The question remains: to what extent should policy-makers rely on fiscal contraction, and to what extent should policy-makers opt for exchange rate adjustment?

Exchange Rate: Centre of Expectation: Case of Argentina and Mexico

For many countries, the exchange rate has become the anchor of expectations. Changes in the exchange rate signal further inflation, so that devaluation simply passes through to upward adjustment in prices. In Argentina, the sentiment was that it is Christmas time, so it is time for devaluation. So let's raise our prices in anticipation. Of course, the government would announce that this year's devaluation could be the very last. The Cavallo stabilization plan of 1991 fixed the exchange rate of the peso at a one-for-one parity with the USD, with full convertibility. The central bank would function as a 'currency board': domestic monetary expansion would be linked on a one-for-one basis with reserve changes. The central bank could neither monetize fiscal deficits nor act as a lender of last resort, to private banks facing liquidity problems.

The fixing of the exchange rate had an immediate effect on price expectations: inflation came down, and stayed down, for many years. However, there has been a chronic trade deficit. The government is faced with a dilemma: it can devalue, and re-ignite inflationary expectations, or it can live with the trade deficit, loose reserves, and leave itself open to a speculative attack, or it can opt for further fiscal contraction. There is no question that the continuing trade deficit in Argentina is a 'warning signal' of an overvalued exchange rate, and that fiscal contraction is called for.

The position of Mexico is different. It also faced a large trade deficit and slow growth, just at the time when the country should be hitting the ground running after the ratification of the North American Free Trade Agreement (NAFTA). Unlike Argentina, however, Mexico has not had a recent history of hyperinflation. The exchange rate is not the anchor of expectations for price setting. There is thus room for a significant devaluation to restore competitiveness and growth, and to reduce the trade deficit. Mexico, unlike Argentina, can make use of the exchange-rate instrument for domestic adjustment.

It should be clear that the advisability of using the exchange rate instrument or the fiscal instrument depends on the 'initial conditions' of a particular country, on its recent history of inflation, on how inflationary expectations are linked to the exchange rate, and on government credibility.

9.11 Marshall–Lerner Conditions

The effectiveness of the devaluation (in a fixed system) or depreciation (in a flexible system) of the currency for reducing a trade deficit depends on 'well-behaved' demand and supply curves for foreign exchange. The precise conditions that guarantee that devaluations 'work' are the Marshall–Lerner (ML) conditions. These conditions simply state that the sum of the absolute values of the elasticities of home demand for foreign goods, and foreign demand for home goods, must be greater than one. The Marshall–Lerner conditions link the effectiveness of a monetary instrument with analysis of the demands for home and foreign goods in the 'real sector'.

The basic idea behind the Marshall–Lerner conditions is that the exchange rate affects the terms of trade between two countries. 'Terms of trade' are defined as the ratio of export prices, **Px**, over import prices, **Pm**. In domestic currency units, the price of imports **Pm** is equal to the exchange rate E multiplied by the world price level **P^w m**.

Thus,

$$Pm = E \cdot P^w m.$$

A devaluation or depreciation thus implies a fall in the terms of trade, in domestic currency units. Similarly, in foreign currency units, a devaluation of the home currency raises the terms of trade of the foreign country. The ML condition states that a depreciation or devaluation of a country's currency will improve its current balance if the sum of the price elasticities of demand for exports and imports is larger than unity.

The effects of devaluation on trade balance can be separated into three factors:

(1) A devaluation will reduce the real quantity of imports, and that will reduce the foreign exchange spent on imports.
(2) The devaluation will increase the real quantity of exports.
(3) Since export price is denominated in domestic currency, export will bring more revenue in foreign exchange if the increase in real exports is much higher compared to reduction in prices.

But the elasticity approach needs another condition and this is:

(4) We assume that the economy is initially in a position of balanced trade. Given this, the necessary and sufficient condition for the devaluation to improve the trade balance is that the sum of the elasticities of demand for exports and imports is greater than unity, or,

$$\varepsilon_X + \varepsilon_M > 1$$

where ε_X and ε_M are elasticities of demand for exports and imports respectively. This is also known as a stability condition in balance of payments.

9.12 The J-Curve

Even when the Marshall–Lerner conditions hold, and the demand and supply curves are well behaved, there is still the possibility that the devaluation, initially, will make the trade balance worse, before making it better. The J-curve is a well-observed phenomenon. The emergence of J-Curve can be explained in the following manner. After the devaluation of the domestic currency, the value of imports in domestic currency increases and the volume does not decline, because of lag effects of prices and contract obligations. On the other hand, the volume of exports does not increase immediately, as price effects take time to be effective. Meanwhile, the value of exports in foreign currency declines if invoices of exports are in domestic currency. The net result is a worsening of the balance of trade situation in the short run. In the long run, the price effects become stronger, exports increase, and imports decline, and balance of trade improves. This happens if the elasticities of demand for imports and supply of exports are smaller in the short run than in the long run. The course of movements of the balance of trade first falling and then moving up gives a shape like J and hence the name of the curve.

Figure 9.1 J-Curve: After Depreciation

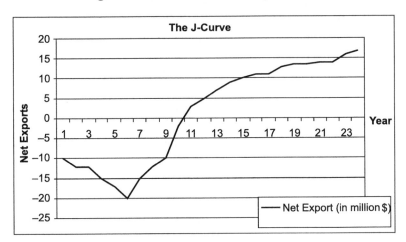

9.13 Contractionary Devaluation

In an exceptional situation, devaluation may lead to a contraction of domestic output if the import intensity of domestic production is high. Further, if the imports are intermediate goods, such as capital equipment, then the devaluation may result in a shrink in industrial production. Also export goods, which use imported capital goods, will become less competitive as a result of the devaluation. Both these effects will lead to a decline in exports and domestic output. This has recently happened in the case of some South Asian countries and Latin American countries.

9.14 Forward Speculation

The participants in forward markets resort to speculation for gain and they generally follow two rules:
(1) if depreciation is expected, buy forward, sell spot;
(2) if an appreciation is expected, sell forward, buy spot.
There are forward markets as well as spot markets. The forward markets exist to diminish risk in foreign currency contracts. If one knows one is to make a payment in USDs in three months, one can negotiate a forward contract to purchase USD now, at an agreed forward price. One then delivers the rupees in three months, and receives the dollar at the agreed price. There is usually a small margin requirement (about 5 per cent, say) at the time the forward contract is signed. But for all practical purposes, the margin is negligible.

The advantage of the forward contract is that it eliminates risk of exchange rate fluctuations. But it eliminates the possibility of gains from exchange rate changes also.

9.15 Market Efficiency

The forward speculation process is a good test of the efficiency of the foreign exchange market. If traders have expectations of an appreciation or depreciation, there will be actions in the forward markets. If there is a rush to buy or sell forward, the traders will adjust their prices for the forward contracts. After all, for every winner in the forward speculation gain, there is a loser. It is a zero-sum game in this particular sense. But in an efficient market, there should be no persistent speculative profit opportunities, though there can be random profits, with gains and losses distributed randomly. But if people are making persistent profits, then forward dealers are taking persistent losses.

It is expected that the forward rate should reflect expectations of next period's spot rate, and it means that the current forward rate should be the best statistical predictor of next period's spot rate. This hypothesis has been verified for the major currency markets.

9.16 Hedging and Interest Arbitrage

Hedging is simple insurance against risk of any kind, and exchange risk is one. If one makes a foreign investment, putting 1000 USD into £500 today in order to invest in a gilt-edge security in the United Kingdom at an interest rate of 7 per cent, maturing in one year, one will have a gross return of £535. However, it is still not clear what your return will be in USD: it may be more or less than 1070 USD assuming that the exchange rate may not stay at the initial one £ 1= ₹ 2. One can remove the risk of exchange rate loss (due to a depreciation of sterling against the USD) by purchasing forward cover. At the foreign investment in gilt-edge securities in the United Kingdom is made, one can sell forward £535 for 1070 USD if the forward rate remains the same as spot.

9.17 Covered Interest Parity and Forward Premium

Hedging does apply to any type of expected return denominated in a foreign currency. The covered interest parity is closely related to the use of forward cover as a hedge against exchange-rate risk in foreign investment. We can do some mathematical exercises. Let 'K' be the initial amount of USD set aside for investment, 'r' the rate of return in the United States, 'r*' the rate of return in India, 'S' the dollar–rupee spot rate, and 'F' the dollar–rupee forward rate. One can simply deposit the K dollars in the United States at an annual interest rate of r, and after one year, receive a gross return of K(1+r). Alternatively, one can convert the dollar capital into rupee K/ S, and after one year, receive a gross rupee return of (K/S) (1+r*). By selling the gross returns forward, one can guarantee a certain return in dollars,

$$(K/S) (1+r^*) F$$

The central insight of covered interest parity is that it should not make any difference where you put your money, in dollar deposits paying a net return r, or in rupee deposits, paying a return r*. Staying in dollars, or round-tripping, going into rupee, and then converting into dollars through forward sales, will not make any difference.

Why? Because if people could get a better return going into rupee, with no exchange rate risk, they would simply borrow in dollars, and invest in rupee, and pocket the difference. If mobility of capital is perfect and if the dollar-denominated and rupee-denominated assets are of equal risk, then we should have the following equality:

$$K(1+r) = (K/S)(1+r^*) F \qquad \text{Equation (9.1)}$$

This relation simplifies to:

$$S(1+r)/(1+r^*) = F \qquad \text{Equation (9.2)}$$

Subtracting S from both sides, we have:

$$S(1+r)/(1+r^*) - [(1+r^*)/(1+r^*)] S \; F - S \qquad \text{Equation (9.3)}$$

This simplifies to:

$$(r - r^*)/(1+r^*) = (F - S)/S \qquad \text{Equation (9.4)}$$

Equation (9.4) is the exact covered interest parity relation. The right-hand side represents the forward premium (when $F > S$) or discount ($F < S$). In most cases, $(1+r^*) \cong 1$, so the approximate covered interest parity (CIP) relation becomes:

$$(r - r^*) = (F - S)/S \qquad \text{Equation (9.5)}$$

Since the forward rate F is the expected spot rate, $E(S_{t+1})$, covered interest parity is a relation between interest rate differentials and exchange-rate expectations:

$$(r - r^*) = [E(S_{t+1}) - S]/S \qquad \text{Equation (9.6)}$$

where the right-hand side of equation (9.6) is the expected rate of depreciation of the home currency.

The implication of the covered interest-parity theory for countries having fixed exchange rates is that they must coordinate their interest rates if they wish to maintain fixed (zero) expectations of exchange rate changes. The central bank should have an interest rate target along with other parameters in the context of the management of monetary policies.

Uncovered Interest Parity

Uncovered interest parity (UIP) assumes that lenders and borrowers in the international markets treat domestic and foreign securities as perfect substitutes. This establishes a relation such as

$$r_t = r^*_t + [(S_{t+1} - S_t)/S_t] \qquad \text{Equation (9.7)}$$

where the second bracketed term is the expected rate of depreciation of the domestic currency. The equation implies that portfolio managers always seek the compensation of the expected depreciation of the domestic currency in case of their investment. When the expected depreciation seems to be high so as to make the nominal interest rate inadequate, to compensate the loss due to depreciation, foreign investors withdraw from the market. This creates a crisis–like situation.

Further from the Purchasing Power Parity (PPP) condition as we have developed in Chapter 2 and Equation (2.4), we can write

$$P = S \cdot P^*, \qquad \text{Equation (9.8)}$$

Or, in logarithmic form

$$\log P = \log S + \log P^* \qquad \text{Equation (9.9)}$$

after differentiating with respect to time t, we can write

$$(1/P) \cdot (dP/dt) = (1/S) \cdot (dS/dt) + (1/P^*) \cdot (dP^*/dt) \qquad \text{Equation (9.10)}$$

or, $\Pi_t = \Delta S_t + \Pi^*_t$
or, $\Delta S_t = \Pi_t - \Pi^*_t$ Equation (9.11)

From Equation (9.11) and Equation (9.7) we get by substitution

$$r_t = r^*_t + \Pi_t - \Pi^*_t$$

or,

$$r_t = (r^* - \Pi^*_t) + \Pi_t$$

or, $r_t = R^*_t + \Pi_t$ Equation (9.12)

or, nominal interest rate is the sum of real interest rate R^* and the expected inflation rate π, that is known as open economy Fisher equation.

9.18 Measuring Capital Mobility

The covered interest parity relation has another important function. It is the most widely quoted measure of capital mobility. One can use this measure to evaluate the degree of capital mobility between two countries. Most measures of capital mobility using the covered interest parity relation in the literature show near perfect capital mobility among the industrialized countries.

An alternative measure of capital mobility is uncovered interest parity. Similar to covered interest parity, it simply replaces the expected future exchange rate with the actual exchange rate at time t+1:

$$(r - r^*) = [S_{t+1} - S] / S \qquad \text{Equation (9.13)}$$

The uncovered interest parity assumes perfect myopic foresight: expectations from time t to t+1 are perfectly realized, without error. It is said that uncovered interest parity is a stronger and more restrictive test of capital mobility, as it is a test of capital mobility with perfect, not just rational expectations.

There is another test of capital mobility, and it is real interest parity: one would expect convergence in real returns for capital among countries where there are few restrictions to the mobility of capital. The real interest rate for any country is simply its nominal interest rate less the expected rate of inflation, π. Hence, we have the following real interest parity relation:

$$r - \pi = r^* - \pi^* \qquad \text{Equation (9.14)}$$

But this test, like uncovered interest parity, is more difficult than covered interest parity. It assumes that the returns adjusted for inflation should be equal across countries. In other words, it tells us that nominal interest differentials should be reflected in inflation differentials, not just expected or actual percentage changes in the nominal exchange rate E:

$$r - r^* = \pi - \pi^* \qquad \text{Equation (9.15)}$$

This relation imposes Purchasing Power Parity as a short-run relation. Expected exchange rate changes, or actual exchange rate changes, linked to interest differentials, are equal to expected inflation differentials.

Feldstein and Horioka Approach

Another measure of capital mobility is the correlation of national saving with national investment, following the work of Feldstein and Horioka (F–H) (1980). Given the national income identity:

$$(S - I) + (T - G) = (X - M) \qquad \text{Equation (9.16)}$$

One sees that there is a link between aggregate savings/investment and the trade balance. Under perfect capital mobility, persistent savings-investment imbalances can be sustained, as capital inflows finance the trade deficits. This is seen in many developing countries including India.

F–H argue that in a world of capital mobility, a country's savings are free to flow to their productive uses anywhere in the world. So, for perfect capital mobility, there should be no relation between a country's domestic savings and its domestic rate of investment. This is placed in the model form that can be estimated using time series data and the equation is:

$$(I/Y)_t = a + b\,(S/Y)_t + u_t \qquad \text{Equation (9.17)}$$

where

I/Y = ratio of gross domestic investment to national income
S/Y = ratio of aggregate savings to national income
u = random error term with a normal distribution

The Null Hypothesis to be tested from the estimation is:

Ho : b = 0

The F–H relation has been estimated by many economists and the results have been a mixed one. Some even tried to measure the correlation between (I/Y) and (S/Y) across countries (Nandi, 1999; Obstfeld, 1995). Again, the inherent puzzle in the F–H relation has been shown to be useful, but it cannot explain fully the weak correlation between saving and investment in the economies of the developed countries (Nell and Santos, 2008).

9.19 The Real Exchange Rate

In the discussion above regarding the exchange rate link to the real world and to the relative prices, we have seen that the exchange rate works through its effect on the terms of trade, or the relative price of a country's exports to its imports, in domestic currency terms. However, a more important link is through the 'real exchange rate', defined as the relative price of tradable goods to non-tradable goods.

Figure 9.2 pictures the production possibility frontier of an economy, as a division of traded and non-traded goods. The relative price of traded/non-traded goods is the equilibrium relative price, which determines the allocation of production between these sectors. The tradable goods sector of the economy is the growth-producing and employment-generating sector of the economy. Countless studies have documented that countries that allocate more of their resources in the tradable goods sector have higher long-term growth rates, higher employment rates, and higher living standards, than countries, which do not. The reason is simple and straightforward: the tradable goods sector is the outward-looking sector of the economy, with a higher learning-curve. Goods that are produced in this sector must be competitive with goods produced internationally. Thus, this sector must respond and adjust to innovations more rapidly than the other sectors of the economy. It is also the sector of producers whose market is not limited by the size of the domestic economy.

By contrast, the non-tradable sector is primarily the service sector, whose goods serve the local economy, with little or no competition from abroad. The need for a fairly high and stable real exchange rate is obvious. With a high and stable real exchange rate there are strong and

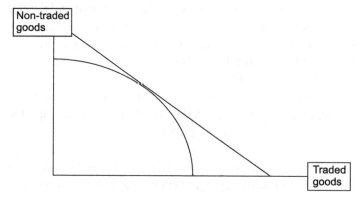

Figure 9.2 *Production Possibility Frontier*

credible incentives for the allocation of resources to this sector. Unstable real exchange rates, by contrast, obstruct development of this sector.

What is the real exchange rate, in operational terms? Since we do not observe price series of tradable and non-tradable goods, one may approximate it with the following relation:

$$REXR = \frac{P(traded)}{P(nontraded)} \approx \frac{SP^*}{P(cpi)} \qquad \text{Equation (9.18)}$$

where P* is the world price (in foreign currency) of tradable (or manufactured) goods, and S is the exchange rate. Given that the world price of tradable goods changes very slowly, one can normalize this relation, by assuming that the world price index P* = 1, so that the real exchange rate is approximated by the ratio of the nominal exchange rate to the consumer price index, P_{cpi}. The consumer price index serves as the proxy for the non-tradable goods price index, since this index incorporates the prices of services and other non-tradable goods. Thus, the ratio of the nominal exchange rate to the CPI price index often serves as the proxy for the real exchange rate, *ceteris paribus*:

$$REXR \approx S/P_{cpi} \qquad \text{Equation (9.19)}$$

However, this definition can give misleading results. For example, a trade liberalization programme reduces the price of tradable goods, and thus lowers the real exchange rate (or causes a real appreciation). This would not be picked up by the ratio of the nominal exchange rate to the consumer price index. One can thus make use of an alternative measure, the ratio of the wholesale price index to the consumer price index:

$$REXR \approx P_{wpi}/P_{cpi} \qquad \text{Equation (9.20)}$$

In the alternative scenario, this ratio gives a measure of real exchange rate, though this is used in a special situation as described.

9.20 Monetary and Fiscal Policy in Open Economies

An economy is 'open' to interaction with the rest of the world through two channels: through international trade, and through capital flows. Analysis of monetary and fiscal policy is at once richer, and more interesting, and more complicated in the open-economy context: the relative effectiveness of these two policy instruments depend on two other policy parameters: the choice of exchange rate regime, and the degree of capital mobility, inflows and outflows, permitted by the government. Complexities apart, the relative effectiveness of monetary and fiscal policy is perhaps the single most important question facing policy makers whose national economies are subject to a myriad of expected and unexpected shocks.

The traditional analysis of monetary and fiscal policy is the IS-LM model of Hicks and Hansen, based on their diagrammatic illustration of the Keynesian system. Their analysis was of a closed economy: no trade, no capital flows, no balance of payments constraint, no exchange rate decision. The two models that we will examine are built on the classical foundations of monetary theory and on the microeconomic analysis of the foreign exchange market. Both models tackle the problem of the appropriate use of monetary and fiscal policy under fixed and flexible exchange rates, and also the way these results depend on the degree of capital mobility.

The analysis creates the backdrop of the Mundell–Fleming and Dornbusch models under full or near-perfect capital mobility. Under fixed rates, monetary policy is weak, and fiscal policy becomes the policy-instrument for intervention. By contract, under flexible rates, fiscal policy loses much of its effectiveness, and monetary policy comes into its own. The reasons why this policy-effectiveness 'switch' takes place, as the economy moves from one exchange rate system to another, will become clear in the analysis of these two models. In a later chapter we will bring the classical 'policy trilemma' where this problem is focused more sharply.

Both the Mundell–Fleming and Dornbusch models show the usefulness of a good economic theory in analyzing real-world situations. Both models use clear, easy-to-accept, and reasonable assumptions. The basic insights about monetary and fiscal policy in the open economy come from the two models.

9.21 Mundell–Fleming Model of Fixed Exchange Rates

The model dealing with balance of payments has also initiated discussion on the role of international capital flow in the determination of the exchange rate. Modern macroeconomics has adopted this approach to analyze exchange rate determination that originated with the papers of Mundell (1963) and Fleming (1962). Their theory known as Mundell–Fleming approach (MF) states that the exchange rate enters the macroeconomic framework of output determination because change in the exchange rate affects the competitiveness of the country in the external front. The depreciation of the domestic currency has the same effects as the fiscal policy regarding its influence on the domestic demand for goods that is associated with each level of output and interest rate. The depreciation of the domestic currency shifts world demand for domestic goods and works in an expansionary manner.

The Mundell–Fleming model rests on the following three-equation set-up:

IS Curve : $I(r) = S(y)$, $I' < 0$, $S' > 0$ Equation (9.21a)

LM Curve: $M/P = L(y, r)$, $L_y > 0$, $L_r < 0$ Equation (9.21b)

FF Curve: $BOP = EX - IM(y) + NKI(r)$, Equation (9.21c)
$IM' > 0$, $NKI' > 0$

Here 'I' means first derivative of 'I(r)' with respect to the variable 'r', and the same is the meaning of others. Similarly, 'L_y' is the first derivative of 'L (y, r)' with respect to variable "y' and the same meaning is applicable to others. The 'balance of payments' (BOP) is defined as net exports (exports minus imports) plus net capital inflow NKI, the latter a positive function of rate of interest. Since exports are autonomous, imports depend on domestic income and net capital inflow is a function of rate of interest, BOP depends on two variables, domestic income and rate of interest.

The IS (Investment-Saving) curve summarizes equilibrium in the goods market, in which investment 'I' must be equal to aggregate saving 'S'. Investment is negatively related to the domestic interest rate 'r', while aggregate saving positively responds to increases in domestic income 'y'. Hence we see I < 0 and S > 0.

Figure 9.3 *Mundell–Fleming Model*

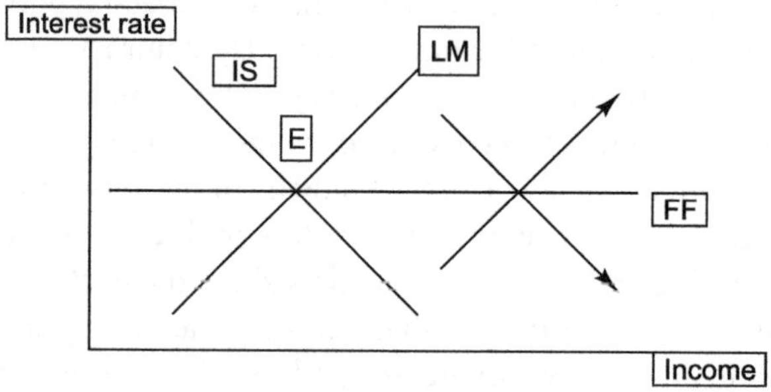

In Figure 9.3, the shift of the IS and LM curves are shown on the right, the three markets are in equilibrium at E. The LM (for Liquidity – Money Demand) curve summarizes equilibrium in the money market. Exogenous supply of real balances M/P must be equal to demand L, which is positively related to income (based on transactions demand) and negatively related to the level of interest rates. The latter is based on an inventory-theoretic cash-management approach. Hence we get Ly > 0 and Lr < 0.

The FF curve is the foreign sector or external constraint. The balance of payments definition includes exogenous exports EX, less imports IM which depend positively on domestic income, and net capital inflows. The latter depends positively on the level of domestic interest rates, relative to a fixed level of foreign interest rates.

The adjustment of the bond market is implicit in the analysis and that is through Walras' Law. The latter states that if there are N markets in the economy, and (N – 1) markets are in equilibrium, then the Nth market is in equilibrium. Once we have equilibrium conditions for goods, money, and the foreign sector, bond market is automatically taken care of. When people are happy holding their money, goods, and foreign assets in equilibrium sense, they have to be happy with the domestic interest-bearing assets they are holding.

The IS curve represents the negatively-sloped locus of (r, Y) points which clear the commodity market. A rise in Y increases savings S; thus, r must fall to induce more investment to match the increase in S. The LM curve gives the positively-sloped locus of (r, Y) points which clear the money market. An increase in Y increases demand for money with a fixed real supply (M/P), only an increase in r will decrease demand for cash balance to maintain overall equilibrium in the money market.

Again, the FF curve represents the positively-sloped (approaching flat) locus of (r, Y) points for external-sector equilibrium. For an increase in Y, there is a deficit due to the increase in imports.

To correct this deficit, an increase in the interest rate generates an incipient inflow of capital. If the capital reacts quickly and strongly to small increases in interest rates around the world, only a small increase in the domestic interest rate would be needed to restore external-sector equilibrium after the increase in Y. Thus, the higher the degree of capital mobility, the flatter the FF curve. The horizontal curve shown in the diagram implies perfect capital mobility.

The MF framework has an important implication for monetary theory. We see that under conditions of perfect capital mobility and with given interest rate of the world, monetary policy works by generating a depreciation and through that a current account surplus, and not through the interest rate channel. It draws attention to the important role of exports in the generation of aggregate demand. It also explains the relation between interest rate and exchange rate.

The MF framework implies an equilibrium exchange rate that can be obtained as the condition of goods market equilibrium or, as the equilibrium condition of the whole system. The model does not allow any role of exchange rate expectation, neither the depreciation has any effects on the domestic price system.

The overall equilibrium of the system is at E. At this point, all three markets clear. How can we be sure that all three markets will clear at the same point? The assumption of convertibility of the money supply under fixed exchange rate guarantees that the LM curve will pass through the intersection of the IS and FF curves. Under full convertibility, the change in the money supply is linked to the reserve (R) changes induced by the balance of payments:

$$\Delta M = \Delta R = BOP(Y, r),$$
$$BOP_Y < 0, BOP_r > 0 \qquad \text{Equation (9.22)}$$

Thus, a displacement of the interest rate above the FF (along the IS curve) will cause a surplus in the balance of payments, an increase in reserves, an increase in the money supply, and a rightward shift of the LM curve. Further, a rightward shift of the LM curve depresses domestic interest rates below world levels, and causes an outflow of capital. The loss of reserves generates a contraction in the money supply, forcing interest rates back up, until the initial equilibrium is restored at E. Under perfect capital mobility, the change in the level of international reserve and the money stock move in tandem. This induces interest rate adjustment, and the latter causes capital movement to stabilize both exchange rate and balance of payments.

Topic for Discussion

Explain the concept of undervalued exchange rate of a currency. In this connection, explain why Chinese renminbi is perceived to be an undervalued currency.

Further reading

Andersen, T.G., T. Bollerslev, F.X. Diebold, and C. Vega , 'Micro Effects of Macro Announcements: Real Time Price Discovery in Foreign Exchange', *American Economic Review,* 93, 38–62 , 2003.

Bogetic, Z., 'Official Dollarization: Current Experiences and Issues', *CATO Journal*, 20(2), 179–213, 2000.

Bussiere, M., G. Chortareas and R.L. Driver, 'Current Accounts, Net Foreign Assets and the Implications of Cyclical Factors', *Eastern Economic Journal,* 29, 269–86, 2003.

Devereux M.B. and C. Engel, 'Exchange Rate Pass-Through, Exchange Rate Volatility, and Exchange Rate Disconnect', *Journal of Monetary Economics*, 49, 913–40, 2002.

http://www.cato.org.

Jeanne, O. and A.K. Rose, 'Noise Trading and Exchange Rate Regimes', *Quarterly Journal of Economics,* 117, 537–69, 2002.

Mussa, M., *Argentina and the Fund: From Triumph to Tragedy*, Washington DC, Institute for International Economics 2002.

Web Resources

http://www.bis.org (accessed 27 August 2013)

http://cnnfn.com/markets/currencies (accessed 27 August 2013)

10
Modern Theory of Exchange Rate Determination and International Parity Relationship

10.1 Introduction

When we discuss the determination of exchange rate of a currency, we mean the equilibrium exchange rate. The latter becomes meaningful as it should bring equilibrium in the balance of payments of the country as well as be consistent with other desirable parameters of the economy.

There has been a tremendous growth of literature on the exchange rate in the past two decades. The success or failure of an open economy depends crucially on the management of its exchange rate. Given this importance, it is no wonder that exchange rate is one of the most heavily researched areas in the economics literature. In the case of an open economy, the exchange rate of the domestic currency is the crucial link between the domestic economy and the world. When a country has a flexible exchange rate regime, the domestic economy is expected to adjust whenever exchange rate changes. This makes the exchange rate change very important. The literature gives several theories that explain the movement of the exchange rate both in the short-run and in the long-run.

The exchange rate reflects the bilateral quantitative relation between two sovereign currencies, which themselves are the numeraire in their domestic markets for the determination of the nominal prices of the commodities. This aspect brings the exchange rate into the central place of the open economy macroeconomics. Further, since it reflects the external price of the sovereign currency, the authorities attach importance to the stability of this rate. Thus, many governments give prestige to the stability of the exchange rate. Moreover, the stability of the exchange rate is important to safeguard the economic interest of the country, and this aspect will be made clearer a little later.

The exchange rate as defined here is the indirect quotation of the same in the foreign exchange market (popularly known as forex market). But the direct quotation (which is more popular) defines the exchange rate of a currency as the price of foreign currency in terms of the domestic currency.

10.2 Determination of Exchange Rate

The existing theories explain the movement of the exchange rate rather than the determination of the rate initially. The initial determination of the exchange rate is done by the gold content of the currency as announced by the sovereign government. In the olden days of the bullion standard, the intrinsic value (read metal value) of the coin had been more or less synonymous with the face value. Thus, the metal content of the respective coin could determine the exchange rate. This system worked smoothly till the first decade of the twentieth century. Subsequently, paper gold standard replaced the gold bullion standard, and paper currency came into circulation to meet the historical needs of the time. The evolution of money in its present form and its intrinsic nature can be discerned from the following passage:

> Currency differs from other things in that an increase in its quantity exerts no direct influence on the amount of the service it renders. Inconvertible paper currencies.
>
> The exceptional character of this "quantity" statement in regard to the value of currency has been described in many ways. But the central fact in the account now submitted is that an increase in the amount of money in a country does not increase the total services which it performs. This statement is not inconsistent with the fact that an increase in the amount of gold in a country's currency increases her means of obtaining goods by exporting gold, and also gives her the power of converting some of her currency into articles of ornament. It merely means that the purpose needs to be clearly defined and generally acceptable. Next, it needs to command a stable purchasing power; such stability can be attained by an inconvertible paper currency, so long as the government (*a*) can prevent forged notes from getting into circulation, and (*b*) can make the people absolutely certain that genuine notes will not be issued in excess. Gold coins may indeed be regarded as currency based on the belief that nature will not countenance a violent increase in the currency drawn from her stores. If we were to discover (in spite of the opinion of geologists and mineralogists that no such thing is physically possible) a mine of gold ore with contents as large in volume as those of a vast coal mine, then gold coin would cease to serve any good purpose (Marshall, 1924; 91–92).

This quote explains in detail the nature of money and how the stability of its price depends on some economic circumstances. From the value of money in general, we can see the determination of the exchange rate. But the process can be further explained by studying the history of the gold standard.

10.3 Gold Standard: A Brief History

The international gold standard dates from 1870, though the oldest known gold coins date from the sixth century BCE. The system lasted until 1914, when the World War I started, and then had a brief revival in the 1920s. Britain was on a full legal gold standard from 1816, but on a de facto gold standard since 1717. Until the late nineteenth century, most countries were on a bimetallic standard. Some countries, particularly China and Mexico, were on silver alone and remained so into the twentieth century. When gold was discovered in California in 1848, Holland and Belgium switched from bimetallism to silver alone in 1850, as gold was considered to be too unstable to provide the basis for the currency. After the Civil War, the United States adopted a de facto gold standard with the resumption of the specie payment on the Civil War greenbacks in 1879. Two decades later, it moved formally into the system with the Gold Standard Act of 1900.

The initial exchange rate system had been nearly a fixed exchange rate, one between the currencies of the countries on the gold standard. Further, the system remained assured by the possibility of profitable gold arbitrage whenever exchange rates reached the gold export or import points, determined by the mint charges and the cost of shipping gold. The fluctuations in the exchange rates had been influenced by the changes in the production costs in the mint, by the gradual decline in the shipping costs and also by the interest rate changes.

The system of gold standard which remained functional in the nineteenth and early twentieth century had been typified by three broad features. First, the nineteenth-century gold standard was a gold coinage standard in which gold coins remained in domestic circulation, and these were interchangeable with notes at the Central Bank, and the latter maintained a gold reserve to maintain and safeguard interchangeability.

Second, within the gold standard of the nineteenth century, British sterling operated as an international currency on equal terms with gold. The sterling was even stronger compared to gold and the latter derived its value as a monetary asset from its convertibility into sterling (Tew, 1948). In the case of settlement of international transactions, both gold and sterling were used, as overseas banks of many countries held working balances in sterling.

Third, it is interesting to compare the gold standard of the period 1870–1914 based on gold, and the internationally acceptable sterling with the gold exchange standard of the post-1918 period. The crucial difference between the two periods had been the much weaker position of sterling, and many other currencies were established in countries on the basis of gold standard. Thus the structure of the gold exchange standard in the post-1918 period had been weak, and before the full realization of its weakness, another World War broke out in the late 1930s, putting an end to the system.

The gold standard had evolved basically into a system of international balance-of-payments adjustment as theoretically developed by the classical economists. The classicists contended that the movement of goods at the international level was the result of the differences of the relative price levels, and the dimension of the movement of goods would be determined by the laws of comparative advantage. While the changes in the relative price level would depend on the supply of money and natural advantages, the surplus and deficits in international transactions were taken care of through the shipment of gold and/or through the accounts in British sterling. Thus the quantity theory of money as developed by Hume and the comparative cost doctrine as developed by Ricardo, supplied the theoretical building blocks of the gold standard (Meade, 1951).

152 • Modern Theory of Exchange Rate Determination

The brief description of the system of gold standard helps in the understanding of the exchange rate mechanism in the world. The salient points which are important can be written as: the cost of production of gold and the stability in the price of it, the system of money supply as in practice in the principal countries, the operation of the law of comparative advantage, the movement of the relative price levels, and the cooperation among the central banks of the countries — these factors used to influence the exchange rate of the principal currencies.

10.4 Models of Exchange Rate Determination

A large number of models have been developed in the literature to explain the fluctuation of the exchange rate, and a systematic grouping in some schematic form is difficult, though not impossible. Broadly, we can put all the models into two categories — the monetary and the non-monetary models. Later on, various subgroups of models have been developed within each group. The aim of this brief survey is to give a broad synoptic view of the whole literature.

Purchasing Power Parity Theory (PPP)

The Purchasing Power Parity (PPP) theory was developed first by Cassel (1918) and since then it has been one principal building block in the monetarist literature. In its simple and absolute form it states the following equation:

$$E = P/P^* \tag{Equation 10.1}$$

Where P and P* are domestic and foreign price levels and E is the exchange rate or the price of foreign currency in terms of the domestic currency.

Expressed as in equation (10.1), the exchange rate between any two currencies is equal to the ratio of their price indices. Thus, the exchange rate is a nominal magnitude on prices. Further, equation (10.1) can be rewritten as:

$$P = E \cdot P^* \tag{Equation 10.2}$$

Or the exchange rate converts the foreign price into the domestic price. In other words, equation (10.2) implies the law of one price, i.e., a tradable commodity like HMT watch should cost the same whether it is purchased at Mumbai or New York, when we ignore the transport cost. The PPP doctrine is often used to explain the long-run movement of the exchange rate. From equation (10.1), after logarithmic transformation, we have:

$$\log E = \log P - \log P^* \tag{Equation 10.3}$$

Differentiating equation (10.3) with respect to t (time), we get:

$$(1/E)\,(dE/dt) = 1/p \cdot (dp/dt) - (1/p^*)(dp^*/dt)$$

or, we can write using symbols

$$g_E = g_P - g^*_P \tag{Equation 10.4}$$

where g stands for rate of growth of the concerned variables.

Thus equation (10.4) explains that the rate of change of the exchange rate (here direct quote) is the difference between the rate of inflation of domestic economy and the foreign country. Thus if India experiences inflation at the rate of 10 per cent, while the United States has an inflation rate of 5 per cent, then the Indian rupee is expected to depreciate by 5 per cent over the year.

As mentioned above, the PPP explains the long-run movement of the price level and the empirical test of the doctrine has been conducted on many occasions by different researchers. A good survey of that can be had in Officer (1976) and Dornbusch (1976).

Empirical evidences on PPP, based on studies for the last three decades, are a mixed one. The studies on time series PPP relationship for aggregate price indices show evidence of persistent deviations. Once relative prices are not strictly constant, PPP is seen to perform differently depending on the type of index chosen for empirical analysis. But the studies of high inflation situation generally lend support to the PPP, as in these situations, close cumulative movements of internal prices, and exchange rates are seen. When an inflationary process is on, wages, prices, and the exchange rate fluctuate with different frequencies and intensity. But if hyper-inflation takes over, the variability of different prices converges on the movement of the exchange rate. Such tests are carried out in Isard (1977) and Kravis and Lipsey (1978). The common experience is that deviations from PPP become the least under the hyper-inflation situations.

Empirical Test of PPP and Experimental Economics

Among the many papers written on the deviations from the PPP doctrine in real life, the study of Noussair, Plott and Riezman (N-P-R) (1994) is interesting, as their work is in the area of experimental economics. The latter consists in generating data from properly designed 'laboratory experiments', mimicking the economics of market-decision making through the behaviour of properly selected persons, who participate in the experiments. These data are then used for the empirical tests of economic theories.

One result of N-P-R study is that the purchasing power theory is not supported when tested with the data. The reasons for the failure of PPP are conjectured to be due to the differing speeds at which markets adjust in different countries. Since market is one of the broader infrastructures in a country conditioned by sovereign rules and regulations, the speed of adjustments should differ depending on the nature of the specific market conditions.

In general, prices within countries do not seem to be adjusting rapidly to local demand and supply conditions, although there is evidence of slow convergence on local market clearing.

Another result of N-P-R study is that the movement of the exchange rate from one market period to the next is influenced by the international demand for and supply of currency. Over the course of the experiment, the exchange rate moves in accordance with the equal system surplus adjustment path.

PPP and Price Level in Poor Countries

There has been an interesting statistical observation in the international scene, and that is the positive relation of a country's price level to the level of per capita real income. To put it differently, it means that the intrinsic value of one USD when converted to Indian rupee, increases much more than what it can buy at the United States. The discrepancy in the price level between rich and poor countries is explained in terms of the prices of non-tradables. It is observed that non-tradables are far more expensive in the rich countries.

Balassa (1964) and Samuelson (1964) have explained the relative lower prices of non-tradables in the poor countries. The Balassa–Samuelson (B S) theory assumes that the labour in poorer countries is less productive in the traded sector, but the international productivity differences in the non-tradable sectors are negligible. PPP ensures equality of prices of tradable goods in all the countries. The lower productivity of labour in the poorer countries will lead to lower wages of labour. This reduces the cost of production of non-tradables in the poorer countries, and so the prices of non-tradables will be lower. Thus rich countries with higher productivity in tradable sector will have higher wages and higher prices for non-tradables. This means that their price levels will also be higher compared to poor countries. The B–S productivity differential postulate has statistical support as observed in some studies.

10.5 PPP and Real Interest Parity

Under the assumption of perfect international mobility of capital and risk neutral speculation, a link can be established between the nominal interest rate and the expected rate of depreciation of the currency in the following way:

$$i = i^* + x \quad \text{(Equation 10.5)}$$

Where i and i^* are the nominal interest rates of the home country and abroad and x is the expected rate of depreciation. Equation (10.5) is also known as open economy Fisher equation. The relation of nominal interest rate and the real interest rate is shown by:

$$i = r + \Pi \quad \text{(Equation 10.6)}$$

Where Π is the expected rate of inflation and r is the real interest rate. Combining equations (10.5) and (10.6) we get the relation of real interest parity (Dornbusch, 1987):

$$R^* = r + R/R \quad \text{(Equation 10.7)}$$

Where R/R is the expected rate of real appreciation. Thus, real interest parity prevails when the difference of the two real interest rates equals the expected real appreciation. The implication of this is clear. Under the exact PPP, real exchange rate is constant. This gives a simple but robust policy guide to the authority who remains cautious about the competitive strength of the country's exports. It is the real exchange rate which is important for the latter.

10.6 Monetary Approach to Exchange Rate

Since an exchange rate is the price of one country's money in terms of that of another country, it makes sense in theory to analyze the determinants of that price in terms of the outstanding stocks of and demand for the monies of two countries. This is the basic rationale of monetarist approach.

The monetary approach to the balance of payments and the exchange rate emphasizes that payment surpluses and deficits reflect the imbalances between the demand for money in each country, and the supply of reserves that result from the monetization of domestic assets. When the demand for money increases at a greater rate than supply based on domestic assets, the supply of commodities will exceed the demand and the country will realize a trade surplus in international transactions. The latter induces more inflow of foreign assets resulting in an increase in the domestic money supply and possibly a higher price level also.

The monetary approach places the problem in a general equilibrium framework. The model in a two-country case can be put as follows following (Frankel, 1983):

$$M - p = b_1 y - b_2 i \quad \text{(Equation 10.8.1)}$$
$$M^* - p^* = b_1 y^* - b_2 i^* \quad \text{(Equation 10.8.2)}$$
$$i - i^* = E(e) + b_3 k \quad \text{(Equation 10.8.3)}$$
$$E(\Delta e) = E(\Delta p - \Delta p^*) - b_4 (e - \bar{e}) \quad \text{(Equation 10.8.4)}$$
$$e = (\bar{p} - \bar{p}^*) \quad \text{(Equation 10.8.5)}$$

Here, 'p', 'm' and 'y' refer to the logarithm of exchange rate, price level, money supply and real income respectively and i is the interest rate, k is the cumulative balance on the external private capital account. The definition of the exchange rate is direct (i.e., value of foreign currency in terms of domestic currency). Further, bars indicate long-run equilibrium value, asterisks indicate foreign country, Δ indicates first difference, and E the expected value in the sense of mathematical expectation.

Equations (10.8.1) and (10.8.2) are money demand function of two countries, where prices are set at long run values and come as a solution of these. Equation (10.8.3) states that interest rate differential is explained by the expected change in the exchange rate and/or in response to accumulation of international credit (K < 0) or indebtedness (K > 0). Equation (10.8.4) states that the expected change in the exchange rate is due to the expected inflation differential and/or deviation of the exchange rate from the equilibrium value. Equation (10.8.5) expresses the PPP doctrine straight away.

The solution of the equations (10.8.1) to (10.8.5) in terms of the exchange rate gives the following expressions in the reduced form:

$$E = (m - m^*) - b_1 (y - y^*) + b_2 E(\Delta p - \Delta p^*) - (1/b_4 - b_2)(r - r^*) + (b_3/b_4)k$$
(Equation 10.9)

Here r is the real interest rate (that means, $r = i - E[\Delta p]$)

The estimation of equation (10.9) means a joint test of a set of hypothesis, and all of these hypotheses are not central to the validity of monetary approach. The latter can be tested by examining the validity and stability of the coefficients in equation (10.9) and by testing when $b_3 = 0$ (which means whether uncovered interest parity holds).

10.7 Overshooting Exchange Rate

Exchange rate exhibits much more volatility compared to other prices. Some analysts argue that in the short run, following a disequilibrium in the money market, prices will adjust slowly to the new equilibrium level, but interest rate and exchange rate adjust quickly. This non-uniform speed of adjustment to the equilibrium level allows some interesting behavior in the movement of the exchange rate.

Suppose the interest rate parity condition holds like the following:

$$i = i^* + (F - S)/S \qquad \text{(Equation 10.10)}$$

Where 'S' and 'F' are spot and forward exchange rates respectively. Now, given the foreign interest rate 'i*', if domestic rate 'i' declines, the second term in the right hand side (RHS), i.e., (F–S)/S, which is the expected depreciation of the domestic currency, must decline to maintain parity. When domestic money supply increases leading to an increase in prices, this higher price level should induce depreciation of the currency by PPP, because

$$S = P/P^* \qquad \text{(Equation 10.11)}$$

This higher expected future spot rate (a higher value of S means depreciation in this case) will be reflected in a higher forward rate (F) now. But if F rises — while at the same time (F – S) must fall to maintain the interest rate parity — S will have to increase more than the forward rate F. But once prices start rising, it reduces real money balances leading to an increase in the interest rate. Over time as interest rate increases, the exchange rate (S) has to decline to maintain parity. This shows that the initial increase in S will be much higher than its long-run value, or the exchange rate will overshoot its long-run value. This non-uniform speed of adjustment of different prices gives an overshooting exchange rate which is the important feature of the model of Dornbusch (1976). Later on, this model has been extended by incorporating PPP into it in Driskell (1981).

10.8 Dornbusch Model of Flexible Exchange Rates

The Dornbusch model was published in 1976, after the start of the post-Bretton Woods system of floating exchange rates. The Dornbusch model shows what a good theory can do to clear up some very widespread misunderstandings. The volatility of the major exchange rates after the switch from a fixed to floating system was quite pronounced. No one ever expected the exchange-rate swings to be so pronounced and so prolonged. The feeling among the policy-makers at the Smithsonian Accords in 1971 and 1973, which killed the Bretton Woods system, was that floating would quickly restore exchange rates to sustainable stable equilibrium rates, in which trade would be balanced. The feeling was that markets could do the job better than finance ministers and central bank governors in smoke-filled rooms could. If the market was efficient, and doing its job, then exchange rates would quickly settle down to correct levels, trade would be balanced, and uncertainty would diminish.

Of course, as data shows, nothing like that happened. Exchange rates went wild; trade imbalances persisted, and actually deteriorated in the 1980s. One reaction was that somehow the market was inefficient, or expectations irrational — that the exchange rate was following a speculative bubble, or was subject to a 'herd instinct', based on expectations not grounded in fundamentals. The contribution of the Dornbusch model is in showing that wild exchange rate fluctuation — far from being a rare occurrence in an efficient market with 'rational' or 'consistent' expectations, based on market fundamentals — are what we should expect. High volatility in the exchange market is a natural consequence of a high degree of international asset arbitrage, coupled with a relatively slow speed of adjustment by price setters in domestic goods markets.

The basic set-up of the Dornbusch model is in three equations:

DD (Demand) Equation : $y = -y^* + d(e - p)$, $d > 0$
LM (Liquidity-money) Equation : $m/p = L(y, r)$, $L_y > 0$, $L_r < 0$
AA (Asset Arbitrage) Equation : $\Delta e = r - r^*$ (Equation 10.12)

The DD equation represents goods market equilibrium. Output demand y is equal to its long run normal level –y when the real exchange rate is constant, with e = p. When the real exchange rate is above its equilibrium level, in the case of a real depreciation, with e > p, demand is above the long-run level, and there is excess demand. For the case of a real appreciation, with e < p, there is excess supply. This DD block simply integrates into a macroeconomic setting, the idea of the real exchange rate, as the key variable for determining resource allocation and equilibrium levels of demand in the real sector of the economy.

The second equation, the monetary sector, is expressed in logarithmic terms. Demand for money is a positive function of output and a negative function of the domestic interest rate. The AA (asset arbitrage block) simply states the uncovered interest parity relation. The expected and actual rate of change in the exchange rate is equal to the interest differential, $r - r^*$.

The diagrammatic exposition of the Dornbusch model appears in the Figure 10.1 below:

Figure 10.1 Dornbusch Model: Monetary Expansion with Overshooting

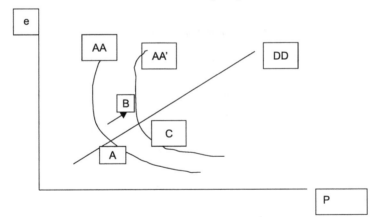

The DD curve summarizes the equilibrium, e.g., pairs for equilibrium in the goods market. We see that the DD curve is simply a straight line through the origin. As long as e and p change uniformly, equilibrium is maintained in this market.

The AA curve integrates the asset-market equilibrium conditions from the money demand-supply relation and the asset arbitrage conditions. It is a downward-sloping curve. Why? An increase in the price level p lowers the real money stock, which in turn forces interest rates to rise.

The rise in interest rate generates an incipient capital inflow, which causes an appreciation of the exchange rate, so e falls. Thus, asset-market equilibrium relations imply a negative relation between p and e. The Dornbusch model makes one important assumption about dynamic speeds of adjustment. Note in the goods market or DD block that the parameter d > 0 is finite: the goods market does not clear instantaneously, but takes time to adjust, in order to ensure that $y = -y^*$.

However, Dornbusch assumes that exchange rate changes take place instantaneously, in order to satisfy the asset-arbitrage condition. This operating assumption guarantees the overshooting of the exchange rate in response to a monetary expansion.

Zero Capital Mobility Issues

There is one important implication of the Dornbusch model as shown in the above diagram. To evaluate the dynamics of the adjustment path under zero capital mobility, simply draw the AA curve as a flat horizontal line. Under zero capital mobility, a rise in price level p lowers real money, which raises domestic interest rates. But this interest rate increase generates no incipient capital inflow, so the exchange rate does not appreciate. The exchange rate stays the same for all levels of prices.

When AA curve is flat, the exchange rate jumps to a new long-run level, and stays there, as p gradually adjusts. Therefore, with zero capital mobility, overshooting vanishes. It follows then that capital mobility is the driving force behind overshooting exchange rates. When capital is mobile, and arbitrage opportunities appear, exchange rates will remain volatile and remain far away from the long-run purchasing power levels. Thus under conditions of efficient markets and rational arbitrage, the exchange rates may remain out of equilibrium for a longer time.

10.9 The Portfolio-Balance Approach

The portfolio-balance approach (PBA) points to the links between the balance of payments flows and adjustments in the asset stocks. It emphasizes that the models of the capital account should be rooted in the behavioural models of the supplies of and demand for the portfolio of stocks. This aspect is same as the monetary approaches. Both the monetary approach and the PBA generally assume that each country's money balances are held entirely by the citizens of that country. But while the monetary approach regards home currency securities, the PBA regards them as imperfect substitutes.

Following Dooley and Isard (1983) and Isard (1995), the basic features of PBA can be explained in the context of a two-country two-currency world, which have two composite private sectors with different sets of asset preferences. The net portfolio holdings of the two private sectors combined correspond to the liabilities of the official sectors of the two countries, and this is net of the liabilities of the official agencies to each other.

The symbols of the model are as follows:
- $\bar{M}$ and $\bar{M}^*$ are the stocks of non-interest bearing claims on the home and foreign governments respectively corresponding to the monetary bases.
- $\bar{B}$ and $\bar{F}$ are the privately held stocks of interest bearing claims on the home and foreign governments, referred to as bond and securities.

The assumptions are the M and B are denominated in the home currency unit and M* and B* are denominated in foreign currency. The net portfolio holding of home private residents, which are assumed to hold the entire stock of home base money, are denoted by M, B and F, and similarly, those of foreign private residents by M*, B* and F*.

The model can be written as:

$$M = \bar{M} \quad \text{(Equation 10.13)}$$
$$M = \bar{M}^* \quad \text{(Equation 10.14)}$$
$$B + B^* = \bar{B} \quad \text{(Equation 10.15)}$$
$$F + F^* = \bar{F} \quad \text{(Equation 10.16)}$$
$$W = M + B + SF \quad \text{(Equation 10.17)}$$
$$W^* = M^* + B^*/S + F^* \quad \text{(Equation 10.18)}$$

Here (10.13) to (10.16) are the relevant market clearing conditions, and (10.17) and (10.18) define the nominal portfolio wealth (W and W*) of the two private sectors, and S is the exchange rate of the home currency (home currency value of one unit of foreign currency).

The size of the stocks of the four categories of financial assets — the stocks of non-interest bearing claims on the home and foreign governments and the privately-held stocks of interest bearing claims — held by private individuals of the two countries is determined by the interactions of the monetary policies, budget deficit, and official interventions in the foreign composition of private portfolios in each country and is assumed to depend on the own-currency rates of return on domestic and foreign bonds, together with a set of other variables. One such variable is the scale of monetary transactions within the country. The rates of return are the own rates of interest on home and foreign bonds, denoted by r and r* respectively. Also the expected rate of appreciation of the home currency unit, n reflects the rate of return partly. Also Z and Z* denote the vectors of other variables that are meaningful to home and foreign nationals respectively. Further, there is no difference between the desired and actual compositions of financial portfolios. Thus, the rest of the model can be written as:

$$M/W = m(r, r^* - P, Z) \quad \text{(Equation 10.19)}$$
$$B/W = b(r, r^* - P, Z) \quad \text{(Equation 10.20)}$$
$$SF/W = f(r, r^* - P, Z) \quad \text{(Equation 10.21)}$$
$$M^*/W^* = m^*(r, r^* + P, Z^*) \quad \text{(Equation 10.22)}$$
$$B^*/S = b^*(r, r^* + P, Z^*) \quad \text{(Equation 10.23)}$$

Also by definition, portfolio shares must add to unity, or

$$M + b + f = 1 \quad \text{(Equation 10.24)}$$
$$M^* + b^* + f^* = 1 \quad \text{(Equation 10.25)}$$

It is assumed that private portfolio holders are risk-averse, and so they perceive home and foreign bonds as imperfect substitutes. Also for the convenience of analysis, we can focus on the case in which the asset stocks are determined exogenous by the policy authorities and the endogenous variables are the interest rate and the exchange rates. The latter adjust to clear the market.

10.10 News and Volatility in the Exchange Rate

The market for stocks has always been in the forefront in the use of the latest technology, so that the market remains organized and economic agents are equipped with full information set. The efficient market hypothesis (EMH) describes the asset market as efficient if the asset price 'fully reflects' available information, some concept of equilibrium expected return or equilibrium prices are required.

In mathematical symbols, using the concept of equilibrium expected return, the excess market return on asset i (W_{it}) can be written as:

$$W_{i,t} = h_{i,t} - E(h_{i,t}/I_{t-1}) \qquad \text{(Equation 10.26)}$$

Where $h_{i,t}$ is one period percentage return, I_{t-1} is the information set, bar denotes the equilibrium value. If the market for asset i is efficient, then the sequence $W_{i,t}$ should be orthogonal to the information set, i.e.,

$$E(W_{i,t}/I_{t-1}) = 0 \qquad \text{(Equation 10.27)}$$

And also it is not serially correlated. Thus, EMH implies two things simultaneously: it assumes that agents in forming their expectations in period (t – 1) are rational in the sense that they cannot make systematic errors in their decisions and also they know the expected equilibrium prices.

The structure of stock market and foreign exchange market is more or less similar. One implication of EMH is that when EMH is operational, whether some agents can make abnormal profit. Also in the foreign exchange market, EMH implies that the forward rate is the best predictor of the future spot rate. When agents on both the sides optimize through their decision, the forward risk premium (B_t) in the equilibrium should consist of two components: a constant risk premium term and a time-varying component of the risk premium.

Putting all the variables in natural logarithm to avoid Siegel paradox in this particular case (Siegel, 1972), we can write:

$$F_t = \Delta S_{t+1} + e_{t+1} + \beta_t \qquad \text{(Equation 10.28)}$$

When ΔS_{t+1} is the actual change in the exchange rate in logarithm, I_{t+1} is a random forecasting error and β_t is the risk premium. In the forex market, the role of news comes through in the equation and this explains why the forward market of the exchange rate is so much volatile.

Researchers have built models to capture the nature of the distribution of I_{t+1} so that a systematic pattern can be discerned about the volatility of the exchange rate. While historical volatility can be modeled with sufficient accuracy, this historical volatility is a poor guide to the prediction of future volatility. This is the essence of all types of uncertainty in the literature.

Another aspect of the forex market is about the role of expectations. Most models are based on the assumption of normality about the fluctuation of the exchange rate, though the empirical basis of this assumption is poor. It is no surprise then that the predictive power of most models is very poor compared to the simple random-walk type model.

In the pursuit of a fair knowledge of the movement of the exchange rate, researchers have emphasized the non-linear dynamic system which can typically describe the movement of the exchange rate in the short-run. One such theory is the chaos model in which chaotic behaviour is defined as a non-linear deterministic system in which all time paths are bounded, though trajectories starting close together, diverge exponentially as time passes. In such a situation, one can venture only a short-run prediction, and a long-run prediction would be hazardous.

10.11 The Foreign Exchange Market

The players in the foreign exchange market have to function with a large stake, in the form of exposure of their portfolio to the fluctuation in the prices. This makes them very sensitive to the slightest change in the market. News, vital economic information and even rumour, can change the perceptions of the agents who then revise their expectations. This is why the premium in the forward market may change though economic fundamentals remain fixed. In the very short run, a sudden shift in demand will change the exchange rate as shown in the Figure 10.2.

Figure 10.2 *Demand and Supply of Dollar Changes the Price: A Shift of the Demand Curve*

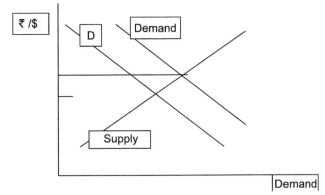

Source: Prepared by the author

Here the vertical axis shows the rupee price of USD (direct exchange rate) and horizontal axis shows the quantity of dollar. As the demand curve shifts up, the price increases, which means a depreciation of rupee.

One school believes in this line of approach for an explanation of the movement of the forward rate. This is the approach of the economists, who of course, place due importance in the interest differential. There is another institutional view, sometime known as the Cambist or dealing-room view, which claims that only interest rate differential matters in the determination of the forward rate. In other words, the Cambist approach predicts that the forward rate is determined by the relative interest differential. But the two approaches give the same result under two different scenarios. In a world full of uncertainty, both the relationships will lead to the same result if the speculators are risk-neutral, whereas in a completely certain world the same result would hold if purchasing power parity holds and Fisher equation guides the determination of the nominal interest rate vis-à-vis the rate of inflation.

10.12 Currency Substitution and Exchange Rate

It is generally assumed that domestic residents do not hold foreign currency for its use as a medium of exchange. This assumption does not hold in countries which have fully convertible currencies and where multinational corporations (MNCs) have significant influence in the gross domestic product. Because of their involvement in the international trade, MNCs hold multiple currencies as a hedging device against potential loss due to the exchange rate depreciation. In this situation, actual supply of money domestically is bound to be quite different from what the central bank supplies, with the result, that both the price level and the exchange rate of the domestic currency will be at variance with what the central bank predicts, depending on its own estimate of monetary aggregates. The situation is much more prominent with the USD. Since the latter is an international currency, many central banks hold the dollar in their portfolios, and as a result, the US money supply has a limited bearing on the US inflation rate.

It is argued that because of the situation as explained in the previous paragraph, the growth of money supply of a country is a poor predictor of its price level movement (Mckinnon, 1981, 1988). When price stability becomes the principal objective, each country should determine the optimum level of the money stock, granted that some foreign currency will be held. Also the sterilization policy of the central bank should be applied with discretion. For example, if it is found that yen/dollar rate is appreciating, the central bank of Japan can buy dollars to correct the rate rather than using sterilization policy to influence the supply of domestic monetary stock. In the context of currency substitution, some sort of cooperation among countries is necessary for the maintenance of stability in the exchange rate.

10.13 Disequilibrium Models

As noted earlier, the instability in the foreign exchange market started in the middle of 1980s, and the volume of trading also increased rapidly. The currency trading assumed a nature of commodity trading with little link to merchandise trade, where money is supposed to be used as a medium.

The market for foreign currencies nowadays reveals turnover of more than a trillion USD per day. Only a tiny fraction of the volume of transactions is due to the international movement of commodities in the market. The market is more concerned about the small changes in the spot rate, and economic fundamentals are not able to predict such type of changes. Thus new types of models are developed which basically assume disequilibrium in the market. For example, some participants in the exchange market rely on 'follow-the-leader' approach and behaviour is guided by conventional wisdom; changes in the exchange market reflect a bandwagon effect. Further, there may be 'speculative bubble' in the exchange rate. As explained in MacDonald and Taylor (1989), if e_t is the spot rate and e^*_t is the equilibrium value, then the relation

$$e_t = e^*_t + b_t \qquad \text{(Equation 10.29)}$$

shows how rational bubble (b) can make the important difference in the expectation of the agents in the market. Such a situation may emerge when the market exchange rate has deviated from the fundamental solution. It is argued in Dornbusch and Frankel (1989) that significant appreciation of the USD in the early 1980s was partly due to the operations of the bubble. An interesting aspect of this 'bubble hypothesis' is that once the nature of the distribution of the bubble, b_t is known or approximated, efficient forecast can be made about the spot rate. This type of approach has some problems. First, the success of the estimation depends on the assumed model of the exchange rate. The model specification may go wrong. Second, 'bubbles' may be generated within the system through a measurement error or through a small sample bias.

10.14 Exchange Rate Systems and Policy

Over a long process of historical evolution and with innovative experiments of countries, a set of exchange systems are seen in the literatures that are being practiced by the countries. In this section, we try to explain these systems briefly.

The system that a developing country chooses depends on its circumstances at the time and also on the long-run goals of economic policy. A country may wish to pursue exchange rate stability because of the instability and perceived disadvantages of floating rates. In that case, it will wish to choose some form of fixed exchange rate regime. Again, a country may wish to use its exchange rate to achieve various real objectives in the domestic economy, such as a faster rate of economic growth and full employment. In which case, it can set a target for the *real* exchange rate. A real exchange rate target will require frequent changes in the nominal exchange rate faced with different price situations. Here the country will wish to choose some form of flexible exchange rate regime.

If a country has liberalized its capital markets and the capital account of the balance of payments, that makes the capital freely mobile, it will be difficult for that country to pursue an exchange rate target and operate an independent monetary policy at the same time. When heavy capital outflows cause the possibility of currency depreciation, the only effective way to stop this is to raise domestic interest rates. The reverse dilemma occurs with capital inflows. The way open to the economy to reconcile internal and external equilibrium is either to control capital movements, or to allow the exchange rate to float. Theoretically, free floating allows a country to pursue an independent monetary policy. But no country is completely indifferent to the value of its exchange rate.

Five main types of exchange rate regime can be distinguished. Proposals for alternative exchange rate regimes fall within one or the other of the five main categories.

The five main types of regime are:
(1) rigidly fixed exchange rates, including the old gold standard; currency boards; currency unions, and 'dollarization' (adopting the currency of another country, e.g., the USD);
(2) pegged exchange rates such as the old Bretton Woods adjustable peg system (or gold exchange standard), and pegging to a basket of currencies;
(3) managed exchange rate flexibility including crawling pegs; exchange rate bands, and crawling bands;
(4) freely floating exchange rates; and
(5) multiple exchange rates, of which dual exchange rates are a special case.

10.15 Rigidly Fixed Exchange Rate

The Gold Standard

The old gold standard was in operation in its purest form between 1880 and 1914, and it collapsed in 1931. It was a fixed exchange rate system under which balance-of-payments adjustment was supposed to be achieved automatically through internal adjustment provided certain rules were adhered to. We have discussed this system in Chapter 2.

10.16 Currency Boards

A Currency Board System (CBS) is an extreme form of fixed exchange rates. It requires each unit of a country's currency to be backed by an equal amount of a reserve currency, such as the USD. The CBS was widely practised in Africa under British colonial rule before independence; and more recently, between 1991 and 2002, Argentina anchored its currency to the USD in this way. Linking a weak currency to a stronger currency can be a useful anti-inflation device to gain monetary credibility. The CBS has similarity with the old gold standard system, where the currency had to be backed by gold, is clear.

There are two major serious disadvantages of CBS. First, credit for entrepreneurs to invest is not elastic to the needs of trade, because it depends on the availability of the reserve currency. Second, if the reserve currency appreciates in value, so too does the currency that is linked to it. This can cause serious problems of competitiveness with other trading partners, and damage exports potential due to loss of competitiveness. A recent example is Argentina. It went into serious recession with the appreciation of the USD in 2000/01, and Argentina's Currency Board was disbanded in 2002.

10.17 Currency Union

Currency Union (CU) is another extreme form of hard peg. In this system, countries decide to adopt a single currency, so that by definition, exchange rates between member countries of the Union disappear. CU is the real life experiment of optimum currency area concept. The ideal conditions for an optimal currency area are:
 (1) economic cycles should be synchronized and economic shocks symmetrical so that a single monetary policy is suitable for all members;
 (2) labour and capital are freely mobile so that the underemployment of factors of production is minimized;
 (3) fiscal prudence is maintained by each member.

European Union is a successful story of currency; 12 countries have initially merged their currencies and have a single currency Euro. It is expected that another set of countries are ready to join the Union soon.

Dollarization is a variant of the Currency Union. In this experiment, the country simply adopts the currency of another country, say USD. As far as monetary and exchange rate policy is concerned, the country becomes an adjunct to the country issuing the currency. This seems to be the last resort for countries unable to manage their own affairs. In recent years, countries such as Ecuador and El Salvador have dollarized.

10.18 Pegged Exchange Rate

An exchange rate is said to be pegged if the central banks accept an obligation to prevent the market rate of exchange from deviating by more than a specified amount from the peg, also called a margin. Some multiple of the margin gives the band — or maximum range within which the exchange rate is allowed to move without a change in the peg. The Bretton Woods system was a pegged exchange rate system. In this, each country's currency was pegged to the USD, so that bilateral rates of exchange between countries were also pegged, and each country was obliged to maintain rates within a margin of 1 per cent either side of the central rate. The system was called the 'adjustable peg system'.

The problem of maintaining the pegged system is the problem of synchronization of monetary and fiscal policies with the country of the currency to which the currency is pegged. In South Asia, some countries like Thailand and South Korea pegged their currencies to the USD. Since the middle of 1990s, these countries found it difficult to closely follow the fiscal and monetary policies of the US because of system rigidities and other reasons. Soon their currencies went out of sync and became over-valued. Once that was revealed in the market perception, crisis came. The rest is history.

Choice of a currency to which the domestic currency would be pegged is a major issue. This issue is called the 'Optimal Peg'. There are two broad choices of peg: (*i*) pegging to a single currency such as, for example, the dollar, pound or euro; and (*ii*) pegging to an individually tailored basket of currencies reflecting the trade of the country concerned.

The choice of the peg will depend on what the country is trying to achieve, or its objective function. If the objective is macroeconomic stability, pegging against a single currency is unlikely to give the desired result, since movements in a country's exchange rate will bear no relation to its own balance of payments, as the currency's exchange rate will move according to the currency to which it is pegged.

Pegging to a basket of currencies where the weights reflect the direction and elasticity of total trade (exports and imports) between the country and its trading partners is much more useful for the stability of the exchange rate, and also the currency movement can be used for the promotion of trade and correction of balance of payments.

10.19 Managed Exchange Rates

With managed exchange rates, there are no rigid pegs or fixed parities that the authorities are obliged to preserve. In this system, the currency is free to vary, but the authorities intervene to avoid excessive appreciation or depreciation. A weak currency may lead to excessive depreciation which the authorities may wish to avoid because of its negative fall-out on domestic front. Again, countries with a strong currency may wish to avoid appreciation if they want to accumulate reserves.

Sometimes, a country may engineer the depreciation of its currency that would otherwise appreciate if the foreign exchange market were left to operate freely. Such behavior is sometimes referred to as 'leaning against the wind'. This is done to achieve special advantage in the external sector, may be to change the term of trade vis-à-vis a particular trade partner.

One type of managed exchange rate system is the crawling peg. In this system, a country maintains its pegged exchange rate within agreed margins, at a level equal to the moving average of the market exchange rate over an agreed previous time period. Both appreciation and depreciation within a tolerable limit are allowed in such a way that it should have minimum impact on the balance of payments.

10.20 Freely Floating Exchange Rate

Only a handful of elite currencies have the system of free floating exchange rate system. In this, the exchange rate is left to find its own level in the market without any official intervention. This implies that theoretically the country is completely indifferent to its exchange rate, though in reality no country can afford to remain aloof in this regard.

Leading currencies like USD, Canadian dollar, yen, euro, Australian dollar and some others are free floating currencies. The fiscal and monetary policies of these concerned countries are always maintained at an efficient level in the sense that inflation is kept at a minimum. The economies are mature in the sense that the balance of payments of these countries can absorb the effects of exchange rate fluctuations without any significant fall-out in the domestic economy.

The three currencies — USD, euro and yen — have additional responsibilities of maintaining stability of the world financial system under the G-3 Agreement in which Japan, Germany and the United States are to synchronize their exchange rate policies so as to avoid unwarranted fluctuations of their currencies.

10.21 Multiple Exchange Rates

Multiple exchange rate systems imply different exchange rates for different transactions either on current or capital account. The official definition of a multiple exchange rate of the IMF is: 'It is 'an effective buying or selling rate which, as a result of official action, differs from parity by more than 1 per cent'.

The IMF has traditionally been hostile to multiple exchange rate practices. It views them as an interference with a free market mechanism internationally. But IMF tolerates this system as they are to be preferred to more direct means of control, which have typically been resorted to, when multiple exchange rates have been abandoned.

Multiple exchange rates can be viewed both as a form of exchange control and as a rational response to the fact that different types of goods have different price elasticity in world trade. When foreign currency is scarce, governments of the developing countries use multiple exchange rates as policy tools for the allocation of resources according to desired objectives. But the discretion used by the governments create distortion in the markets in the form of the operation of black market of foreign currency and capital flight.

10.22 The Relative Merits of Different Exchange Rate Regimes

The basic feature of fixed exchange rates is that they give stability and certainty to the nominal exchange rate and serve to anchor the national price level. But the flexibility exchange rate system has some advantages and these are enumerated ahead.

First, it gives a country an extra degree of freedom in the pursuit of simultaneous internal and external balance. But under fixed rates, the domestic economy must be subordinated to the needs of preserving balance of payments equilibrium.

Second, it offers the possibility for the monetary authorities to pursue an independent monetary policy as money supply is no longer endogenous. It is subject to change through changes in the level of foreign currency reserves which occur under fixed rates.

Third, flexible exchange rates may help to insulate economies against external disturbances like price shocks that would otherwise affect the balance of payments, and feedback to the domestic economy. This is possible by suitable movements of the exchange rate to neutralize the effects.

For a small developing country, the maintenance of a flexible exchange rate system may become a luxury, as the cost of it in the form of independent monetary and fiscal policies, and the adoption of swift measures to insulate the domestic economy from external shocks, may be high. Viewed from this angle, many developing countries go for pegged exchange rate system.

Exchange rate is an important link with the foreign commodity and financial markets, and the swings in this rate trigger movements of money and commodities across national borders. Many countries find it increasingly difficult to maintain stability in the exchange rate in the volatile world of flexible exchange rate regime. Because of this many countries have opted for dual currency system, the second currency being the USD. Even in extreme cases, some countries have adopted USD as the medium of exchange.

It is clear that trans-border movements of money and capital may be both the cause and the effects of exchange rate changes. An efficient combination of fiscal and monetary policies can maintain equilibrium and stability both in the domestic and foreign sector of the economy.

Case of the Appreciating Indian Rupee

Indian rupee was floated in 1993 and the result had been a steady depreciation of the currency from ₹ 31.37 for a unit of USD in 1993–94 to ₹ 48.40 per USD in 2002–03. The Indian economy benefited due to this depreciation in the form of a favourable trend in balance of payments and an upward trend of India's international reserves. The positive trend in the accumulation of international reserves steadily reversed the trend of rupee's movement vis-à-vis USD and other currencies. This prompted the media to comment on the ongoing trend. On 2 September 2003, *Economic Times* reported.

> Hurt by the steady appreciation of the rupee against the dollar, exports during July 2003 slipped to 5.75% as compared to 11% in June 2003. Due to the sluggish growth July 2003, the overall export growth during April–July 2003 declined to 9.29% — below the psychologically signifiant double-digit mark. The flip side is that imports are surging, presumably to feed domestic growth. The export growth target for 2003–04 is 12% and the current trend indicate that even this modest target will provide a tough challenge in view of rupee's appreciation against the dollar.
>
> Since the government expects foreign exchange reserves to cross the $ 100 billion mark, speculation in the forex market is that the rupee would harden further. . Appreciation of the rupee has also resulted in a spurt in imports, with non-oil imports rising 29.03% during April–July.

Topic for Discussion

The intrinsic values of two currencies, say USD and Indian rupee as defined by the purchasing power parity relationship are sharply different than what the exchange rate of Indian rupee reveals. How can you explain this phenomenon?

Further Reading

Calvo, G. and C. Reinhart, 'Fear of Floating', *NBER Working Paper No. 7993,* Cambridge, Mass., 2000.

Eichengreen, B. and R. Hausmann, 'Exchange Rates and Financial Fragility', *NBER Discussion Paper No. 7418,* Cambridge, Mass., 1999.

Michael, P. and R. Nobay and A. Peel, 'Transaction Costs and Non-Linear Adjustment in Real Exchange Rates: An Empirical Investigation', *Journal of Political Economy*, 105(4), 862–79, 1997.

Obstfeld, M. and K. Rogoff, 'The Six Major Puzzles in International Macroeconomics: Is There a Common Cause?', *NBER Discussion Paper No. 7777*, July 2000.

Sarno, L. and M. Taylor, 'Official Intervention in the Foreign Exchange Market: Is it Effective and if so, How does it Work?', *Journal of Economic Literature*, 39(3), 839–69, 2001.

Taylor, M., D. Peel and L. Sarno, 'Non-linear Mean Reversion in Real Exchange Rates; Towards a Solution to the Purchasing Power Parity Puzzles', *CePR Discussion Paper No. 2658*, 2001.

Bacchetta, P. and E. van Wincoop, 'A Theory of the Currency Denomination of International Trade', *Journal of International Economics*, 67(2), 295–319, 2005.

Web Resources

http://www.oecd.org./economy/outlook/economicoutlook.htm

http://www.oanda.com/

http://www.jpmorganam.com.hk/GTMA/en.pdf (provides trade-weighted nominal and inflation adjusted real exchange rates of OECD countries as well as G-7 countries)

11

International Transmission of Interest Rates and Monetary Independence

11.1 Introduction

The global financial crisis of 2008 first came into existence in acute form in the US, and then spread to some European countries through the linkages of financial markets. The way the crisis spread to the real sectors of the concerned countries cannot be easily explained by the dominant economic paradigm of the day, and as a result, it has affected the thinking process of the policy makers all over the world. Many long-held views about the global financial system are being questioned, and some major changes in the financial regulations both at the global and individual countries' levels are expected. The complete relaxation of rules and regulations in the 1990s and the first decade of 2000 is now over, and protectionism is already on the rise, and it is expected that world is to see some degree of control on the inter-country capital movement. Believers of some degree of capital control in the emerging countries — including scholars like Bhagawati (1998), Krugman (1995), Rodrik (2006), and Stiglitz (2002), — have argued that these restrictions keep speculative capital out and thus the system protects countries from volatility of international financial markets.

In order to understand the way in which the possible changes in the financial policies of the countries and the resultant reforms in the global financial system will affect different countries and the outcome, it is necessary to have a well-founded idea on how the system induced transmission of shocks across countries through the inter-connectedness of the financial system. An important question, in this regard, refers to the international transmission of interest rate changes across national boundaries. The significant issue is to what extent and how rapidly changes in the advanced countries' policy interest rate are transmitted into emerging countries like countries in the Asian continent. Equally important is how changes in the advanced countries, term structure of interest rates affect financial conditions, including interest rates, in the emerging countries.

What is the mechanism? Well, central banks in both advanced countries and emerging economies are interested in determining how much their countries' domestic interest rates diverge from the world interest rate (generally the rate announced by Federal Reserve of US is taken as a proxy). For example, countries that are suffering from high inflation will like to have a positive differential with respect to world interest rate (which means domestic interest rate is higher than the world one). Likewise, countries that experience an increase in unemployment will want to reduce the interest rate differential and, in some cases, make it negative. An important question in this regard is to what extent interest rates differentials in emerging markets are affected by the policy actions of the advanced countries. This is the crux of the issue of international transmission of interest rates.

The interest rate and exchange rate of the domestic currency of a country are strongly related, and the policy regarding the exchange rate becomes inter-twined with the maintenance of a specific exchange rate. Before we delve into this issue further, we are to see the relevant theory of exchange rates.

11.2 Exchange Rate

The choice of exchange rate regime — fixed, floating, a combination of two or a pegged one — has been always a favorite question in international macroeconomics. According to the prevalent view, there are two principal advantages in a fixed exchange rate regime and these are: (*i*) reduced transaction cost and exchange rate risk, and, (*ii*) a credible nominal anchor for monetary policy. The first facilitates international trade and investment of foreign capital. The second helps in the stability of the domestic currency.

The flexible exchange rate has the unique advantage that it allows the country to pursue independent monetary policy. There are other advantages also. In the case of an independent currency, the government retains the seignorage and second, floating of the currency can lead to a smooth adjustment to real external shocks even when price frictions exist in the economy. Of course the first one, i.e., monetary independence is very important and we take up this issue now.

Under flexible exchange rate, the monetary independence is maintained and the monetary authority enjoys the advantage of discretion rather than the rules. Suppose the economy is hit by a disturbance in the form of a shift of worldwide demand away from the goods the country produces. In such a situation, the government would like to respond so that the country can avoid a potential recession. The authority can go for a monetary expansion and depreciation of the domestic currency. This will stimulate the demand for domestic commodities and help the economy return to the desired level of output. This adjustment could not have been achieved under a fixed exchange rate regime when monetary policy would have been powerless.

Under a pegged exchange rate and unrestricted capital flows, the traditional literature argues that domestic interest rate cannot be set independently, as it should keep pace with the interest rate of the currency to which the domestic currency is pegged. But under a flexible exchange rate regime, domestic interest rate is less sensitive to changes in the foreign interest rates. Again the countries with intermediate exchange rate regimes should show less sensitivity to the changes in international interest rates compared to the countries that have pegged the exchange rates of their currencies with some major currency of the world.

Against the traditional view, an alternative view stated by Calvo and Reinhart (2001, 2002), and Hausmann, Panizza and Stein (2001) holds that there exists a 'fear of floating' that prevents countries with *de jure* flexible regime from allowing their exchange rates to move freely. This view holds that factors like exchange rate pass through, lack of credibility, and foreign currency liability, prevent countries from pursuing an independent monetary policy irrespective of the nature of exchange rate regime. The result is that many countries with floating exchange rate are following the monetary policies of major-currency countries like the US or some EU countries. It is also suggested that the interest rate may be more sensitive to the US interest rate in developing countries with flexible rates than in countries with fixed rates, as the flexible rate countries suffer from having to pay risk premium (for currency risk and default risk) and this premium is sensitive to international interest rates.

The main question is whether floating exchange rate regime does facilitate a country to follow an independent monetary policy in the sense that domestic interest rates in such countries are less sensitive to the changes in international interest rates. The empirical evidence on this issue is scarce and not decisive. It is also observed that the developing countries do not stick to a particular exchange rate regime, and they often change the nature of the regime in response to both internal and external shocks.

There are several factors that determine the extent to which domestic and foreign interest rate will move together. First, the degree of financial integration of the domestic economy into the world markets moulds the domestic capital market. If there are barriers to international capital flows, the response of the local interest rate to changes in the international rates will be less. This will allow the monetary authorities in countries to maintain different interest rates even under fixed exchange rate regime.

Second, the degree of real international integration influences the co-movement of domestic and foreign interest rates. The movement of the two rates will be close if the business cycles in the two countries are highly synchronized, and the integration of the capital markets in both of them are near perfect with no restriction on capital mobility.

11.3 Financial Integration and Capital Mobility

Many economists now recognize the relentless trend towards globalization and increasing capital mobility. Empirical studies have shown that since the 1980s, there have been a growing degree of capital market integration all over the world and capital mobility has increased tremendously. Many experts believe that these trends are largely inevitable and irreversible too. Because, these are partly driven by new innovations of information technology and better communications, and partly because policy makers are increasingly convinced about the many benefits of regulatory changes that foster financial integration. So capital mobility is irreversible.

The changed world scenario has some important implications. The more openness of the economy along with open environment imply, that changes in monetary policy involve a somewhat different transmission mechanism than what it used to be, in earlier relatively closed regime. For example, the more integrated the economy, the more quickly do divergent policies affect financial markets and capital flows. Also, foreign exchange rate may play an increasingly important role in transmitting changes in monetary policy to the macro economy. Thus, exchange rate movement may contain more useful information about the changes in domestic monetary policies compared to the earlier times, when the world did not experience so much financial integration.

11.4 The Policy Trilemma

The changed world situation of increased capital mobility has placed constraints on the implementation of domestic monetary policy and this Obstfeld describes as follows:

> The limitations that open capital market place on exchange rate and monetary policy are summed up by the ideas of the 'inconsistent trinity' or ... 'the open economy trilemma' ... that is, a country cannot simultaneously maintain fixed exchange rates and open capital markets while pursuing a monetary policy oriented toward domestic goals. Governments may choose only two of the above (Obstfeld, 1998, 14–15).

We see the consensus here about unrestricted capital mobility, and if that is irreversible and given, the policy choices circumscribed by the above trilemma are limited. For the governments of the developing countries, the policy choices are now between flexible exchange rate/domestic monetary policy goal (say, inflation targeting) regimes and fixed exchange rate/no domestic goal regimes. If policy makers go for fixed exchange rate, they lose control of the exchange rate. If they peg the interest rate, they cannot control the exchange rate. Some economists suggest that the choice in recent time has moved in favour of flexible exchange rate/domestic monetary policy alternative, which boils down to a *de facto* informal inflation targeting regime (Eichengreen, 1996). This also goes well with the contemporary political economy of many developing countries, as the authority can exercise control on the domestic monetary policies.

11.5 USD as International Currency

There has been another trend in the international arena, and it is that the USD has appeared in a new role apart from its Bretton Woods role of international currency. Many newly emerging market economies and some Latin American countries have started using dollar as the official currency. USD has replaced the domestic currency. Also, in many countries, people are informally holding dollars. The situation is such that foreigners are holding a large percentage of USD currency outside the US and the amount is no less than 50 per cent (Porter and Judson, 1996). This induces Robert Mundell to state:

> The need for an international unit of account for purposes of international trade and finance was just as great as ever, and the increased uncertainty associated with flexible exchange rates increased, rather than eliminated the need for international reserve assets ... The dollar remained the principal international monetary reserve (in the 1980s and 1990s). The enhanced role of the dollar under flexible exchange rate was reflected in the rapid expansion of dollar reserves which has more than kept pace with the growth of trade (1994, 12).

Thus, dollar continues to provide the principal function of international money and so it remains the dominant international key vehicle and reserve currency[1]. The use of USD as international

---

[1] As of December, 2007, total currency in circulation, both US coins and paper currency in the hands of the public totaled 829 billion USD. According to the estimate of Federal reserve, the majority of cash in circulation is outside the United States (Federal Reserve Bank of New York).

currency suggests that there remains an important demand for the services of an international currency, i.e., *continued demand for a money for other monies*. Given this global demand, the suppliers of this global currency, the Federal Reserve of the US has a responsibility of adjusting the global supply of USD, as and when demands for the dollar changes. This will promote international stability. But it has another implication. When the Federal Reserve of the US tightens policy and as a result money supply gets restricted even globally, other central banks in countries that are using dollar should follow the Federal Reserve. Also the use of dollar as international reserve boils down to the role of the Federal Reserve as the international lender of last resort. All these imply that monetary policy in the developing countries that use dollar as the currency, becomes dependent on the policy of the Federal Reserve of America.

A large body of empirical literature suggests that changes in the monetary policy of the Federal Reserve can have significant impact on the policy of foreign countries, and on the global economy. There are evidences that international capital flows, recent crisis in the international banking and currency markets, and choice of exchange rate regimes may have been influenced by the policy changes of the Federal Reserve (Calvo et al., 1996).

Recent research on the choice of exchange rate regime has also revealed that US monetary policy has significant impact on the foreign interest rates. This is evident when the developing countries adjust their interest rates in response to the interest rate changes by the Federal Reserve. This has been seen in times of Russian devaluation in 1998, in times of Asian currency crisis, and also Mexican crisis. The preferential choice for the USDs in some transition economies over their domestic currencies has helped the Federal reserve of the US, to maintain a relatively lower interest rates to promote domestic investment and generate employment. Because, lower interest rate on USD remains attractive for foreign citizens as they compare the rapidly declining intrinsic value of their domestic currency due to high inflation. This also explains informal dollarization in many transition economies.

Table 11.1 *Countries and their Exchange Rate Regimes*

Country	Period	Exchange Rate Regime
Argentina	March 1991 onwards	Peg to USD
Australia	December 1983 onwards	independently floating
Canada	January 1975 onwards	independently floating
Chile	January 1999 onwards	crawling band
Columbia	January 1999 onwards	crawling Band
Denmark***	Jan 1972–March 1999	LFCA**
Ecuador	January 1999 onwards	crawling band
Egypt	January 1997 onwards	managed floating
Finland	Oct 1996–March 1999	LFCA
Germany	April 1973–March 1999	LFCA
Greece	March 1998–March 1999	LFCA

Country	Period	Exchange Rate Regime
Hong Kong	December 1990 onwards	Peg to USD
India	August 1994 onwards	managed floating
Ireland	January 1979–March 1999	LFCA
Israel	January 1999 onwards	crawling band
Italy	October 1996–March 1999	LFCA
Japan	January 1973 onwards	independently floating
South Korea	December 1997 onwards	independently floating
Mexico	December 1997 onwards	independently floating
Netherlands	January 1972–December 1998	LFCA
New Zealand	March 1985 onwards	independently floating
Norway	May 1994 onwards	managed floating
Portugal	April 1992–March 1999	LFCA
Singapore	July 1987 onwards	managed floating
Spain	June 1989–March 1999	LFCA
Sweden	November 1992–March 1999	independently floating
Thailand	July 1998 onwards	independently floating
United Kingdom	July 1992 onwards	independently floating
Venezuela	January 1999 onwards	crawling band

Note: ** LFCA means limited flexibility with respect to cooperative arrangement
*** means countries against which LFCA are written, are countries who have joined the European Union, and at present their currency is Euro, and it is independently floating.

The evidence indicates that the changes in the US monetary policy affect financial markets in the developing countries through different transmission channels. These further suggest that international financial markets are becoming more integrated, and the interest rates in the developing countries are becoming more sensitive to the interest rate changes in the United States. This is true irrespective of different exchange rate regimes.

As seen in Table 11.1, for many developing countries, USD has become a reference currency. Not only that, there has been a high degree of volatility among the three principal currencies of the world — USD, yen and euro. The exchange rate of both yen and euro vis-à-vis dollar has become volatile and that has created problem for the stability of the exchange rate of many developing countries. The question now is whether the three monetary areas —United States, Japan and European Union — should initiate policies to stabilize the exchange rates as mentioned. A recent study cautions that in case the three currencies are stabilized, that is not a sure guarantee for the stability of the developing countries (Reinhart and Reinhart, 2002).

For the newly emerging market economies, USD has been the *de jure* or at least *de facto* medium of exchange. This type of dollarization has other implications that we have covered in other chapters. What is relevant here is that the central banks in these countries cannot exercise an independent monetary policy. The monetary policy followed by the Federal Reserve has various transmission channels that affect the interest rate policy of not only the new market economies but also other developing countries as well, who have pegged their currencies to the USD.

It has been enquired in the literature, whether the transmission of international interest rate affecting the changes of the local rates are influenced by the type of exchange rate regimes (Frankel et al., 2001). In this debate, the issue of monetary independence has played an important role. Supporters of independent-floating exchange rate regime argue that countries adopting free float would be able to pursue their own monetary policy goals. This strategy has been questioned by the proponents of the fixed exchange rate regime (hard peg) regarding its feasibility in the face of high international capital mobility. This refers to the policy trilemma as we discussed in the beginning of this chapter.

Empirical evidence suggests that in the 1990s, all types of exchange rate regimes showed a high degree of sensitivity of local interest rates to the change in the international interest rate. This is particularly true with full transmission in case of smaller countries. The big industrial countries like Canada and Australia have experienced less than one transmission rate (Frankel et al., 2001). The only major exception is the countries belonging to European Union, as this group in the 1990s has shown interest rate convergence to the German interest rate. The EU countries have shifted from the US monetary area to the deutsche Mark-EU monetary area. But here also the convergence of the two principal rates may not be far away.

Topic for Discussion

In case a country's currency is pegged to USD, the country faces problems in its pursuit of independent monetary policy. Explain the statement and critically evaluate it.

Further Reading

Aizenman, J., 'Financial Opening and Development: Evidence and Policy Controversies', *American Economic Review*, 65–70 May 2004.

———, 'On the Hidden Links between Financial and Trade Opening', *Journal of International Money and Finance*, 372–86 April 2008.

Bhagawati, J.N., 'The Capital Myth: The Difference Between Trade in Widgets and Dollars', *Foreign Affairs*, May/June 1998.

Edwards, S., 'Capital Controls, Capital Flow Contractions, and Macroeconomic Vulnerability', *Journal of International Money and Finance*, April 2008.

———, *Populism and Markets: Latin America's Bumpy Road to Modernity*, University of Chicago Press, 2010.

Krugman, Paul, 'Dutch Tulips and the Emerging Markets: Another Bubble Bursts', *Foreign Affairs*, 75(4), 1995.

Rodrik, D., 'Good Bye Washington Consensus, Hello Washington Confusion?' A Review of the World Bank's 'Economic Growth in the 1990s: Learning from a Decade of Reform', *Journal of Economic Literature*, 44(4), 2006.

Stiglitz, J.E., *Globalization and its Discontents*, New York, W.W. Norton, 2002.

12

Capital Mobility, Currency Crisis and Problems of Contagion

12.1 Introduction

Since the middle of 1980s, some countries in the south Asian region had experienced rapid economic growth in the range of seven to 8 per cent per annum. Most of these countries have a liberal exchange rate regime, and they took advantage of their export expansion and huge inflow of foreign capital. Hong Kong and Singapore became two strong offshore financial centres apart from Tokyo. Over the years, this region also had become a centre of 'Geo Finance' holding a huge amount of international reserve. By June 1997, international reserve of Japan was USD 222 billion, China had USD 121 billion, while Hong Kong had USD 82 billion. To what extent this economic muscle of these three countries affected the strength of the currencies of countries like Thailand, Malaysia, Philippines, and Indonesia remains a matter of conjecture. There is a debate in the literature that the North American free trade bloc NAFTA may have been responsible for the weakness of the Mexican peso, as Mexico is the weakest in the bloc (Torres, 1994). If it is true, one can draw a parallel in the case of the south Asian trade bloc where major economic powers like Japan, China and Hong Kong might have contributed to the weakness of the currencies of the fellow countries. We are to remember that all these countries were pursuing a strategy of economic development that was known as export-led growth. Or, they depended heavily on exports.

12.2 The Crisis

In 1997, Thailand experienced heavy pressure on its currency, baht, as it was perceived to be overvalued. When the pressure became too severe, the government decided not to defend it further and to allow the currency to float in order to avoid defaulting on its obligations to international creditors. This induced a rapid spread of the crisis throughout the region, culminating in the collapse of the currencies of Thailand, Indonesia, Malaysia, the Philippines, and South Korea within a matter of weeks. Along with the currency collapse, there were steep falls in the stock markets of these countries also. This spread to other economies in the region, particularly Hong Kong and Singapore. This regional turmoil rapidly turned into a major world financial crisis and led to a substantial downturn in the world economic growth.

The question that occupied the minds of the academicians was why was this region, previously described by economists and commentators as representing a 'growth miracle', plunged into one of the world's most serious recessions. The traditional explanation of fiscal profligacy and macroeconomic instability, which plagued Latin America in the 1980s and 1990s, were not applicable, because most of the important macroeconomic indicators were generally healthy. The fiscal balance was generally in surplus. Inflation in these countries was low, and domestic saving and investment as a proportion of GDP were among the highest in the world. But these countries were suffering from severe current account deficits. In the two years preceding 1997, the current account deficits as a percentage of GDP were: Thailand (7.9 per cent); Malaysia (7.3 per cent); Philippines (4.7 per cent); Indonesia (3.4 per cent), and South Korea (3.3 per cent) (McCombie and Thirlwall, 1999). These ratios are very high, as from historical experience we see that the maximum sustainable deficit to GDP ratio seems to be of the order of 2 to 3 per cent, beyond which the financial markets start to get nervous for understandable reasons. However, the quick spread of the crisis in the region, known as contagion, has induced the growth of literature to which we now turn.

12.3 Currency Crisis

A currency crisis is defined as a speculative attack on the currency of a country. This is brought out by the high-volume traders when they attempt to alter their portfolio, by selling that particular currency to buy another preferred one that they perceive to be safe. This may happen for a variety of reasons. One explanation is that sometimes investors fear that the government will finance its high prospective deficits through printing money or it may attempt to reduce its non-indexed debt through devaluation. When the pressure comes on the exchange rate, the central bank must step in and it should buy up its currency with international reserve. When the reserve is not adequate, the central bank allows the currency to float and devaluation follows.

The currency crisis in south Asia had been so severe that it induced academic interest in the literature, for a proper explanation of the genesis of the crisis and its effects. The series of models tried to explain the phenomenon and that is known as generation models.

12.4 First-Generation Models

The models of currency crisis developed by Krugman (1979), Flood and Garber (1984) and Obstfeld (1986) and others depend on government debt and the perceived inability of the government to control the budget, as the principal causes for the explanation of the crisis. The argument is that a speculative attack on the currency may result from an insistent current account deficit, and also from an expected monetization of the fiscal deficit. When the attack starts in the form of a high sale of the domestic currency, the central bank initially tries to defend by the buy-back of the domestic currency with foreign reserve, and when it is depleted, it allows the currency to float. The implicit assumption of Krugman's model is that a fixed exchange rate regime with no sound fiscal policy is the inevitable target of attack. The crisis is triggered when the market expects the government to abandon the peg. The potential conflict between the fiscal policy of the government and the fixed exchange rate (peg) regime changes the market perception about the intrinsic worth of the currency, and that creates the environment for attack.

12.5 Second-Generation Models

The second generation models of crisis are provided by Obstfeld (1994), Eichengreen et al. (1996) and others. These models explain self-fulfilling currency crisis that are contagious. Devaluation in one country not only affects the price level and demand for money of that country, but it also affects the current account by a reduction of exports in the partner country, and through trade link, the devaluation in the partner country becomes increasingly likely. Eichengreen et at. finds that there exists a correlation between the likelihood of default across the countries. They have estimated that a speculative attack on currency somewhere in the world increases the probability of a domestic currency crisis by about 8 per cent. The spill-over of the crisis from one country to another is attributed to a number of scenarios, and these are: economic events like oil price hike, a devaluation or default by one country, or collapse of the stock market in a neighboring country. Any combination of such scenarios can help to explain the international linkages that are responsible for the spread of speculative attacks from one country to another.

12.6 Third-Generation Models

The earlier models have not provided a policy recommendation for the central bank when it faces the crisis. The third-generation models of Krugman (1999), Aghion et al., (2000, 2001) and others examine the effects of monetary policy in a currency crisis. These models suggest that a currency crisis is a result of the combination of factors like high debt, low foreign reserves, falling government revenue, increasing expectations of devaluation, and domestic borrowing constraints. Firms' access to domestic credit is constrained by assuming they can borrow only a portion of their wealth. In the face of lending constraints in the economy, credit markets do not clear, and though interest rate increases, the increase is not considered enough to compensate the lenders the potential default risk. Thus, the rise in the interest rate neither increases the supply of loanable funds nor induces the banks to increase the credit.

These models offer a role of monetary policy through a binding credit constraint when the financial market is imperfect. When the firms' leverage in the domestic market is reduced, they go to the foreign market and in the process accumulate foreign debt. In the domestic market, nominal interest rate is important for the amount of available lending and when the central bank raises the interest rate in response to a typical prescription for a currency crisis, it deepens the crisis by reducing the firms' ability to invest. The lowering of investment reduces productive capacity of the economy, and the perceived decline in output puts additional pressure on the exchange rate.

The models of three generations suggest four factors that can influence the onset and magnitude of the currency crisis of a country and these are: domestic public and private debt, expectations generated in the market, state of the financial markets, and pegged exchange rate. These factors either in combination or alone can trigger the currency crisis, and after that the course of the crisis and its magnitude may be influenced by the policies pursued by the central bank and the governments. But the differences in the nuances of the three categories of models being not very prominent, a new explanation in the theoretical literature emerged that emphasized moral hazard as well as contagion as the missing links that could probably explain the differences between the set of models as stated above.

12.7 Contagion: The Definition

The term 'contagion' was first introduced in July 1997, when the currency crisis in Thailand crippled the Thailand economy and then spread throughout East Asia and then as far as Russia and even Brazil. The developed markets in North America and Europe were also affected, as the relative prices of financial instruments shifted and caused the collapse of Long-Term Capital Management (LTCM), a large US hedge fund. The financial crisis beginning from Thailand with the collapse of Thai baht spread to Indonesia, Philippines, Malaysia, South Korea, and Hong Kong in the shortest possible time (less than two months).

The incident of currency crisis that helped the emergence of contagion as a concept has been defined in multiple ways. The World Bank has used three definitions: one broad, one moderately restrictive, and the third very restrictive.

The broad definition defines contagion as the cross-country transmission of shocks — whether real, financial, or from exogenous sunspots. Contagion can take place both during the tranquil period and crisis period, though the latter is generally referred. The examples are Asian currency crisis of 1997–98, the EMS crisis of 1992–93.

The moderately restrictive definition of contagion is that it is the transmission of shocks to other countries, and more generally, this happens when significant cross-country correlation exists beyond any fundamental links between countries and beyond common shocks. This is usually referred to excess co-movement and is explained by herding behavior leading to sunspots.

The most restrictive definition of contagion is that phenomenon, when cross-country correlation increases during the crisis period relative to correlation during the tranquil period. This is tested with econometric tools and as such, it is very exclusive.

Outside the World Bank study, contagion has been defined as a significant increase in cross-country linkages after a shock to an individual country or group of countries (Dornbush et al., 2001). This definition asserts that contagion arises due to a shift in cross-market linkages, and this tendency is sometimes known as 'shift-contagion'.

For the recognition of contagion, researchers have applied the following strategies: correlation of asset returns, conditional probability of currency crises, the transmission of volatility changes, and co-movements of capital flows and rates of returns. The estimation of correlation coefficients among stock returns is the most popular method used in the estimation of contagion effects. Since a study based on correlation has obvious limitation, some researchers go for more refined methods like vector auto regression and causality analysis.

There are several explanations for the happening of contagion. The literature is huge and we report two types of explanations for the financial contagion that affected the economies of some Southeast Asian countries.

One school emphasizes contagious currency crises showing the inter-relation of such crises to various monetary and financial sector vulnerabilities and trade factors. These studies often look for the underlying causes behind a simultaneous set of speculative attacks. Thus, Goldfajn and Valdés (1997) find that the intermediaries' role of transforming maturities is shown to result in larger movements of capital and a higher probability of crisis, which resemble the observed cycle in capital flows: large inflows, crisis, and abrupt outflows.

The second school explains contagion transmission as a result of linkages among financial institutions. Lagunoff and Schreft (2001) analyze financial contagion as a result of linkages among financial intermediaries. They provide a general equilibrium model to explain that a small liquidity preference shock in one region can spread by contagion throughout the economy, and the possibility of contagion depends strongly on the completeness of the structure of interregional claims.

The currency crisis in south Asia has been followed by similar crisis in some Latin American countries like Argentina, Russia and some East European countries. Whatever may be the reasons that first trigger the crisis, the countries suffered in terms of loss of productivity and employment. The IMF came to the rescue to most of these countries with a package that is basically based on a theoretical structure known as 'Washington Consensus'.

12.8 Washington Consensus

The name Washington Consensus (W-C) was given by John Williamson in 1990 to a package of 10 policy recommendations for countries willing to reform their economies and these are:
(1) Tax reforms
(2) Financial liberalization
(3) Fiscal discipline
(4) Redirect public expenditure
(5) Adopt a single competitive
(6) Trade liberalization exchange rate
(7) Eliminate barrier to foreign direct investment
(8) Privatize state owned enterprises
(9) Deregulate market entry
(10) Ensure secure property rights

Later on, Williamson articulated the concept of W-C in subsequent papers (Williamson, 1990, 1993). But the debate continued about the contents of the so-called consensus. Even important persons within the administration of World Bank expressed doubts about the applicability of the general package.

The general ideas derived from the W-C had a huge influence on the economic reforms of the countries that were implementing this. Yet, the way these countries interpreted such ideas varied substantially. Moreover, the original ten policy prescriptions of the W-C reigned unchallenged only for a short time. Changes in the international economic and political environment, and the new domestic realities in the reforming countries created problems, and adjustment and compromises were called for. The newfound answers often complemented the recommendations originally offered by the W-C, though some were opposed to the original package. The wildly gyrating ideas about controls on foreign capital or about exchange rate regimes that have been offered at different times are good examples of the lack of consensus.

When John Williamson summarized what he saw as the consensus that had emerged among the 'political' Washington of the US Congress, within the IMF, World Bank and the think-tanks, he did not suspect that he was fathering one of the brand names that would come to characterize the decade. He even could not imagine that his basic proposal would draw so many disagreements among the academics, and that it would generate political controversy.

From the beginning, advocates of the W-C have been greatly divided about the pace and sequence of the reforms. Even among the specialists of market-friendly reforms, serious differences emerged about the need or desirability of what came to be known as the application of a 'shock therapy' approach to policy reforms. This approach implied the implementation of many reforms as quickly as possible. Some economists argued for a slower, more sequenced pace. This is not a debate just between experts in Washington and others elsewhere. It also raged among insiders.

It would be a mistake, however, to assume that these differences emerged all of a sudden. Early in the decade, Williamson acknowledged that not all of the assertions he included in his original 'ten-best' policy recommendations, enjoyed the same degree of consensus. According to his assessment at the time, in five of the 10 policy prescriptions 'consensus has been established'. Thus the existence of consensus had been assumed. But it was perceived that over time, agreement could be reached on the remaining items, though two conditions — changing public budget priorities and according the same treatment to foreign and domestic firms — is always controversial in nature due to political overtones.

It is important to stress that Williamson was an innocent victim of the success of his useful summary of the prevailing thought among the persons within the think-tank of the IMF. Williamson tried hard to qualify very carefully what he really meant when he framed the W-C. He sought to correct those who misinterpreted the approach and made repeated attempts at clarifying the nuances of his conceptual framework. Wide use and popularity of W-C had a price, and soon it was revealed in the form of distortions of the concept. Williamson's efforts at clarifying the meaning and implication of W-C were not enough to compensate for the distortions already created. Very soon, even the ten prescriptions were not that well known. The concept W-C acquired a life of its own, and it became a brand name known worldwide and used quite independently of its original intent.

But every ideology has an evolutionary process and very soon W-C became an ideology with the IMF. May be one can link it to the early Polak model that may give it the theoretical back up. But the evolution of the idea is interesting.

12.9 Evolution of Washington Consensus

Alfred Marshall had once commented that short words are usually bad economics. By that measure, according to Moises Naim (1999), the decade of the 1990s was full of such expressions: international financial contagion, sequencing, bailouts, the tequila effect, moral hazard, crony capitalism, to name only a few. None of these terms figured in the original formulation of the W-C. But, slowly, with new interpretations by economists, new words were coined. New concepts and names, and the realities they tried to encapsulate, gained importance as a result of the many surprise events that impaired the implementation of market reforms. While this jargon-filled list of terms may sound like a cacophony of jumbled words, they help in understanding the signposts marking the road through which common wisdom about market reforms evolved since 1990. This evolution had a pattern. It usually began with the increase in popularity of a general set of policy recommendations. For sometime, these recommendations embodied the views of an influential majority of academics and high level staff of the IMF and the World Bank. But crises came in some countries in the process of implementation of the reforms. New experiences created learning, and it was realized that the new data would show that the lessons derived from the previous crises missed some important element whose critical importance had now been clearly illuminated by the next crisis. Another new explanation is required and another set of jargons are coined.

The Mexican crisis of 1994 explains how the original W-C remained on the path of evolution. The lesson drawn from this crisis was that a low domestic savings rate made Mexico overly vulnerable to the volatility of foreign capital markets by making it too dependent on foreign funds. Therefore, a higher rate of domestic savings along with sound macroeconomic fundamentals would serve to inoculate a country from a crash induced by the volatility of short-term international capital flows.

Again, the higher saving-income ratio was unable to explain the crisis of south Asia that came in 1997. That crisis came in spite of high savings rate and sound macroeconomic fundamentals of the South Asian economies. So another explanation was required. The concept of 'crony capitalism' came, and that meant the reliance on a private sector highly distorted by the dominance of a few, large 'economic groups' closely associated with those in government. Sound macroeconomics and increasing the savings rate are not discarded as worthy policy goals. But apart from these necessary conditions, something additional was considered necessary, and that was the reforms in the domestic industrial sector to encourage competition. The process continues.

12.10 Globalization

It is ironic that the Washington Consensus missed globalization. Because the elimination of obstacles to international trade and investment that fueled much of the economic integration the world has witnessed, owes a great deal to the influence of the W-C on many liberalizing countries. But the subsequent financial troubles some of these countries faced had little answer in the package of W-C.

The package in the W-C did not provide a set of policies that would enable reforming countries to better cope with the consequences of globalization, especially in the financial sphere. In the 1990s, a large number of countries experimented with market reforms, and most of them experienced periodic financial crashes that rocked these countries, and spread across borders in quick and unpredictable ways. Between 1994 and 1999, some middle-income developing countries like South Korea, Thailand and others had a major financial crisis[1]. These crises wrought havoc in these countries' financial systems, bankrupted them, set the economic clock back by several years. But why these happened and on a massive scale still remains unanswered. For better credibility of the W-C, new explanations are required.

What are the factors that created the crashes of that magnitude still remains unexplained and confusion prevails. Some economists, having ideologies that do not necessarily comply with the mainstream, raise interesting questions of the following nature: Was financial opening in a developing country with questionable infrastructure a good idea? Is trade liberalization necessarily good? Should currencies of the developing countries float freely or are countries better off with a currency board or some sort of pegged rate? Should the IMF be abolished or strengthened? These are just a few examples.

The disagreements as stated in the above paragraph can be grouped into three general categories:

(1) the fix or float debate,
(2) the capital account liberalization debate, and
(3) the inflate versus deflate debate

The fix or float debate is about the nature of the exchange rate regime a country should have. This area is full of controversy largely because monies are fiduciary issues and not adequately backed by the issuing authority. Yet, while a certain convergence has emerged in favor of floating exchange rates, the debate is still far from reaching a kind of expert consensus. Faced with currency crisis, leaders in Mexico, Asia, Brazil, and Russia received a barrage of contradictory advice.

The debate about exchange rate regimes is closely linked to the debate on the liberalization of a country's capital account. In the words of Alan Binder, 'the hard-core Washington Consensus — which holds that international capital mobility is a blessing, full stop — needs to be tempered by a little common sense.' On the other hand, proponents of capital controls do not share the same common sense about what kind of measures are the best. Some radical proponents, like Krugman (1999, 145-46), recognize that 'there is virtually unanimous consensus among economists that exchange controls work badly'. Yet, imposition of currency control was the only alternative left in Asian crisis because of its magnitude and severity.

Some economists, who hold a moderate view, suggest some mechanism that will slow down the flow of hot money. They cite Chile as it is open to foreign banks and allows outflow of capital. But Chile taxes the inflow of short-term capital. But there is disagreement on the effectiveness of this measure.

The prescriptions for the solution in the crisis-ridden countries have been stringent fiscal and monetary policies. These have become the reasons for severe recession in such countries and the question that haunts the economists is: Why a financial crash has to be cured with a recession? This is also the crux of the deflate versus reflate debate.

Some economists argue that the unequivocal priority after a country suffers a financial crash is to stabilize its exchange rate. Protecting the currency sliding down too much requires

---

[1] The countries are Turkey, Venezuela, Argentina, Mexico, Indonesia, South Korea, Malaysia, Philippines, Russia, Brazil, and Thailand.

some drastic measures like cutting public budgets, raising taxes, and hiking interest rates. This combination of measures slows down the economy and boosts unemployment. Also in countries where banks had not been competently supervised and suffer from moral hazard problems, the recession may also create a costly banking crisis. This is bitter medicine, but to many experts this is the solution.

In fact, the debate boils down to the issue of increasing the interest rate. While this is thought necessary to save the currency, it also discourages investment and the result may be severe recession and high unemployment. Thus the consensus on the prescriptions of so-called 'Washington Consensus' remains elusive.

Topic for Discussion

In the context of free capital movement, how can a country safeguard itself to avoid the Asian currency crisis in 1997-type of situation? Explain your view.

Further Reading

Bordo, M.D., B. Eichengreen and D.A. Irwin, 'Is Globalization Today Really Different than Globalization a Hundred Years Ago?', *NBER Working Paper No. 7195*, 1999.

Gerald P. and Paula Tkac. 2009. 'The Financial Crisis of 2008 in Fixed-Income Markets', *Journal of International Money and Finance,* 28 (8), 1293–1316, December 2009.

Goldfajn, Ilan and Rodrigo Valdes, 'Capital Flows and the Twin Crisis: The Role of Liquidity', *IMF Working Paper No. 97/87*, International Monetary Fund, 1997.

Kolb, Robert, *Lessons from the Financial Crisis: Causes, Consequences, and Our Economic Future,* Hoboken, Wiley, 2010.

Kristin J. Forbes and Roberto Rigobon, 'No Contagion, Only Interdependence: Measuring Stock Market Comovements', *The Journal of Finance,* 57(5), 2002.

Lagunoff, Roger D. and Stacey L. Schreft, 'A Model of Financial Fragility', *Journal of Economic Theory,* 99 (1–2), 2001.

Lane, Philip R. and Gisn Maria Milesi–Ferretti 'The External Wealth of Nations: Measures of Foreign Assets and Liabilities for Industrial and Developing Countries', *Journal of International Economics,* 55(2), 263–94, 2001.

Pesaran, M.H. and A. Pick, 'Econometric Issues in the Analysis of Contagion', *Journal of Economic Dynamics and Control,* 31(4), 1245–71, 2007.

Sinclair, P. and Shu Chang, 'International Capital Movement and the International Dimension to Financial Crisis', in R.A. Brealey et al. (eds), *Financial Stability and Central Banks: A Global Perspective,* London, Routledge, 2001.

Torres, Craig. 'How Mexico's Behind-the-Scenes Tactics and a Secret Pact Averted Market Panic', *Wall Street Journal,* 28 March 1994.

13

Foreign Direct Investment in India and Emerging Economies

13.1 Introduction

Foreign direct investment (FDI) occurs when an investor based in one country acquires an asset in another country with the intention of managing the same. Their management dimension distinguishes FDI from the general portfolio investment in foreign stocks, bonds, and other capital market instruments. 'FDI' is defined by the Organization for Economic Co-operation and Development (OECD, 2008) as 'capital invested for the purpose of acquiring a lasting interest in an enterprise and of exerting a degree of influence on that enterprise's operations'.

Total FDI flow in the world in 2009 was USD 2421.08 billion of which European Union accounted for USD 1054.27 billion. The developed countries attracted FDI significantly and it became about USD 1 trillion in 2007, the US being the largest beneficiary (USD 192.9 billion) followed by countries like France, United Kingdom, and Netherlands. FDI inflows in CIS countries[1] increased also in 2007 and in Asia we see that China, Hong Kong, Singapore, and India are the major beneficiaries.

Since 1991–92, India has been trying to attract foreign capital to bridge the gap between the intended investment and the actual saving of the country. To increase the rate of growth of GDP in the range of 7 per cent, the rate of net capital formation should be increased in the vicinity of 28 to 30 per cent. The savings of the country has been hanging around 24 per cent. There is a gap and this gap is to be bridged by (*i*) Portfolio investment by foreign financial institutions, (*ii*) lending by foreign banks and other institutions, and (*iii*) foreign direct investment. Of these three routes, developing countries prefer the third, i.e., Foreign Direct Investment, as this gives certain advantages to the host country. The advantages of FDI are:

---

[1] The Commonwealth of Independent States (CIS) is a regional organization whose participating countries are former Soviet Republics. The organization was founded on 8 December 1991 by the Republic of Belarus, the Russian Federation, and Ukraine, when the leaders of the three countries met in the Belovezhskaya Pushcha Natural Reserve, about 50 km (30 miles) north of Brest in Belarus, and signed a *Creation Agreement* on the dissolution of the Soviet Union and the creation of CIS as a successor entity to the USSR. At the same time, they announced that the new alliance would be open to all republics of the former Soviet Union, as well as other nations sharing the same goals. The CIS charter stated that all the members were sovereign and independent nations, and thereby effectively abolished the Soviet Union.

(1) It increases the capital for investment automatically. If we compare this with the acquisition route, we see that foreign capital replaces the domestic capital by a take-over or purchase. The released domestic capital may be invested in some other sectors of the economy.
(2) FDI in green field ventures brings new technology and modern management technique. In these areas, developing countries are lagging behind.
(3) Foreign capital inflow through FDI route creates a permanent stake of foreign capital in the domestic economy. This may be beneficial for the host country in the sense that it brings a stabilising force in the economy.

The World Investment Report 2010 reveals that South, East and Southeast Asia together received about 20 per cent of the global FDI inflows in the year 2009 and the amount was USD 233 billion. The region's largest recipients were China, Hong Kong and India with the ranking of second, fourth and ninth respectively in the world.

Again South, East and Southeast Asia together experienced an outflow of FDI to the extent of USD 153 billion with the non-financial sectors of China and Hong Kong taking the lead. The FDI flow in the region has been the combined result of some changes in the economic policies in China, Hong Kong and India.

13.2 Objective

The objective of this present chapter is to give a fair account of the status of FDI in India during the recent period. The study focuses attention at three levels of the
(1) states
(2) sectors
(3) industry

This is the usage side of FDI. We are to see also the source side. So far as FDI inflow into India is concerned, the United States and the European Union provides the lion's share of FDI to India. Japan comes next in importance of source. For some years, Mauritius became important, and the role of Non-Resident Indians (NRI) is somewhat complex. Some people argue that many NRIs are taking advantage of the Mauritius route regarding the supply side of FDI. There is another problem, and this is the widening gap between the approval and actual inflow of FDI. If we see the international situation, we find that there is normally a gap of 30 per cent between the approval and the actual inflow. But, in India the gap is much wider and sometimes it becomes difficult to give explanation for that gap.

There have been some studies on the determinants of FDI inflow into the host countries in the literature. The economic parameters often mentioned as explanatory variables are: Growth rate of GDP, state of infrastructure, exchange rate stability, equitable value of the exchange rate, openness of the economy, legal structure of the host country, and the attitude of the government. The models, which are implicit in the study of these variables, are based on a market economy framework. In India, the paradigm shift occurred from 1991–92, i.e, the Indian think-tank became accustomed to exploring the role of market mechanism in explaining the movement of economic variables. This happened from 1991–92 onwards. A broad section of people — executives in the corporate, officials of foreign embassies, academicians, independent consultants, and industrialists — often express the opinion that India has a great problem regarding the mind set, i.e., a popular belief is that foreign capital inflow leads to the exploitation of the domestic economy by the owners of foreign capital. There is another popular belief that India suffers from 'too much government syndrome'. The latter means that the role of government in India is spread everywhere, but ironically the governance is weak in areas where it is called for. The latter are areas of external security, true safeguards of the downtrodden people, preservation of the environment, and a true reform in the financial sector. The perception is partly qualitative in nature. The extent to which this perception exists can be measured only by a survey method, and this is beyond the scope of this chapter.

13.3 Approach towards FDI in India

The exact position of FDI in India will be put up first at three levels: at the level of the State, at the level of the sector, and at the level of the industry. The objective of doing this is to examine several hypotheses like the role of infrastructure in attracting FDI, the role of labour situation, the role of law and order, etc. We are to see also whether the inflow of FDI in India has certain favourable destination, region-wise or sector-wise.

A broad explanation of the above will enable us to zero in on certain areas that could be explored further to ascertain the causes of a slow inflow of FDI. It can facilitate the drawing of our conclusion.

13.4 Role of Infrastructure

There is a popular perception that FDI flows to the region where infrastructure is better. But the state of infrastructure in a particular region covers many aspects. Broadly, infrastructure can be placed under two categories.

(1) Physical infrastructure, which may be called as social capital. This category includes roads, railways and other communication systems, the availability of power and other viable inputs.
(2) The second category includes those aspects which are non-physical in nature like law and order system, availability of efficient work force, education system, work culture and a common growth-oriented human psychology. In many developing countries, the work culture may be not conducive to modern-age industrial society. Also, the overall impression regarding the work culture on the mind of the potential investors is important.

The role of government in the development of the economy is an important factor in the second category of infrastructure. While the government as a facilitator is appreciated everywhere as it helps rapid economic development, too much government control, and particularly bureaucratic red-tape is not liked by foreign investors.

In spite of planned economic development in India during the last five decades, the development of infrastructure has not been uniform in 28 states/regions of the country. One study places the situation of infrastructure in the form of an index. Taking the average India situation as a hundred, the study shows the index of Delhi as 730, Kerala 162, Punjab 172, Tamil Nadu 195, while Gujarat is 105, and West Bengal 102. States like Rajasthan, Meghalaya,

188 ❖ Foreign Direct Investment in India and Emerging Economies

Manipur are lagging behind as their index is far below 100. When we place the flow of FDI in different states in contrast to the indices of infrastructure of different states, we find that while the states successfully attracting FDI are generally the states that have good infrastructure, the converse is not true. The states having good infrastructure index have not always been able to attract FDI.

13.5 Hypothesis of the Study as Pursued in this Chapter

We are trying to test the following hypotheses:
(1). Foreign Direct Investment flows to the region where returns on capital are higher. This is true both in the case of inter-country comparison and intra-country regions. One important factor in this study is the rate of growth of Gross Domestic Product (GDP). The latter has another important role and this is that a higher growth rate of GDP ensures a higher absorption capacity of the economy. It implies that the necessary condition for attracting higher volume of FDI is the higher growth rate of GDP in the region.
(2). While the first hypothesis shows the necessary condition for inflow of FDI in a region, this may not be sufficient. The sufficient condition is the existence of both infrastructure in the region that can facilitate the profitable investment and a long-term sustenance of the investment procedure. By infrastructure we put emphasis on the way we have defined infrastructure in a qualitative way. It implies that while the existence of good physical infrastructure is important, the other aspects of non-physical infrastructure as explained before are also important.

We will test the above two hypotheses with the help of analysis through tables, diagrams and also with some rigorous analysis in the form of testing of models.

13.6 Data and Methodology

This study is based on secondary level data collected from the Ministry of Commerce and Industry, Goverment of India and also Reserve Bank of India. While the traditional method of analysis will be followed, a small model also will be tested with the help of a simple method of econometrics. Charts and diagrams will supplement this.

In the following pages, we try to test these two hypotheses both qualitatively and quantitatively on the basis of the available data. The examples of other countries will be used as supplements, and the major focus will remain on India.

13.7 FDI: A Model in the Making

Foreign Direct Investment is one aspect of foreign capital flow in the domestic economy. In the open economy set-up, capital funds flow will maintain equilibrium by adjustment in the real variables in the external sectors.

In an open economy, aggregate demand [AD] will be

$AD = C + I + G + X + T^*$,   where, C, I, G, and X are consumption, investment, government expenditure and export respectively. T^* is transfer of funds abroad.

The aggregate supply [AS] will be
AS = C + S + T + M + Tr*,   where, C, S, M and T are consumption, savings, import and taxation respectively. Tr* is the funds transfer inflow in the country.

Using traditional macroeconomic assumptions that government budget is balanced, which means G = T, and consumption plan is always satisfied, that means we can eliminate C from both sides; we can write after *imposing equilibrium in the economy,*

$$I + X + T^* = S + M + Tr^*,$$

Or, $T^* - Tr^* = (S - I) + (M - X)$

Or, $Tr^* - T^* = (I - S) + (X - M)$ (Equation 13.1)

In our scheme of things, Tr* – T* is the excess funds inflow into the country that can be taken as the foreign direct investment (FDI). Both S and I are functions of income Y and rate of interest r. Again, X and M are functions of domestic price P, foreign price P* and exchange rate **e**. Also,

$$P = e \cdot P^*$$ (Equation 13.2)

From (13.1) we can write using functions,

$$FDI = \{I(Y, r) - S(Y, r)\} + \{X(P, e) - M(P, e)\}$$

Or, $FDI = f(Y, r, e, P)$ (Equation 13.3)

Since nominal exchange rate and price level move in the same direction ('e' is the price of foreign currency in terms of domestic currency), and nominal interest rate includes inflation expectations, keeping all the three — nominal interest rate, exchange rate and price level — may lead to multi-collinearity, a particular problem in econometrics when some of the independent variables are correlated among themselves. So, we drop price level for the purpose of econometric estimation. So equation (13.3) in estimable form looks like (through logarithmic transformation),

$$\text{Log FDI} = a_0 + a_1 \log Y + a_2 \log e + a_3 r + u$$ (Equation 13.4)

Theoretical value will be $a_1 > 0$, $a_2 < 0$, $a_3 > 0$

The estimation can be made in level form also. That shows the relative strength of the different determinants of FDI in a developing country.

The variable Y will capture the importance of the absorption capacity of the economy. It is expected that a faster growth can absorb larger amounts of capital, domestic or foreign, into the economy. The exchange rate takes care of both the potential return and opportunity cost of investment. Again, the interest rate reveals the reference rate of the feasible return on capital and also the cost of domestic capital.

13.8 Empirical Exercise

The data on FDI in India is available only from 1991 onwards, and as such, the database is weak. We have taken the time series 1991 to 1997 for the econometric estimation of the model (Equation 13.4). The results for India and Malaysia are placed. We find that the coefficient of log e gives wrong sign though the t-value is not satisfactory. Other coefficients are of correct signs.

Table 13.1 Indian Case of Regression Results

Dependent Variable: FDI
Method: Least Squares
Date: 07/06/00 Time: 17:10
Sample: 1991–97
Included Observations: 7

Variable	Coefficient	Standard. Error	t-Statistic	Probability
C	−9973.503	5568.279	−1.791128	0.1712
GDP	0.00696	0.008616	0.807765	0.4783
LR	143.4031	206.9004	0.693102	0.5381
ER	212.8466	130.8458	1.626697	0.2023
R-squared	0.943273	Mean dependent var		1431.571
Adjusted R-squared	0.886545	S.D. dependent var		1307.848
S.E. of regression	440.5233	Akaike info criterion		15.30936
Sum squared resid	582182.2	Schwarz criterion		15.27845
Log likelihood	−49.58277	F-statistic		16.62815
Durbin-Watson stat	1.708655	Prob(F-statistic)		0.022543

Source : Prepared by the author.

The same analysis is applied in case of Malaysia and the results are as follows.

Table 13.2 Malaysia: Regression

Year	Direct Investment	GDP	Lending Rate	Exchange Rate
	Million USD	Million USD		
1984	6510	32737	11.35	2.43
1985	7388	31912	11.54	2.43
1986	6111	27536	10.69	2.60
1987	6806	31978	8.19	2.49
1988	7054	33405	7.25	2.72
1989	8096	37945	7.00	2.70
1990	10318	42852	7.17	2.70
1991	12440	48669	8.13	2.72
1992	16860	56911	9.31	2.61
1993	20591	61187	9.05	2.70
1994	22916	74326	7.61	2.56
1995		86091	7.63	2.54
1996		98618	8.89	2.53
1997		70788	9.53	3.89
1998			10.61	3.80

Source : Prepared by the author.

Table 13.3 *Sectoral Inflows of Foreign Direct Investment in India*

Dependent Variable: FDI
Method: Least Squares
Date: 07/17/00 Time: 12:01
Sample(adjusted): 1986–1994
Included observations: 9 after adjusting endpoints

Variable	Coefficient	Standard. Error	t-Statistic	Probability.
C	−11709.42	10544.32	−1.110495	0.3173
GDP	0.378765	0.028102	13.47845	0
LR	303.9656	223.4611	1.360262	0.2319
ER	1375.409	3515.937	0.391193	0.7118
R-squared	0.977099	Mean dependent variable		9064.778
Adjusted R-squared	0.963358	S.D. dependent variable		3568.531
S.E. of regression	683.0949	Akaike info criterion		16.19225
Sum squared resid	2333093	Schwarz criterion		16.2799
Log likelihood	−68.86511	F-statistic		71.10889
Durbin-Watson stat	1.429221	Prob(F-statistic)		0.00016

Source: Prepared by the author.

13.9 Technology Transfer, Capital Formation and International Trade

Foreign Trade Investment is associated with large multinational Corporations (MNCs). Economic theory explains how FDI induces the firms to undertake international operations. For this, the relationship between the FDI and MNCs is very strong. In the context of FDI, the overseas expansion of a firm is determined by three factors and these are — ownership advantages, location advantages and internalization of incentives. A firm wishing to operate abroad should possess adequate advantages so that it can offset the handicap of working in an alien atmosphere and also cover for higher risk. The advantages mentioned in the beginning come from the ownership of proprietary intangible assets possessed by the firm and these can be employed abroad in an efficient manner. These intangible assets include brand goodwill, technology management skills, access to cheaper sources of raw materials and capital, etc. The firm may exploit these advantages through exports from the home base in the initial stage. Later, production facility is created abroad to cater to the foreign market. This practice is to exploit other advantages like tariffs and quantitative restrictions imposed by host countries, transport and communication cost, and cheaper input prices.

Many factors like imperfect market, licensing of intangible assets and also internalization of incentives available on local production led to the inflow of FDI in the 1970s. The nature of FDI flows changed with the improvement of communication and advance of information technology. Whenever the cost of market transactions of intangible assets becomes very high, firms tend to avoid these costs by internalizing the transactions of the intangible assets. This is done through FDI also.

Literature also reveals that exporting commodities directly from the home base and production of the same in foreign countries, to serve the foreign markets either through licensing or FDI, are two alternative modes of overseas operations. From this angle, it becomes obvious that if trade liberalization becomes extreme, the location advantage of the country for the local market may be lost.

13.10 Inter-Industry Variation in FDI

The hypothesis that some industries in the host country could contract more FDI than others has been tested empirically in the literature. These studies have ignored the possibility of discrimination in licensing and have concentrated on the behaviour of FDI regarding its destination to particular industries. The common elements of the study include FDI intensity to vary positively with the intensity of advertisement, skill intensity, R&D expenditure, capital -output ratio, and certain other factors. Also in the absence of any particular strong policy factor, the choice between FDI and licensing will be determined by the transaction cost. Since transaction costs are quite high for branded consumer goods, there is a pronounced tendency that FDI will be concentrated in those industries. This finding has one implication and this is as follows. A developing country with the desire to contract more FDI should follow a liberalization policy in such a way that it makes the effects of intangible asset and internalization incentives to be more pronounced.

FDI and Economic Growth: There is a common hypothesis in the literature that higher rate of GDP needs a higher inflow of FDI. The literature also compares the relative productivity of FDI vis-à-vis domestic capital. So far as FDI increases the availability of the capital, this should increase the rate of growth of the GDP. Thus, we have a circularity and it is whether higher growth rate leads to higher inflow of FDI, or higher inflow FDI leads to a higher growth rate. This is a standard causality problem in econometrics literature. Many studies have empirically tried to see the direction of causality, and the result is a mixed one (Chen, 2009; Ghatak and Halicioglu, 2006).

13.11 Indian Economy and Foreign Capital

The domination of foreign capital in the Indian industrial scene just before Independence was the result of history. Foreign capital in general, and British capital in particular, played a crucial role in the development of jute textiles and engineering industries in the Indian subcontinent. The philosophy of economic development to be pursued in post-Independent India had changed radically, and it was thought that the least importance should be attached to the role of foreign capital in India's economic growth. The result was a socialist pattern of industrial development based on self-sufficiency.

The import-substitution and inward-looking industrialization led to a minimum role for the foreign capital and the paucity of foreign exchanges induced the authority to enact the stringent law like Foreign Exchange Regulation Act (FERA), 1973. The strictness of this piece of legislation had been responsible for much of capital flight from India in the 1970s and 1980s. Indian planners were so much immersed in self-delusion that they could not believe the reality of capital flight until the national coffer became almost empty in 1990. The gravity of the situation changed the whole perspective and the paradigm shift happened. This led to the attempt of economic reforms.

13.12 Foreign Direct Investment and Emerging Economy Perspective

The political economy of the role of FDI in the development process of an emerging economy like India is full of controversy. The arguments are on both sides. Those who advocate a more liberal regime claim that FDI will provide the much-needed resources and foreign exchange for reviving Indian industry, improve the crumbling infrastructure, and allow India to modernize its technological base. Also greater competition in Indian manufacturing will benefit the Indian consumer. On the other hand, critics point to the poor record of multinational corporations in India, their excessive profitability. Also they argue about the adverse impact of profit remittances on India's balance of payments.

Does foreign investment contribute to growth? Empirical investigation does not offer any clear answer. Countries like China have experienced large FDI inflows and high growth in recent years, while Korea grew rapidly without significant levels of foreign capital. In Latin America, many countries have periods of slow growth despite openness to foreign capital. Even if we did find some positive correlation between FDI and growth, the issue of causality remains unresolved.

13.13 Technology: Policy and Reality

Host country governments often encourage foreign investment in the hope of improving the productivity of domestic firms. Foreign direct investment potentially brings new technologies to the host economy. Technology inflows can also improve the productivity of domestic firms through 'spillovers', as better production and management techniques diffuse in the host economy. In some situations, foreign investment can be a catalyst for growth. The literature isolates two channels for this spillover process. The more disembodied aspects of superior technologies used by foreign firms can spread to domestic firms through the mobility of trained workers and managers, and through technical guidance provided.

13.14 FDI: A Segmented Analysis

In the following paragraphs we will explain the current position of FDI in India in different parts. This method of analysis will help us to have an in-depth analysis of dynamics of the flow of FDI in different sectors of the economy.

A Macro View

The source countries from which FDI flows into Indian economy are large in number but the major partners are the United States, the European Union countries, and a couple of countries in Asia like Japan, South Korea, Singapore, Hong Kong, and Mauritius. An interesting phenomenon is that even after the accession of Hong Kong to mainland China, capital has flowed from Hong Kong into India. All the European Union countries, particularly countries like United Kingdom, Germany, France, and Netherlands are important source countries of FDI. As a single country outside EU block, Japan is very important as a source country.

Table 13.1 (see Annexure) reveals that though the number of countries from which FDI flows into India is impressive, only a handful of countries are important as the source of FDI inflow. Some countries are reluctant to make investment in India; Taiwan is an example. Non-resident Indians (NRI) is a category in Table 13.A which shows that the contribution of NRI in the FDI in India is not impressive.

13.15 Sector-Wise Inflow

The flow of FDI in different sectors of Indian economy is not uniform, and some sectors have been able to attract large volumes of FDI. From this angle, the important sectors are: metallurgical industries, electrical instrument, telecommunication, chemicals, drugs, and pharmaceuticals, textiles, paper and paper pulp, and food processing industries. In Tables 13.B and 13.C, sector-wise approvals and actual incomes are revealed. Table 13.D keeps sector-wise inflow as a percentage of approval. Table 13.E is deriving from Table 13.D in an aggregate form by the period 1991 to 1998. One interesting aspect of Table 13.E is that in some particular sectors the inflow as a per cent of approval are pretty large like drugs and pharmaceuticals (93 per cent), mechanical engineering (61 per cent) trading (46 per cent). But in most other areas the percentage is low like telecommunication, fuel, metallurgical industry, photographic films and other materials, soaps and cosmetics, consultancy services, etc. A very low percentage in these sectors require further research and case studies, to understand the nature of the problem in the implementation stage of the project.

13.16 Nature of FDI Inflow

As indicated here, the nature of FDI inflow into India is not uniform of the two routes of FDI inflow, automatic route and Government route. There has been a steady rise from 1991 to 1997, but after that, there has been a perspective decline inflow to FDI into India. This aspect is revealed in Exhibit 1. The factors responsible for the deceleration of FDI inflows into India from 1997 should be investigated. The same picture in a different format is presented in Exhibit 3.

Between the two routes of FDI inflow into India, the government route is predominant as the percentage of shares through the government route is much higher compared to the automatic route. This aspect is revealed in Exhibit 2.

Though the number of source countries from which FDI inflows into India happens is impressive, the principal sources are: United States, United Kingdom, Japan, Germany, France, South Korea, Mauritius, and NRI. This aspect has been revealed in Exhibit 4.

Exhibit 13.1 *FDI Inflows into India (Rs Million)*

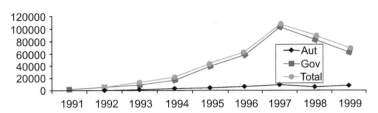

Source : Nandi (2011)

Exhibit 13.2 *Shares of Automatic Route and Government Route in the Total Inflow of FDI*

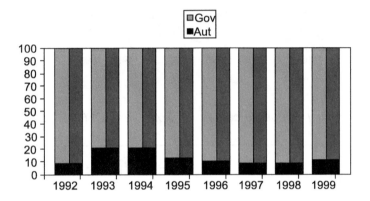

Source : Nandi (2011)

Exhibit 13.3 *FDI in India: Approved to Actual*

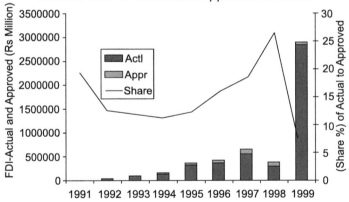

Source : Nandi (2011)

Exhibit 13.4 FDI Inflow into India from Select Countries

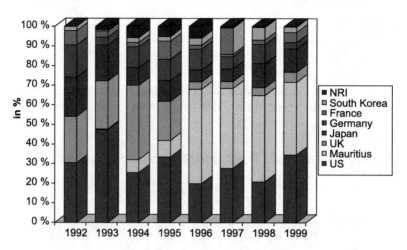

Source: Nandi (2011)

Exhibit 13.5 Actual FDI as Percentage of Approved FDI (1991–99) (Country-wise)

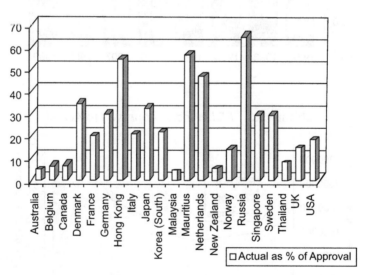

Source: Nandi (2011)

Source : Nandi (2011)

Actual inflow of FDI as a percentage total approval for the period 1991–99 is not uniform country-wise and this interesting aspect is revealed in Exhibit 5. We see that the percentage is quite high for countries like Russia, Netherlands, Mauritius, and Hong Kong. But countries like United Kingdom, United States, and Canada show very low percentage of actual inflow as a percentage of the total approval. One explanation may be that the total volume of inflow from these countries is very high compared to other countries that register a higher percentage, but this fails to give the total explanation.

We have seen earlier that a FDI inflow in major sectors in India during the period 1991–99 is not uniform and the distribution is very skewed. This is revealed in Exhibit 6. We see that while transportation industry comments 7.3 per cent, telecommunication 5.8 per cent, service sector 5.8 per cent, chemicals 5.7 per cent, electrical equipment 6.6 per cent, and fuels 5.2 per cent, other things like hotel and tourism, trading, industry machinery, etc., have failed to attract sizeable FDI inflow.

13.17 Infrastructure and FDI Inflow

We have mentioned in the hypothesis that infrastructure is a condition for FDI inflow. We have composed infrastructure into two parts; physical infrastructure and subjective infrastructure. While the existence of both physical and subjective infrastructure is necessary to attract foreign direct investment, it may not be sufficient if the important elements of qualitative aspect of infrastructure are lagging. This interesting proposition has been confirmed by our analysis of data taking from the states. CMIE has compiled an index of infrastructure for all the states. The average is 100 and the states whose indices are above 100 are termed as better placed regarding the existence of physical infrastructure. Following this criteria the states are: Goa, Haryana, Himachal Pradesh, Kerala, Maharashtra, Punjab, and Tamil Nadu. The states like Andhra Pradesh, Assam, Gujarat, Karnataka, Odisha, Uttar Pradesh, and West Bengal are just above 100 so far as the infrastructure indices are concerned it is important to mention that CMIE indices are based on physical infrastructure only. We find from Exhibit 8 that those states like Goa, Haryana, Kerala, and Punjab having good infrastructure have failed to attract sufficient amount of FDI. But states like Andhra, Odisha, and West Bengal, though relatively weak in infrastructure, have been able to attract sizeable amount of FDI. The relationship between infrastructure index and state-level FDI is also shown in Exhibit 9. The lack of a clear trend is due to the fact that the FDI index is based on physical infrastructure only. The perception about the work culture, supply of qualified labour force, mental preparation about the existence of foreign capital etc., are important, that attract foreign capital in a region.

Regarding FDI inflow and growth rate of state domestic product, we have mentioned in one part of the hypothesis that higher growth rate of GDP helps inflow of FDI. This has been shown in Exhibit 12 that the relationship is positive. But relationship between FDI flow in the states and degree of urbanization is not very clear as we see in Exhibit 11.

The relationship between FDI inflow and the growth rate of gross domestic product has been empirically tested in the literature. The common result is that the relationship is positive. But

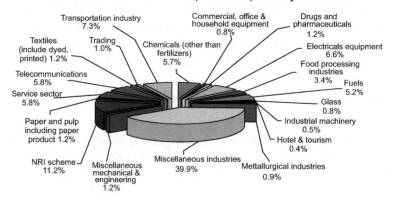

Exhibit 13.6 *FDI Inflows (1991–99) in Major Sectors*

Source : Nandi (2011)

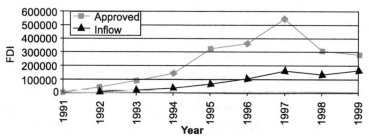

Exhibit 13.7 *FDI (Approved and Inflow)*

Source : Nandi (2011)

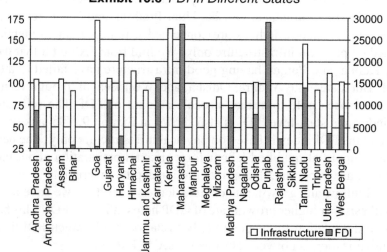

Exhibit 13.8 *FDI in Different States*

Source : Nandi (2011)

Exhibit 13.9 *Relationship between State-level FDI and Infrastructure Index*

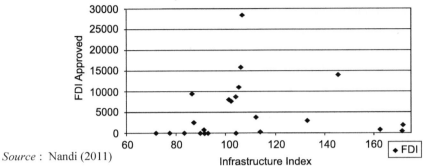

Source: Nandi (2011)

Exhibit 13.10 *Relationship between State-level FDI and Percentage of Man-days Lost*

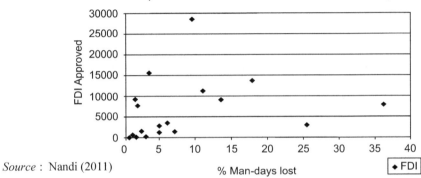

Source: Nandi (2011)

Exhibit 13.11 *Relationship between State-level FDI and Urbanization Growth*

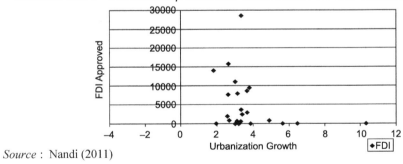

Source: Nandi (2011)

Exhibit 13.12 *Relationship between State-level FDI and GDP Growth Rate*

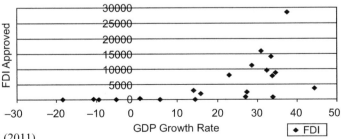

Source: Nandi (2011)

the issue whether higher growth of GDP causes higher inflow of FDI, or higher inflow of FDI causes higher growth of GDP, is a question of causality. The answer to this complex question requires sophisticated treatment for empirical data that has not been done here. We have tested the simple model to determine the empirical influence of the growth rate of State domestic product and the infrastructure index. The result is reported and we find that the effects are positive. This proves that our initial hypothesis is correct.

13.18 A Quantitative Exercise to Ascertain the Role of Infrastructure

In the earlier section, we have estimated a model to determine the quantitative effects of some macro variables on the inflow of FDI in India and other countries. That was basically a time series study. Since, in the second section, we are more concerned about the role of infrastructure in the inflow of FDI in different states of India, we use here a different model and test the model on cross-section data.

We have developed a model for the quantitative estimation of the effects of some economic variables like GDP, infrastructure, exchange rate, and interest rate. We have estimated the model both at the level terms and by logarithmic terms. The latter enables us to get the elasticities of the relevant variables as the effects on the inflow of FDI. This is a cross-section data and so the problem of auto-correlation is not relevant. Also, we have checked the potential problem of heteroskedasticity and this problem does not exist. The following two tables show the results of regressions. These are based on the cross-section data of 26 states in India that are shown in Exhibit 8. We see that both infrastructure and growth rates of state-level domestic products have coefficients that are statistically significant. Also adjusted R^2 0.447 approximately. Thus both infrastructure and GDP growth rates can explain the inflow of FDI in the regions. Our comment on heteroskedasticity is based on the figure in Table 13.5 that shows the plot of residuals against the infrastructure indices.

Table 13.4 *Regression: Level Terms*

Dependent Variable: FDI
Method: Least Squares
Sample: 1 26
Included Observations: 23
Excluded Observations: 3

Variable	Coefficient	Standard Error	t-Statistic	Probability
C	−671.7450	2098.041	−0.320177	0.7522
INFRASTRUCTURE	40.58214	10.48555	3.870290	0.0010
SDPGR	114.1215	45.86812	2.488036	0.0218
R-squared	0.497407	Mean dependent variable		6397.589
Variable	Coefficient	Standard Error	t-Statistic	Probability

(Contd.)

(Contd.)

Adjusted R-squared	0.447148	Standard Deviation dependent variable	8733.885
Standard Error of regression	6493.995	Akaike information criterion	20.51625
Sum squared residuals	8.43E+08	Schwarz criterion	20.66436
Log likelihood	−232.9369	F-statistic	9.896823
Durbin–Watson statistic	2.834082	Probability (F-statistic)	0.001028

Source : Prepared by the author.
Note : SDPGR is Growth Rate of State Level Domestic Product

Table 13.5 *Regression: Residual Plot*

Observation	Actual	Fitted	Residual	Residual Plot
1	8685.40	7501.23	1184.17	|.|*.|
2	11.0600	142.445	−131.385	|.*.|
3	1.49000	5210.26	−5208.77	|.*|.|
4	831.180	6907.09	−6075.91	|.*|.|
5	30267.6	29967.8	299.821	|.*.|
6	502.260	−5121.22	5623.48	|.|*.|
7	11083.5	6871.21	4212.25	|.|*.|
8	2938.81	6337.38	−3398.57	|.*|.|
9	360.310	4035.34	−3675.03	|.*|.|
10	8.41000	3719.23	−3710.82	|.*|.|
11	15820.2	7165.75	8654.43	|.|.*|
12	808.020	9005.45	−8197.43	|*.|.|
13	28467.8	7939.63	20528.1	|.|.*|
14	3.19000	1641.84	−1638.65	|.*|.|
15	52.9600	1255.19	−1202.23	|.*|.|
17	9491.51	6539.22	2952.29	|.|*.|
19	7986.74	6063.26	1923.48	|.|*.|
20	1926.62	8111.68	−6185.06	|*|.|
21	2441.15	5991.08	−3549.93	|.*|.|
23	14059.9	9066.60	4993.32	|.|*.|
24	0.68000	2525.70	−2525.02	|.*|.|
25	3707.99	8937.51	−5229.52	|.*|.|
26	7687.81	7330.87	356.935	|.*.|

Source : Prepared by the author.
Note : SDPGR is Growth Rate of State Level Domestic Product

Table 13.6 Regression: Log Transformation

Dependent Variable: LOG(FDI)
Method: Least Squares
Sample: 1 26
Included Observations: 18
Excluded Observations: 8

Variable	Coefficient	Standard. Error	t-Statistic	Probability
C	−5.995820	6.406615	−0.935879	0.3642
LOG(INFRASTR)	1.999758	1.199575	1.667055	0.1162
LOG(SDPGR)	1.377390	0.597440	2.305488	0.0358
R-squared	0.311402	Mean dependent variable		7.703807
Adjusted R-squared	0.219589	Standard Deviation dependent variable		2.662105
Standard Error of regression	2.351727	Akaike information criterion		4.699189
Sum squared residual	82.95928	Schwarz criterion		4.847584
Log likelihood	−39.29270	F-statistic		3.391699
Durbin–Watson statistic	2.421010	Prob(F-statistic)		0.060918

Source : Prepared by the author.

13.19 Conclusion

The developing countries will need FDI to supplement the inadequate domestic savings in the face of growing requirement of capital to maintain a crucial rate of economic growth so that the people below the poverty line can be lifted within a reasonable time. We have seen that the share of FDI inflow in the developing countries is very much high, with some countries like China having been able to attract a huge amount of foreign capital. Though the comparison with China regarding the inflow of FDI is not truly justified, India should have been able to attract the relatively larger volume of foreign capital than what she has done so far. In the earlier paragraphs, attempts have been made to point out the factors which are responsible for the inflow of FDI. In certain quarters, studies have been made to analyze the nature of FDI inflow in developing countries particularly in South Asian and Latin American countries. Filtering down the studies available in the literature help us to identify certain factors, which are also relevant in Indian situation. We should be clear that some of these variables are qualitative in nature. But China is an example of how export orientation can be properly utilized to attract foreign capital and also to maximize the growth process. Not only that, China has been able to use FDI on a selective basis to maximize the rate of growth, but China has one unique advantage which India is lacking, and this should be mentioned to keep the comparison straight.

China is lucky to have two highly-developed regions like Hong Kong and Taiwan. The first it has obtained from the United Kingdom in 1997 and a large chunk of FDI in China is from Hong Kong. Taiwan is a breakaway province of China and in spite of the political row, Taiwan invests a huge amount of capital in China. Apart from these two highly–developed regions and a large supplier of foreign capital, China has a large ethnic diaspora in South Asian countries. This group is financially very rich and they invest huge amounts in the mainland.

These two factors i.e., the existence of Hong Kong and Taiwan, and a large Chinese Diaspora having strong economic linkage, make China unique among the developing countries regarding the inflow of FDI. This is true in spite of a political regime which is totally opposite of the capitalist system. This aspect is interesting. China has become a capitalist economic system with a totalitarian political set-up as only Chinese Communist Party is the legitimate political party there.

The inflow of FDI is sometimes associated with the level of technological development in the country. In this case again, the China example should be mentioned. So long as foreign capital is flowing in and particularly in areas where China is lacking, the Chinese authority is not bothered about the type of technology the foreign investor is bringing. The system is regimented and it has ruled out any debate in political circles regarding the appropriateness of the technology brought by the MNCs. This type of system has been found to be very suitable for the foreign investors. South Korea also has been able to import modern technology in crucial industries so that it can maintain competitive edge on the export front.

Sometimes the export performance requirements are tagged with the inflow of FDI and the authority of developing countries puts emphasis on this aspect. On this point, several questions are important.

(1) How well do international markets work in apportioning FDI in line with comparative advantage?
(2) What investment-diverting actions are being taken by other countries to set a location of international manufacturing production in their own direction?
(3) What obstacles inhibit international markets from functioning more effectively?

These questions are crucial to understand the nature of FDI inflow in developing countries. It is a fact that the developing countries are competing among themselves to attract foreign capital.

Sometimes the location issue becomes important for the inflow of FDI, and the nature of industry becomes related to that. Some particular industries like automobile, petrochemical and electronics are mentioned for the initial phase of investment. The sources of inputs and location of cheap labour becomes important sometimes in the determination of the location of particular industries.

Another important issue has come up in a study related to the dynamism of FDI in developing countries. While the host government tries to convince the international investor to commit the capital to develop a new production side, a country would have to spend more resources to build up infrastructure so that the foreign firm's commitment remains. But the concern of the host country does not end here. Literature in this particular area has identified five broad categories of concern in developing countries which are in the process of transition:

(1) Cultural factors (worker's motivation, cultural preparation)
(2) Labour regulations (Flexibility in hiring and laying of workers)
(3) Responsiveness of the surrounding economy in providing supporting goods and services
(4) Institutional base of commercial law to give guidance when dispute arises
(5) The credibility of public sector commitments about taxes, infrastructure and other regulatory issues.

Literature also reveals the concern of foreign investors regarding the credibility of the promises of the host government and the institutional factors like the judicial systems of security. These are the patterns of information gap which the foreign companies desire to bridge in order to evaluate the returns associated with the investment opportunity. The MNCs are most often oligopolies and the countries where they have their headquarters behave also as oligopolies. They introduce entry barriers and transfer knowledge only when it becomes a public good. In most cases, technological knowledge is strictly kept under control. This practice prevents dissemination of latest technology in the host country. In this case experience with all the countries is not the same.

Topic for Discussion

Explain the process how foreign direct investment can help diffusion of superior technical efficiency to the domestic firms of the country.

Further Readings

Agosin, M.R. and R. Machado, 'Foreign Investment in Developing Countries: Does it Crowd in Domestic Investment?', *Oxford Development Studies*, 33(2), 2005.

Borenzstein E., J.D. Gregorio and Jong–Wha Lee, 'How does foreign Direct Investment affect Economic Growth', *Journal of International Economics*, 45, 1998.

Eichengreen, B. and H. Tong, 'Is China's FDI Coming at the Expense of Other Countries?', *Journal of Japanese International Economics*, 41, 2007.

Javorcik, B.S. and M. Spatareanu, 'To Share or Not to Share: Does Local Participation Matter for Spillovers from Foreign Direct Investment?', *Journal of Development Economics*, 85 (1–2), 2008.

Lipsey, R.E., 'Home and Host Country Effects of FDI', *NBER Working Paper No. 9293*, 2002.

Saggi, K., 'Trade, Foreign Direct Investment, and International Technological Transfer: A Survey', *World Bank Research Observer*, 17 (2), 2002.

Annexures

Table 13A Total FDI (Approvals and Inflows)
Value in ₹ Million

Country Name	App. 1991	Inf. 1991	App. 1992	Inf. 1992	App. 1993	Inf. 1993	App. 1994	Inf. 1994	App. 1995	Inf. 1995	App. 1996	Inf. 1996	App. 1997	Inf. 1997	App. 1998	Inf. 1998	App. 1999	Inf. 1999	App. Total	Inf. Total
Argentina	0	0	0	0	0	0	0	0	0	0	183.8	0.38	0.2	0.38	0	0	0	0	184	0.38
Australia	26.1	0	776.2	0.19	295.6	23.98	3885	18.81	15042.2	327.27	8344.32	515.89	4316.72	213.18	26377.2	593.78	6489.62	870.52	65552.46	2563.64
Austria	15.9	0	61.4	34.57	155.7	15.06	249.7	8.04	296.1	41.14	828.08	310.66	258.94	157.77	554.79	133.68	326.77	3.1	2747.37	704.03
Bahrain	0	0	4	0	4.1	0	48.4	17.53	0	8.95	530.2	2.95	6	2.47	633	26.5	641.97	673.05	1867.67	731.44
Belgium	16.1	0	237	20.23	60	7.32	76.6	102.26	1659	76.82	1947.14	11.4	2163.27	1648.81	32887.7	116.82	139.96	496.87	39186.8	2480.52
Belorussia	0	0	0	0	0.5	0	0	23.77	0	0	0	0	0	0	0	0	0	0	0.5	23.77
Bermuda	0	0	33.2	42.67	0	12.52	260.3	14.2	207.2	190.15	1765.2	0	237.31	300	2660.5	402.5	158.54	57.43	5322.25	1019.47
Brazil	0.1	0	1.1	0	0	0	0	0.11	0	22.97	0	0	0	0	5.1	0	0	0	6.3	23.09
Canada	48.6	0	7.8	0	272.8	14.37	420.8	0.5	13735.6	141.76	1965.42	257.38	3842.64	395.92	3156.79	395.63	368.42	450.46	23818.87	1656.02
Cayman Islands	0	0	0	0	33	0	35	30	0	0	86.9	0	36058.8	0	5	0	108.4	0	36327.1	30
Channel Islands	0	0	0	20	0	0	12.5	0	20	0	0.7	1.56	67.5	0	20	0	0	0	120.7	21.56
China	7.5	0	0	1.35	616.6	0	272.5	0	5810.6	0.18	139.73	0	3.6	15.4	68	2	210.85	0.04	7129.38	18.98
Cyprus	0	0	0	0	0	0	0.3	2.59	4.5	4.09	0	166.71	60.69	196.89	70	434.34	68.36	169.96	203.85	974.59
Czech Republic	0	0	0	0	4.4	0	0	4.2	20.7	0.7	0	0	70	5.75	450	35.28	2352	124.85	2897.1	170.77
Denmark	111.7	12.2	252.3	8.81	319.9	36.01	533	49.4	1224.7	751.86	729.01	436.77	1067.15	200.49	295.41	66.46	761.65	271.63	5294.84	1833.64
Egypt	0	0	0	0	0	0	0	0	0	0	0	12.03	3.15	0	0	3.15	0	0	3.15	15.18
Estonia	0	0	0	0	70	0	0	0	3.1	31	0	0	0	0	0	3.1	0	0	73.1	34.1
Finland	25.3	0	105	105.8	20.7	23.91	103.7	14.82	131.9	111.87	539.62	100.13	1186.97	200.38	495	0.07	2.92	99.47	2611.12	656.45
France	193.3	60.6	296.4	267.0	1290.3	314.3	897.3	292.98	4203.6	2405.24	16716.9	961.96	7134.12	1123.14	5135.57	1588.24	14486.17	2624.94	50354.3	9638.43
Germany	418	65.4	862.7	612.5	1759.3	401.5	5694	1396.53	13394.9	2370.8	15378.9	4726.48	21558.14	5686.84	8537.58	6269.2	11429.46	1981.54	79032.6	23510.8
Gibraltar	0	0	0	0	0	0	0	0	0	0	0	0	0	0	0	0	7	7	7	7
Greece	0	0	0	0	0	0	0	0	6	0	0	0	0	80.08	0	15.4	14.4	0	20.4	95.48
Hong Kong	211.5	12.7	570.8	124.3	879.5	252.9	1648	687.79	4071.7	3348.26	5078.81	1669.31	2585.7	1509.06	2380.25	1909.19	441.36	159.85	17867.42	9673.31
Hungary	0	0	0	0	22.7	0	1.6	0	0	1.78	0	4.25	0	0	10	0	0	0	34.3	6.03

(Contd.)

(Cond.)

Country Name	App. 1991	Inf. 1991	App. 1992	Inf. 1992	App. 1993	Inf. 1993	App. 1994	Inf. 1994	App. 1995	Inf. 1995	App. 1996	Inf. 1996	App. 1997	Inf. 1997	App. 1998	Inf. 1998	App. 1999	Inf. 1999	App. Total	Inf. Total
Iceland	0	0	0	0	0	0	0	0	0	0	3.41	0	10.05	0	0	9.73	0	0	13.46	9.73
Indonesia	0	0	19	0	3.8	0	0	0	3133	0	375	32.46	105	80	294	79.89	0	40.11	3929.8	232.46
Iran	0	0	0	240.6	0	35.4	0	0	0	70	109.3	0	0	0	600	278.6	1.5	0	711.3	624.6
Ireland	0	0	0.1	0.89	1656.4	8.68	64.1	75.52	312.6	41.3	63.57	35.7	228.3	13.44	42.7	15.36	64.11	26.7	2431.88	217.59
Isle of Man	0	0	0	0	0	0	0	4.5	7.3	14.18	2.42	9.28	0	0	1560	0	0	7.2	1569.72	20.98
Israel	178.1	0	12.7	0	14.6	6.51	85.2	6.26	41372.2	14.18	150.49	55.5	514.16	1220.72	120.8	42.65	77.33	31.81	42347.48	1377.62
Italy	178.1	24.0	893.9	46.48	1173.5	53.98	3909	69.47	4603.4	320.48	1388.76	698.44	11949.96	1134.05	2783.53	4291.33	17594.76	2582.38	44475.3	9220.65
Japan	527.1	55.8	6102	716.5	2574.3	810.0	4009	2758.14	15142.6	2271.66	14882.5	3008.28	19063.5	5911.39	12828.2	7805.56	15947.28	6356.38	91076.81	29693.65
Jordan	0	0	0	0	0	0	0	0	0	0	0.06	0	0	0.09	20	0	2.5	0	22.56	0.09
Korea (S)	61.5	0	394	83.89	293.3	64.75	1069	336.13	3141.9	522.24	32209.2	1587.41	19559.76	12279.58	3683.54	4389.06	36489.3	1657.79	96901.01	20920.85
Kuwait	0	0	0.9	0	0.5	0.44	345.9	2.47	1500	0	2600	0.3	1393.54	35.74	2	40.14	0.77	0.19	5843.6	79.28
Liechtenstein	0	1.48	0	0	0	0	0	2.96	0	1.24	0	4.75	308.74	43.42	0	0.08	0	0	308.74	53.93
Luxembourg	0	0	0	46.46	29	0	0	0	531.4	109.91	93.26	42.23	1737.22	19.05	6.4	192.53	65.55	13.16	2462.84	423.33
Malaysia	1.8	0	744.3	0	84.8	5.1	252.2	94.75	13860.9	209.4	423.31	120.23	21046.41	513.24	18031.0	380.12	1161.46	195.46	55606.2	1518.3
Maldives	0	0	0	0	0	0	6	0	0	0	0	0	0	0	3.7	0	3.07	1.54	12.77	1.54
Malta	0	0	1.3	0	0	0	0	1.25	0	0	0	0	0	0	0	0	0	0	1.3	1.25
Mauritius	0	0	0	0	1242.4	37.5	5347	903.22	18084.9	16380.1	23340.2	22768.3	104278.9	36643.22	31659.1	29020.2	38030.48	18906.4	221983.3	124659
Mexico	0	0	52.8	0	2389.8	0	0.1	0.06	81.6	0	0	0	0	0	0	0	0	0	2524.3	0.06
Nepal	0	0	0	0	0	0	0.2	0	0	0	0	0	0	5.04	0	0	0	0	30.3	5.04
Netherlands	559.2	15.0	967.9	148.4	3216.5	1611	2070	1489.12	9664.6	1237.6	10487.1	4693.9	8705.43	5236.78	4962.56	3719.89	6322.14	3591.58	46955.07	21743.34
New Zealand	0	0	3.2	0	0.5	0	0	0	503.3	0	371.35	0	0.51	0	1908.82	70	0	63.35	2787.68	133.35
Norway	3.8	0	9.2	2.03	26.7	1.91	3.2	35.62	48.1	3.61	68.77	41.68	91.73	21.91	246.41	26.15	452.68	1.64	950.59	134.54
NRI	197	0	4391.3	0	10433.2	175.71	4908.8	760.34	7097.1	1190.49	21906.97	2181.69	18171.79	658.41	7503.39	296.66	4548.08	103.46	79157.63	5366.76
Oman	0	0	0	0	5429.8	0.05	173.8	40	58.5	33.6	7.5	0	27.64	5.5	18.32	10.45	71.58	6	5787.14	95.59
Panama	0	0.01	0	54.93	25.5	6.5	0	4.8	0	0	0.5	0	6188.4	4.07	0	36.99	191.05	24.05	6405.45	131.34
Philippines	0	0	50	27.5	132.42	39.5	41	146.4	729.5	111.91	2836.84	0	49	929.42	0	610.14	0	0	3838.76	1864.88
Poland	0.4	0.4	0	0	1.5	0	0	3.1	16	0	32.98	0	0.75	0	100	0	0	1.91	151.63	5.41

Country Name	App. 1991	Inf. 1991	App. 1992	Inf. 1992	App. 1993	Inf. 1993	App. 1994	Inf. 1994	App. 1995	Inf. 1995	App. 1996	Inf. 1996	App. 1997	Inf. 1997	App. 1998	Inf. 1998	App. 1999	Inf. 1999	App. Total	Inf. Total
Portugal	1.6	0	12	0	140	0	0	0	1735.6	0	0	0	42.3	0	0	12.56	0	7.5	1939.03	20.06
Qatar	0	0	45.3	0	0	0	0	0	0	0	0	0	270	0.03	0	0	0	0	315.3	0.03
Romania	0	0	0	0	0	0	0	0	0	0	20	0	0	0.71	0	0	0	0	20	0.71
Russia	86.1	24.74	115.9	0.8	19.5	62.74	1056.9	65.93	1161.3	2.5	2.99	7.98	0.48	0	145.48	11	87.58	1572.93	2676.23	1748.63
Saudi Arabia	0	0	3.1	20	108.7	0.1	0	5.01	1.2	0	6094	0	61.79	0	584.68	396.35	1265.3	0.75	8118.77	422.21
Singapore	13.7	0	602.1	114.97	667.4	223.78	2655	172.71	9910.4	2431.72	3197.72	2220.16	8619.01	1346.99	7673.39	4071.82	8258.94	1811.04	41597.66	12393.18
Slovakia	0	0	0	0	0.5	0	0	0.25	0	0	0	0	0	0	0.8	0.8	0.25	0	1.55	1.05
South Africa	0	0.01	0	0	0	0	2.5	0	157.8	0	567.5	21	925.97	0	17077	0	250.86	0	18981.63	21.01
Spain	3.3	0	19.2	0	98	22.05	20.2	10.02	227.1	0.44	91.7	110.72	593.25	14.2	627.22	25.97	1810.35	66.93	3490.32	250.34
Sudan	0	0	0	0	0	0	0	0	0	0	0.25	0	0.05	0	0	0.25	0	0	0.3	0.25
Sweden	69.8	0	484.1	59.92	6.2	422.91	116.4	150.96	5022.5	536.26	5330.19	2087.13	1089.99	630.55	2154.25	388.02	2739.34	701	17012.77	4976.75
Switzerland	355	1.87	6897.6	544.43	4268	1073.58	483	930.59	3094.8	263.49	1597.53	2378.52	4936.63	942.35	2850.48	646.57	2912.14	1169.84	27395.18	7951.23
Syria	0	0	0	0	0	0	0	0	0	0	0	0	0	0	1.2	0	0	0.22	1.2	0.22
Taiwan	4.5	2.4	180	3	100.1	9.15	102	115.65	38.8	91.89	778.63	21.15	13.23	39.97	35.74	6.98	74.49	19.65	1327.49	309.84
Thailand	0	0	25.2	0	3684.2	0	99.8	17.94	19680.9	166.79	765.22	881.67	259.44	523.91	3.45	100.75	70	8	24588.21	1699.05
UAE	2.2	0	64.5	7.5	4044.9	7.24	512.3	56.21	143.6	34.44	526.14	40.83	935.56	20.7	162.92	124.79	101.2	75.76	6493.33	367.47
UK	321	479.12	1176.7	871.78	6227.3	2422.7	12991.5	4967.58	17258.6	2236.82	15245.99	1809.37	44907.19	3323.18	32008.44	2208.52	29630.47	3959.95	159767.18	22279.01
US	1858.5	277.67	12315	1148.28	34618.5	4527.72	34880.9	3731.16	70543.7	6769.51	100558.7	9484.26	135698.2	25780.72	35619.6	13710.95	35751.7	18112.05	461844.82	83542.33
Ukraine	0	0	8.4	0	2.8	0	4.5	0	0	4.02	40.15	0	33.57	0	0	0	0.42	0.86	89.85	4.88
West Indies	0	0	3	0	0	0	0.5	1.02	0	7.39	16	0	999.8	15.9	4185	22.12	1270	0	6474.3	46.43

Note : App.-Approvals Inf.-Inflows.

Table 13B Sector-Wise Approval of FDI

₹ Million

Sectorwise Approvals	1991	1992	1993	1994	1995	1996	1997	1998	1999	Total
Metallurgical Industries	8.3	777.8	12565.3	9173.9	18442.3	23163.8	25167.2	22198.4	14001.5	125498.5
Fuels	23	15073.1	28225.4	38090.5	35614.7	57525.9	264326.1	138917.7	56734.7	634531.1
Boilers and Steam Generating Plants	7.2	1.2	538.3	34.7	384.5	134	66.5	13.8	286.4	1466.6
Prime Movers other than Electrical	0	0	0	22.5	153	358.9	128.9	250	4	917.3
Electricals Equipment	878.3	3689.8	6113.5	6922.5	10124.9	31221.9	21929.9	14274.9	25498.5	120654.2
Telecommunications	133.9	1190.7	469.8	164.4	178230.3	44362.1	71856	31001.3	39017.8	366426.3
Transportation Industry	201.1	1511	3046.7	12090.9	12897.3	28790.4	37900.7	15628.8	62207	174273.9
Industrial Machinery	450.8	634	868.4	6581.2	5810.8	1976.2	2181.8	1080.9	2694.2	22278.3
Machine Tools	43.9	67.3	107.3	188.9	213.6	740.8	1280.1	143.6	972.2	3757.7
Agricultural Machinery	0	55.5	0	1558	0.5	563.8	0	2163.4	7.3	4348.5
Earth-Moving Machinery	0.8	5.6	6	117.3	0	0	699.8	3.9	18.5	851.9
Miscellaneous Mechanical and Engineering	4.8	371.8	303.7	696.7	1140.6	2956.6	3833.2	1892.7	2753	13953.1
Commercial, Office and Household Equipment	0	637.7	90.8	87.1	2096.1	1575	2523.1	2808	853.3	10671.1
Medical and Surgical Appliances	2.8	36.3	81.5	64.3	1521.6	28.6	424.7	258.5	38.4	2456.7
Industrial Instruments	19	148.1	16.9	8.4	421.2	425.1	118	9.1	49.4	1215.2
Scientific Instruments	15.4	327.7	1.9	3.4	119.1	17.8	117.7	11.4	3	617.4
Mathematical, Surveying and Drawing	0	0	0	0	1.2	0	2.5	380	0	383.7
Fertilizers	10	0	16.6	9.9	0	2420.4	12	0	0	2468.9
Chemicals (other than fertilizers)	1358.2	4292.6	3701.2	14486.9	11754.9	30298.9	28271.8	18137.3	8104.1	120405.9

(Cond.)

(Cond.)

Photographic Raw Film and Paper	0	79	107.3	20	42.5	3	1962.7	0	83.3	2297.8
Dye-Stuffs	0	0.8	21.7	37	197.8	45.1	28.9	735.9	45	1112.2
Drugs And Pharmaceuticals	8	291.1	299.1	1629.6	1869.7	1182.1	1828.9	911.4	797.8	8817.7
Textiles (Including Dyed, Printed)	141.3	962.6	787.6	9742.1	4002.4	4154.3	5953.2	2325.5	3227.6	31296.6
Paper and Pulp Including Paper Product	0	201.5	1135.7	2587.2	618.6	10626.6	6846.8	1071.2	6857.7	29945.3
Sugar	0	0	535	0	0	132.5	9340	0	0	10007.5
Fermentation Industries	0	119.4	1724.5	235	5801.5	833	2536.7	5.1	22.2	11277.4
Food Processing Industries	1104.3	3246.8	9524.6	6856	3231.9	33847.7	19269.3	6325.4	1414.2	84820.2
Vegetable Oils and Vanaspati	13.2	51.8	107	116.8	149.1	40	1452.9	8.5	483	2422.3
Soaps, Cosmetics and Toilet Preparations	0	184.6	4.7	250.3	580.4	286	1450.3	605.5	12.4	3374.2
Rubber Goods	10.9	23.7	602.7	324.8	210.5	3431.6	458.3	5512.5	1237.1	11812.1
Leather, Leather Goods and Pickers	7.9	284.5	164.4	252.5	662.7	291.3	590.6	488.3	265.6	3007.8
Glue and Gelatin	0	0	0	0	0	0	0	0	12	12
Glass	7.5	437.4	505.8	857.6	1986.3	3029.5	4663.4	1929.3	4253.3	17670.1
Ceramics	98.3	193.8	285.8	2099.1	1099.3	1945.6	1245.9	935.8	680.9	8584.5
Cement and Gypsum Products	120	67.9	267	3354.9	167.8	1561.5	591.3	895.9	6810.6	13836.9
Timber Products	0	0	1.1	0	62.6	25	67.2	7.3	0	163.2
Defence Industries	0	0	0	0	0	0	34.7	0	0	34.7
Consultancy Services	72.8	85.7	84.1	163.8	1375.1	5244.9	3693.7	6362.2	2536.2	19618.5
Service Sector	3.8	608.1	11258.5	12117.3	7670.7	52697.1	14369	16971.2	22879	138574.7
Hotel and Tourism	160	1990.7	3794.9	4381.3	8002.2	4490.9	7281.1	4805.2	7844.9	42751.2
Trading	0	56.3	351.5	345.3	537.9	2852.6	1193.6	6851.1	2382.8	14571.1
Miscellaneous Industries	143.6	473.2	901.7	6184.6	3520.8	8218.1	3215	2214	8576.3	33447.3
Total	5049.1	38179.1	88618	141856.7	320716.4	361498.6	548913.5	308135	283665.2	2096632

Table 13 C Sectoral Inflows

Rs. Million

Sectorwise Inflows	1991	1992	1993	1994	1995	1996	1997	1998	1999	Total
Metallurgical Industries	1.6	249.2	140.18	169.99	581.37	1275.84	1014.39	1258.96	1641.81	6333.34
Fuels	16.68	97.36	539.91	884.96	3121.58	3493.26	15245.9	5635.55	7484.58	36519.77
Boilers and Steam Generating Plants	0	1.26	0	28.82	14.02	26.01	21.5	62.9	2.87	157.38
Prime Movers other than Electrical	0	0	0	13.69	277.9	443.25	161.33	94.49	62.6	1053.25
Electricals Equipment	72.16	910.54	1589.72	2917.37	5050.15	7670.49	13312.38	7865.89	7036.06	46424.75
Telecommunications	0	0	16.63	140.19	1274.47	7529.76	11850	17410.18	2155.58	40376.82
Transportation Industry	40.13	1081.53	579.62	1308.66	2307.37	4993.91	15138.31	14769.16	11301.98	51520.67
Industrial Machinery	6.97	74.81	129.79	372.4	575.6	296.16	1039.63	139.19	993.35	3627.9
Machine Tools	3.2	6.08	8.13	62.68	62.9	746.39	369.54	256.01	99.87	1614.8
Agricultural Machinery	0	0	1.5	8.15	1362.63	0.51	0	0	510.69	1883.49
Earth-Moving Machinery	0	0	0	0	8.97	0	11.52	256.39	1.02	277.9
Miscellaneous Mechanical and Engineering	199.31	561.11	628.38	700.49	1585.05	884.14	2142.5	1181.14	629.07	8511.2
Commercial, Office and Household Equipment	0	4.97	534.75	202.8	3181.84	544.15	81.51	179.49	677.69	5407.19
Medical and Surgical Appliances	0	2.13	23.59	24.89	14.7	72.34	245.95	391.15	91.67	866.42
Industrial Instruments	0	35.41	10.65	141.35	28.78	116.81	57.34	1.31	6.35	397.99
Scientific Instruments	0	0.75	3.3	5.08	40.04	24.5	38.62	0.39	31.38	144.06
Fertilizers	0	240.61	35.4	2.46	86.78	10.98	320.4	0	0	696.63
Chemicals (other than Fertilizers)	373.12	714.45	2299.27	4258.48	2726.35	5880.76	8212.65	10640.01	4756.19	39861.28
Photographic Raw Film and Paper	0	0	0	0	0	0	287.08	0	2.45	289.53
Dye-Stuffs	0	0	20.88	0	9.8	198.9	177.74	56.82	0	464.14
Drugs and Pharmaceuticals	112.26	60.45	1326.99	391.28	426.74	2426.87	1881.48	838.36	757.34	8221.75
Textiles (Including Dyed, Printed)	2.85	186.51	354.18	1407.72	1478.83	1520.72	1590.32	503.53	1248.83	8293.49
Paper and Pulp Including Paper Product	0	0.21	0	136.97	1114.34	3080.8	1471.66	2341.71	513.65	8659.35
Sugar	0	0	0	0	15.31	0.75	244	0	0	260.06

(Cond.)

(Cond.)

Sectorwise Inflows	1991	1992	1993	1994	1995	1996	1997	1998	1999	Total
Fermentation Industries	0	0	0	291.95	67.25	125.31	320.17	0	0	804.69
Food Processing Industries	21.16	580.91	1428.06	2094.83	1547.27	6411.5	5177.4	2368.8	4046.97	23676.92
Vegetable Oils and Vanaspati	0	3.75	0	371.36	8.32	0	0	0	86	469.43
Soaps, Cosmetics and Toilet Preparations	0	0	0	0	0	0	0	0	24.17	24.17
Rubber Goods	0	99.26	36.24	241.09	40.64	476.58	1625.49	362	177.59	3058.89
Leather, Leather Goods and Pickers	1.3	0	294.34	53.54	80.8	82	554.24	53.25	1.53	1120.98
Glue And Gelatin	0	0	0	0	0	0	0	1180	0	1180
Glass	0	0	575	2.55	1056.64	198.17	646.13	1454.85	1718.08	5651.42
Ceramics	1.45	19.25	102.56	350.62	80.11	594.38	464.37	69.25	37.46	1719.45
Cement and Gypsum Products	0	6.82	146	354.88	562.71	102.27	118.16	279.35	93.36	1663.54
Consultancy Services	0	0	0	0	0	0	0	5.82	214.19	220.02
Service Sector	0.3	48.3	1214.87	943.08	11014.94	10106.94	5411.44	7679.8	4023.82	40443.49
Hotel and Tourism	0	7.42	2.92	532.97	219.07	444.29	1031.94	399.49	405.38	3043.49
Trading	0	1.93	55	240.86	3320.06	650.73	945.1	519.98	980.55	6714.21
Miscellaneous Industries	180.88	386.99	727.57	4087.82	6129.73	22920.07	62651.83	51548.61	113375.7	262009.2
NRI Scheme	1622.96	1529.97	5794.15	11452.59	19878.38	20620.63	10396.19	3594.8	3488.3	78377.98
Total	2656.31	6911.99	18619.57	34196.62	69351.43	103970.2	164258.2	133398.6	168678.2	702041.1

Table 13D Sector-Wise Inflows as a Percentage of Approvals

	1991	1992	1993	1994	1995	1996	1997	1998	1999	Total
Metallurgical Industries	19.27711	32.03908	1.115612	1.852974	3.152373	5.507905	4.030603	5.6714	11.72596	5.046546
Fuels	72.52174	0.645919	1.912852	2.323309	8.764864	6.0725	5.767838	4.056754	13.19224	5.755395
Boilers and Steam Generating Plants	0	105	0	83.05476	3.646294	19.41045	32.33083	455.7971	1.002095	10.73094
Prime Movers other than Electrical	Na	Na	Na	60.84444	181.634	123.5024	125.159	37.796	1565	114.8207
Electricals Equipment	8.215872	24.67722	26.00344	42.1433	49.87852	24.56766	60.70424	55.10294	27.59402	38.47753
Telecommunications	0	0	3.539804	85.27372	0.715069	16.97341	16.49132	56.15952	5.524607	11.01908
Transportation Industry	19.95525	71.5771	19.02452	10.82351	17.89033	17.34575	39.94203	94.49964	18.16834	29.56304
Industrial Machinery	1.54614	11.79968	14.94588	5.658543	9.905693	14.98634	47.65011	12.87723	36.86994	16.28446
Machine Tools	7.289294	9.034175	7.576887	33.18158	29.44757	100.7546	28.86806	178.2799	10.27258	42.9731
Agricultural Machinery	Na	0	Na	0.523107	272526	0.090458	Na	0	6995.753	43.31356
Earth-Moving Machinery	0	0	0	0	Na	Na	1.646185	6574.103	5.513514	32.6212
Miscellaneous Mechanical and Engineering	4152.292	150.9172	206.9081	100.544	138.9663	29.90394	55.89325	62.40503	22.85035	60.99863
Commercial, Office and Household Equipment	Na	0.779363	588.9317	232.8358	151.7981	34.54921	3.23055	6.392094	79.4199	50.67135
Medical and Surgical Appliances	0	5.867769	28.94479	38.70918	0.966088	252.9371	57.91147	151.3153	238.724	35.26764
Industrial Instruments	0	23.90952	63.01775	1682.738	6.832858	27.47824	48.59322	14.3956	12.85425	32.75099
Scientific Instruments	0	0.228868	173.6842	149.4118	33.61881	137.6404	32.81223	3.421053	1046	23.33333
Mathematical, Surveying and Drawing										
Fertilizers	0	Na	213.253	24.84848	Na	0.453644	2670	Na	Na	28.21621
Chemicals (other than Fertilizers)	27.47165	16.64376	62.12228	29.39538	23.19331	19.40915	29.04891	58.66369	58.68869	33.10575
Photographic Raw Film and Paper	Na	0	0	0	0	0	14.62679	Na	2.941176	12.60031
Dye-Stuffs	Na	0	96.2212	0	4.954499	441.02	615.0173	7.721158	0	41.7317
Drugs and Pharmaceuticals	1403.25	20.76606	443.661	24.0108	22.82398	205.3016	102.875	91.98596	94.92855	93.24143

(Cond.)

(Contd.)

	1991	1992	1993	1994	1995	1996	1997	1998	1999	Total
Textiles (Including Dyed, Printed)	2.016985	19.37565	44.96953	14.44986	36.94858	36.60593	26.7137	21.65255	38.69222	26.49965
Paper and Pulp Including Paper Product	Na	0.104218	0	5.29414	180.139	28.9914	21.49413	218.6062	7.490121	28.91723
Sugar	Na	Na	0	Na	Na	0.566038	2.61242	Na	Na	2.598651
Fermentation Industries	Na	0	0	124.234	1.159183	15.04322	12.62152	0	0	7.135421
Food Processing Industries	1.916146	17.89177	14.99339	30.5547	47.87493	18.9422	26.86865	37.44902	286.1667	27.91425
Vegetable Oils and Vanaspati	0	7.239382	0	317.9452	5.580148	0	0	0	17.80538	19.37952
Soaps, Cosmetics and Toilet Preparations	Na	0	0	0	0	0	0	0	194.9194	0.716318
Rubber Goods	0	418.8186	6.012942	74.22722	19.30641	13.88798	354.6782	6.566893	14.35535	25.89624
Leather, Leather Goods and Pickers	16.4557	0	179.0389	21.20396	12.19255	28.14967	93.84355	10.90518	0.576054	37.2691
Glue and Gelatin	Na	Na	Na	Na	Na	Na	Na	Na	0	9833.333
Glass	0	0	113.6813	0.297341	53.1964	6.541343	13.85534	75.40818	40.39405	31.98295
Ceramics	1.475076	9.932921	35.88523	16.70335	7.287365	30.54996	37.27185	7.400085	5.501542	20.0297
Cement and Gypsum Products	0	10.04418	54.68165	10.57796	335.3456	6.549472	19.98309	31.18094	1.370804	12.02249
Timber Products										
Consultancy Services	0	0	0	0	0	0	0	0.091478	8.445312	1.121492
Service Sector	7.894737	7.942773	10.79069	7.782922	143.5976	19.17931	37.66052	45.25196	17.58739	29.18533
Hotel and Tourism	0	0.372733	0.076945	12.16465	2.737622	9.893117	14.17286	8.313702	5.167434	7.119075
Trading	Na	3.428064	15.64723	69.75384	617.2263	22.81182	79.18063	7.58973	41.15117	46.07895
Miscellaneous Industries	125.961	81.78149	80.6887	66.09676	174.1005	278.8974	1948.735	2328.302	1321.965	783.3494

Table 13E *Sector-Wise FDI Inflows as a Percentage of FDI Approved from 1991 to 1998*

Sector	Percentage
Metallurgical Industries	5.05
Fuels	5.76
Boilers and Steam Generating Plants	10.73
Electricals Equipment	38.48
Telecommunications	11.02
Transportation Industry	29.56
Industrial Machinery	16.28
Machine Tools	42.97
Agricultural Machinery	43.31
Earth-Moving Machinery	32.62
Miscellaneous Mechanical and Engineering	61.00
Commercial, Office and Household Equipment	50.67
Medical and Surgical Appliances	35.27
Industrial Instruments	32.75
Scientific Instruments	23.33
Fertilizers	28.22
Chemicals (other than Fertilizers)	33.11
Photographic Raw Film and Paper	12.60
Dye-Stuffs	41.73
Drugs and Pharmaceuticals	93.24
Textiles (including Dyed, Printed)	26.50
Paper and Pulp Including Paper Product	28.92
Sugar	2.60
Fermentation Industries	7.14
Food Processing Industries	27.91
Vegetable Oils and Vanaspati	19.38
Soaps, Cosmetics and Toilet Preparations	0.72
Rubber Goods	25.90
Leather, Leather Goods and Pickers	37.27
Glass	31.98
Ceramics	20.03
Cement and Gypsum Products	12.02
Consultancy Services	1.12
Service Sector	29.19
Hotel and Tourism	7.12
Trading	46.08

14

International Reserve and Liquidity

14.1 Introduction

One important fact of the international monetary system is that some East Asian countries are holding huge amounts of international reserve. This phenomenon has emerged mainly after the Asian currency crisis of 1997, when several countries in the region faced high volatility of the exchange rates and capital flight. After those events, countries like Japan, China, South Korea, Taiwan, and Malaysia have accumulated huge amounts of international reserve.

People in general, and the economists in particular, have been conscious nowadays about the desirability of holding a critical minimum level of international reserve on the portfolio of a country, to meet the import expenditure. What determines the critical level is altogether a different matter, but six to ten months' import bill is taken as a good measure for the determination of that level. Alternatively, in today's world of fiat money, the reserve of gold and foreign exchange of a country gives some credibility to the currency of the country, as people in general consider the level of international reserve as the amount of backing the currency enjoys.

In the 1960s, a debate arose about the imperative of increasing international liquidity, and that was the concern at the global level. Since USD had been the international currency through the Bretton Woods agreement, the Federal Reserve of the US agreed to bear the burden of providing necessary liquidity to the world trade and commerce. At that time, Professor Triffin (1959) raised the interesting question of the ability of the world monetary system to maintain sufficient liquidity for the smooth functioning of international trade and commerce.

Triffin's Point and Prescription

Professor Triffin's contribution has been in the clarity with which he explained the growing inadequacy of the post-war international financial system, in the context of rapid economic growth experienced by the Western countries. The interesting dilemma that Triffin revealed was that the prevailing monetary system would not be able to provide the additional reserve required by the expanding world economy. If the overall balance of payments deficit of the United States had been eliminated in the 1950s, that would have deprived the rest of the world of the source of two-thirds of the accretion to world monetary reserves during the same period. While there is no consensus among the economists regarding the optimum growth rate of international reserves, there is no debate regarding the fact that supplies of new monetary gold (which furnished the remaining one-third of reserve growth during the 1950s) would have been inadequate. On the other hand, if the United States fails to achieve overall balance in the international trade, then foreigners will have doubts about the strength of the USD. Thus, Robert Trifin comes to the conclusion, that the international financial system is having two central problems at the core. First, the system is not capable of providing adequately for future reserves growth, and second, the total quantity of reserves in existence is both undependable and inconsistent.

Triffin himself provided the solution to the above dilemma through the creation of new sources of liquidity, based on issuing more IMF special drawing rights that would not be the liability for any one country. But this way the reliance of the system on USD and US treasuries and supplementing them with other reserves is a necessary step to reduce the fragility of the system. Thus special drawing rights (SDR) of the International Monetary Fund came into existence, to augment the world financial liquidity in the face of rapid economic growth of the countries of the world.

Definition

According to Palgrave Dictionary of Economics, international liquidity is considered as that stock of asset which is available to a country's monetary authorities to cover payments imbalances (when exchange rate is fixed), or to influence the exchange value of the currency (when the exchange rate is flexible).

The standard level of international reserve (IR) of a country consists of the following four elements:

(1) Gold
(2) Short-term foreign exchange holding in convertible currencies
(3) Special drawing rights (SDR)
(4) Reserve position in International Monetary Fund (IMF)

If we see the elements, it becomes clear that the level of international reserve can be considered as a stock of reserve which represents the purchasing power of the country as a whole, and at the disposal of the monetary authority which can be used to moderate the domestic economic impact of the decline in foreign exchange receipt.

The literature on the international reserve has explored varied aspects of the same and some of these are as follows:

First, with the growth of trade and commerce, volatility of the inflow of the foreign exchange will rise and this necessitates the maintenance of a minimum level of international reserve as a cushion to meet that sort of situation.

Second, there is a close parallel between the income elasticity of cash balance in the domestic money market and the income elasticity of holding IR.

Third, the changes in the level of IR may be independent of the movement of trade and the operation of international capital market can change the level of IR. When the currency of the country is fully convertible and free movement of capital is allowed, the significance of IR becomes sharply different compared to the case of typical developing countries with fixed exchange rate regime and restriction on the movement of capital.

The present study is concerned about the demand for international reserve of some countries. The argument of Prof. Triffin has been explained rather briefly. With the limited objective, we have reviewed the literature in Section 2. Section 3 brings the theoretical aspects of the study. A model is explained and elaborated. Then empirical estimation has been done using both the cross-section and time series data. The analysis of the result has been done also. The last section comes in the form of a conclusion.

14.2 Review of Literature

Since the late 1950s, many papers have been written on the theme of international reserve, and these come under broadly two categories: The world reserve problem and how the IMF would solve the problem of inadequate world-level liquidity, so that rising trade among the member countries are not adversely affected; the second channel of research continued regarding the optimal level of reserve from the stand point of a single country. The latter problem has assumed importance in view of the floating exchange rate regime established after the collapse of the Bretton Woods Agreement in the early 1970s. There are at least eight reviews of the literature on the subject since 1960 and these are: Clower and Lipsey(1968), Niehans (1970), Salant (1970), Grubel (1970), Williamson (1973), Aizenman and Marion (2003), and Aizenman and Lee (2007).

Almost all the studies explain that countries hold international reserve so that they can meet sudden temporary excess demand for foreign exchange and/or to meet short-run adjustment in the balance of trade. The central banks often intervene in the foreign reserve market by selling/ buying foreign exchange. International reserves are defined to be assets or credits which can be used directly for intervention, or which can be converted into foreign exchange quickly and with certainty. In practice, it has been necessary to pick up arbitrary cut-off point on such a scale, and define international reserve as assets which are acceptable at all times to foreign economic agents (Machlup,1966). IMF has to forward estimates of international reserve and these estimates have been widely used in literature for different purposes (Clark, 1971; Flanders, 1971; Kelly, 1970).

A country can have international reserve at the macro level and also private liabilities towards foreign exchange. Some authors consider whether international reserve should be adjusted for such private liabilities (Brown, 1964; Kenen and Yudin, 1967). In the monetary theory literature, portfolio theory and financial intermediation have been developed and these tools have been used to explain the movement of international reserve in Kane (1965). Such a framework has some relevance with the discussion in Machlup (1966) and the studies of reserve assets composition (Hageman, 1969; Kenen, 1963). The portfolio model employed in Hageman computed stock-adjustment equation for 11 major countries on quarterly data of the 1950s and early 1960 and the study found good evidence that adjustment was far from instantaneous.

Triffin (1978) first explained the dilemma of the gold-exchange standard in the sense that either liquidity would be progressively deficit, and it would lead to a deterioration in the US reserve ratio, and in the process, confidence in dollar would be undermined. The latter would provoke countries to make an attempt to convert dollars into gold in a big way which might give signal for the collapse of the system. The first part of the Triffin thesis provoked the literature on the demand for international reserve. The second part of the Triffin's thesis led to a discussion in the literature about the discretion of the member countries for the selection of their portfolio, and its possible impact on the stability of the system (Gilbert, 1968; Mundell, 1968).

Mundell (1968) assumed that Europe's portfolio choice is determined by its views as to whether there should be an expansion of world income. When dollar is converted into gold in a big way, this sends a signal to the US that income should contract, and the latter is forced to restrict monetary expansion so as to restore its reserve ratio. Mundell prefers the US to select a monetary policy appropriate to the requirement of the expansion of the world income, and Europe should compliment this by selecting a proper gold/dollar mix in the portfolio.

While IMF and the United States are the major suppliers of international reserve, some economists have developed a 'demand-oriented theory' of supply (Johnson 1964; Kindleberger, 1965; Krause, 1970; Mckinnon, 1969). According to this theory, the deficit of the US is determined by the desire of the world regarding the accumulation of reserve, and thus it is the residual. If it tries to reduce the deficit, the readjustment of policies of other countries would frustrate that effort. Thus, some critical level of that deficit of the US is not a measure of disequilibrium of the economy, but the result of 'mutually-beneficial financial intermediation' among the nations. To some extent, this readjustment procedure of the member countries, related theoretically to what is known in the literature as the international quantity theory, is that reserve changes influence monetary policies on gold standard lines, and the monetary policies produce changes in the nominal income that reflects the price rather than quantity changes except in the very short run. On that basis, one important conclusion of the theory is that the real level of reserve cannot be manipulated through the variation in the created nominal reserve, because of the reactions of these affected with access or deficient reserve holdings (Mundell, 1971).

The discussion on the issue of international reserve has attracted the attention of economists in the recent time. Thus, Ben-Bassat and Gottlieb (1992) have analyzed the quantum of optimal reserve and the probability of default risk. Also using simulation technique, optimum reserve (in case of Israel) has been calculated and then compared with actual reserve. The changes in the exchange rate regime can also affect the level of reserve (Heller and Khan, 1978). In another paper, Ford and Huang (1994) have employed an error correction model (ECM) for the computation of optimum reserve in China. One important conclusion of the paper is that reserve holding in China have maintained the long-run relationship and a stable dynamic relationship with several economic parameters.

Exchange rate changes and the system should have some bearing on the growth of reserve which is explored in Frankel (1978), while he has attempted to explain the problem of international liquidity and monetary control (Frankel 1983). Also a probabilistic framework has been attempted in the explanation of the growth changes in international reserve in Frankel and Jovanovic (1981) and Hamada and Ueda (1977). Recently, the stability of the demand for international reserve has been discussed in Landell-Mills (1989), and Lizondo and Mathieson (1987). Also Edwards (1984) has explained the dynamic relationship between foreign borrowing, foreign debt and the level of reserve.

Willet (1980) provides a public choice analysis of the incentives that the governments faces with respect to the policy of holding international reserve. Bar-Ilan et al. (2007), and Li et al. (2008) show that a country may perform a comparative analysis regarding the cost of holding international reserve and then proceed to accumulate international reserve.

Another set of studies (Aizenman and Lee, 2007; Ben-Bassat and Gottlieb, 1992; Lee, 2004) offer precautionary demand explanation in the sense that accumulated international reserve can provide protection against sudden stop of capital flows and thus provide self-insurance for nations.

When public finance problems persist, a country can hold international reserve to keep consumption smooth (Aizenman and Marion, 2003). It can deliberately keep exchange rate undervalued to maintain competitiveness in international trade and accumulate international reserve as is the case with China (Aizenman and Lee, 2007; Dooley et al., 2003).

14.3 Adequacy of and Demand for Reserve

There is a close parallel between the traditional demand for cash balances (explained by Quantity Theory of Money) and the demand for reserve. The theory postulates a stable relationship in the demand for cash balance. If aggregate levels of imports be the measure of the total international transactions, a stable relationship can be postulated between the demand for international reserve and the volume of imports. The IMF report of 1953 and 1958 on international liquidity have stressed the importance of imports/reserve ratio as a rough indicator of the adequacy of reserve (IMF, 1953, 1958). The reserve/import ratio also has its limitation (Niehans, 1970). Also it has been pointed out by Heller (1968) that during the period 1951–66, the aggregate exchange holding of commercial banks to imports increased. International reserve can be considered as a buffer stock of the medium of exchanges, and the relationship between the two is much less tight compared to the relation between medium of exchange, and transaction. This defect is sought to be corrected by Brown (1964) by relating reserve to the net external balance of the country. His analysis emphasizes the holding of international reserve by a country to address effectively in the context of economic turbulence when disequilibrium creeps in international trade situations.

Reserve and Money Supply Nexus

Instead of imports, Scitovsky (1958) relates adequacy of reserve with the premium that a reduction in reserve is equivalent to, and excess of aggregate expenditure over receipts. Such excess expenditure means a reduction in cash balance. Thus BOP deficits and reserve losses should be interpreted essentially as monetary phenomena. The Scitovsky argument can be put as follows:

The individual should be able to do collectively what they think they can do individually. The implication of this can be explained with the help of a Keynesian type trade model. In equilibrium, aggregate income Y must be equal to domestic demand plus export demand, which is treated as exogenous. If domestic demand is a function of income,

$$Y = A + qY + X \qquad \text{Equation (14.1)} \quad \text{A is constant}$$

Again, import is a function of income Y, or

$$M = B + mY \qquad \text{Equation (14.2)} \quad \text{B is constant}$$

If there is change in A and B, import will change. If export is not exogenous, this change will depend on the reaction of export. But assuming the latter exogenous, we get

$$dM = (m/1-q) \, dA + dB \qquad \text{Equation (14.3)}$$

Scitovsky then postulates that the shifts in dA and dB are identified with the desired spending out of cash balance dL.

Every monetary unit of that spending is assumed to be distributed between domestic goods and imports in the same way as marginal income dollars. Thus we get

$$dA = (q/m + q) \, dL, \text{ and} \qquad \text{Equation (14.4)}$$

$$dB = (m/m + q) \, dL \qquad \text{Equation (14.5)}$$

By substitution from Equations 14.3, 14.4 and 14.5

$$dM = (m/1-q)\left(\frac{q}{m+q}\right)dL + \left(\frac{m}{m+q}\right)dL$$

$$= dL\left(\frac{q}{m+q)}\right)\left(\frac{m}{1-q}\right)$$

$$= dL\left(\frac{q}{m+q}\right)\left(\frac{m+1-q}{1-q}\right)$$

Or

$$\frac{dM}{dL} = \frac{q}{m+q}\left(\frac{m+1-q}{1-q}\right) \qquad \text{Equation (14.6)}$$

Thus, for exogenous exports, Equation (14.6) gives the desirable minimum ratio of external reserve to domestic money supply. But Scitovsky's analysis shows that the ratio is subject to change for changes in m and q. Nonetheless, this analysis puts emphasis on the important relationship between external reserve and domestic money supply. Though the domestic money supply is not backed by gold, every central bank keeps the promise of converting domestic currency into foreign currency at fixed rate when demanded. This makes it imperative that the central bank keeps a minimum international reserve.

The analysis of Scitovsky can also be extended to the macroeconomic analysis (Niehans, 1970). Sometimes, the relation between the level and the growth of international reserve is emphasized (Fleming, 1967). Fleming postulates that social welfare depends positively both on the level and the growth of reserve[1].

Also Triffin (1960), Machlup (1967) and Gilbert (1968) have assembled huge evidence to show that the proportion of total reserve to aggregates like imports, money supply and liabilities of central back cannot be expected to reveal simple regularities.

An early attempt to determine the need for international reserve and even to measure it is available in Marquez (1970), who also postulates that the need for reserve on the part of developing countries is much greater compared to the developed world, when the fixed exchange rate regime prevails. But Marquez opines that in the process of creating international reserve, the countries are required to demonetize gold. This point refers to the analysis of Triffin (1960). As Patel (1971) mentions, if the possibility of gold revaluation were kept alive, there would always be pressure for countries not to use gold holdings, and gold would be frozen, and the need for other reserve would increase.

The arguments that the developing countries have greater need for holding and maintaining international reserve for a number of reasons (instability in price of raw materials, instability of balance of payments, etc.) are well established in the literature. Also factors like rigidities introduced by debt payments, volatility in the prices of primary factors in trade, and the inability of the poorer countries to attract short-term capital inflow, all these justify the greater need for maintaining higher reserve for the developing countries.

14.4 Reasons for Holding Reserve

Though in normal circumstances a country should hold a certain amount of reserve, the holding of it is not costless. The opportunity cost of holding reserve is the differential income the country is to forego, which is the difference between the productivity of capital when invested domestically and the interest earned through the holding of the reserve. Still, there are important reasons why reserve should be held. At least three reasons are cited in the literature.

First, holding of reserve gives credibility to the monetary authority regarding financial strength. A visible strong financial position will prevent flight from the currency, whether it

---

[1] This refers to the effects of changes in external situation of a country on the welfare of population. On this Professor H. G. Johnson once remarked:
'I would like to suggest that theoretical analysis of the problems of the international monetary system has been dominated and excessively restricted by concern with the mechanics of the analysis, and time has come for introducing some elements of welfare economics into the study of international monetary problems ... What can be said in theory about the welfare aspects of financing a deficit by borrowing, or suppressing it by controls, instead of eliminating it by deflation as rapidly as required by the limitations of the reserve available? These are problems of great concern to practical policy makers, with respect to which rigorous economic theory should be capable of contributing much more than it has done so far' (cited in Willet and Tower, 1971).

is by residents or non-resident creditors who might otherwise be tempted to sell a currency short. Further, a national 'fiat' currency should be backed, at least partially, so that monetary authority remains ready to keep the promise of converting the liquidity liabilities (currency) into foreign exchange when desired. Also a large reserve enables the country to borrow foreign capital and enhance the liquidity by a multiplier if the country faces the possibility of capital flight.

Second, a certain level of reserve of the country can be used against 'the contingency that the country may some day want to absorb resources from the rest of the world at a time when it cannot borrow or liquidate other foreign asset' (Cooper, 1968). These reasons for holding reserve refer to exceptional circumstances when normal internal or external economic relationship comes to the point of breakdown.

Third, international reserve can be used to meet payments imbalances — something like those that are reversible or those that are once-for-all. The first type may come from seasonal patterns, in payments, or from cyclical development in the economy. When alternative means of financing imbalances are costly, or not easily available, while adjustment is needed, use of international reserve in the short run is preferable.

14.2 Monetarist Controversies and Reserve: A Macro World View

Two controversies in monetary theory are related to the question of international reserve. First is the question whether financial intermediation destroys the possibility of central bank control. Second is whether prices can be taken as autonomous so that variations in the nominal quantity of money imply variations in the real quantity of money, or whether prices in the long-run adjust so as to make real balances correspond to what holders of money would demand.

The first question is related to the issue whether it is justified if one assumes that the global nominal quantity of reserve can be controlled through the control of the issue of SDR.

The second question is related to the issue whether one is justified in the assumption that, even if the nominal aggregate of reserve can be controlled, such control will regulate the real quantity of international money.

Regarding the first question, Johnson (1970) is of the view that the essence of the concepts of reserve needs is that of the international monetary system and that is, special drawing rights. In the national monetary system this is a fact, and this leads to the conclusion that financial intermediation cannot frustrate central bank control, because the intermediaries themselves require reserves and the latter constitute a demand for the ultimate reserve money. This becomes a fact in the international monetary system if monetary policy in the US is constrained by the same need to maintain adequate reserves like any other country. But if such constraints are not there, and other countries are obliged to hold dollars, the US effectively controls the nominal quantity of world reserves.

As for as the second question is concerned, the theoretical answer is simple and this is as such: the economic agents will vary the price level so as to reduce any given nominal quantity of money into the real quantity they desire. But when it comes to the policy level, it becomes an empirical question. Whether within the time span permissible under the policy plan, changes in the nominal reserve have effects on the quantity of real reserve or on prices. The implication of this empirical issue is much more complex. According to this, any undesirable consequences due to the shortage of international reserves in any country can be prevented as the country can utilize the special drawing rights from the IMF.

When there is an increase in the level of international reserve in a country due to a mix of fiscal and monetary policies, it will affect other parameters of the economy in a pattern which are expected to follow a pattern quite predictable by the theory. Such a thing can be put up in a schematic form following Rhomberg (1970).

Table 14.1 Possible Effects of a Rise in Reserves on a Country's Policies

	Description of Policy Change	*Effect on Domestic Demand (Increase +; Decrease –)*
1.	Reduce level of international liquidity (swaps, fund quotas)	0
2.	Increase foreign aid grants	+
3.	Untie foreign aid	–q
4.	Relax restrictions on capital exports or tighten restrictions on capital imports	(–)*
5.	Relax restrictions on imports of goods and services	–
6.	Reduce tariffs and import equalization taxes or reduce export subsidies and border tax rebates	–
7.	Revalue exchange rate	–
8.	Reduce interest rate or level of credit restraint and offset employment effect through fiscal policies	0
9.	Expand domestic demand for goods and services	+

Source: Rhomberg (1970a, 176).

Note: * The effect is uncertain though. The relaxation on the restrictions posed on capital export is likely to increase interest rate and therefore have a negative effect on demand. But an increase in capital exports may facilitate an increase in exports in merchandise and this leads to the net effect being somewhat ambiguous.

14.6 Theory, Model and Estimation

The literature on the demand for international reserve has developed broadly on two complementary traditions. One tradition develops general equilibrium cost-benefit models and the estimation equation is derived from it (Kelly, 1970; Frankel and Jovanovic, 1981; Ben-Bassat and Gottlieb, 1992). The second tradition is purely empirical (Frankel, 1974, 1978; Heller and Khan, 1978; Edwards, 1983, 1984).

While every country maintains a decent level of international reserve, the dynamic behaviour of international reserve has been explained in literature in two alternative ways. One school has postulated that the movement of reserve responds to discrepancies between the desired reserve and the actual reserve held by the country (Clark, 1970; Iyoha, 1976; Heller and Khan, 1978; Bilson and Frenkel, 1979; Edwards, 1983). The second school offers an explanation through a simplified version of the monetary approach to the balance of payments. This school postulates that changes in the international reserve will be functionally related to the disequilibrium in the domestic money market. That is, international reserve will increase if there exists an excess demand for money, given the constant domestic credit; and again, international reserve is a residual (Frenkel and Johnson, 1978). In a fixed exchange rate system, if actual reserve is less than the desired one, other things being given, it will tend to rise and in order to make it feasible, there will be a tendency to reduce domestic credit. Again the possible simultaneity between the determination of the international reserve and the domestic credit has been explored in Genberg (1976).

The Model

Following standard literature (Archibald and Richmond, 1971; Ben-Bassat and Gottlieb, 1992; McDonald, 1982) a simple model for the demand for international reserve can be constructed in the following way.

The cost of the depletion of international reserve comes from the effects of the reduction of imports on the domestic product. The form is needed to restore this level of international reserve. If the ratio of imports to gross domestic product (m) is taken as the openness of the economy, a higher value of the openness (m) means the effect of import cut on the gross domestic product (GDP) will be less severe. This means that the cost is inversely related to the size of m. As cost is reflected in the loss of GDP, it can be written as

$$Co/y = f1(m) \qquad \text{Equation (14.7)}$$

Again, holding international reserve is not costless. This opportunity cost of holding reserve depends on the difference between the economy's marginal productivity of capital (h) and the interest on the level of reserve (i). If $r = (h-i)$, then the cost of reserve holding can be written as

$$C_1 = rR \qquad \text{Equation (14.8)}$$

Where R is the level of international reserve. Without loss of generality, it can be assumed that productivity of capital at home will be higher than the borrowing cost, mainly because of the existence of controls on international capital movement.

In the backdrop of these two types of cost (of depletion and of holding), the central bank of a country is to hold a certain amount of international reserve. Thus, the total expected cost consists of two parts: (*i*) first foregone earnings C_1 in the case of positive reserve (quantified by the difference between h and i) and (*ii*) the social cost of the depletion of reserve Co. Thus we get

$$EC = \lambda Co + (1-\lambda) C_1 \qquad \text{Equation (14.9)}$$

Where λ is the probability of reserve depletion and $(1 - \lambda)$ is the probability of reserve being positive.

Sovereign Risk

Since a sudden depletion of the international reserve reduces the lender's confidence in the financial viability of the country, the risk of reserve depletion is taken as the same as the sovereign risk. Further, the probability of the depletion of the reserve depends on some economic factors like the ratio of reserve to imports (R/M), ratio of exports to imports (X/M), ratio of debt service to exports (D/X), and some other macroeconomic factors (a catch all variable Z). We can write

$$\lambda = f(R/M, X/M, D/X, Z) \qquad \text{Equation (14.10)}$$

An increase in the reserve ratio (R/M) will reduce the risk of default (sovereign risk), an increase in the ratio X/M will again reduce, but an increase in debt services ratio (D/X) will increase the default risk.

Rational Behaviour of the Central Bank

It can be postulated that the central bank will minimize the expected cost of holding international reserve with respect to the level of reserve.

Substituting Equations (14.7) and (14.8) into Equation (14.9) we can write

$$EC = \lambda C_0 + (1-\lambda) C$$
$$= \lambda f_1(m) \cdot y + (1-\lambda) r R \qquad \text{Equation (14.11)}$$

The wealth constraint of the economy as a whole can be written as

$$K + A + R = W + DB \qquad \text{Equation (14.12)}$$

Where K = aggregate capital stock of the economy
R = level of international reserve
A = other assets of the economy
W = net wealth and
DB = gross external debt

Further, from Equation (14.12) we write

$$DB = K + A + R - W \qquad \text{Equation (14.12a)}$$

Which implies that gross external debt is endogenous?
Substituting Equations (14.6) and (14.7) into Equations (14.8) we get the objective function as

$$\text{Minimize } \frac{EC}{R} = \lambda C_0(m, y) + (1-\lambda) r R \qquad \text{Equation (14.13)}$$

$$\text{Subject to } \lambda = (R/M, X/M, D/X, Z) \qquad \text{Equation (14.14)}$$

And also the wealth constraints.
The first and the second order condition for the optimization process are

$$\frac{dEC}{dR} = 0 = \frac{d\lambda}{dr} C_0(m, y) + \lambda \frac{dC_0(m1, y)}{dR} + (1-\lambda)r \qquad \text{Equation (14.15)}$$

and
$$\frac{d^2 EC}{dR^2} = EC_{RR} > 0 \qquad \text{Equation (14.16)}$$

Assuming that second order condition holds, the solution to the first order condition Equation (14.15) can give the optimum level of reserve as

$$R^* = f(Co, y, r, X/M, D/X, Z) \qquad \text{Equation (14.17)}$$

Assuming that the function in Equation (14.17) is separable and additive, the optimum level of reserve is determined by the cost of reserve depletion, rate of interest, and other economic variables.

It is clear from Equation (14.17) that international reserve depends on gross domestic product, rate of interest, ratio of exports over imports, ratio of debt burden to exports, and a scale variable. For the purpose of estimation, we can take a proxy like the ratio of imports to GDP of the debt–export ratio. Further, the interest rate variable is dropped. Thus, in the modified form, the equilibrium demand for international reserve can be written as

$$R = F(GDP, M/Y, X/M) \qquad \text{Equation (14.18)}$$

And in linear logarithmic term it becomes

$$\ln R = bo + b1 \ln GDP + b2 \ln (M/Y) + \ln (X/M) + U \qquad \text{Equation (14.18A)}$$

Where U is assumed to be stochastic and it obeys all the necessary properties.

Thus (Equation 14.18A) can be called as Model 1.

The expected sign of the coefficients are:

$$b1 > 0, b2 > 0 \text{ and } b3 > 0.$$

This is because an increase in gross domestic product will induce more imports, and so, an increase in international reserve is warranted. Similarly, an increase in import propensity will require an increase in international reserve, and the same explanation holds for a change in export–import ratio.

Model 1 has been estimated with time series data of 13 countries and these are: India, Poland, France, Malaysia, Australia, Japan, Argentina, Canada, China, Chile, Brazil, Germany, and South Korea. The period taken is 1980–2006. The empirical results are shown in Table 14.2.

Since time series data in selected countries do suffer from autocorrelation (as experimented with regression and the value of the Durbin–Watson statistic being far away from the theoretical value 2[2], Cochrane–Orcutt method of estimation has been used in case of all estimations.

One significant aspect of the econometric result has been that the estimated coefficients of logarithm of GDP in all cases are positive and significant. But in cases of average propensity to import and the ratio of export to imports, the estimated coefficients have not been in accordance to the theoretical expectation in all cases.

---

[2] In the case of the autocorrelation of the disturbances the value of the Durbin–Watson statistic will be significantly different from two.

Table 14.2 *Regression Results of Countries*

Model: Ln R = b0 + b1 Ln GDP + b2 Ln (M/Y) + b3 Ln (X/M) + u
Period: 1980 to 2006 (For All Countries)

Country / Parameters	b0	b1	b2	b3	adj.R^2	DW	F
1. India	10.0534	0.5535	2.227	−0.2386	0.95	0.956	152.38
	(3.644)	(3.28)	(4.713)	(−0.357)			
2. Poland	3.70	1.0818	0.8715	0.68	0.99	2.23	916.18
	(19.15)	(19.33)	(13.03)	(4.594)			
3. France	2.439	2.13	1.8582	−4.109	0.936	1.633	123.34
	(3.588)	(17.49)	(19.46)	(−5.35)			
4. Malaysia	−4.6486	1.207	0.0284	−0.0288	0.955	0.89	192.9
	(−2.3)	(7.7236)	(0.068)	(−0.055)			
5. Australia	−12.37	1.585	−1.065	−0.705	0.959	1.52	208.45
	(−5.778)	(16.17)	(−2.098)	(−1.33)			
6. Japan	−29.46	3.331	1.1899	0.2263	0.95	0.64	1.997
	(−5.963)	(8.868)	(2.449)	(0.3322)			
7. Argentina	−0.4986	1.0228	0.6725	0.2977	0.954	1.87	139.5
	(−0.606)	(11.99)	(7.487)	(2.387)			
8. Canada	7.2494	0.9826	1.0168	−0.05	0.92	0.667	122.3
	(3.87)	(4.98)	(1.987)	(−1.32)			
9. People's Republic of China	6.0635	1.3103	1.3762	2.55	0.966	1.18	118.9
	(19.6)	(17.35)	(5.52)	(3.76)			
10. Chile	3.134	0.5829	−0.3879	−0.8247	0.958	1.12	209
	(5.03)	(18.963)	(−1.537)	(−5.36)			
11. Brazil	−9.083	4.3836	0.4141	−0.42	0.871	0.62	61.86
	(−3.579)	(7.72)	(0.482)	(−0.676)			
12. Germany	0.5829	1.999	1.2228	−0.5356	0.927	1.05	89.5
	(0.436)	(11.46)	(1.95)	(8.48)			
13. South Korea	0.4232	0.7082	2.6679	1.3869	0.973	1.336	143.12
	(0.2112)	(2.25)	(4.79)				

Source: Prepared by the author.

Note: Figures in parentheses are t-values of respective parameter estimates.

Model 2

As noted in the previous section, the maintenance of a critical level of international reserve on the part of a country is necessitated mainly for two purposes — to meet short-run adjustments in the deficit of the current account, and to maintain stability in the exchange rate in the floating exchange rate world. Regarding the first objective, it is obvious that the changes in the exports and imports of the country causing changes in the current account will trigger changes in the level of international reserve. Thus forces which work behind the movements of the exports and imports influence the size and changes of the international reserves. In this connection, two economic parameters can be mentioned, and these are the gross domestic product of the country and the ratio of domestic price level to foreign price level.

An increase in the gross domestic product will increase the level of imports, as absorption capacity of the economy increases and marginal propensity to import is positive. So far as exports are concerned, an increase in gross domestic product (GDP) will increase the supply of commodities in general, and that facilitates exports expansion. Since an increase in imports increases the probability of deficit in current account which is to be met by drawing down the reserve, the expansion of income at home has a negative effect on the reserve through import expansion. But simultaneously, the expansion of exports will help in building up the reserve. Thus the effect of the expansion of GDP on the level of reserve is uncertain.

The inflation differential of a particular country affects its competitive power in the international trade. Thus, if domestic inflation rate is higher compared to the inflation of the foreign country, the exports of the country suffer while imports increase, which leads to a depletion of the international reserve. Thus a change in the ratio (Pd/Pf), Pd being the price level of the domestic country and Pf the foreign country, will negatively affect the level and change of the reserve.

On the basis of the theoretical discussion above, we can write the equation depicting the movement of reserve.

$$R = F(Y, P_d/P_f, r_d/r_f) \qquad \text{Equation (14.19)}$$

Where Y is gross domestic product.

The function in linear estimable form can be written as

$$R = a_0 + a_1.Y + a_2(P_d/P_F) + a_3(r_d/r_f) + u \qquad \text{Equation (14.20)}$$

Where u is the stochastic error term, which is normally distributed and follows usual assumptions. The expected signs of the coefficients are: $a_1 > 0$ $a_2 < 0$; $a_3 > 0$.

We denote Equation (14.20) as Model 2 and the results of estimation is shown in Table 14.2

We see that the same 13 countries' data are used for the estimation, and the period of estimation remains the same i.e., 1980–2006.

The empirical estimation on Table 14.3 shows that the sign of the coefficients comply with the theoretical positions in the case of most of the countries, but not for all countries. All the estimations are done with Cochrane–Orcutt method of estimation to take care of the potential autocorrelation problem of time series data as explained earlier. The values of the adjusted R^2 is satisfactory in most of the cases.

Table 14.3 Regression Results of Some Countries

Model: $R = a0 + a1\, GDP + a2\, (CPI/CPI^*) + a3\, (R_d/R_f) + u$
Period 1980–2006 [for all countries]

Countries/Parameters	a0	a1	a2	a3	adj. R^2	DW	F
1. India	10.053 (3.643)	0.5535 (3.281)	2.227 (4.712)	−0.2386 (−0.356)	0.945	0.955	152.38
2. Poland	3336.42 (2.45)	0.0907 (6.914)	−25328.02 (−2.469)	85.429 (1.203)	0.963	0.353	231.70
3. France	2756066 (2.4599)	15.174 (0.6275)	−2575810 (−2.075)	294635.4 (1.302)	0.06	0.198	123.8
4. Malaysia	29718.26 (0.612)	0.1707 (14.94)	−28648.36 (−0.6439)	−8932.87 (−1.4356)	0.91	0.705	92.68
5. Australia	47069.02 (1.763)	0.1376 (12.448)	−89021.77 (−2.5793)	−7281.13 (1.313)	0.899	0.836	78.9
6. Japan	5567788	−1.238	−3520534	3741.323	0.933	0.628	4.3
7. Argentina	17595.46 (1.9528)	0.06336 (6.105)	−13952.62 (−1.36)	−1047.957 (−2.619)	0.903	1.786	153.8
8. Canada	285640 (1.682)	161.01 (9.012)	−343680 (−1.81)	25350 (0.657)	0.855	0.678	34.8
9. People's Republic of China	276760 (3.483)	5582.5	597070	6861.5	0.96	0.4379	1.9
10. Chile	3078.29 (1.505)	11740.57 (21.91)	−746.176 (−1.4825)	0.11909 (3.929)	0.95	0.666	190.9
11. Brazil	−158189.3 (−2.7037)	2515.187 (2.9)	−20219.05 (−0.6517)	−12.703 (0.5133)	0.679	0.746	20.02
12. Germany	−393686.9 (−1.4439)	270.932 (7.283)	128164.1 (0.5515)	−25775.96 (−0.5258)	0.91	1.666	76.9
13. South Korea	−359.01 (−4.949)	0.08388 (0.989)	546.17 (4.505)	−75.986 (−2.226)	0.755	0.379	112.4

Souce: Prepared by the author.

Note: Figures in parentheses are t-values of respective parameter estimates.

14.7 Conclusion

The demand for international reserve has the wider implication in the sense of the concern of the economists for the maintenance of an optimum level of international liquidity, so that the world trade and commerce can be run smoothly. This is another implication of the maintenance of international reserve of a signal country, and that is that the level of international reserve can be used to stabilize the exchange rate of the country's currency, apart from utilizing the reserve to meet imbalance in the current account in the short-run. This is the subject matter for the study of this present research.

The present analysis is basically empirical in nature. It examines existing literature and analyses the models developed for this purpose. It then tests the models in the context of current data set of some countries including India. The presence of some countries in the data set facilitates comparison with India's position.

Many developing countries suffer from the apprehension of default of their import bill due to inadequate international reserve. Because such an eventuality hampers the country's credit rating, and it becomes difficult for the country with poor rating to raise finance in the international capital market. Therefore, many countries set a target of the level of international reserve equivalent to six to eight months' import bill, though there is no hard-and-fast rule about the exact number of months.

As indicated earlier, holding a sizeable international reserve is costly for a developing country because the opportunity cost of holding it is positive. One can argue that maintenance of a high level of international reserve is equivalent to giving subsidized credit to the rich and developed countries, as it is the latter whose currencies are convertible, and other countries keep in their portfolio.

From a theoretical standpoint, export of a country depends on the purchasing power of the rest of the world, though import depends on the domestic purchasing power. Sometimes, an asymmetry in the rates of growth of national income at home and abroad can create a gap in the balance of trade (current account), and this is to be bridged by the change in the international reserve or by capital movement. In either case, a decent level of international reserve can give the country both a breathing space and a respectability, regarding the financing of a negative current account gap.

Further, one should consider the size of foreign debt of a country along with the size of the international reserve. A higher volume of foreign debt necessitates a higher liability of redemption of the debt along with the volatility of the amount of payments due to exchange-rate fluctuations. In this situation same level of comforts can be preserved only by a higher level of international reserve.

Topic for Discussion

In general, countries maintain a certain amount of international reserves as a caution against the sudden possibility of adverse current account, but there is an opportunity cost of holding large amount of international reserves. Explain the statement.

Further Reading

Bacus, D.K., P.J. Kehoe and F.E. Kydland, 'Dynamics of the Trade Balance and the Terms of Trade : The J-Curve', *American Economic Review*, 84(1), 84–103, March, 1994.

Baily, A., S. Millard and S. Wells, 'Capital Flows and Exchange Rates', *Bank of England Quarterly Bulletin*, Autumn, 2001.

Heathcote, J. and F. Perri, 'Financial Autarky and International Business Cycles', *Journal of Monetary Economics*, 49(3), 601–27, 2002.

Lane, P.R. and G.M. Milesi-Ferretti, 'The External Wealth of Nations: Measures of Foreign Assets and Liabilities for Industrial and Developing Countries', *Journal of International Economics*, 55(2), 263–94, 2001.

15

Optimum Currency Area, European Union and the Euro

15.1 Introduction

In the early 1960s, Robert Mundell discussed the concept of the optimum size of a region in which a single currency can be in operation efficiently. That he has Europe in mind becomes clear from this observation: 'In Western Europe the creation of the Common Market is regarded by many as an important step toward eventual political union, and the subject of a common currency for the six countries has been much discussed.' (Mundell, 1961, 661).

But the movement for the formation of the European Union started a little earlier. In the 1957 Treaty of Rome, two treaties were signed on 25 March 1957, which created the European Economic Community (EEC) and the European Atomic Energy Community (Euratom). The signatories to the agreement were Christian Pineau of France, Konrad Adenauer of Federal Republic of Germany, Antonio Segni of Italy, Josepf Bech of Luxemburg, Paul Henri Spaak of Belgium, and Joseph Luns of Netherlands. Later on, the treaties were ratified by the respective national parliaments and came into force on 1 January 1958.

The new institution was a customs union and the member countries agreed to remove all tariff barriers over a 12-year transitional period. But the success of the experiment of tariff removal induced the member countries to shorten the period, and in July 1968, all tariffs among the EEC countries were removed and a common tariff was established for all commodities coming from third countries.

Though a common market was established among the six nations, it was reflected in the free movement of goods only, as the inter-country movements of capital and persons were subject to many restrictions. This was achieved in the European Union Treaty in 1992. The Treaty of Rome also adopted a Common Agricultural Policy (CAP) that created a free market of agricultural products inside the EEC, and established protectionist policies to safeguard the interests of the farmers, so that they get fair and remunerative prices for the agricultural products.

The Treaty of Rome heralded the triumph of a gradualist approach to the building of European Union. With that aim in mind, the new strategy sought to adopt a process of integration that slowly incorporated diverse economic sectors and created supranational institutions with political competences. Thus, from the start, the EEC was based on a series of institutions: the European Commission, the European Assembly later known as European Parliament, the Court of Justice, and the Economic and Social Committee.

15.2 The British Problem

The British government's attitude towards governments in the mainland Europe is conditioned by the public opinion as both the main political parties — the Labour Party and the Conservatives — are famous for making it an issue in their electoral battle. However, a common ground exists, and that is the skepticism of average British citizens towards a successful functioning of united Europe.

Even among those in the United Kingdom who would be termed as 'pro-European', there is a deep contempt for the European institutions within the European Union, in particular the European Commission and the European Parliament. This is because they are seen as being in competition with well-established British institutions. Moreover, the British official and political elite have never fully internalized the concept of a 'United Europe', of which the central European institutions are the guarantors. This unwillingness on the part of the British political elite, to engage realistically with the deep underlying structure of the EU, is at the heart of much British popular dissatisfaction with the European Union.

Put in perspective, as explained here the refusal of the British government to participate in the EEC can be explained by the following reasons: First, the importance of the commercial, political and sentimental bonds of the British government with its former colonies in the form of Commonwealth had not been considered consistent with the membership of EEC. Second, the British government supported the creation of a free trade area, but it was strongly in favour of national governments maintaining their competence of enacting their own tariffs with respect to third countries. Third, the British government was opposed to any project whose long term was to surrender the sovereignty of the national states to supranational European institutions.

The initial reluctance of Britain to join EEC created antagonism within EEC, and when British government started negotiations for joining EEC in 1962, President De Gaulle of France opposed it. After some waiting, the United Kingdom could join EEC in 1972 and two other countries — Denmark and Ireland — also joined EEC taking the number of members to nine. In 1981 Greece joined EEC, followed by Spain and Portugal in 1986.

15.3 Maastricht Treaty, 1992

Maastricht is one beautiful city in Holland and its historical connection is well known. The European leaders had chosen this city for their historical meeting and thus the Treaty on European Union was signed in Maastricht on 7 February 1992. This is known as Maastricht Treaty. This Treaty become operational on 1 November 1993. The Treaty addresses the following objectives:
(1) strengthen the democratic legitimacy of the institutions;
(2) improve the effectiveness of the institutions;
(3) establish economic and monetary union;
(4) develop the Community social dimension, and
(5) establish a common foreign and security policy.

The Maastricht Treaty has a complex structure. Its preamble is followed by seven titles. Title I contains provisions shared by the member states, common foreign policy, and judicial cooperation. Title II contains provisions amending the EEC Treaty. Title III and Title IV amend European Coal and Steel Community (ECSC), and European Atomic Energy Community (EAEC or Euratom) Treaties respectively. Title V introduces provisions related to common foreign and security policy (CFSP). Title VI contains provisions on cooperation in the fields of justice and home affairs (JHA), and Title VII contains some final provisions.

The Maastricht Treaty created the European Union (EU), and that consists of three pillars: (*i*) the European Communities, (*ii*) common foreign and security policy and (*iii*) police and judicial cooperation in criminal matters.

The first pillar consists of European Community, the European Coal and Steel Community (ECSC), and the Euratom and concerns the domains in which the Member States share their sovereignty via the Community Institutions.

The second pillar establishes common foreign and security policy (CFSP), that belongs to Title V of the Treaty on European Union. This replaces the provisions of a single European act. It also allows member states to take joint action in the field of foreign policy, as it involves an intergovernmental decision-making process relying mainly on unanimity.

The third pillar accommodates cooperation in the field of justice and home affairs (JHA), provided for in Title VI of the Maastricht Treaty. European Union is expected to undertake joint action so as to offer European Citizens a high level of protection in the area of security, justice, and freedom of expression. The decision-making process is intergovernmental.

The Maastricht Treaty expands the role of the European Parliament in the context of a Single European Act. The scope of the cooperation procedure and the assent procedure has been extended to new areas. The Treaty has also created a new *co-decision procedure* that allows the European Parliament to enact acts in conjunction with the European Council.

The Maastricht Treaty represents a key stage in post-WW II European construction. By establishing the European Union, by creating an economic and monetary union, and also by extending European integration to newer areas, the European Community has acquired a political dimension. Aware of the fluidity of the political situation in Europe, the Member States inserted a revision clause in the Treaty, and Article N provided for an Intergovernmental Conference to be convened in 1996. The conference culminated in the signature of the Amsterdam Treaty in 1997.

The Treaty of Amsterdam (1997) increased the power of European Union by creating a Community employment policy. To that end, it has transferred to the Communities some of the areas which were subject to intergovernmental cooperation in the field of justice and home affairs, introducing measures aimed at bringing the Union close to its citizens. This has also enabled closer cooperation between certain member states.

The Treaty of Nice (2001) dealt with issues that could not be taken up in Amsterdam Treaty. These were mainly institutional problems linked to the enlargement of the Union which were not resolved in 1997. The Treaty dealt with the make-up of the Commission, the weighting of votes in the council, and the extension of the areas of qualified majority voting. It simplified the rules on the use of the enhanced cooperation procedure and made the judicial system more effective.

The Treaty establishing a Constitution for Europe was signed in October 2004. It was designed to repeal and replace by a single text all the existing treaties, and consolidate 50 years of European treaties. The Treaty establishing the Constitution had to be ratified by all the member states in accordance with each one's constitutional rules, i.e., either parliamentary ratification or national referendum.

15.4 The European Union

The European Union at present consists of 27 sovereign member states and they are: Austria, Belgium, Bulgaria, Cyprus, the Czech Republic, Denmark, Estonia, Finland, France, Germany, Greece, Hungary, Italy, Latvia, Lithuania, Luxembourg, Malta, Netherlands, Poland, Portugal, Republic of Ireland, Romania, Slovakia, Slovenia, Spain, Sweden, and the United Kingdom.

The present membership of 27 members has grown over the years from the original six founding states — Belgium, France, Germany, Italy, Luxembourg, and the Netherlands— by successive enlargements as countries acceded to the Maastricht Treaty and in the process, pooled their sovereignty in exchange for representation in the institutions. Of the 27 members, 21 have adopted Euro as the national currency being the only medium of exchange, and six states are maintaining their separate national currencies. These states are: Denmark, Sweden, the United Kingdom, Poland, Lithuania, and Latvia.

A member state of the European Union is a state that is party to the treaties of the European Union, and has undertaken the privileges and obligations that the membership of European Union (EU) entails. Unlike the membership of an international organization, being a member state of EU places a country under binding laws in exchange for representation in the legislative and judicial institutions of the European Union. But unlike being a member of a federal structure as a state in the US, EU states maintain a great deal of autonomy, including maintaining their national defense and foreign policies.

The European Union may have expansion in future as some European states are eager to join the Union. Before being allowed to join the Union, a state must fulfill the economic and political conditions generally known as Copenhagen criteria[1]. Following this the membership criteria require the following:
(1) the candidate country must have achieved stability of institutions guaranteeing democracy, the rule of law, human rights and respect for and protection of the minorities,
(2) the country should ensure the existence of a functioning market economy as well as the capacity to cope with competitive pressure and market forces,
(3) the country should have the ability to take on the obligations of membership including adherence to the aims of political, economic and monetary union.
The Copenhagen criteria also require that the candidate country must have created the conditions for its integration through the adjustment of its administrative structures, as had

---

[1] Membership requires that candidate country has achieved stability of institutions guaranteeing democracy, the rule of law, human rights, respect for and protection of minorities, the existence of a functioning market economy as well as the capacity to cope with competitive pressure and market forces within the Union. Membership presupposes the candidate's ability to take on the obligations of membership including adherence to the aims of political, economic and monetary union. (Presidency Conclusions, Copenhagen European Council 1993, 7.A.iii)

been underlined by the Madrid European Council in December 1995. Again, it is important that European Community legislation is to be transposed into national legislation; but is more important that the legislation is implemented effectively through the proper process of administrative and judicial structures. This is the prerequisite of the mutual trust required by the membership of European Union.

15.5 Euro as the Single Currency of the European Union

The birth of Euro as the common currency of the member states of the European Union is a watershed in the post-WW II history of European integration. After World War II, fifty years of endeavour to create a closer union and a cooperative future for the people of Europe, culminated in the advent of a single common currency. The process that had led to Economic and Monetary Union (EMU) with the Euro as its currency had been accomplished in three distinct stages. The first stage was the removal of all restrictions on capital movements between member states. With the full liberalization of capital, the European single market had a deeper financial dimension. But greater fluidity of financial markets increased the stakes regarding the intrinsic value of financial assets (bonds denominated on other currency) on possible tensions within an exchange rate regime of currency bands. The second stage laid out the blue print for a new institutional architecture to form and operate the common currency (Euro) area, including the establishment of the European Monetary Institute as the precursor to the European Central Bank. The third stage started on 1 January 1999, when 11 countries fixed their exchange rates to the Euro.

The second and third stages provided for a compact enshrined in the Treaty of European Union (Maastricht Treaty), setting the groundwork for the Euro. Maastricht Treaty specified nominal criteria for the proper convergence of the economies of future participants in the common currency Euro in four areas: inflation, interest rates, exchange rates, and government finances.

Adopting the single currency also implied adopting a single and uniform monetary policy by the member states. Under the Maastricht Treaty, the independent European Central Bank (ECB) safeguards the value of Euro by pursuing its primary objective i.e., maintaining price stability. Apart from the Maastricht Treaty, the legal basis of single monetary policy of the member states is the Statute of the European System of Central Banks (ESCB) and the European Central Bank (ECB). The statute established both the ECB and also ESCB from 1 June 1998. The European Central Bank was established as the core of the Eurosystem and also European system of Central Banks.

Article 127 of the Treaty of the Functioning of European Union (TFEU) states the monetary policy of the European Union as the following:

The Primary objective of the European System of Central Banks [herein after referred to as the ESCB] shall be to maintain price stability. Without prejudice to the objective of price stability, the ESCB shall support the general economic policies in the Union with a view to contributing to the achivement of the objectives of the Union as laid down in Article 3 of the Treaty on European Union. The ESCB shall act in accordance with the principle of an open market economy with free competition, favouring an efficient allocation of resources, and in compliance with the principle set out in Article 119 (Eur-lex, 2008).

Since all the European Union states have not joined the euro system, the ESCB could not be used as the monetary authority of the Euro zone. For this reason, the euro system (which excludes all the National Central Banks [NCB] that have not adopted the euro as the medium of exchange) became the institution in charge of those tasks which in principle had to be managed by the ESCB. Apart from maintaining price stability (to preserve the value of the euro), the Euro system supports the general economic policies of the Community and act in accordance with the principles of an open economy. The basic tasks to be carried out by the Euro system are the following:

(1) to define and implement the monetary policy of the Euro zone,
(2) to conduct foreign exchange operations,
(3) to hold and maintain the official foreign exchange reserve of the Member States, and
(4) to promote the smooth operations of the payments system.

Moreover, the Eurosystem contributes to the smooth conduct of policies pursued by the competent authorities relating to the prudential supervision of credit institutions and the stability of the financial system. The European Central Bank has an advisory role vis-à-vis the European Community and national authorities on matters that fall within its field of competence, particularly where European Community or national legislation is concerned.

Over the last 10 years, the Euro has established itself as a world currency, acting as a pole of stability for the world economy, and also an inspiration for the world economy. On the global stage, the Euro has played a role second only to the USD. For example, regarding the currency denomination of instruments in the international debt market at the end of 2009, the global measure of euro-denominated debt stood at about 30 per cent of the global issuance. According to the narrow measure, international debt, including money market instruments, denominated in euro stood at about 31.4 per cent of the total issuance. By comparison, the ratio of international debt securities denominated in USD to total issuance was about 38 per cent according to global measure, and almost 46 per cent according to the narrow measure (see Table 15.1).

Table 15.1 *Alternative Measure of Debt Securities and Share of Currencies (4th Quarter of 2009, value at current exchange rate)*

	Share (percentages %)		
	USD	Euro	Yen
Narrow Measure	45.8	31.4	5.8
Global Measure	38.2	29.8	13.4

Source: BIS and ECB calculation as reported in ECB (2010).

The euro and the European Monetary Union became a reality in 1999 with the irrevocable locking of the exchange rates of the participating countries against the common currency euro. On 1 January 2001, euro notes and coins replaced the national currencies in 12 European countries, and the original currencies became legacy currencies of the member states. Since its introduction, the euro has been the second most widely held international reserve currency after the USD. The share of the euro as a reserve currency increased from 17.9 per cent in 1999 to 26.5 per cent in 2008. At the same time, the share of the USD as international reserve currency declined from 70.9 per cent in 1999 to 64 per cent in 2008, and that of the Japanese yen declined from 6.4 per cent to 3.3 per cent during the same period. That euro has become a good rival of the USD is evident from one estimate of International Monetary Fund[2] that reveals that the total of euro held as a reserve in the world at the end of 2008 was equal to USD 1.1 trillion, with a share of 22 per cent of all currency reserves in advanced economies, and a total of 31 per cent of all currency reserves in the emerging and developing economies.

Outside the Euro zone, a good number of countries have currencies that are directly pegged to the Euro including 14 countries in mainland Africa, one Balkan country (Bosnia and Herzegovina), and three French Pacific territories. These countries had earlier a currency peg with major European currencies like the French Franc and the German Mark.

The international status of the Euro has conferred certain benefits on Euro-area members. First, and the most important advantage is that, by attracting more investors, it contributes to the deepening and development of the Euro area's financial markets. Thus the financial system of the EU has become more developed and well integrated. The single currency also reduces the cost of doing trade internationally, by making trading partners more willing to pay and accept payments in Euro.

Second, the Euro area member states jointly enjoy the international seigniorage as Euro has acquired the credibility to be used as reserve currency by non-member states. A related benefit is that Euro-denominated government bonds become more liquid, and that helps the governments in the Euro area to borrow at a relatively lower interest rates.

Third, there is the so-called 'exorbitant privilege', that enables the issuer of an international currency to cash in on the fact that its foreign assets are denominated in other currencies, while its foreign liabilities are denominated in its own currency, and this transfers the exchange rate risks to the trading partners. This, along with the liquidity premium on its government bonds, contributes to producing an excess return on its foreign assets over its foreign liabilities, and this makes it easier for an issuer of an international currency to finance large current account deficits, while limiting its negative fall-out on its net foreign debt position.

15.6 Euro vis-à-vis USD

There is debate in recent literature regarding the issue whether the Euro may eventually displace the USD as international currency. Bergsten (2002) points out that the supremacy of US dollar since the WW II is due to the fact that there was no credible national currency with sufficient standing. From that standpoint, euro is the first currency that can challenge the supremacy of US dollar owing to the economic size of the European Union.

In fact, the dominance of a currency in international financial transactions can come into the picture, when the use of national currencies depend heavily on international trade in goods and services. Again, this may not be a persuasive argument always in a world where global financial transactions become preponderant. A single national currency, say USD, which is identified as the numeraire and medium of exchange in foreign exchange trading, is economically more

---

[2] Currency Composition of Official Foreign Exchange Reserve (OCFER), International Monetary Fund, 2009.

efficient. But the liberalization of world capital markets and the increased allocation of world savings in global portfolio equity securities, call for risk management including currency risk. Here the stability of the currency of denomination is important, as investors use currencies to hedge their risks through diversification across international currencies. Here the comment of Mundell (1998, 228) is very important:

> The introduction of euro will represent the most dramatic change in international monetary system since President Nixon took the dollar off gold in 1971 [and when] the era of flexible exchange rates began ... the euro is likely to challenge the position of the dollar [and hence] this may be the most important event in the history of international monetary system since the dollar took over from the pound the role of dominant currency in World War I.

In spite of Professor Mundell's doubt, the strength of USD is that it is the currency of the largest economy of the world, and it is managed by a well-organized Federal Reserve System. On the other hand, Euro is the currency of European Union and the latter is still searching a much needed cohesion among the economies within the area.

15.7 Conclusion

The emergence of euro is an important experiment in the international financial system, and it has brought a healthy competition with USD regarding its use as an international currency. One positive fall-out of the emergence of euro is that countries are now able to diversify their portfolio of international reserve, and the latter is not totally exposed to the real value of a single currency, i.e., USD.

Within the policy framework of the Economic and Monetary Union created by the Maastricht Treaty, the European Central Bank (ECB) has been assigned the fundamental task of safeguarding the intrinsic value of the euro currency. So far ECB has been managing well as Euro has gained the confidence of the European Union citizens.

Topic for Discussion

Being a member of the European Union and adopting the common currency Euro, the member state loses the power to adjust both fiscal and monetary policies in response to specific situations arising out of disequilibrium in macroeconomic fundamentals of the economy. Explain the statement with examples.

Further Reading

Bergsten, Fred C., 'The Dollar and the Euro', *Foreign Affairs*, 83–95, July–August 1997,
———, 'I was a Euro Enthusiast', *Economic Journal Watch*, 7(1), 2002.
Cohen, Benjamin J., 'The Macro-Foundations of Monetary Policy', in David M. Andrews (ed.), *International Monetary Power*, Ithaca, Cornell University Press, 2006.
Detken, Carsten, and Philipp Hartmann, 'Features of the Euro's Role in International Financial Markets', *Economic Policy*, 35(2), 2002.

Dunne, Peter, Michael Moore and Richard Portes, *European Government Bond Markets: Transparency, Liquidity, Efficiency*, London, Centre for Economic Policy Research (CEPR), 2006.

Eichengreen, Barry, 'Sterling's Past, Dollar's Future: Historical Perspective on Reserve Currency Competition', National Bureau of Economic Research, Cambridge, Massachusetts, Working Paper No. 11336, May 2005.

Kirshner, Jonathan, 'Dollar Primacy and American Power: What's at Stake?', *Review of International Political Economy*, 15(3), August 2008.

Select Bibliography

Adams, Charles, Donald J. Mathieson, Garry Schinasi, and Bankim Chadha, *International Capital Markets: Developments, Prospects, and Key Policy Issues*, World Economic and Financial Surveys, Washington DC, International Monetary Fund, 1998.

Aghion, P., P. Bacchetta and A. Banerjee , 'A Simple Model of Monetary Policy and Currency Crisis', *European Economic Review*, 44(4–6), May 2000, 728–38.

———, 'Currency Crisis and Monetary Policy in an Economy with Credit Constraints', *European Economic Review*, 45(7), June 2001, 1121–50.

Aghion, P., Philippe Bacchetta, R. Ranciere, and K. Rogoff, 'Exchange Rate Volatility and Productivity Growth: The Role of Financial Development', Working Paper No. 12117, National Bureau of Economic Research, March 2006.

Aizenman J. and J. Lee , 'International Reserve: Precautionary vs. Mercantilist Views, Theory and Evidence', *Open Economic Review*, 18(2), 2007, 191–214.

Aizenman J. and Marion N., 'The High Demand for International Reserves in the Far East: What's Going On?' *Journal of the Japanese and International Economies*, 17(1), 2003, 370–400.

Akelis, Stephen B., *Technical Analysis from A to Z*, Moscow, Diagramma, 1999.

Alexander, S.S., 'Effects of a Devaluation on a Trade Balance', *Staff Papers — International Monetary Fund*, 2(2), April 1952, 263–78.

Archibald G.C. and J. Richmond, 'On the Theory of Foreign Exchange Requirement', *Review of Economic Studies*, 38(2), April 1971, 245–63.

Argy, V., 'The Mundell–Fleming Model: Its Strength and Limitations', in *International Macroeconomics: Theory and Policy*, New York, Routledge, 1994.

Balassa, Bela, 'The Purchasing Power Parity Doctrine: A Reappraisal', *Journal of Political Economy*, 72(6), December 1964, 584–96.

Bank for International Settlement (BIS), *International Banking and Financial Market Development*, Basle, November 1991.

Bar-Ilan A., N. Marion and D. Perry, 'Drift Control of International Reserves', *Journal of Economic Dynamics and Control*, 31(9), 2007, 3110–37.

Barro, Robert J., 'Are Government Bonds Net Wealth?' *Journal of Political Economy*, 82(6), 1974, 1095–1117.

———, 'On the Determination of the Public Debt', *Journal of Political Economy*, 87(5), 1979, 940–71.

———, 'Measuring the Fed's Revenue from Money Creation', *Economic Letters*, 10(3–4), 1982, 327–32.

———, 'The Ricardian Approach to Budget Deficits', *The Journal of Economic Perspectives*, 3(2), Spring 1989, 37–54.

Baumol, W.J., 'The Transaction Demand for Cash', *Quarterly Journal of Economics*, 66, November 1952, 545–56.

Ben-Bassat A. and D. Gottliab, 'Optimal International Reserves and Sovereign Risk', *Journal of International Economics*, 33(3–4), 1992, 345–62.

Bergin, Paul and Robert Feenstra, 'Pricing-to-Market, Staggered Contracts, and Real Exchange Rate Persistence', *Journal of International Economics*, 54(2), August 2001, 333–59.

Bergsten, C.F., 'The Euro Versus the Dollar: Will There be a Struggle for Dominance', *Journal of Policy Modeling*, 24(4), 2002, 307–14.

Betts, Caroline and Michael B. Devereux, 'Exchange Rate Dynamics in a Model of Pricing-to-Market', *Journal of International Economics*, 50(1), February 2000, 215–44.

Bilson, John F.O. and A. Jacob. Frenkel, 'International Reserves: Adjustment Dynamics', *Economics Letters*, 4(3), 1979, 267–70.

Bhagawati, J.N. (ed.), *Illegal Transactions in Foreign Trade*, Amsterdam, North-Holland, 1974.

———, *Anatomy and Consequences of Exchange Control Regimes*, Cambridge, MIT Press, 1978.

———, 'The Capital Myth: The Difference between Trade in Widgets and Dollars', *Foreign Affairs*, 77(3), May/June 1998, 7–12.

Black, F. and M. Scholes, 'The Pricing of Options and Corporate Liabilities', *Journal of Political Economy*, 81(3), May–June, 1973, 637–54.

Black, S., 'Seignorage', in J. Eatwell, M. Milgate and P. Newman (eds), *The New Palgrave Money*, New York, Norton, 1989.

Black, S.W., 'Exchange Policies for Less Developed Countries in a World of Floating Rates', in D. M. Leipziger (ed.), *The International Monetary System and the Developing Nation*, Washington DC, Bureau for Program and Policy Coordination, Agency for International Development, 1976.

Blejer, M., 'Exchange Restriction and the Monetary Approach to the Exchange Ratio', in J.A. Frenkel and H.G. Johnson (eds), *The Economics of Exchange Rates: Selected Studies*, Reading, Addison Wesley Publishing Co., 1978.

Blejer, M. and A. Cheasty, 'The Measurement of Fiscal Deficits: Analytical and Methodological Issues', *Journal of Economic Literature*, 29(4), December 1991, 1644–78.

Blinder, Alan S., 'Central Bank Credibility: Why Do We Care? How Do We Build It?' Working Paper No. 7161, National Bureau of Economic Research, 1999.

Branson, W.H., 'Asset Markets and Relative Prices in Exchange Rate Determination', Reprint Series No. 98, Institute of International Economic Studies, 1977.

Bresman, H., J. Birkinshaw and R. Nobel, 'Knowledge Transfer in International Acquisitions', *Journal of International Business Studies*, 30(3), 1999, 439–62.

Brown, W.M., *The External Liquidity of an Advance Country*, Princeton Studies in International Finance No. 14, Princeton, Princeton University Press, 1964.

Buckley, P. and M. Casson, 'Analyzing Foreign Market Entry Strategies: Extending the Internalization Approach', *Journal of International Business Studies*, 29(3), 1998, 539–61.

Cagan, Phillip, *Persistent Inflation*, New York, Columbia University Press, 1979.

———, 'Hyperinflation', in P. Newman, M. Milgate and J. Eatwell (eds), *The Palgrave Dictionary of Money and Finance*, vol. 2, London, Macmillan, 1992.

Calvo, G. and Carmen R. Reinhart, *Fixing for your Life*, Washington DC, Brookings Trade Forum, 2001, 1–39.

———, 'Fear of Floating', *Quarterly Journal of Economics*, 117(2), 2002, 379–408.

Calvo, G, L. Leiderman and Carmen R. Reinhart, 'Inflows of Capital to Developing Countries in the 1990s', *Journal of Economic Perspective*, 10(2), Spring 1996, 123–39.

Cassel, G., 'Abnormal Deviations in International Exchange', *Economic Journal*, 28(112), December 1918, 413–15.

Caves, R.E., 'International Liquidity: Toward a Home Repair Manual', *Review of Economics and Studies*, 46(2), May 1964, 173–80.

———, *Multinational Enterprises and Economic Analysis*, Cambridge, Cambridge University Press, 1996.

Chang, R., 'Financial Integration with and without International Policy Coordination', *International Economic Review*, 38(3), 1997, 547–64.

Chen, H., 'The Analysis of Simultaneous Multi-Equation Model on the Relationship between Trade and Economic Growth in China', *International Journal of Business and Management*, 4(1), 2009.

Clark, P.B., 'Interest Payments and the Rate of Return on International Fiat Currency', Duke University, mimeo, 1971.

———, 'Demand for International Reserve: A Cross Country Analysis', *Canadian Journal of Economics*, 3(1), February 1970a, 577–94.

———, 'Optimum International Reserve and the Speed of Adjustment', *Journal of Political Economy*, 78(2), March–April 1970b, 356–76.

Clower, R. and R. Lipsey, 'The Present State of International Liquidity Theory', *American Economic Review*, 58(2), May 1968, 586–95.

Colby, Robert W. and Thomas A. Meyers, *The Encyclopedia of Technical Market Indicators*, Homewood IL, Dow Jones-Irwin, 1988.

Cooper R.N., 'The Relevance of International Liquidity to Developed Countries', *The American Economic Review*, 58(2), May 1968, 625–36.

Corsetti, G. and P. Pesenti, 'Welfare and Macroeconomic Interdependence', *The Quarterly Journal of Economics*, 16(2), August 2001, 421–45.

Courchene T.J. and G.M. Youssef, 'The Demand for International Reserve', *Journal of Political Economy*, 75(4), August 1967, 404–13.

Devereux, M.B., 'Real Exchange Rates and Macroeconomics: Evidence and Theory', *Canadian Journal of Economics*, 30(4), 1997, 773–808.

———, 'Exchange Rate Pass-Through, Exchange Rate Volatility, and Exchange Rate Disconnect', Working Paper No. 8858, National Bureau of Economic Research, April 2002.

Dollar, D., 'Outward Oriented Developing Economies Really Do Grow More Rapidly: Evidence from 95 LDCs, 1976–85', *Economic Development and Cultural Change*, 40(3), April 1992, 523–44.

Dominguez, Kathryn M., 'The Role of International Organization in the Bretton Woods System', in Michael D. Bordo and B. Eichengreen (eds), *A Retrospective on the Bretton Woods System: Lessons for International Monetary Reform*, Chicago, University of Chicago Press, 1993.

Dooley, M.P. and P. Isard, 'The Portfolio Balance Model of Exchange Rates and Some Structural Estimates of the Risk Premium', *IMF Staff Papers*, 30(4), 1983, 683–92.

Dooley, M.P., 'A Survey of Literature on Controls over International Capital Transactions', *IMF Staff Papers*, 43(4), December 1996, 639–87.

Dooley, M.P., David Folkerts–Landau and Peter Garber, 'An Essay on the Revived Bretton Woods System', Working Paper No. 9971, National Bureau of Economic Research, September 2003.

Dornbusch, R., 'Expectations and Exchange Rate Dynamics', *Journal of Political Economy*, 84(6), 1976, 1161–76.

———, 'Special Exchange Rates for Capital Account Transactions', Working Paper No. 1659, National Bureau of Economic Research, 1985.

———, 'Lessons from the German Inflation Experience of the 1920s', in R. Dornbusch, S. Fischer and J. Bossons (eds), *Macroeconomics and Finance: Essays in Honor of Franco Modigliani*, Cambridge, Massachusetts, MIT Press, 1987.

Dornbusch, R. and J.A. Frankel, 'The Flexible Exchange Rate System: Experience and Alternatives', Working Paper No. 2464, National Bureau of Economic Research, 1989.

Dornbusch, R. and S. Fischer, 'Exchange Rates and Current Account', *American Economic Review*, 70(5), 1980, 960–71.

Dornbusch, R., Y.C. Park and S. Claessens, 'Contagion: How It Spreads and How It Can Be Stopped', Proceedings of the World Bank Conference on International Financial Contagion, Washington DC, 3–4 February 2001.

Drazen, Allen, 'A General Measure of Inflation Tax Revenue', *Economic Letters*, 17(4), 1985, 327–30.

———, 'Capital Controls and Seigniorage in an Open Economy', in M. de Cecco and A. Giovannini (eds), *A European Central Bank? Perspectives on Monetary Unification after Ten Years of the EMS*, Cambridge, Cambridge University, 1989.

Driskill, Robert, 'Exchange-Rate Dynamics: An Empirical Investigation', *Journal of Political Economy*, 89(2), 1981, 357–71.

———, 'A General Measure of Inflation Tax Revenue', *Economic Letters*, 17(4), 1985, 327–30.

Duarte, Margarida, 'International Pricing in New Open-Economy Models', *Economic Quarterly*, 87(4), Fall 2001, 53–70.

Dunbar, Nicholas, 'Meriwether's Meltdown', *Risk*, October 1998, 32–36.

Edison, H. and J T Klovland, 'A Quantitative Reassessment of the Purchasing Power Hypothesis: Evidence from Norway and the United Kingdom', *Journal of Applied Econometrics*, 2(4), 1987, 209–33.

Edwards, F.R., 'Hedge Funds and the Collapse of Long-Term Capital Management', *Journal of Economic Perspectives*, 13(2), Spring 1999, 198–210.

Edwards, S., 'The Demand for International Reserves and Exchange Rate Adjustments: The Case of LDCs, 1964–1972', *Economica*, 50(199), 1983, 269–80.

———, 'The Demand for International Reserves and Monetary Equilibrium: Some Evidence from Developing Countries', *The Review of Economics and Statistics*, 66(3), 1984a, 495–500.

———, 'The Role of International Reserve and Foreign Debt in the External Adjustment Process', in Joaquin Muns (ed.), *Adjustment, Conditionality and International Financing*, Washington DC, International Monetary Fund, 1984b.

———, 'On the Interest Rate Elasticity of the Demand for International Reserve: Some Evidence from Developing Countries', *Journal of International Money and Finance*, 4(2), 1985, 287–95.

Eichengreen, Barry, 'International Monetary Stability Between the Wars: Structural Flaws or Misguided Policies?' Discussion Paper No. 348, Centre for Economic Policy Research, 1989.

———, *Globalizing Capital*, Princeton, Princeton University Press, 1996.

———, *Towards a New International Financial Architecture: A Practical Post-Asia Agenda*, Washington DC, Institute for International Economics, 1999.

Eichengreen, Barry, A. Rose, and C. Wyplosz, 'Contagious Currency Crisis', *Scandinavian Journal of Economics*, 98(4), December 1996, 463–84.

Engel, Charles, 'Real Exchange Rates and Relative Prices: An Empirical Investigation', *Journal of Monetary Economics*, 32(1), August 1993, 35–50.

EUR-Lex, 'Consolidated Version of the Treaty on the Functioning of the European Union', *Official Journal of the European Union*, C 115/47, 2008.

European Central Bank (ECB), *The International Role of the Euro*, Frankfurt, European Central Bank, July 2010.Evans, M. and R. Lyons, 'Order Flow and Exchange Rate Dynamics', *Journal of Political Economy*, 110(1), 2002, 170–80.

Ewijk, Casper Van, 'The Distribution of Seigniorage: A Note on Klein Neumann', *Weltwirtschaftliches Archiv (Review of World Economics)*, 128(2), 1992, 2346–51.

Feldstein, M. and C. Horioka, 'The Domestic Saving and International Capital Flows', *Economic Journal*, 90(358), 1980, 314–29.
Financial Action Task Force (FATF), '1998–1999 Report on Money Laundering Typologies', FATF Secretariat, Paris, 1999.
Fiorentini, G. and S. Peltman, *The Economics of Organized Crime*, Cambridge: Cambridge University Press, 1997.
Fischer, S., 'Seignorage and the Case for a National Money', *The Journal of Political Economy*, 90(2), 1982, 295–313.
Fischer, S. and W. Easterly, 'The Economics of the Government Budget Constraint', *World Bank Research Observer*, 5(2), July 1990, 127–42.
Flanders M.J., 'International Liquidity is Always Inadequate', *Kyklos*, 22(3), 1969, 519–29.
———, *The Demand for International Reserves*, Princeton Studies in International Finance No. 27, Princeton, Princeton University Press, 1971.
Fleming, J.M., 'Domestic Financial Policies under Fixed and under Floating Exchange Rates', *IMF Staff Papers*, 9(3), November 1962, 369–79.
———, *Towards Assessing the Need for International Reserves*, Essays in International Finance No. 58, Princeton, Princeton University Press, 1967.
Flood, Robert and P. Garber, 'Collapsing Exchange Rate Regimes: Some Linear Examples', *Journal of International Economics*, 17(1–2), 1984, 1–13.
Ford, J.L. and G. Huang, 'The Demand for International Reserve in China: An ECM Model with Domestic Monetary Equilibrium', *Economica*, 67, 1994, 379–97.
Frankel, J.A., 'The Demand for International Reserves by Developed and Less-Developed Countries', *Economica*, February 1974, 14–24.
———, 'International Reserves: Pegged Exchange Rates and Managed Float', in K. Brunner and A.H. Metzler (eds), *Public Policies in Open Economies*, Carnegie–Rochester Conference Series on Public Policy, vol. 9, Amsterdam, North Holland, 1978.
———, 'International Nominal Targeting (INT): A Proposal for Monetary Policy Coordination in the 1990s', *The World Economy*, 13(20), 1990, 263–73.
Frankel, J.A., S. Schmukler and L. Serven, 'Verifiability and the Vanishing Intermediate Exchange Rate Regime', *Journal of Development Economics*, 66(2), 2001, 351–86.
———, 'Global Transmission of Interest Rates: Monetary Independence and Currency Regime', Working Paper No. 8828, National Bureau of Economic Research, March 2002.
Frenkel, J.A., 'Flexible Exchange Rates, Prices and the Role of News: Lessons from the 1970s', *Journal of Political Economy*, 89, 1981, 665–705.
———, 'International Liquidity and Monetary Control', in G.M. von Furstenbug (ed.), *International Money and Credit: The Policy Roles*, Washington DC, International Monetary Fund, 1983.
Frenkel, J.A. and B. Jovanovic, 'Optimal International Reserve: A Stochastic Framework', *The Economic Journal*, 91(362), 1981, 507–14.
Frenkel, J and H. Johnson (eds), *The Economics of Exchange Rates: Selected Studies*, Reading, Addison Wesley Publishing Co., 1978.
Friedberg, Arthur L., Ira S. Friedberg and Robert Friedberg, *Gold Coins of the World: From Ancient Times to the Present — An Illustrated Standard Catalogue with Variations*, Clifton NJ, Coins and Currency Institute, 2003.
Friedman, Milton, *The Optimum Quantity of Money*, Chicago, Aldine Publishing Company, 1969.
———, *Money Mischief: Episodes in Monetary History*, Chicago, Harcourt Brace Jovanovich, 1992.
Friedman, Milton and A. Jacobson Schwartz, *A Monetary History of the United States, 1867–1960*, Princeton, Princeton University Press, 1963.

Fry, M.J., *Money, Interest and Banking in Economic Development*, Baltimore, John Hopkins University Press, 1988.
Gandolfo, Giancarlo, *International Finance and Open Economy Macroeconomics*, Heidelberg, Springer-Verlag, 2001.
Ganesh, S., 'Who is Afraid of Foreign Firms? Current Trends in FDI', *Economic and Political Weekly*, 32(2), March 1997, 1265–74.
Ghatak, A. and F. Halicioglu, 'Foreign Direct Investment and Economic Growth: Some Evidence from Across the World', MPRA Paper No. 3563, Munich Personal RePEc Archive, 2006.
Genberg, A. Hans, 'Aspects of the Monetary Approach to the Balance of Payment Theory: An Empirical Study of Sweden', in Jacob A. Frenkel and Harry G. Johnson (eds), *The Monetary Approach to the Balance of Payments*, London, George Allen and Unwin Limited, 1976.
Gibson, Rajna, *Option Valuation: Analyzing and Pricing Standardized Option Contracts*, New York, McGraw-Hill, 1999.
Gilbert, M., *Problems of the International Monetary System*, Essays in International Finance, Princeton, Princeton University Press, 1968a.
———, *The Gold-Dollar System: Conditions of Equilibrium and the Price of Gold*, Essays in International Finance, Princeton, Princeton University Press, 1968b.
Giovannini, Alberto, 'How Do Fixed Exchange-Rate Regimes Work: The Evidence from the Gold Standard, Bretton Woods and the EMS', in Marvin Miller, Barry Eichengreen and Richard Portes (eds), *Blueprints for Exchange Rate Management*, London, Center for Economic Policy Research, 1989, 13–46.
———, 'Bretton Woods and Its Precursors: Rules versus Discretion in the History of International Monetary System', in Michael Bordo and Barry Eichengreen (eds), *A Retrospective on the Bretton Woods System: Lessons for International Monetary Reform*, Chicago, University of Chicago Press, 1993.
Giovannetti, G., 'A Survey of Recent Empirical Test of the Purchasing Power Parity Hypothesis', *Banca Nazionzle del Lavaro Quarterly Review*, 180, March 1992, 81–101.
Goldberg, Pinelopi and Michael Knetter, 'Goods Prices and Exchange Rates: What Have We Learned?' *Journal of Economic Literature*, 35(3), September 1997, 1243–72.
Goldfajn, Ilan and Rodrigo Valdés, 'Capital Flows and the Twin Crises: The Role of Liquidity', IMF Working Paper No. 97/87, International Monetary Fund, Washington DC, 1997.
Goldstein, Morris, *The Case for an International Banking Standard*, Washington DC, Institute for International Economics, 1997.
———, 'The Asian Financial Crisis: Causes, Curses and Systematic Implications', Policy Analyses in International Economics No. 55, Institute for International Economics, Washington DC, 1998.
Goldstein, Morris and Phillip Turner, 'Banking Crises in Emerging Economies: Origin and Policy Options', BIS Economic Papers No. 46, Bank for International Settlements, October 1996.
Goodhart, Charles A.E., 'The Two Concepts of Money: Implications for the Analysis of Optimal Currency Areas', *European Journal of Political Economy*, 14(3), 1998, 407–32.
———, 'A Reply to the Contributors', in S. Bell and E. Nell (eds), *The State, the Market and the Euro*, Cheltenham, Edward Elgar, 2003, 184–96.
Gottlieb, D., 'On the Determinants of a Country's Credit Worthiness: The Case of the Israel 1971–1983', *Journal of Economic Development*, 14(1), 1989, 65–91.
Grauwe, Paul De, 'Is the European Monetary System a DM – Zone?' *Business and Economics*, Centre for Policy Research, London, 1989.
Grubel, H.G., 'Gold and the Dollar Crises Five Years Later', *National Bank Review*, 3(1), September 1965, 89-99.

———, *The International Monetary System: Efficiency and Practical Alternatives*, Baltimore, Penguin Books, 1970.

———, 'The Demand for International Reserves: A Critical Review of the Literature', *Journal of Economic Literature*, 9(4), December 1971, 1148–66.

Gurley, J. and E. Shaw, *Money in a Theory of Finance*, Washington DC, Bookings Institutions, 1960.

Hageman, H.A., 'Reserve Policies of Central Banks and their Implications for US Balance of Payments Policy', *American Economic Review*, 59(1), March 1969, 62–77.

Hamada, K., *The Political Economy of International Monetary Independence*, Cambridge, MIT Press, 1985.

Hamada, K. and K. Ueda, 'Random Walks and the Theory of Optimal International Reserve', *Economic Journal*, 87(348), 1977, 722–42.

Hanke, S.H. and K. Schuler, *Currency Boards for Developing Countries: A Handbook*, San Francisco, ICS Press, 1994.

Harberger, A., 'Currency Depreciation, Income and the Balance of Trade', *Journal of Political Economy*, 58(1), 1950, 47–56.

Hartmann, Phillip, *Currency Competition and Foreign Exchange Markets; the Dollar, the Yen and the Euro*, Cambridge, Cambridge University Press, 1998.

Hau, Harald, 'Exchange Rate Determination: The Role of Factor Price Rigidities and Nontradeables', *Journal of International Economics*, 50(20), April 2000, 421–47.

Hausmann, R., Ugo Panizza and Ernesto Stein, 'Why Do Countries Float the Way they Float?' *Journal of Development Economics*, 66(2), 2001, 387–414.

Heller, H.R., 'Optimal International Reserves', *The Economic Journal*, 76(302), June 1966, 296–311.

———, 'The Transaction Demand from International Means of Payments', *Journal of Political Economy*, 76(1), January–February 1968, 141–45.

Heller, H.R. and M.S. Khan, 'The Demand for International Reserve under Fixed and Floating Exchange Rates', *IMF Staff Papers*, 25(4), 1978, 623–49.

Heller, H.R. and R.R. Rhomberg (eds), *The Monetary Approach to Balance of Payments*, Washington, International Monetary Fund, 1977.

Henry, J.F., 'The Social Origins of Money: The Case of Egypt', in L.R. Wray (ed.), *Credit and State Theories of Money: The Contributions of A. Mitchell Innes*, Cheltenham, Edward Elgar, 2004, 79–98.

Hoover, Kevin D., *Causality in Macroeconomics*, Cambridge, Cambridge University Press, 2001.

Hudson, M., 'The Archaeology of Money: Debt versus Barter Theories of Money's Origins', in L.R. Wray (ed.), *Credit and State Theories of Money: The Contributions of A. Mitchell Innes*, Cheltenham, Edward Elgar, 2004, 99–127.

Hull, Cordell, *The Memoirs of Cordell Hull*, vols 1 and 2, New York, Macmillan, 1948.

Hume, David, *The Philosophical Works of David Hume*, vol. 3, London, Adam Black and William Tait, 1828.

———, *A Treatise of Human Nature*, Oxford, Clarendon Press, 1888 [1739].

———, *Essays: Moral, Political, and Literary*, Indianapolis, Liberty Classics, 1985 [1754].

International Monetary Fund (IMF), 'The Adequacy of Monetary Reserve', *IMF Staff Papers*, 3(2), 1953, 181–227

———, *International Reserve and Liquidity*, Washington DC, International Monetary Fund, 1958.

———, *International Reserves: Needs an Availability*, Washington DC, International Monetary Fund, 1970.

———, 'Currency Composition of Official Foreign Exchange Reserves', International Monetary Fund, 1995–99, 2006–10.

———, 'Currency Composition of Official Foreign Exchange Reserves', International Monetary Fund, 2010.

Isard, P., 'How Far Can We Push the Law of One Price', *American Economic Review*, 67(5), December 1977, 992–98.

———, *Exchange Rate Economics*, New York, Cambridge University Press, 1995.

Iyoha, M.A., 'The Optimal Balance-of-Payments Strategy of a Less Developed Country', Discussion Paper No. 161, February, Department of Economics, State University of New York at Buffalo, 1971.

———, 'Demand for International Reserve in Less Developed Countries: A Distributed Lag Specification', *Review of Economics and Statistics*, 58, August 1976.

Ize, Alain and Eduardo L. Yeyati, 'Financial Dollarization', *Journal of International Economics*, 59(2), 2003, 323–47.

Jevons, William Stanley, *Money and the Mechanism of Exchange*, New York, D. Appleton and Company, 1875.

Johnson, H.G., *International Trade and Economic Growth*, Cambridge, Harvard University Press, 1958.

———, 'Tariffs and Economic Development: Some Theoretical Issues', *Journal of Development Studies*, 1(1), 1964, 3–30.

———, 'The International Competitive Position of the United States and the Balance of Payments Prospect for 1968', *The Review of Economics and Statistics*, 46(1), February 1964, 14–32.

———, 'The Monetary Approach to Balance of Payment Theory and Policy: Explanations and Policy Implications', *Economica*, 44(175), 1968, 217–29.

———, *Efficiency in Domestic and International Money Supply*, vol. 3, Guildford, International Economics, University of Surrey, 1970.

Kaldor, N., 'The Effects of Devaluation on Trade in Manufactures', in *Further Essays on Applied Economics*, London, Duckworth, 1978.

Kane, E J., 'International Liquidity: A Probabilistic Approach', *Kyklos*, 18(1), 1965, 27–48.

Kelly, M.G., 'The Demand for International Reserves', *American Economic Review*, 60(4), September 1970, 655–67.

Kenen, P.B., *Reserve Asset Preferences of Central Banks and Stability of the Gold Exchange Standard*, Princeton Studies in International Finance, Princeton, International Finance Section, Department of Economics, Princeton University Press, 1963.

———, (ed.), *Understanding Interdependence: The Macroeconomics of the Open Economy*, Princeton, Princeton University Press, 1995.

Kenen, P. and E. Yudin, 'The Demand for International Reserves', *The Review of Economics and Statistics*, 47(3), August 1965, 242–50.

———, 'The Demand for International Reserves: A Reply', *The Review of Economics and Statistics*, 49, 1967, 626–27.

Keynes, J.M., *The Economic Consequences of the Peace*, New York, Harcourt, Brace and Howe, 1920.

———, *A Treatise on Money: The Pure Theory of Money*, vol. 1, New York, Harcourt Brace-Jovanovich, 1930.

———, 'Social Consequences of Changes in the Value of Money', in *Essays in Persuasion*, New York, W. W. Norton, 1963.

———, *The General Theory of Employment, Interest, and Money*, New York, Harcourt, Brace & World, 1964.

Kindleberger, C.P., 'Balance-of-Payments Deficits and the International Reserves', *The Review of Economics and Statistics*, 47, August 1965, 242–50.

———, *Balance-of-Payments Deficits and the International Markets for Liquidity*, Princeton Essays in International Finance, No. 46, Princeton, Princeton University Press, 1965.

———, 'International Public Goods without International Government', *American Economic Review*, 76(1), 1986, 1–13.

Klein, Martin and Manfred J.M. Neumann, 'Seigniorage: What is it and Who Gets it?' *Weltwirtschaftliches Archiv*, 126(2), 1990, 205–21.

Knapp, G.F., *The State Theory of Money*, New York, Augustus M. Kelley, 1973.

Kokko, A., 'Technology, Market Characteristics and Spillovers', *Journal of Development Economics*, 43, 1994.

Kollmann, Robert, 'Incomplete Asset Markets and the Cross-Country Consumption Correlation Puzzle', *Journal of Economic Dynamics and Control*, 20(5), May 1996, 945–61.

Krause, L.B., 'A Passive Balance-of-Payments Strategy for the United States', *Brookings Papers on Economic Activity*, 3, 1970.

Kravis, I. and R. Lipsey, 'Price Behaviour in the Light of Balance of Payments Theories', *Journal of International Economics*, 8(2), May 1978, 193–246.

Krugman, Paul, 'A Model of Balance of Payments Crisis', *Journal of Money, Credit and Banking*, 11(3), August 1979, 311–25.

———, 'Dutch Tulips and the Emerging Markets: Another Bubble Bursts', *Foreign Affairs*, 75(4), 1995, 28–44.

———, 'Saving Asia: It's Time to Get Radical', *Fortune Magazine*, 7 September 1998, 75–80.

———, 'Balance Sheets, the Transfer Problem, and Financial Crisis', *International Tax and Public Finance*, 6(4), November 1999a, 459–72.

———, *The Return of Depression Economics*, New York, WW Norton, 1999b.

Kumar, N., *Multinational Enterprises and Industrial Organization: The Case of India*, Delhi, Sage Publications, 1994.

Lagunoff, Roger D. and Stacey L. Schreft, 'A Model of Financial Fragility', *Journal of Economic Theory*, 99, 2001, 220–64.

Laidler, David, 'The Quantity Theory is Always and Everywhere Controversial — Why?' *Economic Record*, 67(4), December 1991, 289–306.

Landell-Mills, J.M., 'The Demand for International Reserves and their Opportunity Cost', *IMF Staff Papers*, 36(3), 1989, 708–32.

Lapittus, J.R., 'The Demand for Official Reserves to Finance International Trade under a System of Fixed Exchange Rates', Unpublished Ph.D. Dissertation, Yale University, 1970.

Lee, Jaewoo, 'Insurance Value of International Reserves; An Option Pricing Approach', IMF Working Paper No. 04/175, International Monetary Fund, 2004.

Li, J., O. Sula and T.D. Willet, 'A New Framework for Analyzing Adequate and Excessive Reserve Levels under High Capital Mobility', in Yin-Wong Cheung and Kar-Yiu Wong (eds), *China and Asia: Economic and Financial Interactions*, London, Routledge, 2008, 230–45.

Lilley, Peter, *Dirty Dealing: The Untold Truth about Global Money Laundering*, London, Kogan Page Ltd, 2006.

Lincoln, A., 'Many Free Countries Have Lost Their Liberty', A Speech on the Sub-Treasury, Springfield, 26 December 1839.

Liu, Henry C.K., 'US Dollar Hegemony Has Got to Go', *Asia Times online Co Ltd*, 11 April 2002.

Lizondo, J.S. and D.J. Mathieson, 'The Stability of the Demand for International Reserves', *Journal of International Money and Finance*, 6, 1987, 251–82.

Lucas, Robert E., 'Interest Rates and Currency Prices in a Two–Country World', *Journal of Monetary Economics*, November, 10(3), 1982, 335–59.

Lyons, R.K., 'Foreign Exchange: Macro Puzzles, Micro Tools', *Economic Review*, Federal Reserve Bank of San Francisco, 2002.

MacDonald, R., *Floating Exchange Rates: Theories and Evidence*, London, Unwin Hyman, 1988.
Machlup, F., 'The Need for Monetary Reserves', *Banca Nazionale del Lavoro* Quarterly Review, 19, September 1966, 175–222.
———, 'From Dormant Liabilities to Dormant Assets', *The Banker*, 117, 1967, 788–97.
Makin, J.H., 'The Composition of International Reserve Holdings: A Problem of Choice Involving Risk', *American Economic Review*, 61, December 1971, 827.
Markovitz, H., *Portfolio Selection: Efficient Diversification of Investments*, New York, Wiley, 1959.
Marquez, J., 'Reserves, Liquidity, and the Developing Countries', in International Monetary Fund, *International Reserves: Needs and Availability*, Washington DC, International Monetary Fund, 1970, 97–111.
Marshall, A., *Money, Credit and Commerce*, London, Macmillan, 1923.
McCombie, J. and A.P. Thirlwall, 'East Asian Financial Crisis: Retrospect and Prospect', *Asia and Australasia: Regional Overview*, 3rd Quarter, Economist Intelligence Unit, 1999.
MacDonald, Ronald and Mark P. Taylor, 'Economic Analysis of Foreign Exchange Markets: An Expository Survey', in *Exchange Rates and Open Economy Macroeconomics*, Oxford, Basil Blackwell, 1989, 1–108.
McDonald, D.C., 'Debt Capacity and Developing Country Borrowing: A Survey of the Literature', *IMF Staff Papers*, 29(4), 1982, 603–46.
McKinnon, R.I., *Private and Official International Money: The Case for the Dollar*, Princeton Essays in International Finance No. 74, Princeton, Princeton University, 1969.
———, *Money in International Exchange : The Convertible Currency System*, New York, Oxford University Press, 1979.
———, 'The Exchange Rate and Macroeconomic Policy: Changing Postwar Perceptions', *Journal of Economic Literature*, 19, June 1981, 531–57.
———, 'Monetary and Exchange Rate Policies for International Financial Stability', *Journal of Economic Perspective*, Winter 1988, 83–103.
———, 'Mundell, the Euro, and the World Dollar Standard', *Journal of Policy Modeling*, May 2000.
McNamara, K., 'A Rivalry in the Making? The Euro and International Monetary Power', *Review of International Political Economy*, 15(3), 2008, 439–59.
Meade, James E., *Theory of International Economic Policy*, London, Oxford University Press, 1951.
Meese, R.A. and K. Rogoff, 'Empirical Exchange Rate Models of the Seventies: Do They Fit Out of Sample?' *Journal of International Economics*, 14, 1983, 3–24.
Meyer, D., 'Protest and Political Opportunities', *Annual Review of Sociology*, 30, 2004, 125–45.
Misselden, E. and Gerard Malynes, *The Center of the Circle of Commerce*, London, J. Dawson for N. Bowne, 1623.
Moore, B.J., *An Introduction to the Theory of Finance*, New York, Free Press, 1968.
Mundell, R.A., 'A Theory of Optimum Currency Areas', *American Economic Review*, 51(4), 1961, 657–65.
———, 'Capital Mobility and Stabilization Policy under Fixed and Flexible Exchange Rates', *The Canadian Journal of Economics and Political Science*, 29(4), 1963, 487–99.
———, *International Economics*, New York, Macmillan, 1968.
———, *Monetary Theory: Inflation, Interest and Growth in the World Economy*, Pacific Palisades, California, Goodyear Publishing Company, 1971.
———, 'The Future of the Exchange Rate System', paper prepared for the Rocca de Salimbeni Conference, Siena, November 1994.
———, 'What the Euro Means for the Dollar and the International Monetary System?' *Atlantic Economic Journal*, 26(3), September 1998.

Murphy, John J., *Technical Analysis of the Futures Markets: A Comprehensive Guide to Trading Methods and Applications*, New York Institute of Finance, Prentice-Hall, 1986.

Naim, Moisés, 'Washington Consensus or Washington Confusion?' *Foreign Policy Magazine*, 26 October 1999.

Nandi, Sukumar, 'Exchange Rate Behavior of Indian Rupee: A Cointegration Approach', *Journal of Indian School of Political Economy*, January–March 1994.

———, 'An Empirical Study of Demand for International Reserve', *Journal of Foreign Exchange and International Finance (JFEIF)*, April–June 1996a.

———, *Essays on International Finance: The Indian Perspective*, Pune, National Institute of Bank Management, 1996b.

———, *Growth, Financial Cycles and Bank Efficiency: An Analysis of Indian Money Market*, Mumbai, Business Publications Inc., 1998a.

———, 'Hong Kong Dollar and Chinese Renminbi (RMB), Two Currencies in One Country', *Journal of Foreign Exchange and International Finance*, July–September, 1998b.

———, 'Exchange Rate of Indian Rupee and Price Level Behaviour in India', in D.K. Das (ed.), *Trade and Development: Experiences and Challenges*, New Delhi, Deep and Deep Publications, 1999a.

———, *International Money and Capital*, Mumbai, Business Publications Inc., 1999b.

———, *International Money and Finance*, New Delhi, Samskriti, 2001.

Nayyar, D., 'Transnational Corporations and Manufactured Exports from Poor Countries', *The Economic Journal*, 88, 1978.

Nell, S. Kevin and Luis D. Santos, 'The Feldstein–Horioka Hypothesis versus the Long–Run Solvency Constraint Model: A Critical Assessment', *Economic Letters*, 98(1), 2008, 66–70.

Niehans, Jurg, in International Monetary Fund, *International Reserve: Needs and Availability*, Washington DC, International Monetary Fund, 1970.

———, *International Monetary Economics*, Baltimore, Johns Hopkins University Press, 1984.

Neumann, M.J.M., 'Seigniorage in the United States: How Much Does the US Government Make from Money Production?' *Federal Reserve Bank of St. Louis Review*, 74 (2), March–April 1992, 29–40.

North, John, *Roman Religion*, London, Cambridge University Press, 2000.

Noussair, C.N., C.R. Plott and R.G. Reizman, 1994. 'The Principles of Exchange Rate Determination in an International Finance Experiment', Papers 94–021, Center for International Business Education and Research (CIBER), Krannert Graduate School of Management, Purdue University.

———, 'The Principle of Exchange Rate Determination in an International Finance Experiment', *Journal of Political Economy*, 105, 1997, 822–61.

Nuruzzaman, Mohammed, 'Economic Liberalization and Poverty in Developing Countries', *Journal of Contemporary Asia*, 35(1), March 2005, 109–27.

Obstfeld, Maurice, 'Rational and Self-Fulfilling Balance-of-Payments Crises', *American Economic Review*, 76, March 1986, 72–81.

———, 'The Logic of Currency Crises', *Cahiers Economiques et Monetaires 43*, Bank of France, 1994, 189–213.

———, 'International Capital Mobility in the 1990s', in Peter Kenen (ed.), *Understanding Interdependence: The Macroeconomics of the Open Economy*, Princeton, Princeton University Press, 1995.

———, 'The Global Capital Market: Benefactor of Menace?' *Journal of Economic Perspective*, 12(4), Fall 1998, 9–30.

Obstfeld, Maurice and A.M. Taylor, 'Globalization and Capital Markets', in M.D. Bordo, A.M. Taylor and J.G. Williamson (eds), *Globalization in Historical Perspective*, Chicago, University of Chicago Press, 2003.

Obstfeld, Maurice and Kenneth Rogoff, 'Exchange Rate Dynamics Redux', *Journal of Political Economy*, 103, 1995a, 624–60.

———, 'The Intertemporal Approach to the Current Account', in G. Grossman and Kenneth Rogoff (eds), *Handbook of International Economics*, 3, Amsterdam, 1995b.

———, *Foundations of International Macroeconomics*, Cambridge, MIT Press, 1996.

———, 'Risk and Exchange Rates', Working Paper No. 6694, National Bureau of Economic Research, August 1998.

———, 'New Directions for Stochastic Open Economy Models', *Journal of International Economics*, 50, February 2000, 117–53.

Officer, L.H., 'The Purchasing Power Parity Theory of Exchange Rates: A Review Article', *IMF Staff Papers*, 23, 1976, 1–60.

Olivera, Julio H.G., 'A Note on the Optimal Rate of Growth of International Reserves', *Journal of Political Economy*, 77(2), March–April 1969, 245–48.

Organisation of Economic Cooperation and Development (OECD), *OECD Benchmark Definition of Foreign Direct Investment*, Paris, Organisation for Economic Co-operation and Development, 2008.

Patel, I.G., 'Aid Relationships for the Seventies', in Barbara Ward, Lenore D'Anjou and J. D. Runnalls (eds), *The Widening Gap: Development in the 1970s*, New York, Columbia University Press, 1971.

Payne, R., 'Informed Trade in Spot Foreign Exchange Markets: An Empirical Investigation', *Journal of International Economics*, 61, 2003.

Pick, F., *Pick's Currency Yearbook*, New York, Pick Publishing Corporation, 1968 [1960].

Pigou, Arthur C., 'The Classical Stationary State', *The Economic Journal*, 53(212), 1943, 343–51.

Pisani-Ferry, Jean and Adam S. Posen, *The Euro at Ten: The Next Global Currency?* Washington DC, Peterson Institute for International Economics, 2009.

Polak, J.J., 'Monetary Analysis of Income Formation and Payments Problems', *IMF Staff Papers*, 6, 1957.

———, 'The IMF Monetary Model at Forty', IMF Working Paper No. 97/49, International Monetary Fund, Washington DC, April 1997a.

———, 'The IMF Monetary Model: A Hardy Perennial', *Finance and Development*, December 1997b, 16–19.

Porter, R.D. and R.A. Judson, 'The Location of the US Currency: How Much is Abroad?' *Federal Reserve Bulletin*, October 1996, 883–903.

Prahalad, C.K. and Kenneth Lieberthal, 'The End of Corporate Imperialism', *Harvard Business Review*, 76(4), July–August 1998.

Quirk, Peter J., 'Money Laundering: Muddying the Macroeconomy', *Finance and Development*, International Monetary Fund, 34(1), 1997.

Reinhart, C.M. and Kenneth Rogoff, 'This Time is Different: A Panoramic View of Eight Centuries of Financial Crisis', NBER Working Paper No. 13882, National Bureau of Economic Research, April 2008.

Reinhart, C.M. and V. Reinhart, 'What Hurts Most? G-3 Exchange Rate or Interest Rate Volatility', NBER Working Paper No. 8535, National Bureau of Economic Research, 2002.

Rhomberg, Rudolf R., 'Estimation of Effects of Changes in International Reserves', in *International Reserves: Needs and Availability*, Washington DC, International Monetary Fund, 1970a, 157–93.

———, 'Possible Approaches to a Model of World Trade and Payments', *IMF Staff Papers*, 17, March 1970b, 1–26.

Ricardo, David, *On the Principles of Political Economy and Taxation*, London, John Murray, 1817.

———, 'Essay on the Funding System', in J. R. McCulloch, *The Works of David Ricardo, With a Notice of the Life and Writings of the Author*, London, John Murray, 1888.
Rodrik, D., 'Goodbye Washington Consensus, Hello Washington Confusion? A Review of the World Bank's Economic Growth in the 1990s: Learning from a Decade of Reform', *Journal of Economic Literature*, 44(4), 2006, 973–87.
Rogoff, Kenneth, 'The Purchasing Power Parity Puzzle', *Journal of Economic Literature*, 34(2), June 1996, 647–68.
Sachs, J.D., A. Tornell and A. Velasco, 'The Collapse of the Mexican Peso: What Have We Learned?' *Economic Policy*, 11(22), April 1996, 13–63.
Sachs, J.D. and F. Larrain B., *Macroeconomics in the Global Economy*, Englewood Cliffs, Prentice Hall, 1993.
Salant, W. A., 'The Reserve Currency Role of the Dollar: Blessing or Burden on the US?' *The Review of Economics and Statistics*, 46(2), May 1964, 165–72.
———, in International Monetary Fund, *International Reserve: Needs and Availability*, Washington DC, International Monetary Fund, 1970.
Samuelson, Paul, 'Theoretical Note on Trade Problems', *The Review of Economics and Statistics*, 46, May 1964, 145–54.
———, 'What Classical and Neoclassical Monetary Theory Really Was', *Canadian Journal of Economics*, 1(1), 1968, 1–15.
Sargent, T., 'The Ends of Four Big Inflations', in Robert E. Hall (ed.), *Inflation: Causes and Effects*, Chicago, University of Chicago Press, 1983, 41–97.
———, *Dynamic Macroeconomic Theory*, Cambridge, Harvard University Press, 1987.
Sarno, Lucio, 'Toward a New Paradigm in Open Economy Modeling: Where Do We Stand?' *Federal Reserve Bank of St. Louis Review*, 83(3), May–June 2001.
Scitovsky, T., 'A New Approach to International Liquidity', *American Economic Review*, 56, 1966, 1212–20.
———, *Economic Theory and Western European Integration*, Stanford, Stanford University Press, 1988.
Siegel, J. E., 'Risk, Interest Rates and the Forward Exchange', *Quarterly Journal of Economics*, 86, 1972.
Simmel, Georg, *The Philosophy of Money*, trans. Thomas Burton Bottomore and David Frisby, Boston, Routledge and Kegan Paul, 1978.
Smith, V.L., 'Experimental Methods in Economics', in *The New Palgrave Dictionary of Economics*, vol. 2, London, Macmillan, 1987.
Stekler, L. and R. Piekarz, 'Reserve Asset Composition for Major Central Banks', *Oxford Economic Papers*, 22(2), July 1970, 260–74.
Stern, R., The *Balance of Payments: Theory and Economic Policy*, London, Macmillan, 1973.
Stiglitz, J.E., Globalization *and its Discontents*, New York, WW Norton, 2002.
———, *Making Globalization Work*, New York, W.W. Norton, 2006.
Taylor, Alan, 'Potential Pitfalls for the Purchasing-Power-Parity Puzzle? Sampling and Specification Biases in Mean-Reversion Tests of the Law of One Price', *Econometrica*, 69(2), March 2001, 473–98.
Temin, Peter, *Lessons from the Great Depression*, Cambridge, MIT Press, 1989.
Tew, Brian, 'Sterling as an International Currency', *Economic Record*, 24(1), June 1948, 42–55.
———, *The Evolution of the International Monetary System: 1945–88*, London, Hutchinson, 1988.
Thorn, R, 'The Demand for International Reserves: A Note in Behalf of the Rejected Hypothesis', *The Review of Economics and Statistics*, 49(4), November 1967, 623–26.

Tobin, J., 'The Interest-Elasticity of Transactions Demand for Cash', *The Review of Economics and Statistics*, 38(3), August 1956, 241–47.

———, 'Liquidity Preference as Behaviour towards Risks', *The Review of Economic Studies*, 25, February 1958, 686.

———, 'A Proposal for International Monetary Reform', *Eastern Economic Journal*, 4, 1978, 153–59.

———, 'Agenda for International Coordination of Macroeconomic Policies', in *International Monetary Cooperation: Essays in Honor of Henry C. Wallich*, Essays on International Finance No. 169, Princeton, Princeton University Press, 1987, 61–69.

Torres, Craig. 'How Mexico's Behind-the-Scenes Tactics and a Secret Pact Averted Market Panic', *Wall Street Journal*, 28 March 1994.

Triffin, R., *Tomorrow's Convertibility: Aims and Means of International Policy*, Quarterly Review No. 49, Rome, Banca Nazionale del Lavoro, 1959.

———, *'Gold and the Dollar Crisis: The Future of Convertibility'*, New Haven, Yale University Press, 1960.

———, *Gold and the Dollar Crisis: Yesterday and Tomorrow*, Essays in International Finance No. 132, Princeton, Princeton University, December 1978.

Tsang, Eric W.K., *Internationalization as a Learning Process: Singapore MNCs in China*, Academy of Management Executives, vol. 13(1), February 1999.

Ugur, Mehmet, 'Extensions on the Mundell–Fleming Model; Perfect Capital Mobility and Flexible Prices', in *An Open Economy Macroeconomics Reader*, New York, Routledge, 2002, 42–50.

United Nations Conference on Trade and Development (UNCTAD), *World Investment Report 1998: Trend and Determinants*, Geneva, United Nations Conference on Trade and Development, 1998.

———, *World Investment Report 1999: Foreign Direct Investment and the Challenge of Development*, Geneva, United Nations Conference on Trade and Development, 1999.

von Hayek, F.A., 'The Use of Knowledge in Society', *American Economic Review*, 35(4), September 1945, 519–30.

———, *Denationalization of Money: An Analysis of the Theory and Practice of Concurrent Currencies*, London, Institute of Economic Affairs, 1976.

Wacziarg, R., 'Measuring the Dynamic Gains from Trade', *World Bank Economic Review*, 15(3), 2001, 393–429.

Wallich, H. C., 'Institutional Cooperation in the World Economy', in J.A. Frenkel and M.L. Mussa (eds), *The World Economic System: Performance and Prospects*, Dover, Auburn House, 1984.

Walter, Andrew, 'Domestic Sources of International Monetary Leadership', in: David M Andrews.(ed.), *International Monetary Power*. Ithaca, Cornell University Press, 2006, 51–71.

———, 'Global Imbalances and Currency Politics: The US, EU, and China', in Robert Ross, Øystein Tunsjø and Zhang Tuosheng (eds), *US-China-EU Relations: Managing the New World Order*, Abingdon, Routledge, 2010.

Wang, J.Y. and M. Blomstrom, 'Foreign Investment and Technology Transfer: A Simple Model', *European Economic Review*, 36(1), 1992.

Willett, Thomas D., 'Adequacy of International Means of Payments', *The Review of Economics and Statistics*, 51(3), August 1969, 373–74.

———, *International Liquidity Issues*, Washington DC, American Enterprise Institute, 1980.

Willett, Thomas O. and Edward Tower, 'The Welfare Economics of International Adjustment', *The Journal of Finance*, 26(2), May 1971, 287–302.

Williamson, J., 'International Liquidity: A Survey', *Economic Journal*, September 1973.

———, *The Failure of World Monetary Reform, 1971–1974*, Sunbury, Thomas Nelson and Sons, 1977.

———, 'A Survey of the Literature on the Optimal Peg', *Journal of Development Economics*, 11(1), 1982, 39–61.

———, 'On the System in Bretton Woods', *American Economic Review*, 75(2), May 1985, 74–79.

——— (ed.), *Latin American Adjustment: How Much has Happened*, Washington DC, Institute of International Economics, 1990.

———, 'Democracy and the "Washington Consensus"', *World Development*, 21(8), 1993.

Williamson, J. and M.H. Miller, *Targets and Indicators: A Blueprint for the International Coordination of Economic Policy*, Policy Analyses in International Economics, 22, Washington DC, Institute for International Economics, 1987.

World Bank, *The East Asian Miracle: Economic Growth and Public Policy*, Washington DC, World Bank, 1993.

Wray, L.R., 'Understanding Modern Money: Clarifications and Extensions', CofFEE Conference Proceedings, Centre of Full Employment and Equity, Newcastle, December 2001.

Yeager, L.B., 'The Misconceived Problem of International Liquidity', The *Journal of Finance*, vol. 14(3), September 1959, 347–60.

Yeoman, R.S., *A Guide Book of United States Coins*, ed. Kenneth Bressett, New York, Whitman Publishing, 2011.

Zhao, Laixun, 'Labour-Management Bargaining and Transfer Pricing in Multinational Corporations', *Canadian Journal of Economics*, 31(4), October 1998.

About the Author

Sukumar Nandi is Professor of Economics at Indian Institute of Management, Lucknow. He has a PhD in Economics from Utah State University, US. Prior to this, he has taught and conducted researches at Utah State University; Massachusetts College of Liberal Arts, US; Vidyasagar University, West Bengal; National Institute of Bank Management (NIBM), Pune; Indian Institute of Foreign Trade, New Delhi, India and was Visiting Professor at the School of Management, Asian Institute of Technology, Bangkok on an assignment for the Government of India in 2003.

Index

absorption approach, 14–16
Asian crisis, 62, 183

Basle Committee, 57
Bretton Woods
    Agreement, 1, 3, 44, 48, 50, 52, 56, 86, 101, 133, 215, 217
    system, 1, 28, 51, 55, 59, 65, 69, 75, 89, 99, 156
    par value system, 48

Cambridge school, 9
competing currencies, 85
covered interest parity (CIP), 140–42
contagion, 5, 63, 176–77, 179–80
currency basket, (Indian Rupee), 89, 93, 98–100
Currency Board (CB), 77, 85, 115, 137, 163–64, 183
currency crises, 59, 179–80
    First-Generation Models, 177
    Second-Generation Models, 178
    Third-Generation Models, 178
currency union, 163–64

dollarization, 85, 113–16, 118–19, 128, 148, 163–64, 173–74
    cost of, 118–19
Dollar as international currency, 78–79, 172–75
Dornbusch model of exchange rate, 156–58

Egmont Group, 123–24
elasticity approach, 14–15
emerging economies, 5, 64, 80, 169
European Union (EU), 67–68, 235–39
European System of Central Banks (ESCB), 70, 236
equilibrium exchange rate, 4, 21, 94, 147, 149
euro, 66–68, 70, 236–39
Eurodollar system, 111–12

EuroPEN system, 135
exchange rate arrangement, 57, 60–61, 77, 89
    black market, 88, 90, 98, 101–03, 121, 129, 166
    exchange rate determination, 4, 12, 18, 96, 145, 149, 151–52, 167
    managed exchange rate, 165
    monetary approach, 16, 23–24, 154, 155, 158, 224
    overshooting model, 155–58
    pegged exchange rate, 164
    portfolio-balance approach, 158–59
exact exchange rate, 93–96
    real exchange rate, 18, 22, 91, 93–94, 96, 112, 143–44, 154, 157, 163, 168
    volatility in exchange rate, 159–60

Federal Reserve of US, 29, 70, 111, 169, 173, 215
Feldstein–Horioka model, 142–43
fiat money, 3, 10, 29–31, 34, 83, 85–87, 114, 215
Financial Action Task Force (FATF), 124–25
financial integration, 171
Fixed Coefficient Model, 110–11
foreign exchange market, 130–34, 161–62
foreign direct investment, 5, 37–38, 43, 73, 106, 180, 185, 188–89, 193, 197, 204
    role of infrastructure, 200–02
forward speculation, 139

globalization, 182–84
gold exchange standard, 46–47
gold pool, 54–55, 57
gold standard, 7, 14, 28, 45–47, 52, 69, 84, 86, 150–52, 163–64, 218
gold
    demonetization of, 49, 55, 86
    sales by IMF, 76–77
Gresham's law, 55–56
Greenfield investment, 39–41

Group of Seven (G-7) countries, 52, 57–58, 62–65, 124
Group of Twenty (G-20) countries, 64, 74, 76

hawala transactions, 121–22

Indian economy and foreign capital, 192–97
Indian rupee, 4, 61, 87–90, 96–98, 100, 102, 107, 120, 130, 134–35, 153–54,167
   black market exchange rate, 88, 90, 101–03, 121
International Bank for Reconstruction and Development (IBRD), 48, 55
International Economic Order, 65– 66
International Monetary Fund (IMF), 50–61, 64–66,73–77, 133, 216, 238
   decline of the system, 56–57
   Second Amendment of IMF Article, 57
   new arrangement to borrow, 74
interest arbitrage, 140
international liquidity, 54, 65, 215–16
international reserve, 215–30

J-Curve phenomenon, 138–39

law of one price (LOOP), 18, 20, 152
London Gold Pool, 54–55
Louvre Accord, 58

Maastricht Treaty, 233–35
managed float, 57
Marshall–Lerner condition, 137–38
Money
   origin of, 82
   Chartalist, 82
monetary theory of exchange rate, 12, 23–25
monetarist approach, 10, 14, 16, 23, 154
monetarist arithmetic, 13
money laundering, 119–21
Money-Laundering Bill (India), 1999, 125–27
Multilateral payments mechanism, 49
Multinational corporation (MNC), 37–41
Mundell–Fleming model, 112, 145

New Arrangement to Borrow (IMF), 74
Nostro account, 135

offshore centres, 108–09, 121, 127
offshore banking, 107–09
open economy trilemma, 5, 172
optimum currency area argument, 67
overshooting of exchange rate, 155

Pass-through, 21–22
pegged exchange rate, 164
Plaza Accord, 58
Polak model, 23–25
policy trilemma, 173
portfolio-balance approach , 158–59
Purchasing Power Parity (PPP), 11–13, 152–54
PPP and Experimental Economics, 153–54

quantity theory of money, 8
quotations (forex), 134

rational expectation, 11
real exchange rate
   determination of, 143–44
Reimbursement Claim Solution (RCS), 135–36
representative money, 7

seigniorage, 28–35
   and exchange rate, 33
   cost of, 34–35
   measurement of, 31
sequential market entry, 43
specie flow mechanism, 8
Special Drawing Rights (SDR), 53–54, 74–77

tax havens, 109
Tobin tax, 61–62

uncovered interest parity, 141–42
USD, 58, 77–78, 172, 238

Vienna Convention, 122, 124
volatility of exchange rate, 25–27
vostro account, 135

Washington Consensus, 180–84
World Development Report 2002, 65–66

Zero Capital Mobility Issue, 158